IRIS MURDOCH AND THE OTHERS

IRIS MURDOCH AND THE OTHERS

A Writer in Dialogue with Theology

Paul S. Fiddes

LONDON • NEW YORK • OXFORD • NEW DELHI • SYDNEY

T&T CLARK

Bloomsbury Publishing Plc

50 Bedford Square, London, WC1B 3DP, UK
1385 Broadway, New York, NY 10018, USA
29 Earlsfort Terrace, Dublin 2, Ireland

BLOOMSBURY, T&T CLARK and the T&T Clark logo are trademarks of
Bloomsbury Publishing Plc

First published in Great Britain 2022

Copyright © Paul S. Fiddes, 2022

Paul S. Fiddes has asserted his right under the Copyright, Designs and Patents Act, 1988, to be identified as Author of this work.

For legal purposes the Acknowledgements on p. ix–x constitute an extension of this copyright page.

Cover image © Sophie Bassouls / Getty

All rights reserved. No part of this publication may be reproduced or transmitted in any form or by any means, electronic or mechanical, including photocopying, recording, or any information storage or retrieval system, without prior permission in writing from the publishers.

Bloomsbury Publishing Plc does not have any control over, or responsibility for, any third-party websites referred to or in this book. All internet addresses given in this book were correct at the time of going to press. The author and publisher regret any inconvenience caused if addresses have changed or sites have ceased to exist, but can accept no responsibility for any such changes.

A catalogue record for this book is available from the British Library.

Library of Congress Cataloging-in-Publication Data
Names: Fiddes, Paul S., author.
Title: Iris Murdoch and the others : a writer in dialogue with theology / Paul S. Fiddes.
Description: London ; New York : T&T Clark, 2022. |
Includes bibliographical references and index. |
Identifiers: LCCN 2021027906 (print) | LCCN 2021027907 (ebook) |
ISBN 9780567703347 (hardback) | ISBN 9780567703385 (paperback) |
ISBN 9780567703354 (pdf) | ISBN 9780567703378 (epub)
Subjects: LCSH: Murdoch, Iris–Criticism and interpretation. |
Murdoch, Iris–Religion. | Murdoch, Iris–Philosophy.
Classification: LCC PR6063.U7 Z6525 2022 (print) |
LCC PR6063.U7 (ebook) | DDC 823/.914–dc23
LC record available at https://lccn.loc.gov/2021027906
LC ebook record available at https://lccn.loc.gov/2021027907

ISBN: HB: 978-0-5677-0334-7
ePDF: 978-0-5677-0335-4
ePUB: 978-0-5677-0337-8

Typeset by Newgen KnowledgeWorks Pvt. Ltd., Chennai, India

To find out more about our authors and books visit www.bloomsbury.com and sign up for our newsletters.

For Jakob Lothe and Elin Toft
Valued friends and important 'others'

CONTENTS

Acknowledgements   ix

INTRODUCTION: WHAT KIND OF DIALOGUE?   1

Chapter 1
IRIS MURDOCH AND LOVE OF THE TRUTH   7
    The fall into lack of truth   7
    The breaking of false worlds   15
    The dangers of magic   23
    A theological perspective: Dietrich Bonhoeffer and the world come of age   28
    False saviours: A Murdochian critique of religion   36
    Another theological perspective: Dietrich Bonhoeffer and facing death   42

Chapter 2
IRIS MURDOCH ON 'GOD' AND 'GOOD': A DIALOGUE WITH MODERN THEOLOGY   47
    From *The Time of the Angels* to *The Good Apprentice*   49
    God is not a person   53
    The unity and necessity of Good   59
    Demythologizing and Christology   65
    Beyond the void   73

Chapter 3
THE SUBLIME AND THE BEAUTIFUL: BRINGING MURDOCH AND GERARD MANLEY HOPKINS INTO CONVERSATION   81
    Iris Murdoch and revising Kant   82
    Visions of the sublime in Murdoch's novels   86
    Theological reflection on the sublime   95
    The beautiful and the sublime in Gerard Manley Hopkins   102
    A theological place for the negative sublime   108

Chapter 4
THE SUBLIME, THE CONFLICTED SELF AND ATTENTION TO THE OTHER: BRINGING IRIS MURDOCH AND JULIA KRISTEVA INTO CONVERSATION   109
    The Kantian and the Murdochian sublime: *Nuns and Soldiers*   111
    The Kristevan sublime   115
    The sublime and sublimation: Kristeva's *Murder in Byzantium*   119

    Attending to the other and the sublime   121
    Internal and external conflict: *The Bell*   125
    The sublime: A theological dialogue   129

Chapter 5
LANGUAGE AND WRITING: MURDOCH IN DIALOGUE WITH JACQUES DERRIDA   133
    Why Murdoch and Derrida?   133
    A curious account of Derrida   134
    Real differences between Derrida and Murdoch   139
    The Black Prince: Contingency and coherence   142
    Love, art and the detail of the world   144
    Voice and writing: Undermining Murdoch's own thesis   147
    Attending to the other: A theological horizon   150

Chapter 6
THE VOID AND THE PASSION: A DIALOGUE WITH SIMONE WEIL   155
    Iris Murdoch and Simone Weil: An enigma   155
    Affliction, gravity and attention: An early talk   158
    Early reception of Weil: *The Flight from the Enchanter*   167
    The waiting and the passion   175
    Reworking Weil: *The Green Knight*   182
    Angels and avatars   192

CODA. WITH AND BEYOND SIMONE WEIL: THE DIALOGUE BETWEEN MURDOCH AND THEOLOGY   199

Bibliography   205
Index   215

ACKNOWLEDGEMENTS

Four chapters in this book began as essays or chapters in other books. 'Iris Murdoch and Love of the Truth: Perspectives from Dietrich Bonhoeffer' (Chapter 1) is a revised version of the chapter 'Iris Murdoch and Love of the Truth', in Paul S. Fiddes (ed.), *Freedom and Limit. A Dialogue between Literature of Christian Doctrine* (Basingstoke: Macmillan, 1991). 'Language and Writing: Murdoch and Jacques Derrida' (Chapter 5) is a revised version of 'Murdoch, Derrida and *The Black Prince*', in Anne Rowe and Avril Horner (eds), *Iris Murdoch: Texts and Contexts* (Basingstoke: Palgrave/Macmillan, 2012), pp. 91–109. I am grateful to Palgrave Macmillan (Macmillan Publishers) for permission to reuse both these pieces. 'The Sublime and the Beautiful: Bringing Murdoch into Conversation with Gerard Manley Hopkins' (Chapter 3) is a revised version of 'The Sublime and the Beautiful: Intersections between Theology and Literature', in Heather Walton (ed.), *Literature and Theology – New Interdisciplinary Spaces* (Aldershot: Ashgate, 2011), pp. 127–52. I am grateful to Taylor & Francis for permission to reuse this essay. 'The Sublime, the Conflicted Self and Attention to the Other: Bringing Murdoch into Conversation with Julia Kristeva' (Chapter 4) is a revised version of 'The Sublime, the Conflicted Self and Attention to the Other: Towards a Theopoetics with Iris Murdoch and Julia Kristeva', in Roland Faber (ed.), *Theopoetic Folds: Philosophizing Multifariousness* (New York: Fordham University Press, 2013), pp. 159–78. For permission to reuse this essay I am grateful to Fordham University Press.

I am very grateful for the gracious help given me by the archivist Dayna N. Miller at the Iris Murdoch Archive, the Kingston School of Art, Kingston University. I am also grateful to the Registrar of Kingston University who has granted permission to reproduce marginalia from Murdoch's own copies, from her Oxford Library, of Paul Tillich, *Systematic Theology*, vols 1 and 2 (1978; Iris Murdoch Oxford Library [IML] 1106 and 1107), Donald Mackinnon, *The Problem of Metaphysics* (1974; IML 1049) and Don Cupitt, *Taking Leave of God* (1980; IML 1105).

For permission to reproduce material from the following works of Iris Murdoch, I am grateful to The Random House Group with regard to distribution in the UK and Commonwealth: *A Fairly Honourable Defeat*, copyright © Iris Murdoch 1970; *Metaphysics as a Guide to Morals*, copyright © Iris Murdoch 1992; *Nuns and Soldiers*, copyright © Iris Murdoch 1980; *The Bell*, copyright © Iris Murdoch 1958; *The Black Prince*, copyright © Iris Murdoch 1973; *The Flight from the Enchanter*, copyright © Iris Murdoch 1956; *The Sea, The Sea*, copyright © Iris Murdoch 1978; *The Time of the Angels*, copyright © Iris Murdoch 1996; *The Unicorn*, copyright © Iris Murdoch 1963.

I am very grateful for the generosity of Norah Perkins at Curtis Brown who has permitted me to quote from the works of Iris Murdoch listed above with regard to distribution worldwide (including the USA), as well as from the following novels of Iris Murdoch without restriction of area: *The Good Apprentice*, copyright © Iris Murdoch 1985; *The Green Knight*, copyright © Iris Murdoch 1993.

INTRODUCTION: WHAT KIND OF DIALOGUE?

The title of this book is a deliberate play on the words of the title John Bayley gave to the second memoir of his wife – *Iris and the Friends*. In that story of the last year of Iris Murdoch's life, the friends are the 'companions' that Bayley finds appearing in the experience of those who suffer from Alzheimer's disease and of those who care for them. Among the friendly 'uses of adversity', he names: unexpected pleasures in being alive, mutual dependence, solitude, an indifference to responsibilities, and finally death itself; to these he adds imaginary friends who emerged in his wife's confused consciousness, and – especially – his own memories of childhood and early life. Weaving through these 'companions' in affliction are more literal friends across the years, 'people with whom she could argue about the arts and discuss literature, people with whom she could fall in love'.[1] Unaccountably, the title of the American edition of the memoir draws attention only to the last of these companions, being called *Iris Murdoch and Her Friends*.[2]

The 'others' of this present book are makers of theology, or philosophers and creative writers who took an interest in theology. At least one of them – D. M. Mackinnon – is to be counted among the literal friends, or 'pals' (a term Murdoch often uses) of Iris Murdoch and John Bayley. Others of them – such as Simone Weil, Dietrich Bonhoeffer, Rudolph Bultmann, Karl Barth, Jacques Derrida and Paul Tillich – Murdoch met only in her consciousness over the years, by way of the written page. Addressing these, Murdoch conducted her own dialogue with theology which was evidently of central importance to her. I aim to bring this 'historic' dialogue to attention through careful analysis. But I also aim to set that dialogue within another one that I am conducting myself as a theologian with a writer of literature, and here I venture to bring into the conversation some partners with whom Murdoch never conversed in any way, notably among them the poet Gerard Manley Hopkins and the philosopher Julia Kristeva. They provide, I believe, significant insights for the larger dialogue. I am encouraged here by the way Bayley himself, in *Iris and the Friends*, takes the liberty of introducing characters whom

1. John Bayley, *Iris and the Friends: A Year of Memories* (London: Gerald Duckworth, 1999), p. 81.
2. John Bayley, *Iris and Her Friends: A Memoir of Memory and Desire* (New York: W.W. Norton, 1999).

Murdoch never knew into his story of Murdoch's last year, in order to understand their relationship more deeply.

All of these partners in the dialogue of this book are 'others' in the sense that Murdoch gave to the word: they are those whose existence and ideas she recognized, or would recognize if she came across them, as having a reality of their own, to whom she could give attention, and whom she would welcome as having the power to break open any attempt to build a world around her own ego-self.

The project of this book, then, is to create a dialogue between Murdoch and theology, to bring Murdoch into relation with theological 'others'. In other books I have written I have already attempted such a dialogue, by which I mean a two-way relationship between literature and theology which aims to be entirely respectful to both disciplines.[3] Poetry, novels and plays are not being dragooned into the role of providing mere 'illustrations' for a theology that has been entirely already constructed. Rather, on the one hand, creative literature is drawn upon in the task of 'making' a theology which is shaped by imagination. The theology could not be made in the way that it is without this interaction. On the other hand, theology provides a perspective for reading literature, and may enable the reader to see aspects within it that would otherwise be hidden, sometimes even detecting breaks and strains which give an openness of meaning to the text, and enable it to be reconstructed. It is essential that the two movements of this dialogue should not be short-circuited, which would happen if the contribution of literature in making theology were simply the reflex of reading from an already-conceived theological perspective. Literature will only make its imaginative (and perhaps surprising) contribution to constructing theology if it is read and analysed from its own perspective and tendencies, out of its own linguistic inventiveness and in the context of its own distinctive cultural heritage. In the dialogical cycle, theology which is re-formed in this way can then, in turn, offer a new lens through which to view the text.

As a theologian, I believe that I am obliged to explain how this kind of dialogue is possible at all. For Christian theologians, 'theology', or talking about God, cannot simply be a study of the phenomenology of religious experience. Since God is infinite mystery, talk about God must always be in analogy and metaphor, but it is also impossible unless the unique and ultimate reality we call 'God' takes the initiative in self-disclosure. Theology always begins in gift. The question then is where that self-revelation takes place, and the dialogue I have been describing assumes that it happens universally. It is only possible for creative literature to be of use in *making* theology if its words can become places where God unveils God's own self, or where – using an appropriate metaphor – God 'speaks'. This does not rule out there being places where there is a particular intensity, or focus of divine self-revelation, and for Christian theologians this will be pre-eminently in the

---

3. See Paul S. Fiddes, *Freedom and Limit: A Dialogue between Literature and Christian Doctrine* (Basingstoke: Macmillan, 1991), pp. 27–46; Fiddes, *The Promised End: Eschatology in Theology and Literature* (Oxford: Blackwell, 2000), pp. 5–8.

person of Jesus Christ, and then derivatively in the Holy Scriptures that witness to Christ and have shaped the Christian community. Those who stand within a different religious tradition will, of course, find other places where revelation has this particular 'density'.

Revelation by its very nature cannot be objectively examined, but we may find traces of revelation open to literary criticism in the form of a human reaching towards mystery, a recognition of mysterious 'excess' in experience, a sense that there is an inexhaustible gift of life. In every case, in response to the disclosure of God's own being, there will be the subsequent exercise of the tools of human discourse in articulating and conceptualizing what has been revealed, a process conditioned by history and cultural context.[4] Literature will aim at openness towards this mystery, placing a premium on images, ambiguity and plurivalent meaning, where doctrine will have elements of closure, or a tendency to put boundaries around concepts. Both, however, will be responding to a self-opening of mystery and love.

This is not the place for elaboration of this theology of revelation. I have attempted this elsewhere.[5] But it offers a framework within which there is space for different kinds of participation in a dialogue between literature and Christian theology. There will be writers who profess a Christian conviction themselves, writers who have no religious belief, writers who use images and symbols from the Christian tradition but with no personal commitment to the belief that lies behind them – such as Jacques Derrida and Julia Kristeva, to whom I appeal in this volume – and writers who stand in a different religious tradition entirely. No religious intentions should be imputed to authors when these are clearly absent from the text itself. But theologians who have the kind of theology of revelation I have described (and I count myself within them) will consider it legitimate to draw on any of this creative writing to assist in the *making* of theology.

There are also writers who may blend the last three categories to different degrees, and Murdoch appears to be one who stands at the intersection of genres, or to be continually crossing their boundaries. Rejecting, by her own account, belief in a 'personal' God from the early 1950s, she remains intensely interested in the theology and images of Christianity, recognizing the power they can have, and by the 1970s styling herself at times as a 'Christian Buddhist'.[6] Her very Platonism, some have judged, amounts in itself to a kind of religion, let alone her attachment to a 'mystical Christ'. Her elusiveness to categorization is, in fact, precisely what her own chosen biographer, A. N. Wilson, another novelist, witnesses to when he

---

4. Here Rahner draws a helpful distinction between 'transcendental' and 'categorical' revelation: see Karl Rahner, *Foundations of Christian Faith: An Introduction to the Idea of Christianity* (trans. W. V. Dych) (London: Darton, Longman and Todd, 1978), pp. 153–62.

5. See Paul S. Fiddes, 'Concept, Image and Story in Systematic Theology', *International Journal of Systematic Theology* 11.1 (2009), pp. 3–23.

6. See Anne Rowe, *Iris Murdoch: Writers and Their Work* (Liverpool: Liverpool University Press/British Council, 2019), pp. 69–70.

ends his account: 'Her mystery – what was going on behind that face – remains a mystery to me.'[7]

Though I refer here to a dialogue between 'creative literature' and theology, this book will in fact be drawing on Murdoch's works in philosophy, as well as her novels. This is not because I am ignoring the distinction she always insisted on making between the writing of philosophy and the writing of novels. Several times in interviews Murdoch claimed that her novels were not 'philosophical novels'.[8] While the novels contain philosophical discussions, this was just – she maintained – to set the atmosphere and because the characters themselves happen to be interested in philosophical ideas. She strived, she maintained, to keep her philosophy and her fiction in separate compartments, and denied that she was dramatizing philosophical questions in her stories. However, to take just one topic, Bran Nicol has pointed out that the whole idea of contingency pervading her novels – that events are accidental, or could have been otherwise, or are dependent on a particular time and place – 'is a fundamental property of her philosophical system'.[9] What is contingency if not a philosophical category? The plots of most of her novels turn at some key point on the failure to respect contingency, or on the successful attention to some contingent detail of life. She appears to be deceiving herself if she thinks that she is not dramatizing a philosophical idea. What we may surely accept is that the novels are not structured to deliver a selected philosophical theory to the reader, as for example the novels of Jean-Paul Sartre seem designed to do. She present us with characters who speak, or live, by different – and often conflicting – perspectives on life. But we can see what those approaches might look like, incarnated in flesh and blood and a moment in history. As she writes herself, 'Good art "explains" truth itself, by *manifesting* deep conceptual connections.'[10]

We might then be tempted altogether to ignore the distinction she makes, especially since her philosophy is written with so much more imagination than is characteristic of Oxford analytic philosophy (Wilson, though tongue-in-cheek, calls it 'sermonising').[11] Yet we can respect her own intentions, expressed in the dictum that 'philosophy is clarification, but literature is mystification',[12] when we

---

7. A. N. Wilson, *Iris Murdoch as I Knew Her* (London: Hutchinson, 2003), p. 265.

8. E.g. see Murdoch's conversation with John Haffenden in his *Novelists in Interview* (London: Methuen, 1985), pp. 191–209.

9. Bran Nicol, 'Philosophy's Dangerous Pupil: Murdoch and Derrida', *Modern Fiction Studies* 47.3 (2001), pp. 580–601 (591). Nevertheless, Elizabeth Dipple rightly warns that 'a fruitful reading' of the novels 'should be aware of but significantly separated from heavy reliance on Murdoch's ... philosophical work': Dipple, 'The Green Knight and Other Vagaries of the Spirit; or Tricks and Images of the Soul; or the Uses of Imaginative Literature', in Maria Antonaccio and William Schweiker (eds), *Iris Murdoch and the Search for Human Goodness* (Chicago: University of Chicago Press, 1996), pp. 138–70 (147).

10. Iris Murdoch, *Metaphysics as a Guide to Morals* (London: Chatto & Windus, 1992), p. 321, original emphasis.

11. Wilson, *Iris Murdoch*, p. 28.

12. See later, pp. 17, 24–5.

see the books and essays of philosophy as taking their place within the *dialogue* that she herself is conducting with theology. Because she is always interested in religion and reads a great deal of Christian theology, her philosophy and novels form a kind of internal dialogue which enriches any dialogue we might ourselves construct. The whole body of her work thus bears out what she wrote to a close friend in 1953, explaining that 'I have by now in effect drifted out of the Christian church', but continuing 'not that I have "finished" with religion. I haven't begun yet'.[13]

Finally, I draw readers' attention to the fact that – as indicated on the acknowledgements page – four chapters in this book began as essays or chapters in other books. These previous pieces, with revisions and expansions, now stand in a new relationship to each other and to much new thinking. This, I hope, is in accord with Murdoch's own sense of ever-new beginning, and in accord with her words that 'ideas in art must suffer a sea-change'[14] – an instruction that she herself amply fulfilled in her writing.

---

13. Iris Murdoch to Raymond Queneau, 11 January 1953, in Avril Horner and Ann Rowe (eds), *Living on Paper: Letters from Iris Murdoch 1934–1995* (London: Chatto & Windus, 2015), p. 152.

14. 'In Conversation with Bryan Magee', *Men of Ideas: Some Creators of Contemporary Philosophy* (Oxford: Oxford University Press, 1982), p. 227.

Chapter 1

IRIS MURDOCH AND LOVE OF THE TRUTH

'Good art is truthful.'[1] On this text Iris Murdoch based twenty-six novels and four books of philosophy, aiming to show in her technique of writing that the artist is a truth-teller and to show in her themes that all people should be no less lovers of the truth if they are to be truly human. In fact, Murdoch believes (following her great mentor, Plato) that the quest for the truth is the search for the Good, and to love the one is to love the other. Even a passing experience of falling in love can make someone more keenly aware of what is true in the world around them. In Murdoch's vision of reality, there is thus an indissoluble bond between truth, love and goodness, and the reader of her novels becomes a traveller through regions of moral value as well as intense passion. Murdoch does not profess to believe in an objectively existing and personal God, but the interest of her work for a Christian theologian is summed up in a remark of one of her characters: 'That's what God is for, to make our lies truth.'[2]

The fall into lack of truth

The characters in Iris Murdoch's novels learn, or fail to learn, to be truthful, which means giving attention to what is real around them. At one level of reality (we shall see that there is another, more transcendent level), this means noticing people as they actually are, rather than as we want them to be for our convenience. It means delighting in all the contingent details of the world, recognizing the 'otherness' of people and things and living with all the hazards of accident. At the very least the disciples of goodness accept the 'muddle' of the world, and at the best they experience its amazing variety as being the sublime. Jenkin has learned to look upon the world like this, so that walking the streets of London was to walk through 'a great collection or exhibition of little events or encounters'.[3]

---

1. Iris Murdoch, *The Fire and the Sun: Why Plato Banished the Artists* (repr., Oxford: Oxford University Press, 1988), p. 79.
2. Iris Murdoch, *The Good Apprentice* (London: Chatto & Windus, 1985), p. 488.
3. Iris Murdoch, *The Book and the Brotherhood* (London: Chatto & Windus, 1987), p. 131.

A prominent symbol for the 'hardness'[4] and separateness of objects in their own right is the stones with which Murdoch strews her landscapes. Characters marvel at the myriad of pebbles upon the beach, each different from the other; Sinclair has made a notable collection of these and 'had known each individual stone personally and given some of them names'.[5] When Anne Cavidge meets Jesus Christ in a vision, he shows her a small stone, reminiscent of the Lady Julian's account in her mystical treatise of how she was shown 'a little thing the size of a hazel-nut'.[6] Ann is in the agonizing predicament of loving a man who has loved her friend Gertrude devotedly (and without reward) for many years; should she tell him her own love? By showing her a stone, Christ makes clear that there is no easy answer, no instant salvation. She must find the truth of her situation, which is there like the integrity of the stone, existing in its own truth.

Like other modern writers, then, Murdoch is presenting the need for a balance between our freedom and the limits that confront us.[7] As in Hopkins's vision of the world, where

> Each mortal thing does one thing and the same:
> ... *myself* it speaks and spells,

the limitations lie in respecting the otherness of things. The characters who search for the Good imitate the creative Demiurge in Plato's myth, who 'realises his limits' when faced by the 'jumble' of the world.[8] The 'very small area of freedom' in human life does not consist in the mere exercise of will power, but is 'that in us which attends to the real and is attracted by the good'.[9] Living in the tension between freedom and limit is frequently pictured as the skill of swimming; the sea is an apt symbol for the multiplicity and vastness of worldly phenomena, and to succeed in swimming is to keep one's balance amid the 'ocean of accident'[10] in daily life. Murdoch's good characters are strong swimmers, or like Dora at the end

---

4. The word is used in Murdoch, *The Fire and the Sun*, p. 80.

5. Murdoch, *The Book and the Brotherhood*, p. 241.

6. Iris Murdoch, *Nuns and Soldiers* (London: Chatto & Windus, 1980), p. 292; Julian of Norwich, *Revelations of Divine Love* (trans. Elizabeth Spearing) (Harmondsworth: Penguin, 1998), pp. 47–8.

7. See Fiddes, *Freedom and Limit*: I explore this theme in William Blake, Gerard Manley Hopkins, D. H. Lawrence and William Golding, in addition to Iris Murdoch.

8. See Murdoch, *The Fire and the Sun*, p. 52. The 'good' character Tallis is always to be found 'wherever there is a muddle': Iris Murdoch, *A Fairly Honourable Defeat* (London: Chatto & Windus, 1970), p. 158.

9. Iris Murdoch, *The Sovereignty of Good* (London: Routledge and Kegan Paul, 1970), p. 75. Murdoch calls for 'a vocabulary of attention' in 'Against Dryness' (1961), in Iris Murdoch, *Existentialists and Mystics: Writings on Philosophy and Literature* (ed. Peter Conradi) (London: Chatto & Windus, 1997), pp. 287–96 (293).

10. Iris Murdoch, *The Nice and the Good* (London: Chatto & Windus, 1968), p. 309.

of *The Bell*, they learn to swim, 'buoyant and fearless in the water'.[11] Those who are not in quest of the Good frequently drown, not only in metaphor but in fact.[12]

Murdoch emphasizes that keeping a balance between one's freedom and one's limits means the death of the self. To give attention to other things and people is to love goodness as well as truth because it means 'unselfing'[13] or 'decentring' from oneself. In a moment of revelation, facing death by drowning in a bog, Effingham Cooper discovers 'the passion of a lover' for 'all that was not himself':

> This then was love, to look and look until one exists no more, this was the love that was the same as death. He looked, and knew with a clarity which was one with the increasing light, that with the death of the self the world becomes quite automatically the object of a perfect love.[14]

This 'death of the self' bears three characteristics in Murdoch's thought, all of which concern the love of truth and which appear in her work in constant dialogue with the Christian tradition. First, she concentrates upon the link between such a death and 'attention' to the contingent facts of the world. From this perspective she fleshes out in her novels an experience of untruth which can be aptly called sin, fallenness and hell. Second, she links this moral theme with a theory of art, in which such religious concepts as revelation, grace, salvation and images of God are brought into play. Third, she reflects upon the relationship between the death of the self and human suffering, where she has some critical things to say about the failures of Christianity in its attempt at the 'long task of unselfing'.[15]

In the first place, then, Murdoch vividly depicts the feelings of characters who fail to give attention to others and build a self-enclosed world around themselves. Jake, in her very first novel, sets the tone for a long list of successors when he exclaims that 'I hate contingency' and remarks of his companion that 'I count Finn as an inhabitant of my universe, and cannot conceive that he has one containing me'.[16] Murdoch exposes the tragic fact that we all manufacture worlds for ourselves; our

---

11. Iris Murdoch, *The Bell* (London: Chatto & Windus, 1958), p. 303.

12. Murdoch's characters drown in a swimming pool (*A Fairly Honourable Defeat*), a bath (*An Accidental Man*), the sea (*The Sea, The Sea*), a flash-flood (*The Unicorn*), the Thames (*A Word Child*) and public baths (*The Philosopher's Pupil*). Murdoch herself was a strong swimmer; see Peter J. Conradi, *Iris Murdoch: A Life* (London: HarperCollins, 2001), pp. 563–4, but she confessed to nearly drowning in the sea; see Peter J. Conradi, *The Saint and the Artist: A Study of the Fiction of Iris Murdoch* (repr., London: HarperCollins, 2nd edn, 2001), p. 138.

13. Murdoch, *Sovereignty of Good*, p. 84.

14. Iris Murdoch, *The Unicorn* (London: Chatto & Windus, 1963), p. 198.

15. The phrase is by Brendan in Murdoch, *Henry and Cato* (London: Chatto & Windus, 1976), p. 174.

16. Iris Murdoch, *Under the Net* (London: Chatto & Windus, 1954), pp. 24, 9.

minds are the 'sacred and profane love-machines' which she explores in her novel of that title.[17] Other images for the cosmic artefacts that we build and imprison ourselves within are boxes, dark cupboards, cages and eggs.[18] This self-centring takes the social form of intimate circles or 'courts' of relatives and friends, usually middle class, professional and university educated; in the plots of the novels, there are continual reminiscences of the in-bred social groups of Shakespeare's comedies which need to be broken open by comic tricks.[19] The mythical form in which this human condition is presented is the fable of the 'imprisoned princess'. In some novels women are literally imprisoned, as, for example, Charles Arrowby shuts up his former childhood sweetheart, Hartley, now an elderly woman, in a dark room in order to protect her from her husband and recapture her love.[20] In others, characters fantasize about finding an imprisoned damsel or keeping her safe from others.[21]

Behind all these images of confinement there lies the Platonic myth of the cave and the inhabitants of a world of shadows. In Murdoch's synthesis of Freud and Plato, the fire in the cave is the ego, aping the sun outside and producing illusions in which the cave-dwellers are content to live.[22] So perpetual and ingrained is this tendency of her characters to construct worlds according to their own patterns that we are not surprised to find Murdoch pronouncing judgement upon modern philosophy in these terms: 'We have lost the vision of a reality separate from ourselves, and we have no adequate concept of original sin.'[23] Some Christian theologians have envisaged the human situation as a paradox of 'fallenness', in which failure to seek God as the Supreme Good is not logically *necessary* but *inevitable* in practice because of the anxiety that arises from living in the tension

---

17. Iris Murdoch, *The Sacred and Profane Love Machine* (London: Chatto & Windus, 1974). For the same image, see also *Fairly Honourable Defeat*, pp. 98, 171, 251, 339. In *Sovereignty of Good*, p. 78, the psyche is described as a 'machine', manufacturing dreams to escape reality.

18. For the image of boxes, see Murdoch, *Book and the Brotherhood*, pp. 377, 595; for cupboard, *The Time of the Angels* (London: Chatto & Windus, 1966), p. 184; for cage, *The Sea, The Sea* (London: Chatto & Windus, 1978), p. 442; for egg, *Sacred and Profane Love Machine*, p. 92 and *Time of the Angels*, p. 251.

19. On 'courts' and social identity, see Richard Todd, *Iris Murdoch: The Shakespearian Interest* (London: Vision, 1979), pp. 72–4, 85–8.

20. Murdoch, *Sea, The Sea*, p. 159. Similarly, Hannah is imprisoned in *The Unicorn*, p. 275, as 'sequestered, immaculate'.

21. E.g. the fantasies of Leo in *Time of the Angels*, p. 72, and the obsessions of Austin in *An Accidental Man* (London: Chatto & Windus, 1971), pp. 311, 331.

22. Murdoch, *Fire and the Sun*, p. 43. On her synthesis of Freud and Plato, see David Tracy, 'Iris Murdoch and the Many Faces of Platonism', in Antonaccio and Schweiker, *Iris Murdoch and the Search for Human Goodness*, pp. 54–75 (59–61).

23. Murdoch, *Sovereignty of Good*, p. 47.

between freedom and limitation.[24] Paul Tillich named a fall into estrangement as 'the original fact'[25] – it just is the case. The characters portrayed in Murdoch's novels give substance to this theory; we sense that they are morally responsible beings, and yet we know also that they cannot help falling – though at different depths – into a self-made universe. When Murdoch came to read Tillich in 1979, she appears to have recognized his diagnosis of the human situation as familiar; her copy of his *Systematic Theology* carries numerous marginal notes at the point of his discussion of fallenness, summarizing his argument; she notes, for example, the nature of estranged existence as a 'tension' between 'ethical freedom & tragic destiny', adding in brackets 'original sin'.[26]

For some, who wilfully cultivate their own world and ignore the 'separate reality' of others, the fall is very deep. When Duncan sins against the truth by spying on his wife rather than confronting her openly about her love affair with his former friend Crimond, he finds himself in hell: 'We are all a vile lot of rotten, stinking sinners, black as hell';[27] his fall down the stairs after a fight with Crimond is symbolic of a moral fall, and the partial loss of sight that results is also a spiritual blindness.[28] When Edward plays the magician and tricks Mark into taking a hallucinogenic drug against his wish, he is failing to recognize his friend as a person in his own right. After Mark's consequent fatal accident, Edward is plunged into a state of hopelessness: 'This is hell, where there is no time.'[29]

Now, it is characteristic of this hell to find that the contingent details of the world, the 'jumble' of life, are not a delight but a horror. The experience of the sublime has been reversed into vertigo, a negative vision. As Duncan stares at the fragments of a broken teapot, he experiences 'as in a mystical vision ... the pointlessness of life'.[30] Morgan, in *A Fairly Honourable Defeat*, descends into the Underground as into the underworld, and emerging finds unbearable the shabby details of the streets, 'the houses which were stripped and wrenched and torn': 'The horror, the horror of the world.' This anti-vision is triggered, it seems, by the

---

24. Reinhold Niebuhr, *The Nature and Destiny of Man: A Christian Interpretation, Vol. I: Human Nature* (London: Nisbet, 1941), pp. 179–83, 194–6; Paul Tillich, *Systematic Theology, Vol. 2, Existence and the Christ* (repr., London: SCM, 1978), pp. 29–36, 43–4.

25. Tillich, *Systematic Theology*, vol. 2, p. 36, cf. p. 44, 'coincidence of creation and the Fall'.

26. Murdoch's marginal notes in Tillich, *Systematic Theology*, vol. 2, p. 38, copy in the Iris Murdoch Oxford Library (IML 1107), Iris Murdoch Archive, Kingston School of Art, Kingston University.

27. Murdoch, *Book and the Brotherhood*, p. 85.

28. Marcus, in *Time of the Angels*, similarly falls into a coal cellar.

29. Murdoch, *The Good Apprentice* (London: Chatto & Windus, 1985), p. 12.

30. Murdoch, *Book and the Brotherhood*, p. 186. In her study of Sartre, Murdoch sets out to explain why he finds 'the contingent over-abundance of the world nauseating': Iris Murdoch, *Sartre, Romantic Rationalist* (repr., London: Collins/Fontana, [1953] 1967), pp. 21–3.

memory of an abortion in which she had felt no regret for the unborn child, no respect for it as a unique object in its own right: 'She had killed it so casually and drunk half a bottle of bourbon afterwards.'[31]

The myriad stones upon the beach that can symbolize joy in the variety of the world can also become the occasion for nausea at the sheer contingency of things. Theo, in *The Nice and the Good*, has some sense of the demands of the Good, but has not been strong enough to pursue it, and he finds the stones on the Dorset coast to be terrible in their factuality. The mauve and white pebbles 'were a nightmare to Theo. Their multiplicity and randomness appalled him.' What was for the children who lovingly collect the stones 'a treasury of lovable individuals' was for Theo a dead 'opacity of matter' and 'an expanse of abomination where the spirit had never come'. The stones are 'jumble and desolation', and he goes on to wonder 'was not all jumble and desolation, was it not all an expanse of senseless random matter, and he himself as meaningless as these stones, since in real truth there is no God?'[32] There may be a clue to his mood in the fact that he is using the pebbles to decorate the bare body of the teenage Pierce, asleep on the beach, with whom he is hopelessly in love. In turn, Pierce is desperately in love with Theo's niece, and when children give him a beautiful stone, an almost perfect ammonite, as a gift of their love and concern, he expresses his feeling that 'everything's black' by throwing the stone far out to sea.[33]

In *The Message to the Planet* Murdoch gathers together, as it were, all the characters in her novels who collect stones into a tribe of New-Agers called 'the Stone People', who collect stones, carry them around and place them in homage at holy places; in this story, a site of great veneration is a massive Neolithic-age stone, the Axle Stone. As one of them explains, 'only good is everywhere, and we see that all things are holy, all the little accidental jumbled things, like little stones, like bits of earth and dust, like little nothing – things –'.[34] But characters who are more out of tune with the planet experience the stones as hostile: the painter and philosopher Marcus Vallar, who has come to a 'void' he cannot cross,[35] explains to his former pupil Alfred Ludens that being required to think things out was 'a nightmare – it was like walking barefoot on sharp stones, or breathing black dust with a sack over one's head'.[36] Ludens himself dreams of 'walking with difficulty up a steep path covered with small sharp stones upon which he often slipped', and when he fingers in his pocket a pebble he has picked up, one of the 'little accidental stones', he feels 'the awful randomness of human life, the suffering, the remorse, the cruelty, the inescapable cruelty'.[37] Aptly, when Vallar disappoints the crowd

---

31. Murdoch, *Fairly Honourable Defeat*, pp. 295–6. Tamar in *Book and the Brotherhood*, pp. 364–5, has a similar descent into hell, for similar reasons.

32. Murdoch, *Nice and the Good*, pp. 152–3.

33. Ibid., p. 155.

34. Iris Murdoch, *The Message to the Planet* (London: Chatto & Windus, 1989), p. 328.

35. Ibid., pp. 54, 88.

36. Ibid., p. 342.

37. Ibid., pp. 366, 375.

of 'Seekers' who have venerated him as a holy man and a healer, he and Ludens become the targets of stones thrown at them.

The theological paradox of fallenness, the human predicament where the sin of self-centredness is not logically necessary but seems inevitable,[38] is fleshed out by such experiences. Even characters who want to be disciples of the Good, and know that only love is necessary, find that they easily slip from vision to anti-vision. The sufferings of people and the inhumanity of their torturers is naturally one of the pressures that makes us turn inward, away from facing the world as it is, to construct our own fantasy one. Stuart, the 'apprentice' of the Good, sums up the horror of the Jewish Holocaust in a single contingent fact; a girl who plaited her hair one morning was dead by the evening, and her hair recycled for other uses: 'Oh it was the details, the details that were so unendurable.'[39] Yet such intolerable details must not be forgotten; suffering must be confronted and the truth must be told about it, not in order to indulge ourselves by lamenting our own sinfulness and abasing ourselves but to lead us to death of the self. If suffering is not recognized and faced, we shall only inflict it on others as we feed our 'fat relentless ego'.[40]

A complementary image to that of constructing the world around oneself appears in one novel, and it includes within its own detail the violence and suffering that will be caused by forcing others into one's own orbit and failing to allow them to be themselves. The image and at the same time the title of the novel is *A Severed Head*. At first Martin builds his own world in which he imagines he 'possesses' neatly both his wife, Antonia, and Georgie, his mistress;[41] Georgie protests that 'I began to feel I didn't exist',[42] and later Martin admits that 'I had never taken sufficient trouble to find out exactly what Antonia herself was thinking and feeling'.[43] Then Antonia leaves him for the charismatic psychiatrist, Palmer Anderson, and Palmer even more powerfully builds a universe in which he intends to hold both Antonia and Martin himself in a dreadful love: 'We shall hold on to you, we shall look after you.'[44] Martin comments that 'I was their prisoner, and I choked with it. But I too much feared the darkness beyond.'[45] Martin's brother, Alexander, a famous sculptor, is practising his own kind of control of others, symbolized by his crafting stone heads detached from the whole person. The prison is his studio: collecting heads is an 'obsession', he boasts[46] – and actually he is collecting, through sexual affairs, all the women who

---

38. For a statement of the paradox of 'inevitable but not necessary', see Niebuhr, *Nature and Destiny of Man*, vol. I, pp. 179–83, 194–6.
39. Murdoch, *Good Apprentice*, p. 248.
40. Murdoch, *Sovereignty of Good*, p. 52.
41. Iris Murdoch, *A Severed Head* (London: Chatto & Windus, 1961), p. 11.
42. Ibid., p. 105.
43. Ibid., p. 149.
44. Ibid., p. 39.
45. Ibid., p. 67.
46. Ibid., p. 54.

have loved Martin, including Antonia and Georgie. Honor Klein, an enigmatic and intimidating Cambridge don (and Palmer's half-sister) makes clear to Martin that she will not be a mere severed head; in a ritual exercise with a Samurai sword she 'decapitates' two napkins, and to Martin's assumption 'you believe in the dark gods', she replies, 'I believe in people'.[47] When, unexpectedly, Martin falls desperately in love with her, with a 'monstrous love', she warns him that 'your love for me does not inhabit the real world … I am a terrible object of fascination for you. I am a severed head … But that is remote from love and remote from ordinary life. As real people we do not exist for each other.'[48]

Murdoch elsewhere identifies both a Freudian and a Sartrean interpretation of the mythical severed head of the Medusa,[49] the first concerned with fear of castration[50] and the second with fear of being observed by others.[51] She notes that 'it is interesting to speculate on how one would set about deciding which interpretation was "correct"'. In her own myth-making, the image is – I suggest – about being treated as less than a whole person, as a 'disembodied' object of another's control. Though the Freudian aspects of the novel have been often explored,[52] Murdoch's employment of the image is a variation on her theme of being a victim of another person's 'dream' or fantasy universe, and so is more related to her rebuttal of Sartre's fear of the way that others impinge on one's own being-in-itself. As she comments in the context of her note on the Medusa, 'Whereas for Freud the deepest human impulse is sexual, for Freud it is the urge towards "self-coincidence" which is

---

47. Ibid., pp. 120–1.
48. Ibid., p. 225.
49. Murdoch, *Sartre* (1953, repr. 1967), p. 97.
50. Sigmund Freud, 'Medusa's Head', in *Standard Edition of the Complete Psychological Works of Sigmund Freud*, 18 vols (trans. James Strachey and Anna Freud) (London: Hogarth Press, 1953–74), vol. 18, pp. 273–4. Freud writes of castration fear as an Oedipal symptom, as it arises from a boy's catching sight of female genitalia 'essentially those of his mother'. In the novel, Palmer and Honor have an incestuous relationship, also associated by Freud with the Oedipus complex. Alexander mentions 'Freud on Medusa. The head can represent the female genitals, feared not desired' (p. 54) and Martin, who was over-attached to his mother, dreams of a severed head when he thinks of the incest between Honor and Palmer (p. 243).
51. Jean-Paul Sartre, *Being and Nothingness: An Essay on Phenomenological Ontology* (trans. Hazel E. Barnes) (London: Routledge, 2003), p. 531.
52. See Antonia Byatt, *Degrees of Freedom: The Early Novels of Iris Murdoch* (London: Vintage, 2nd edn, 1994), pp. 127–9. Byatt's own character Maud in her novel *Possession: A Romance* (London: Chatto & Windus, 1990), p. 315, is writing a paper on the Medusa head as a 'castration-fantasy, female sexuality, feared and desired', so contradicting Alexander's phrase 'feared, not desired' (*Severed Head*, p. 54). Also Deborah Johnson, *Iris Murdoch. Key Women Writers* (Brighton: Harvester, 1987), pp. 17–19, 25–9; Mike Leeson, *Iris Murdoch: Philosophical Novelist* (London: Continuum, 2010), pp. 51–3, 66–8 (more cautiously).

the key to our being.'[53] The image has the advantage of including the element of violence within the symbol itself, but is not, however, repeated in other novels where Murdoch prefers images of dream and containment.

The breaking of false worlds

To escape from our own box, to 'crack the hard ego',[54] to wake from the dream[55] or to smash the shell of the egg in which we are sheltering cannot be achieved simply by an act of our will. Christian theologians speak of 'grace' as a gift from beyond us which enables us to turn from the security of idols and to live courageously in the tensions of life. Grace must be understood not as an impersonal supernatural substance but as God's own gracious encounter with human persons, inviting and eliciting trust in place of anxiety.[56] Now, Murdoch believes that the defeat of egoism requires moral effort, but she also discerns the need for something analogous to 'grace', something to enable the 'reorientation of an energy which is naturally selfish'.[57]

The first form which these ministers of grace assume in Murdoch's novels is the shock of an unexpected event or unlikely relationship. The contingent, accidental events of the world which her characters try to shut out can break in suddenly to disturb their neat, self-enclosed worlds. They are shocked into noticing others, jolted towards the truth.[58] At the same time, of course, the shock operates upon the reader. For instance, the love affairs which develop are 'odd', challenging our tidy ideas of how people behave. They cut across the usual barriers – old and young fall in love together, brothers and sisters love each other incestuously or in a manner that borders on it, people move from heterosexual to homosexual relationships and back again, class divisions are crossed, one member of a long-established circle of intimates falls in love with an outsider, and someone who is hated at one moment becomes the object of passionate love at another. Critics protest, 'But people don't behave like this!', yet Murdoch is unveiling the unpredictability of human nature to which we are often blind. At the same time, of course, she has made the relationships and passions she describes even more erratic because she wants to startle us out of our self-created worlds. As we shall see, she allows that

---

53. Murdoch, *Sartre* (1953, repr. 1967), pp. 96–7.

54. Murdoch, *Metaphysics*, p. 62.

55. As Martin assures Honor, 'we must … hope that we can keep hold of each other through the dream and out into the waking world': Murdoch, *Severed Head*, p. 252.

56. See John Macquarrie, *Principles of Christian Theology* (London: SCM, rev. edn, 1977), pp. 82–3, 266–7. Murdoch possessed the 1966 edition of this volume, as an inscribed gift from the author, but it is unmarked (copy, IML 397).

57. Murdoch, *Sovereignty of Good*, p. 54.

58. See Murdoch, *Book and the Brotherhood*, p. 362: 'Shock tactics do things, they break barriers, they open vistas.'

literature must resort to tricks and 'magic' in order to reveal what is real; good art can lie its way into the truth.

As with unlikely relationships, random and haphazard events can shock Murdoch's characters – and the reader – into awareness of the truth. In *The Sacred and Profane Love Machine*, for example, she uses an ingenious 'magical' device which enables us to share in the main character's experience of having his machine-made worlds blown open by the accidental. The novel begins with a small boy of eight or nine standing outside a garden and staring in. The house belongs to Blaise Gavender, a successful psychiatrist, and for the first sixty pages of the novel we explore the life of his family, residing in a fashionable area of South London. Then the narrator switches the scene to a rather squalid flat in a very unfashionable area of London, where lives an unsuccessful schoolteacher called Emily McHugh. We learn that her small son Luca is difficult to handle, awkward and introverted. So we explore in turn two very different worlds. Suddenly, even casually, half-way through a sentence we read that 'for some time now Emily had been trying to persuade Blaise to go to see Luca's form master'.[59] With a shock we discover that the two worlds connect. Blaise has two families; unknown to his wife Harriet, Emily is his mistress and Luca his son. Blaise thinks he has constructed two separate, carefully sealed worlds around himself, and that he alone crosses between them as he crosses Putney Bridge. His own ego is the centre of them both, with Harriet as his sacred love and Emily his profane love.[60] But now the boy, Luca, has crossed between; he was the boy looking into the garden as the novel opened. He has done the unthinkable thing of finding his own way across London, and Blaise finds that a life he thought he had got neatly ordered is in chaos. His two cosmic eggs are broken.

The casual explosion half-way through a sentence thus enables us to experience the same sensation of Blaise, discovering that the occupants of his two worlds have lives of their own and are going to make demands on him. Our accidental movement in reading reflects the contingent nature of the boy's journey, dethroning Blaise from the centre of his solar system. His feeble attempts at making a moral choice are finally ended by another random happening; his wife Harriet is gunned down in a terrorist attack at Hanover airport while attempting to make a new life for herself with Luca. Her death is brutally accidental, seemingly unconnected to the rest of the action which is not in the style of an international thriller but a social tragi-comedy. Yet, as Emily reminds Blaise earlier in a row about her domestic miseries, life is full of such contingencies: 'God, sometimes I feel like people who go to an airport with a machine gun and just shoot everyone within sight. You simply have no idea how much I suffer.'[61]

---

59. Murdoch, *Sacred and Profane Love Machine*, p. 51.

60. Ibid., p. 306. As Luca joins Blaise's two worlds, so Cupid unites the two Venuses in Titian's painting of 'Sacred and Profane Love'. Tamar, in *Book and the Brotherhood*, p. 168, unites Jean's two worlds of Crimond's and Gerard's circles.

61. Murdoch, *Sacred and Profane Love Machine*, p. 79.

Murdoch thus designs an accidental event or unlikely relationship to disturb her characters and her readers into noticing the truth. This is the proper craft of an artist, who can only reflect what is real through some artifice. Here we are already considering the second of Murdoch's means of grace, which is the art-object itself and especially literature. In her essays on philosophy and art, as well as through the conversations in her novels, Murdoch makes clear that 'good art reveals the minute ... random details of the world'.[62] Murdoch believes that art should be mimetic of reality, and she vigorously attacks those who write mere 'fantasy', fulfilling their own wishes through their characters, indulging themselves with a purely private consolation. Yet she insists that good art does nevertheless console us, 'cheering us up' by giving form to what often seems a formless life. Imagination uses image and story to impose a pattern on what is otherwise chaotic, as I argued in the first chapter of this book. Murdoch is well aware of these 'magical tricks' of art and is contriving a pattern of unlikely relationships and accidental events in order to break our fantasies and bring us to truth. As she expresses it in a gnomic sentence: 'Philosophy is clarification, but literature is mystification.'[63]

Art thus achieves liberation from self and an awakening to truth through its patterns and consoling forms. This is because a work of art is, in Murdoch's definition, 'a quasi-sensuous *self-contained* unity'.[64] Because it is an attempt (though always a failed one, as it recognizes itself) at making a complete statement in an incomplete world, it is an object which clearly exists over against us with a reality all its own. It is 'thingy'[65] (or, in philosophical terms, contingent) and by its intense 'otherness' it diverts our attention from ourselves and prompts a quest for the truth. Indeed, if it is good art the artist has already been attending to what is particular, other than himself or herself, in the making of the artefact. Dora, in *The Bell*, looks at her favourite pictures in the National Gallery and sees them as 'something real outside herself, which spoke to her kindly and yet in sovereign tones', destroying 'the dreary, trance-like solipsism'.[66] In *The Sandcastle*, the painter Rain Carter sees the agonizing truth that there is no future in her relationship with

---

62. Murdoch, *Sovereignty of Good*, p. 84.

63. In interview with Brian Magee, in the series *Men of Ideas*, BBC TV, April 1978. The phrase is slightly revised in the published version, Magee, *Men of Ideas*, p. 230.

64. Murdoch, 'Salvation by Words' (1972), in Murdoch, *Existentialists and Mystics*, pp. 235–42 (239), my emphasis. Cf. 'The Sublime and the Beautiful Revisited' (1959), in Murdoch, *Existentialists and Mystics*, pp. 261–86 (263); Murdoch writes that according to Kant 'in art we enjoy an immediate inexplicable understanding of a unique quasi-sensible object'.

65. Magee, *Men of Ideas*, p. 231; cf. Murdoch, 'Salvation by Words', p. 242: 'The work of art, as a pseudo-thing, is profoundly suitable to the nature of beings who inhabit a thingy planet.'

66. Murdoch, *The Bell*, p. 192. Cf. Murdoch, 'Christ and Myth', interview with F. W. Dillistone, *Frontier*, Autumn 1965, pp. 219–21: 'Great art destroys the cloud of comfortable images with which each one of us surrounds himself in his daily living.'

the young married schoolmaster Mor even as she works, with tears, on the canvas of her sitter, Demoyte. She also knows that no work of art reaches the completeness to which it testifies, since she is continually reworking the portrait, and at this very moment of crisis is repainting the head of what was thought to be the finished work, exclaiming ambiguously, 'I see what to do now.'[67]

Even a book of political theory can create the liberating effect of a work of art, if (unlike philosophy proper) it makes the ambitious attempt at a complete vision of reality. In her novel *The Book and the Brotherhood*, the book of the title is said to be 'about everything ... an attempt to think the whole thing through' and so has an 'inert separateness, [an] authoritative thereness'.[68] The brotherhood of friends who had years before commissioned one of their number, Crimond, to write the book have since drifted away from sympathy with his Marxist outlook. Gerard, for example, passionately disagrees with the message of the book when he finally reads it, but believes it to be a wonderful work because 'it will force its opponents to think'.[69] Art loosens us from ourselves, and so attention to it is analogous to 'respect' for morals (what Kant calls *Achtung*); art is not itself exactly morality but should lead to moral action as the self is turned outwards.[70] Indeed, Murdoch suggests that reflection upon art is a kind of religious experience, since it

> perhaps provides for many people, in an unreligious age without prayer or sacraments, their clearest experience of something grasped as separate and precious and beneficial and held quietly and unpossessively in the attention. Good art which we love can seem holy and attending to it can be like praying.[71]

This effect is intensified when the work of art is already a religious symbol, whether in visual art or story. In *The Bell* two visitors to the religious community at Imber, Dora and Toby, find the old Abbey bell at the bottom of the lake where it has lain hidden for centuries, and they raise it secretly at night. Gazing on it, Dora feels reverence for it as she had for the portraits in the gallery: 'It was a thing from another world.' The gospel story of the life of Christ, as graven by the mediaeval artist on the bell, has power to arouse the attention of the observer to reality:[72]

> The squat figures faced her from the sloping surface of the bronze, solid, simple, beautiful, absurd, full to the brim with something which was to the artist not an object of speculation or imagination. These scenes had been more real to him than his childhood and more familiar. He had reported them faithfully.

---

67. Iris Murdoch, *The Sandcastle* (London: Chatto & Windus, 1957), p. 306.
68. Murdoch, *Book and the Brotherhood*, pp. 292, 307; it is also a 'magic book', p. 140.
69. Ibid., p. 565.
70. See Murdoch, 'The Sublime and the Good' (1959), in Murdoch, *Existentialists and Mystics*, pp. 205–20 (212, 216).
71. Murdoch, *Fire and the Sun*, pp. 76–7; cf. Murdoch, *Sovereignty of Good*, p. 75.
72. Murdoch, *The Bell*, pp. 222, 270.

The members of the community at Imber certainly need to have their attention drawn to the truth of the world and other people. Though they are a lay religious community, living in the grounds of an active Abbey, they fail to exercise their spiritual impulses in a way that makes for truth. Both their leaders, in their different ways, fail to notice others as they really are; James is blinded by legalism, and Michael by guilt over a homosexual incident in the past. The inscription on the bell is apt for them and also leads us to consider a third means of grace which Murdoch finds for the egocentric self: the bell announces, *Vox ego sum Amoris. Gabriel vocor* – 'I am the voice of love. I am called Gabriel.'

Falling in love can be an annunciation, the message of an angel shocking the ego into awareness of someone else's distinct being. Through the energy of the dark Eros 'the centre of significance is suddenly ripped out of the self'.[73] The lover's attention is turned to the beloved and thence outwards to live in 'the dangerous, real, contingent world'.[74] When Edmund, at the end of *The Italian Girl*, finally sees Maria as she is, 'separately and authoritatively there', rather than just 'the maid' or a host of other 'Italian girls', then 'even as I apprehended her as my happiness I apprehended her too as my unhappiness'.[75] Thus Eros can also be an inspiration for art, as in the experience of Bradley Pearson in *The Black Prince*. Bradley has the potential to be a good writer, but his creativity is blocked by an exaggerated restraint, a failure to open himself to the life of the world which is the material of his art. Through his passionate affair with Julia Baffin, nearly forty years younger than himself and the daughter of a rival novelist, Bradley feels he has been filled with 'previously unimaginable power which I knew that I could and would use in my art'.[76] Ironically, however, he destroys this potential and the whole relationship by his failure at a critical moment to tell Julia the truth. From that point events gather pace, beyond Bradley's control, and he dies in prison wrongfully convicted of murdering Arnold Baffin.

The pain of 'unselfing', whether through art or Eros, is symbolized in the Greek myth of Marsyas, which long intrigued Iris Murdoch.[77] As the loser in a musical competition with the god Apollo, the mortal Marsyas suffers the punishment of being flayed alive. In Neoplatonism this myth was used to express the ordeal of purifying the self through divine illumination, and Murdoch combines this with the function of Apollo as God of Art. Thus in Bradley's own exegesis of Shakespeare,

---

73. Murdoch, *Fire and the Sun*, p. 36.

74. Murdoch, *Book and the Brotherhood*, p. 306. Sophie-Grace Chappell, 'Love and Knowledge in Murdoch', in Gary Browning (ed.), *Murdoch on Truth and Love* (Cham: Palgrave Macmillan, 2018), pp. 89–108, demonstrates that attention is a form of both knowing and loving.

75. Iris Murdoch, *The Italian Girl* (London: Chatto & Windus, 1964), pp. 212–13.

76. Iris Murdoch, *The Black Prince* (London: Chatto & Windus, 1973), p. 172.

77. She comments on its iconic meaning in an interview with Eric Robson, ITV Channel 4, September 1984, printed in Ronald Lello (ed.), *Revelations* (London: Border Television, 1985), pp. 89–90.

Hamlet represents 'the empty, tormented sinful consciousness of man seared by the bright light of art, the god's flayed victim'.[78] But since Eros, or Dionysius, can also be identified as one aspect of Apollo, both art and love can 'flay' the self, stripping off the egocentric shell we grow around ourselves. This composite figure of Apollo-Eros is the Black Prince of the novel's title, and he takes form in the mysterious figure of P. Loxias who befriends and comforts Bradley in his last years:

> I felt as if he had suffered the lack of me throughout his life; and at the end I suffered with him and suffered, at last, his mortality. I needed him too. He added a dimension to my being.[79]

Bradley's ordeal also thus affirms that the higher Eros, or love of the Good, can be reached through the lower Eros, or sexual desire. Through great passion, lovers can arrive at an 'impersonal' state in which they are no longer absorbed in each other but simply exposed to what is real. To Bradley, after their lovemaking, Julia had 'the dazed, empty look of a great statue', and she confesses to feeling 'quite impersonal … I'm in a place where I've never been before'.[80] In such moments there is what Murdoch has called a revelation, a 'flash from a higher level'.[81] Art can act like this, 'revealing the really real',[82] and Murdoch's characters, like Dora in *The Bell*, sometimes have such experiences looking at pictures in galleries. Beyond the good of accepting the reality of others, beyond loving the contingent details of the world, there is an ultimate Good. There is a supreme moral value, which Murdoch calls (after Plato) 'the sovereignty of good'. Goodness is there, transcending all the particularities of life; it is not a subjective illusion or a merely pragmatic motivation for good acts. Yet this sovereign Good is strictly unreachable; it is the 'unnameable good' of Plato, or the 'imageless God' of St John of the Cross. As the priest, Brendan, explains in Henry and Cato:

> It's the greatest pain and the greatest paradox of all that personal love has to break at some point, the ego has to break, something absolutely natural and seemingly good, perhaps the only good, has to be given up. After that there's darkness and silence and space. And God is there. Remember St. John of the Cross. Where the images end you fall into the abyss, but it is the abyss of faith. When you have nothing left you have nothing left but hope.[83]

---

78. Murdoch, *Black Prince*, p. 164; thus Shakespeare is 'king of Masochists'. Axel, in *A Fairly Honourable Defeat*, p. 31, interprets the image as the agony involved in love.
79. Murdoch, *Black Prince*, p. 364.
80. Ibid., pp. 282–3.
81. Murdoch in Lello, *Revelations*, p. 86. However, Murdoch finds the experience ambiguous.
82. Murdoch, *Fire and the Sun*, p. 77.
83. Murdoch, *Henry and Cato*, p. 336.

We cannot possess the ultimate Good. Revelations can be deceptive because they are only intuitions of the whole of reality; we cannot build too much upon them, for they do not put the transcendent Good into our hands. Rather, we can only undertake the discipline of striving towards it, doing good for no reward. We are to be 'good for nothing',[84] always questing towards and obedient to the Supreme Good while knowing it is unattainable in itself. Here Murdoch disagrees with Plato in the final part of his myth of the cave, where he pictures the good man as finally able to look at the sun. Nevertheless, Murdoch believes that the Good itself can be loved and meditated upon; it can be 'a central point of reflection' even though it is invisible and cannot be represented. Talk of 'God' can be an apt symbol for this transcendent Good, since the idea of God provides, for believers, a 'non-degradable love-object'.[85] This, then, is a fourth means of grace for human beings caught in a box of their own making; we can attend to and serve the Good itself. As the critic Elizabeth Dipple neatly puts it, we are to reach towards 'reality' through love of 'realism'.[86] To attend to the 'goods' that are visible, to the many contingent things that are 'lovely, pure and of good report', will lead to an increasing awareness of the unity of the moral world,[87] even though that one Good cannot be directly experienced.

In religious terms, these traces of the Good are like one divine spirit dispersed into the many particulars of the world. As Rose looks at her brother's collection of stones, with 'so much individuality, so much to notice' in each one, she muses, 'How accidental everything was, and how spirit was scattered everywhere, beautiful, and awful.'[88] In mythical terms, as expounded by Carel Fisher in *The Time of the Angels*, 'the death of God has set the angels free':

Angels are the thoughts of God. Now he has been dissolved into his thoughts which are beyond our conception in their nature and their multiplicity and their power. God was at least the name of something which we thought was good. Now even the name has gone and the spiritual world is scattered.[89]

In this novel, Murdoch is responding to the 'Death of God' movement in the church of the 1960s.[90] In the face of the modern consciousness of loss and absence of God, the question is whether it is possible to go on striving for the

---

84. Murdoch, 'Existentialists and Mystics' (1970), in Murdoch, *Existentialists and Mystics*, pp. 221-34 (233); cf. Murdoch, *Nice and the Good*, p. 350: love which is good for nothing has a blank face.

85. Murdoch, *Good Apprentice*, p. 245; cf. *Sovereignty of Good*, pp. 59-60.

86. Elizabeth Dipple, *Iris Murdoch: Work for the Spirit* (London: Methuen, 1982), p. 30.

87. In a significant conversation in Iris Murdoch, *The Philosopher's Pupil* (London: Chatto & Windus, 1983), pp. 193-4. Father Bernard affirms this unity, while Rozanov denies it.

88. Murdoch, *Book and the Brotherhood*, p. 533.

89. Murdoch, *Time of the Angels*, p. 185.

90. See Chapter 2 for this context.

Good. Carel is an Anglican rector who has come to the conviction that there is no God; aptly he has been moved to a parish in the middle of London which is nothing more than a demolition site, the rectory standing in the middle of a waste area of mud with neither church nor houses to serve. Carel's reaction to the loss of God is to surrender to evil; he knows that the single Good has been scattered into the many, but these he regards as forces of chance which are inevitably hostile to human life. They are not indications of any unified, transcendent Good but simply roaming and malicious powers. He realizes that 'good is only good if one is good for nothing',[91] but he believes such a stance to be totally impossible. If there is no God then there is no single, universal good to be grasped, and consequently there is no goodness at all. This conclusion is not, of course, a necessary one; it is a choice he makes, where other characters in Murdoch's novels adopt *her* own stance of serving the Good 'for nothing' and so find the particulars of the world, though 'awful', to be also 'beautiful'. Thus Carel creates his own universe around himself, and the contingent becomes a horror to him as to all who do so. In his own language, the angels become terrors and he is their 'prey'. He is in a hellish underworld, of which the underground railway that rumbles away beneath the rectory is a constant reminder.

Carel replaces God with himself, playing God-games such as throwing paper darts as his own angelic messengers to signify his approval or disapproval of those who receive them. He exercises a destructive willpower over the inhabitants of the rectory, holding them prisoner by their mingled fear and love of him. In his solipsism he constructs his own mythologies, with two objects of his desire: 'Lucky the man who has the sugar plum fairy and the swan princess.'[92] Pattie, the Irish-West Indian maid, is his sugar plum fairy – 'my black goddess, my counter-Virgin, my anti-Maria' – and from her ample body he believes he gets love incarnate in the flesh. His swan princess is his supposed niece, Elizabeth, who is an invalid with a back ailment; he also calls her his 'sleeping beauty', keeping her confined to her room in a prison of apathy or a contented daze. From her he imagines he gets a more spiritual love. He is in fact secretly having sexual relationships with both of them, even though he knows that Elizabeth is his illegitimate younger daughter. He is perhaps making a parody of the Trinity, with himself as the Father, Pattie as the Son (love in the flesh) and Elizabeth as the Holy Spirit.[93] In other novels Murdoch explores the way that religious belief can become a *means* of reinforcing our cosmic shells; here she demonstrates that *loss* of belief can lead to the same kind of deistic solipsism. By creative fantasy of every kind we try to fit others into our world.

---

91. Murdoch, *Time of the Angels*, p. 186.
92. Ibid., p. 169.
93. This is argued by Dipple, *Iris Murdoch*, pp. 71–2.

The dangers of magic

Murdoch shows herself acutely aware that all the means of grace she presents can be corrupted into a means of self-interest. What ought to be instruments of truth can be bent into tools of fantasy and manipulation, and the word 'magic' resounds continually through the pages of her novels as a cipher for this corruption. Instead of being pulled out of themselves, her characters fall into a deeper prison of the self. It is not only the conflict between truth and magic, but also (as we shall see) the *ambiguity* that her work displays about the status of such 'magic', that provides the most fertile ground for dialogue with Christian doctrine. From this perspective we must now explore again the several means of grace that I have already outlined.

While accidental events and unlikely relationships can shock people into noticing the truth, it is a mark of self-centredness to want to *procure* shocks for others. This is to don the robe of the magician,[94] to wield a magical power over others' lives. It is not an acceptance of contingency and limits but a false attempt at freedom over them, by sheer act of will.[95] Even the grace of art can be corrupted. An art-object can be used for the black magic of self-indulgence: 'Magic in its unregenerate form as the fantastic doctoring of the real for consumption by the ego is the bane of art.'[96] The things that should disturb us can be woven into a net for trapping reality. In *The Bell*, for example, Dora plans a 'miracle' which she hopes will shake the community out of its self-righteousness, with its patronizing view of her as 'the penitent wife'. She is going to use the bell to make an accidental thing happen. A new bell is to be installed at the Abbey, led there in a procession, veiled in white. She plans to substitute the mediaeval bell, raised in secret from the bottom of the lake, for the modern one:

> 'Think of the sensation ... it would be like a real miracle, the sort of thing that makes people go on pilgrimages! ... I should like to shake everybody up a bit' ... She felt as if by the sheer force of her will she could make the great bell rise. After all, and after her own fashion, she would fight. In this holy community she would play the witch.[97]

In the end, although she does raise the bell successfully with the aid of a young visitor to the community, Toby, she does not carry her plot through. Gazing upon the bell, she knows that to use it for a trick would be to betray its truth; 'she had thought to be its master and make it her plaything, but now it was mastering her and having its will'.[98] She remembers a phrase, 'the truth-telling voice that must not

---

94. Murdoch, *Good Apprentice*, p. 1.
95. There is an instance of planning to procure a shock for others in *Time of the Angels*, p. 114; see later, pp. 50–51.
96. Murdoch, *Fire and the Sun*, p. 79.
97. Murdoch, *The Bell*, pp. 199–200.
98. Ibid., p. 270.

be silenced'. So she gives voice to the truth, by throwing herself against the bell and making its mighty tongue ring out, calling people to the barn where the bell had been hidden. We are reminded of Hopkins's bell in his poem 'As kingfishers catch fire', which – like Murdoch's bell – is an example of a particular object in the world which commands attention in its own right:

> Each hung bell's
> Bow swung finds tongue to fling out broad its name;
> … Selves – goes itself; *myself* it speaks and spells;
> Crying *What I do is me: for that I came.*[99]

The bell speaks what it is and alerts us to what we are. Toby, however, also wants to use it as a magical charm, thinking that he will impress Dora and win her love by the enormous undertaking of raising the bell from the lake. When it is safely stored in the barn, he falls upon Dora and they roll in passion into the mouth of the bell. This makes it ring – a slight, muffled ring unlike the mighty roar which Dora is later to draw from it, but still a ring of truth.

A third attempt to manipulate the bell is made by Catherine Fawley, who uses it to reinforce her own image of herself which she wants to project to others. Neglecting the truth of her own inner feelings of passion, Catherine has vowed to enter the enclosed part of the Abbey as a nun and is to be received as a novice on the same day that the new bell is to be installed. Both are dressed in white, both dedicated to God, both go in procession. For her and the whole lay community, spirituality is much a matter of certain external behaviour, and this pride is given a severe jolt as the bridge over the lake collapses and the new bell is tipped into the water.

Art-objects are abused when they are used as magical charms, and yet Murdoch admits that there is an inevitable component of 'magic' within them. As we have seen, a novel offers a completeness that is in the end illusory; it has a neatness of structure and pattern that is not true of life, and it can play the kind of tricks of accident that we have seen Murdoch delights in. In an address in 1972, Murdoch declared that 'any dictator attempts to degrade the language because this is a way to mystify'; wanting to achieve 'mystification' they blunt the 'verbal precision' of language as practised in literature, which is 'the most practically important' of all the arts 'for our survival and salvation'.[100] Yet in an interview broadcast in 1978 she states that 'philosophy aims to clarify … Literature is full of tricks and magic and deliberate mystification'.[101] In both cases Murdoch is in fact making a consistent case for literature as a vehicle of truth, which calls for a 'purification' of thought,[102] but her wavering over the suitability of the word 'mystification' reveals

---

99. Gerard Manley Hopkins, *Poems* (ed. W. H. Gardner and N. H. Mackenzie) (London: Oxford University Press, 4th edn, 1967), p. 90, original emphases.
100. Murdoch, 'Salvation by Words', p. 241.
101. Magee, *Men of Ideas*, p. 230.
102. Ibid., p. 231.

the necessary ambiguity that remains. A philosopher in one of her novels rejects art (in the spirit of Plato), as 'magic that joins good and evil together',[103] but in her own philosophical work she has a more balanced view: 'Sophistry and magic break down at intervals, but they never go away and there is no end to their collusion with art and to the consolations which, *perhaps fortunately* for the human race, they can provide.'[104]

The dangerously thin line between a 'consolation' that is healthy and promotes unselfing and one that is mere fantasy becomes even thinner for Murdoch when she portrays the effect of religious symbolism. I have already mentioned her belief that talk about God may be a way of directing the attention to the 'undegradable love-object' that is the Good. On the other hand, religion becomes fantasy if we expect a personal God to intervene and supply us with 'instant salvation', or, as her philosopher John Robert describes it, 'salvation by magic, being totally changed'.[105] In *The Time of the Angels*, Carel's brother Marcus has no such belief in a personal God, and yet he also wants to use the old Christian images as magic talismans. He hopes that the faith of others, in a magical way, will act as charms against the threats of evil in our world: 'He did not believe in the Father, the Son and the Holy Ghost, but he wanted others to believe. He wanted the old structure to continue there beside him, near by, something he could occasionally reach out and touch with his hand.'[106] So he is horrified when he meets a modern (and well-fed) bishop who also thinks that God is dead, that 'those who have come nearest to God have spoken of blackness, even emptiness', so that 'obedience to God must be an obedience without trimmings, an obedience, in a sense, for nothing'.[107] When Marcus protests that this takes away all the guarantees, the bishop laughs and remarks, 'That's where faith comes in.'

Yet in the world of Murdoch's novels, the use of religious symbols as 'magic' is not unreservedly bad. After all, there is a legitimate magic in all art-objects, and Murdoch tends to treat the images of Christian belief – whether verbal or pictorial – as an intense form of the 'mystification' that art employs generally, even though they have an even greater capacity for unhealthy illusion. The girl Tamar in *The Book and the Brotherhood*, for example, finds that the Christian symbols of Christ and divine forgiveness release her from the hell of self-loathing in which she has become trapped after an abortion. Like a previous character, Morgan, she has neglected the 'miraculous other being' of a child,[108] and she is now obsessed by a daemon of otherness, believing that the dead child is persecuting her, and that it finally even kills her friend Jenkin. Announcing that she has become a Christian, she explains she must be saved from destruction:

103. Murdoch, *Philosopher's Pupil*, p. 192.
104. Murdoch, *Fire and the Sun*, pp. 87–8, my emphasis.
105. Murdoch, *Philosopher's Pupil*, p. 186.
106. Murdoch, *Time of the Angels*, p. 103.
107. Ibid., p. 102.
108. Murdoch, *Book and the Brotherhood*, p. 324.

I can't do it myself, and you can't do it either. I need supernatural help. Not that I believe it's supernatural or that there is any supernatural. But perhaps there is help somewhere, some force, some power … When you're drowning you don't care what you hold onto. I just don't care whether God exists or who Christ was. Perhaps I just believe in magic. Who cares? It's up to me, it's my salvation.[109]

Like Father Brendan in Henry and Cato, her spiritual advisor Father McAlister has no real belief in the objective existence of God or the resurrection of Christ either. But 'he believed in prayer, in Christ as a mystical Saviour, and in the magical power which had been entrusted to him when he was ordained a priest, a power to save souls and raise the fallen'.[110] Like other characters in Murdoch's novels,[111] he finds that he can know a 'mystical Christ' who is the way of truth for him, a Christ who is not literally resurrected but who faced the fact of death in all its terrible contingency and thus enables us to love God/the Good. So he takes Tamar through a process of 'getting to know her Christ' and tells her that 'if Christ saves, Christ lives … That is the resurrection and the life'.[112] The reality of this 'mystical Christ', of whom one can say 'I know that my Redeemer lives' in a way that cannot be rationally analysed, is vividly hinted at in the experience of Anne Cavidge. As a result of her visionary 'meeting' with Christ she is convinced there is no personal God. Yet the finger with which she tried, like Mary Magdalen in the Gospel narrative (John 20:17) to grasp him and keep him with her, will not heal up: 'It came to her that he was real, that he was unique. She was an atom of the universe and he was her own Christ, the Christ that belonged to her, laserbeamed to her alone from infinitely far away.'[113]

Father McAlister knows that to use the symbols of God, the divinity of Christ, eternal life, salvation and forgiveness without a basis in an objectively existing God is a kind of magic. Though he rejoices in his 'magical power' as a priest, guarding and wielding these weapons, he is also uneasy; contemplating a children's nativity play, with the crib 'a glowing radiant object, so holy', he reflects that 'the power which I derive from my Christ is debased by its passage through me. It reaches me as love, it leaves me as magic. That is why I make serious mistakes.'[114]

He has good reason to be uneasy: we notice danger signs in Murdoch's narrative, such as his rejoicing in 'the fire of instant salvation'[115] and the final effect of his ministry on Tamar; though she does recover from her personal hell, she develops

---

109. Murdoch, *Book and the Brotherhood*, p. 452.

110. Ibid., p. 488; cf. Murdoch in Lello, *Revelations*, p. 84: 'Christ whom I regard as a mystical figure.'

111. Such as Father Brendan (*Henry and Cato*), Stuart Cuno (*The Good Apprentice*), Father Bernard (*The Philosopher's Pupil*) and Anne Cavidge (*Nuns and Soldiers*).

112. Murdoch, *Book and the Brotherhood*, p. 490.

113. Murdoch, *Nuns and Soldiers*, p. 304.

114. Murdoch, *Book and the Brotherhood*, p. 516.

115. Ibid., p. 488.

a kind of self-preserving calculation that falls short of true love. The question put by 'The Good Apprentice', Stuart, persists: 'Is magic bad?'[116] 'All the magic's gone' cries Beautiful Joe, the street urchin and petty criminal of Henry and Cato, when he sees Cato without his cassock;[117] he no longer wants to go away with a man who now looks like a middle-aged pervert in a corduroy jacket. Cato protests that 'a priest is just a symbol' and affirms his love for Joe, but we know that a symbol is not 'just' anything; his failure to grasp its power sets a series of events in train that finally ends in his humiliating kidnap by Joe and Joe's death at his hands.

The ambiguity about the magic of religious symbols is an acute form of the ambiguity attaching to any work of art. When a religious symbol is captured in an art-object the danger is most intense, since 'art materialises God' and tempts us to take the image 'for real'.[118] Yet all art inclines to make us content with images.[119] The ambivalence Murdoch displays over this is well illustrated in the incident of the loss of the icon in *The Time of the Angels*. For the caretaker, Eugene, the icon of the Trinity, which he has preserved from his childhood home in St Petersburg, is the only fixed point in a shifting existence. Having endured many years in a refugee settlement, he has found the whole world since then to be a kind of transit camp, affording no permanent home. He has lost his faith in the 'bearded Russian God [who] had listened in the darkness to his supplications', yet in the darkness he loves the icon 'as a blank image of goodness from which all personality had been withdrawn'.[120] Like the bell at Imber, the icon can draw attention to the good, and Eugene has a basic respect for truth and goodness that gives him a dignity in his basement quarters and makes him an attractive and comforting figure to several of the distressed souls who inhabit the novel. Significantly the icon depicts the Trinity in the only permissible way in Orthodox tradition, as three identical angels; we recall that the dispersion of goodness from one Absolute into the many particulars of the world is mythologized by Murdoch as 'the time of the angels'.[121] 'How can those three be one?' demands Carel when he confronts the icon.[122] Seen through the eyes of Pattie, the West Indian-Irish maid, the angels have the particularity of everyday things: 'It glows as if it were on fire ... It shows three angels confabulating round a table. The angels have rather small heads and very large pink haloes and anxious thoughtful expressions.'[123]

When Eugene's feckless son, Leo, steals the icon and sells it to an antique shop, Eugene is at first devastated. But he begins to see that he has been treating it as

116. Murdoch, *Good Apprentice*, p. 518.
117. Murdoch, *Henry and Cato*, p. 192.
118. Murdoch, *Fire and the Sun*, p. 70.
119. Ibid., p. 66.
120. Murdoch, *Time of the Angels*, p. 62.
121. See above and also cf. Murdoch, *Philosopher's Pupil*, p. 187, 'our time of the angels ... Spirit without God'.
122. Murdoch, *Time of the Angels*, p. 188.
123. Ibid., p. 11. The scene is based on Genesis 19:1-3.

a talisman of his lost childhood, a magical charm shielding him from the reality of the present: 'Let it go, let it go. Now he was a stripped man and better for it; so he told himself; *but he could not really think in this way*.'[124] There is the sharp ambivalence. If God is dead, must images of God also be lost in the cause of truth? Such images of the Good cannot be totally evacuated of magic, and they will always be manipulated for the sake of fantasy; yet they have a place in the devotion of disciples of the Good. Muriel, into whose hands it comes, wants to misuse it to make a miracle, as Dora wants to use the bell; by returning it to Eugene she will win his gratitude and his love – 'the miraculous return of the icon would open the gates of communication between them'.[125] We feel it right that the icon in fact gets back to Eugene by the black hand of Pattie; symbols of reality must not be exploited to buttress the self.

A theological perspective: Dietrich Bonhoeffer and the world come of age

When we place Murdoch's stories alongside the Christian story, as she herself frequently does,[126] then makers of Christian doctrine should take account of her portrayal of characters who use and misuse religious images. Living through these stories should alert the theologian to the way that images of God and Christ have been used to dominate others and to bolster the will to power of the self. For instance, modern political theology has shown how images of God as sole ruler of the universe have been used to legitimate sole human rule in the state. The lordship of Christ has been used to sanction the lordship of bishop and monarch as Christ's representatives on earth.[127] But an empathetic entrance into the experience of Murdoch's characters should also enable the theologian to be imaginative about the many ways in which images of God are invoked in order to impose a world upon others and increase one's own security.

At the same time, the theologian who lives these lives vicariously cannot avoid grappling with the modern sense of 'loss of God' from the world. The fact that there is a widespread consciousness of the 'death of God' will no longer seem peripheral to the making of doctrine, if it did before; the need to interpret this consciousness will become central and urgent. There is a connection here with the misuse of images for the sake of human power; if God *were* present in the world as a *deus ex machina*, as an irresistible cause of events, then this God would coerce the world into submission and feed a religion of domination. The secular feeling

---

124. Ibid., p. 120, my emphasis.
125. Ibid., p. 202.
126. In addition to examples already given, the parable of the Good Samaritan is echoed in *An Accidental Man*, and the Prodigal Son in *The Good Apprentice*.
127. See, e.g., Alistair Kee, *Constantine versus Christ* (London: SCM Press, 1982), pp. 153–75; Jürgen Moltmann, *The Trinity and the Kingdom of God: The Doctrine of God* (trans. Margaret Kohl) (London: SCM Press, 1981), pp. 191–202.

that cause and effect in the world can be explained perfectly well without God's being behind it goes with a sense of human autonomy, of a 'coming of age' in which human beings want no longer to be mere children in the Father's house but to take the adult responsibility of running the estate. Twenty years before the 'death of God' movement in the 1960s, the Lutheran theologian Dietrich Bonhoeffer had written fragmentary comments from a Nazi prison on the necessity of living *etsi deus non daretur* – 'as if there were no God' – as part of God's own intention for human beings 'come of age'.[128] Bonhoeffer had found the phrase *as if there were no God* in Wilhelm Dilthey as an expression of the modern sense of the autonomy of the world.[129] God, he now suggested, was deliberately veiling God's self in order to wean us away from a childish dependency upon what we have imagined as a dominating father-figure or a *deus ex machina*. His words have deservedly become a classic text:

> And the only way to be honest is to recognise that we have to live in the world *etsi deus non daretur*. And this is just what we do see – before God! So our coming of age leads us to a true recognition of our situation *vis à vis* God. God is teaching us that we must live as men who can get along very well without him. The God who is with us is the God who forsakes us (Mark 15.34). The God who makes us live in the world without using him as a working hypothesis is the God before whom we are ever standing. Before God and with him we live without God. God allows himself to be edged out of the world and on to the cross. God is weak and powerless in the world, and that is exactly the way, the only way, in which he can be with us and help us ... Man's religiosity makes him look in his distress to the power of God in the world; he uses God as a *Deus ex machina*. The Bible however directs him to the powerlessness and suffering of God; only a suffering God can help.[130]

Murdoch was well aware of this programmatic statement. She had read and underlined a copy of the first English edition of Bonhoeffer's *Letters and Papers*

---

128. The first appearance of the exact phrase 'world come of age' is in Bonhoeffer, *Letters and Papers from Prison* (trans. Isabel Best, Lisa E. Dahill, Reinhard Krauss and Nancy Lukens), Dietrich Bonhoeffer Works (DBW) 8 (Minneapolis: Fortress Press, 2010), pp. 426–8. Bonhoeffer is echoing the image of the Apostle Paul, Galatians 4:1–7. The passage is heavily underlined in Iris Murdoch's copy of the earlier (1953) English translation of Bonhoeffer's *Letters and Papers from Prison* (repr., London: Collins/Fontana, 1966), pp. 108–10, IML 741.

129. Bonhoeffer also traces the phrase to H. Grotius in *Letters and Papers*, DBW 8, pp. 476–8; see esp. notes 18–28. See also Kevin A. Lenehan, '*Etsi deus non daretur*: Bonhoeffer's Useful Misuse of Grotius' Maxim and Its Implications for Evangelisation in the World Come of Age', *Australasian Journal of Bonhoeffer Studies* 1.1 (2013), pp. 34–60.

130. Letter to Eberhard Bethge of 16 July 1944; cited from Murdoch's edition of Bonhoeffer, *Letters and Papers*, p. 122.

from Prison sometime between 1966 and 1967,[131] and her comment on this passage appears in her Leslie Stephen Lecture for 1967 on 'The Sovereignty of Good over Other Concepts':

> We are what we seem to be, transient mortal creatures subject to necessity and chance. This is to say that there is, in my view, no God in the traditional sense of that term; and the traditional sense is perhaps the only sense. When Bonhoeffer says that God wants us to live as if there were no God I suspect he is misusing words.[132]

In a later chapter I intend to analyse her assertions in this context that the word 'God' needs to be abandoned in favour of 'Good', and that Bonhoeffer's attempt to preserve the word has, in view of his own theology, no future in a world of demythologization. Here I want to develop the implications of Bonhoeffer's declaration as a perspective on Murdoch's novelistic portrayal of giving attention to the Good as it is 'scattered' into the truth of the many particular details of the world.

Murdoch correctly summarizes Bonhoeffer as saying that God 'wants' us to live *etsi non deus daretur*, 'as if there were no God'.[133] It is not altogether clear, however, why she thinks that this is a misuse of words. Murdoch seems to have had no problem with the *logic* of the 'as if' formulation in itself as applied to God. With regard to its positive use (equivalent to saying 'as if there *were* a God') she comments several times on Kant's presentation of moral imperatives coming 'as if' from God as a supreme lawmaker,[134] and she finds an echo here from Plato's 'as if' in his *Meno*, where the spiritual force and energy which moves us towards virtue comes 'as if' from a divine source.[135] In both, 'mythical pictures' can give us an insight into the pattern of the moral life.[136] Murdoch does not appear elsewhere to cite the negative form – 'as if there were *no* God' – but she paraphrases it when she writes that, in the moral life, Kant believes that 'man must proceed as if everything depended upon him; only on this condition dare he hope that higher wisdom will grant the completion of his well-intentioned endeavours'.[137] Here, 'as if everything depended on man' is surely equivalent to 'as if there were no God'.

---

131. For more detail, see Chapter 2. It is a complicated matter to draw conclusions from markings in Murdoch's copy of *Letters and Papers*, because the book appears to have been obtained second-hand, and it had apparently already been marked (mostly, it seems, in red ink) by its previous owner.

132. Murdoch, *Sovereignty of Good*, p. 79.

133. Murdoch's edition oddly omits the phrase in the German edition, 'God himself compels us to recognize it': see *Letters and Papers*, DBW 8, p. 478.

134. Murdoch, *Metaphysics*, p. 266, cf. pp. 11, 26, 488.

135. Ibid., p. 435, cf. pp. 10, 148, 402–3, 477, 505. See Plato, *Meno*, 86bc.

136. Ibid., p. 11.

137. Ibid., p. 447.

Moreover, she goes on to associate its logic with the positive 'as if' form, saying that 'this "as if" may remind us of sayings of Plato in the *Meno* and the *Republic*'. We are left with the conclusion that Murdoch thinks the misuse of words is not the notion of acting 'as if there were no God', but that of a God who actually *wants* us to live *etsi non deus daretur*. Such a God would, in her view, not be a God at all; the idea is incompatible with the 'traditional sense' of 'God', and 'the traditional sense is perhaps the only sense' possible. In *The Green Knight*, Bellamy seems to be echoing Bonhoeffer's words in reflecting on a 'mystical' Christ – 'It is almost *as though* He were telling us not to believe in Him!'[138] – but Bellamy regards Christ as essentially human, and so there is no mismatch with Murdoch's linguistic objection.

For Bonhoeffer himself, the notion that God 'wants' us to live 'as if there were no God' derives its meaning from his following statement that 'God lets himself be pushed out of the world onto the cross'. Either Murdoch does not notice this expansion of the contentious phrase, or she objects to it (as I suggest below). Bonhoeffer is speaking not of an absent God – and so no God at all – but of a God who 'is with us and helps us' precisely because God shares our suffering as 'weak and powerless in the world'. The world out of which God is 'edged' is one where things are under the control of a *deus ex machina*. Bonhoeffer means that God wants us to live 'as if' there were no God, because there *is* no God in the traditional sense of one who could intervene and dominate. In response to the sense of 'death of God' that became widespread in the 1960s, theologians have gladly admitted that the image of a dictatorial cosmic ruler is indeed dead, but affirmed that God is present in the world in a mode of weakness and suffering. It is because God really participates in the human experience of pain and death that God is not dead – that is, irrelevant – to the world. As the theologian Eberhard Jüngel expresses it, we can only think and talk about God in a perishable world because God is 'related to perishability', as the cross of Jesus makes clear.[139] The theologian can therefore interpret the modern lack of consciousness of God not as evidence for the absence of God but as a sign of God's deliberate self-hiddenness for the sake of human freedom.

This means in turn, as Rudolph Bultmann explains in commenting on Bonhoeffer's words, that we must be in a constant state of readiness for unexpected encounters with the hidden God: readiness 'consists in openness in allowing something really to encounter us that does not leave the I alone, the I that is encapsulated in its purposes and plans, but whose encounter transforms us, permits us to become new selves again and again'. This, Bultmann adds, 'can be a questioning readiness, but it can also be completely unconscious. For, surprisingly,

---

138. Iris Murdoch, *The Green Knight* (London: Chatto & Windus, 1993), p. 41, my emphasis.

139. Eberhard Jüngel, *God as the Mystery of the World* (trans. D. Guder) (Edinburgh: T&T Clark, 1983), pp. 185-6.

God can encounter us where we do not expect it.'[140] Such unexpected meetings happen in the midst of the world we know and can explain without God, not in the gaps of the unknown. God is not necessary to explain the world, but 'he is more than necessary', as Eberhard Jüngel puts it. Reflecting on Bonhoeffer's phrase *etsi non deus daretur*, Jüngel suggests that a world which is already self-evident and interesting without God becomes even more interesting when lit up by the self-unveiling of the God who veils God's self in the world.[141]

There are obvious and striking parallels here with Murdoch's portrayal of characters who are surprised by unexpected hints or reminders of the Good, and so shocked out of the orbit of their own self. Murdoch has in fact commended a 'waiting' upon the Good and acknowledges the influence of Simone Weil's notion of attention[142] which Weil identifies as 'Waiting On God':

> I quoted Simone Weil earlier on the subject of patient attention which waits for the insight which has not yet been given. The artist or thinker concentrates on the problem, grasps it as a problem with some degree of clarity, and waits. Something is apprehended as *there* which is not yet *known*. Then something comes; as we sometimes say from the unconscious. It comes to us out of the dark of non-being, as a reward for loving attention.[143]

The artist, Murdoch suggests, waits for what is good, for the 'right thing, the best thing', just as religious people 'wait' in prayer for God, as 'the spirit and light of goodness … to be made manifest'.[144] She reflects that what the artist is waiting for is hidden: 'We have to wait and attempt to formulate for ourselves and convey to others what is initially beyond and hidden.'[145] The artist who 'concentrates and waits' finds that the poem, picture or music is waiting for *her*, 'veiled but present'.[146]

As the theologian recognizes the God who is hidden in the midst of the world, so Murdoch finds that the Good is scattered into the Many, and though her characters have their own moral responsibility they still need help from this hidden but not absent Good. But Murdoch has something further to say which

---

140. Rudolph Bultmann, 'The Idea of God and Modern Man', in R. Gregor Smith (ed.), *World Come of Age: A Symposium on Dietrich Bonhoeffer* (London: Collins, 1967), pp. 256-73 (271).

141. Jüngel, *God as the Mystery of the World*, pp. 30-4, 59-63, 378-89.

142. Iris Murdoch, 'The Idea of Perfection' (1962), in Murdoch, *Existentialists and Mystics*, pp. 299-336 (327): 'a just and loving gaze directed upon an individual reality'. see Weil, *Gravity and Grace* (trans. Emma Craufurd) (London: Routledge and Kegan Paul, 1952), pp. 107-8.

143. Murdoch, *Metaphysics*, p. 505, original emphasis.

144. Ibid., p. 418.

145. Ibid., p. 283.

146. Ibid., p. 400.

is of importance for the shaping of a theology which waits upon the hidden God. How shall we recognize God's presence, veiled in the midst of the world? That is a moral as well as a spiritual question, and for Christians who find God incarnate in Christ it takes the particular form of how to know the Christ who is present in the world. In her moral vision of what is real, Murdoch depicts characters who pay (or fail to pay) attention to contingent details of the world, to the facts. Waiting upon the Good means noticing the particular reality, the truth, of persons and things in the world. Bonhoeffer is curiously in tune with this way of thinking when he declares that 'whatever human weaknesses, miscalculations and guilt there are in what precedes the facts, God is in the facts themselves'.[147]

Attention to 'the facts' is a key part of Bonhoeffer's Christology. For Bonhoeffer, the reality of the world is permeated by Christ, since it is in Christ that God has taken human nature to God's self. Christ then 'takes form' in every time and place in human history, and we can only speak about 'what the good is, can be, or should be' by speaking about 'how Christ may take form among us today and here'.[148] Christians thus make ethical decisions by conforming themselves to the Christ who so takes form. The form of the Christ in the present can only be found by a careful analysis of the situation itself, for Christ is there in the truth of the concrete facts and the contingent details.

> There are not two realities [of Christ and the world], but only one reality, and that is God's reality revealed in Christ as the reality of the world. Partaking in Christ we stand at the same time in the reality of God and in the reality of the world. The reality of Christ embraces the reality of the world in itself.[149]

Bonhoeffer is 'situational' in his ethics in so far as he refuses to base them upon any moral laws which enshrine what is good once and for all; rather, the question is 'how Christ takes form among us today and here – in other words, how we are conformed to Christ's form',[150] and we shall only know that by giving attention to the 'facts' that are really there. He is, however, more than situational in that what is 'good' transcends the particular situation; it is actually the demand of the *Christ* who is present there.[151] We are not just finding what our minds judge to be 'the loving thing to do'; we are being conformed to a Christ who is objectively present, and through whom we encounter the will of God who has a purpose for creation. Murdoch's figure of the liberal bishop in *Time of the Angels*, object of Murdoch's

---

147. Bonhoeffer, *Letters and Papers*, DBW 8, p. 265. The edition used by Murdoch translates 'in the events': *Letters and Papers* (1966), p. 63.
148. Dietrich Bonhoeffer, *Ethics* (trans. Reinhard Krauss, Charles C. West and Douglas W. Scott), Dietrich Bonhoeffer Works 6 (Minneapolis: Fortress Press, 2009), pp. 100–1.
149. Ibid., p. 58.
150. Ibid., p. 100, cf. p. 323.
151. Ibid., pp. 378–81.

gentle mockery as he is, appears to have absorbed this message from Bonhoeffer; when asked about Jesus Christ he observes that 'it is a time when mankind is growing up', that 'God lives and works in history' and that 'obedience to God must be … an obedience, in a sense, for nothing'.[152]

Now, from this perspective, the dialogue of the theologian with Murdoch's thought becomes a critical comment upon her work. We have already noted her ambiguous stance towards the 'magic' of art and religious symbol, and now the theologian, following the track laid down by Bonhoeffer, can proffer a critical perception into what is happening. For Murdoch the Many into which the Good is scattered, the many good things in art and nature upon which we meditate, are impersonal fragments of spiritual reality and sources of 'good energy' like sacraments.[153] Appealing again to the idea of 'waiting', Murdoch writes: 'We wait, we reflect, we conjure up good things out of our soul, lights, sacraments, attachments. Seen here, freedom must be thought of as a love of good which enables a unity of thought and desire.'[154]

Father Bernard in *The Philosopher's Pupil* surely voices her opinion when he claims that 'anything can be a sacrament – transformed – like the bread and wine'.[155] But these fragmentary traces of the Good are not truly analogous to the Christian sacraments, since they are not places of encounter with a personal God. For Bonhoeffer, the God who wants us to live 'as if there were no God' is hidden in the many 'facts' of the world and so unveils God's own self to the one who waits and watches. Truth is in meeting. Rejecting the God who intervenes from outside as a mere 'stopgap' at the 'limits of our possibilities', Bonhoeffer affirms that in a world come of age 'God wants to be recognized in the midst of our lives'.[156] Despite Bonhoeffer's criticism of what he calls, in *Letters and Papers*, the 'positivism of revelation' of Karl Barth,[157] they thus express themselves similarly about the self-revelation of the hidden God. In revelation, as Barth puts it, God takes objects in the world and uses them to make God's self manifest; God is 'veiled' in the mystery of secularity and only indirectly 'unveiled' through it. Thus objects in the world, including words and the humanity of Christ, are 'sacramental' in

---

152. Murdoch, *Time of the Angels*, pp. 101–2. On Murdoch's bishop, and Bishop John Robinson of *Honest to God* fame, see later, pp. 53–4.

153. Murdoch, *Sovereignty of Good*, p. 69. On 'writing sacraments', see Rowe, *Iris Murdoch*, pp. 70–2.

154. Murdoch, *Metaphysics*, p. 457.

155. Murdoch, *Philosopher's Pupil*, p. 192.

156. Bonhoeffer, *Letters and Papers*, DBW 8, p. 406.

157. Ibid., pp. 363–4, 373, 429–30. Regin Prenter, 'Dietrich Bonhoeffer and Karl Barth's Positivism of Revelation', in Smith, *World Come of Age*, pp. 93–130 (105), proposes that by the phrase Bonhoeffer means 'that proclamation of God's revelation which presents its truths … without being able to show clearly how they are related to the life of the world come of age' and argues that this criticism of Barth needs qualification.

that God 'gives himself to be known' in them.[158] We cannot make God an object of our own knowing, and although God never speaks the divine Word except through secular symbols, we must never confuse the two. This freedom of God to unveil or veil God's self in worldly objects demythologizes nature of any divine qualities and always resists the 'magic' of manipulating objects as things of power in themselves.

Murdoch, similarly, does not confuse the Good itself with the many goods that symbolize it and make it visible. Indeed, she herself quotes Karl Barth to this end.[159] The Good in itself is unattainable, and we are to serve it 'for nothing'. Yet a theologian will observe that because there is no objectively existing, personal God according to Murdoch to be met in and through the signs or sacraments in which the Good is scattered through the world, there is the constant danger that the signs will necessarily become powerful talismans in themselves. By contrast, the hidden presence of God as personal Creator and Reconciler of the world – though not in the mythological form of 'a person', or a superior personal being[160] – acts as a control over the deifying of things. Murdoch, to be sure, develops the sense from the 1970s onwards of a 'mystical Christ' who is present here and now and who directs us towards the Good,[161] and already in her 1966 edition of *Letters and Papers*, Murdoch appears to have underlined and side-lined passages about the presence of Christ in the world.[162] But this does not mean any kind of personal encounter with the 'sovereign' Good itself; in finding a limited place for 'as-if' sayings about the existence of an impetus behind a moral life which transcends the present moment with divine force, Murdoch is clear that, in a world come of age, there is no place for relating to a 'personal God'. She comments that 'such acting "as if" would not be like the mythical "as-if" in the *Meno*'. The fiction would be 'hardly discernible from a wishful thought'.[163]

The peril for Murdoch is always that of seeking 'consolation' and so distracting us from the death of the self. But the irony is that symbols of the Good can become such a consolation. The danger of magic becomes most acute with religious symbols but, as we have seen, it is an incipient problem with all art and natural things of beauty. The Christian theologian observes the uncertainties about 'magic' that appear in the novels and proffers an explanation for the phenomenon from a theological perspective, incisively developed by Bonhoeffer.

---

158. Karl Barth, *Church Dogmatics* (trans. and ed. G. W. Bromiley and T. F. Torrance), 14 vols (Edinburgh: T&T Clark, 1936–77), I/1, pp. 163–5; II/1, pp. 50–4.
159. For Murdoch's quotations of Karl Barth, *The Epistle to the Romans* (trans. Edwyn C. Hoskyns) (repr., Oxford: Oxford University Press, 1968), commenting on Rom. 1:20, 8:21–4; see later, p. 58.
160. For this distinction, see Chapter 2.
161. See further Chapter 2.
162. Bonhoeffer, *Letters and Papers* (1966), pp. 108, 130, 165.
163. Murdoch, *Metaphysics*, p. 469.

False saviours: A Murdochian critique of religion

In reviewing the false shapes into which the instruments of the good can be warped by the self, we have not yet considered the distortions of love. While falling in love can decentre the self, shaking it into noticing the existence of another and, together with the beloved, the reality of the contingent world, yet the experience can end in a deeper fall into self. Among several different ways this may happen to Murdoch's characters is the making of a saviour. Characters may impose the role upon another, seeking salvation from their love, or they may assume it voluntarily themselves. Either way, the result is an evasion of the truth that must be faced, a turning away from the hard details of the world and a loss of moral responsibility.

Murdoch's characters often seek a saviour by confessing some misdeed and then believing themselves to be 'saved' if the beloved goes on loving them despite it. They think they have told the truth and been forgiven, but they have shrugged off the proper quest for truth and the good. When Blaise, in *The Sacred and Profane Love Machine*, tells Harriet about his mistress Emily he carefully shapes the account in a letter to her (which he himself finds very moving), stating that the relationship lasted only briefly, that he long ago ceased to find Emily attractive and that he visits her only 'at intervals' for the sake of the child. When Harriet forgives him, he believes himself to be saved:

> In now confessing this [I] can only cast myself on your love as a religious person casts himself onto God ... I ask you, madly perhaps, for your love as the only instrument of salvation ... The extra power which can save the world can only come from your perfect love, my angel and my wife.[164]

Blaise, however, is using her forgiveness to avoid dealing with the situation of Emily, which is becoming more and more intolerable to Emily herself. Having confessed, in an edited version, to his wife, he thinks he has done everything needful, but Emily has already protested, 'I wanted you to tell her because I thought this meant honesty and truth and a square deal for me ... The fact remains that I love you (yes, I must be stupid), and I want you to be my husband, my real husband, and live with me in a real house and look after your son.'[165] This is the 'real' situation, Blaise's 'real' dilemma in which – appointing Emily as another saviour ('the way, the truth and the life')[166] – he fails to make a responsible choice.

This false salvation is a kind of magic, as Edward partly realizes in *The Good Apprentice*. He has sought out his father, the once god-like and now senile Jessie Baltram, in order to confess his responsibility for the death of his friend Mark and ask his forgiveness. 'I love you so much,' he tells him, 'You could do everything for me, you could make me all over again.'[167] But now that Mark's sister Brownie has

---

164. Murdoch, *Sacred and Profane Love Machine*, pp. 121–2.
165. Ibid., p. 119.
166. Ibid., p. 194.
167. Murdoch, *Good Apprentice*, p. 234.

spoken her own forgiveness, his father's vague words pale into nothing: 'What he had taken for redemption had all been illusions, effects of magic.'[168] The irony is that he is about to make a similar saviour out of Brownie. The novel begins with the words from the parable of the prodigal son, 'I will arise and go to my father, and will say to unto him, Father I have sinned,' but the true father is not Jesse but the 'Father and Maker of all' whom Plato identifies as the supreme form of the Good.

Part of the salvation syndrome is the consent of the saviour, and this is no less an evasion of the real world. Tamar's plight in *The Book and the Brotherhood*, made pregnant by Duncan, has arisen from her desire to redeem him from despair by her love. 'You're saving me by pity,' whimpers Duncan in her arms.[169] Similarly Henry, in *Henry and Cato*, tells his unsuitable fiancée that 'I love you because I've taken you on'.[170] Harriet, in *The Sacred and Profane Love Machine*, casts herself in the same role of saviour with Blaise; now that the world in which she was once so placidly content has been broken up and 'she sees the world as terrible', she constructs a number of redemption myths to try and deal with it. Having failed to save Blaise by forgiveness she attempts to apply saving love to her friends Monty and Edgar and finally spins a fantasy in which her love will save Blaise's most difficult and frequently suicidal patient, Magnus Bowles. Unfortunately he turns out to be a fiction, invented for Blaise by Monty (the author of mediocre detective novels) in weekly instalments in order to cover up for his frequent absences with Emily. Magnus is the very epitome of everyone's failure to face reality; he has the most interesting dreams of all the characters, and these are Monty's only real works of art. Dreams, like art, have both the power to draw our attention to what is real, but can also be used to manipulate the truth.

In these examples we can already see the parallel Murdoch is drawing between false salvation in human love and the dangerous desire for instant salvation from God. The two types of magic begin to fuse in the parody-religion of Carel in *The Time of the Angels*. The black Pattie is to be for Carel 'his dark angel', saving him by her love: 'Do you understand the doctrine of the redemption? ... Will you be crucified for me, Pattie? ...You might make a miracle for me.'[171] He plans for her to be crucified by learning that he is having sexual relationships with his daughter Elizabeth; she will save him by remaining faithful in her love for him. Actually, she finds she cannot save him as he wants: 'She loved him but could do nothing with her love. It was for her own torment only and not for his salvation.'[172] This portrayal, with its linking of salvation and suffering, hints at a defect Murdoch finds at the heart of the Christian doctrine of redemption; in the words of another of her characters, 'The West studies suffering, the East studies death.'[173]

168. Ibid., p. 281.
169. Murdoch, *Book and the Brotherhood*, pp. 231–2.
170. Murdoch, *Henry and Cato*, p. 261.
171. Murdoch, *Time of the Angels*, p. 168.
172. Ibid., p. 228, cf. p. 237.
173. Murdoch, *Accidental Man*, pp. 105–6.

Murdoch's critique of redemptive suffering is of great interest for Christian theologians, alerting them to problems within their tradition. For Murdoch, the false magic that lies in confession to a saviour God is not just that this can divert the believer from his or her own moral effort, though we have seen from human examples of evading the truth that this can be a real danger. Even more subtly, Murdoch perceives that abasement before a personal God can lead to sadomasochism, and several of her characters find this typified in the scene in the Book of Job which they read as the grovelling of Job before a thundering Jehovah (Job chapters 38–42). The tirade of Tallis's father, for instance, clearly refers to the narrative of Job's sufferings (ch. 1), to God's answer to Job in the whirlwind, showing up his ignorance of creation (chs 38–41) and consequently to Job's repentance for his complaints to the Almighty (ch. 42):

> What are they for after all but to kiss the foot that kicks them in the teeth? And when they've had the boils and the cattle have died and the children have died and they're scraping themselves with potsherds or whatever ... and after all that and the damned irrelevant rubbish about the elephants and the whales and the morning stars and so on, there they are still whining and grovelling and enjoying being booted in the face.[174]

The 'rubbish about the elephants and the whales and the morning stars' seems to allude to Job 38:7 (morning stars), 40:15 (Behemoth) and 41:1 (Leviathan) and colourfully illustrates a reading that God is pointing to aspects of creation beyond Job's control in order to intimidate him. I shall shortly want to question this exegesis of Job, but this does not affect Murdoch's main point, that confession and a seeking for salvation from God ('whining and grovelling') can mask the fact that we find our sins an interesting and absorbing subject. Suffering the torments of remorse about them can be a self-indulgence, which is simply another form of creating our own world around us. In *The Good Apprentice*, Harry says that 'Stuart wanted to be like Job, always guilty before God, an exalted form of sadomasochism'.[175] Murdoch is condemning an attitude which substitutes suffering for death, that is, the true death of the self. As Father Brendan expounds it (in *Henry and Cato*),

> Death is the great destroyer of all images and all stories, and human beings will do anything rather than envisage it. Their last resource is to rely on suffering, to try to cheat death by suffering instead. And suffering we know breeds images, it breeds the most beautiful images of all.[176]

---

174. Murdoch, *A Fairly Honourable Defeat*, p. 91.
175. Murdoch, *Good Apprentice*, p. 54.
176. Murdoch, *Henry and Cato*, p. 337.

Cato objects that 'Christ cheated death by suffering instead',[177] but Brendan, like other priests in Murdoch's tales, believes in a Christ who is not resurrected and so has really faced death. He is content to let 'Christ look after my Christology'. Christianity has gone wrong by replacing death by suffering, degrading the cross by the resurrection, whereas Christ was obedient to the Good unto a death whose horror he fully comprehended; as Nolan puts it in *The Unicorn*, 'True obedience is without illusion. A common soldier will die in silence, but Christ cried out.'[178] This is being good for nothing, without reward of resurrection. So the mystical Christ can turn us to the Good, and in this sense only he is alive: 'If Christ saves, he lives'[179] and conversely, in an anti-Pauline text, 'if Christ be risen our faith is vain'.[180] The failed man of letters and poet, Lucius, dies in making his best Haiku, a miniature work of art celebrating death as 'the great teacher'.[181] The myth of Marsyas expresses the same truth, as a pagan version of the cross.

All this is exquisitely summed up in the visionary appearing of Christ to Anne Cavidge. In response to her plea that she wants to be saved, 'to be made good' and 'to be washed whiter than snow', he gently insists that 'you must do it all yourself' and 'I am not a magician'. She cannot push away her responsibilities onto him, for he bids her (as he did Mary Magdalen) 'Love me if you must my dear, but don't touch me.' She cannot cling to an easy saviour, but must find the way of truth for herself through the tangles of her love, though Christ can be followed and even loved as one who took the path of truth himself. Christ has certainly suffered wounds on the cross and on the way to it, but they themselves cannot save; when she looks at his unscarred hands he says paradoxically, 'my wounds are imaginary'. That is, the suffering is 'not the point … though it has proved so interesting to you all!' Suffering has passed like a shadow: what remains is the challenge of facing death, which 'is one of my names'.[182]

Living through the experience of Murdoch's characters should thus prompt Christian theologians to rethink what they mean when speaking of salvation as being achieved through the suffering of Christ, resulting in a summons to his disciples to 'share' in his sufferings. The Christian tradition in the West has indeed focused thought upon Christ's sufferings on the cross, and the story Murdoch tells can exert a shaping influence at a point of theological decision about their redemptive significance. On the one hand, atonement through the cross of Jesus might be understood as achieved through suffering inflicted upon Christ by God the Father. The idea may take the older, Calvinistic form that the justice of God is satisfied by the imposing of a vicarious penalty upon Christ as a substitute for

---

177. Ibid., p. 338. Cf. Murdoch, *Metaphysics*, p. 119: 'Death is transformed into visionary pain.'
178. Murdoch, *The Unicorn*, p. 77.
179. Murdoch, *Book and the Brotherhood*, p. 490 (Father McAlister).
180. Murdoch, *Philosopher's Pupil*, p. 188 (Father Bernard).
181. Murdoch, *Henry and Cato*, p. 330.
182. Murdoch, *Nuns and Soldiers*, pp. 290–4.

guilty sinners;[183] so we 'have a share' in the benefits of the cross. But it may also take the very different form proposed by the modern theologian Jürgen Moltmann, who speaks of the Father as 'rejecting' or 'casting out' the Son in order that the rejected and outcast of the world may identify with him and so share fellowship in the divine life.[184] On the other hand, the suffering of Christ may be understood not as inflicted by the Father at all but as the form which participation in the predicament of a fallen world must inevitably take. On this view, the suffering of Christ is his complete identification with our estranged and broken lives, entered into in order to create a change in human response to God and to one another. In a phrase of Tillich's, 'Not substitution, but free participation, is the character of the divine suffering.'[185]

In considering these doctrinal options, novels which test out feelings about the nature of salvation, dependence and suffering are relevant witness. They cannot, of course, prove that one theological path is correct, but stories and images have their own kind of truth that can affect a theological judgement. In my opinion, the depiction of false saviours in Murdoch's novels adds weight to the verdict of one feminist theologian, Dorothee Soelle, that worship of a God who inflicts suffering is 'Christian masochism' and 'theological sadism'.[186] They will also incline us, I believe, towards the view of a liberation theologian, Leonardo Boff, that the concept of such a God 'sacramentalizes' and 'legitimates' the exercise of violence by human authorities.[187] This question, as Murdoch shows so well, has wide implications for the image of God which we hold. A God who inflicts suffering, and who offers or withholds salvation as an instant boon, is a dominating figure whose favour we hope to gain at the expense of facing up to the reality of our own selves.

This is not actually the God whom Job encounters. When God appears and speaks from the whirlwind, the description God offers of a vast and complex creation (chapters 38–41) is not, as Leonard supposes, 'irrelevant rubbish' about elephants and whales and the morning stars; nor is it simply a heavy underscoring of the power of a thundering Jehovah before whom Job has to tremble. It opens out the mysteries of a creation which eludes Job's grasp and prompts him to gaze on the manifold particularity of things; as Simone Weil stresses a number of

---

183. John Calvin, *Institutes of the Christian Religion* (trans. Ford Lewis Battles, ed. John McNeill), 2 vols (London: SCM Press, 1961), II, 17.4–5, pp. 531–4.

184. Jürgen Moltmann, *The Crucified God: The Cross of Christ as the Foundation and Criticism of Christian Theology* (trans. R. A. Wilson and John Bowden) (London: SCM Press, 1974), pp. 241–5.

185. Paul Tillich, *Systematic Theology*, vol. 2, p. 203. Unfortunately, Murdoch's markings of this volume in her own copy end at page 119.

186. Dorothee Soelle, *Suffering* (trans. E. Kalin) (London: Darton, Longman and Todd, 1975), pp. 22–8.

187. Leonardo Boff, *Passion of Christ, Passion of the World* (New York: Orbis, 1987), pp. 113–14.

times, referring to this scene, God 'reveals the beauty of the world' to him.[188] The result is that Job sees the absurdity of demanding that God should act in one way or another; he repents not of failing to submit to God but of insisting that God should intervene to give him the rewards that he feels he deserves. In fact Job himself comes to see, like Murdoch's characters, that there is no magical solution, no easy consolation.[189] Murdoch's concern that we should be 'good for nothing' comes surprisingly close to the question posed about Job: 'does Job serve God for nothing?' (Job 1:9). Perhaps Murdoch herself perceives this in giving to her character Carel a passing reference to Job 41, that 'one must be good for nothing, without sense or reward, in the world of Jehovah and Leviathan'.[190]

The bidding to Anne Cavidge of Murdoch's Christ that 'you must do it all yourself' and 'the work is yours' awakens echoes of the classic debate between Augustine and Pelagius, with their respective successors. However, when we consider the ministers of grace Murdoch recognizes and which I have already outlined, together with her opposition to the autonomous will cultivated by Sartre,[191] it would be too crude to dub her as a Pelagian. It is hard to be satisfied with either traditional account of the relationship between human freedom and divine grace, when faced by the complex experience of such characters as Ann and Tamar. Living through their lives should shape the work of the theologian in creating new ways to understand the balance between human and divine freedom. It might well lead the theologian to explore a cooperative venture between the world and God, in which God freely and humbly chooses to allow created beings to contribute something genuinely their own to God's own creative project.

Such a God would accept self-limitation, risk and consequent suffering. This is precisely what Bonhoeffer means when he declares that God wants us to live 'as if there were no God' and goes on to explain that 'only a suffering God can help'. Murdoch considers that Bonhoeffer is 'misusing words', apparently because she thinks that his declaration is not compatible with the classical understanding of the word 'God', and that this is the only intelligible meaning for the word. Perhaps she is also objecting to the attributing of suffering to God because it contradicts

---

188. Simone Weil, *The Notebooks of Simone Weil* (trans. Arthur Wills) (repr., London: Routledge, 2004), pp. 261, 524, 553; Simone Weil, *Waiting on God* (trans. Emma Craufurd) (London: Routledge and Kegan Paul, 1951), pp. 66, 113. On Weil and beauty, see later, pp. 161–3.

189. For this exegesis, in detail, see Paul S. Fiddes, *Seeing the World and Knowing God: Hebrew Wisdom and Christian Doctrine in a Late-Modern Context* (Oxford: Oxford University Press, 2013), pp. 236–8; cf. David J. A. Clines, *Job 38–42* (Word Biblical Commentary 18B; Nashville: Thomas Nelson, 2011), pp. 1088–92.

190. Murdoch, *Time of the Angels*, p. 186. But Carel follows this up, p. 187, with a quotation of Job 38:4, 'where was thou when I laid the foundations of the earth', uttered by him in the tone of a dominating deity. The bishop also quotes this text, *Time of the Angels*, p. 102, and correctly observes that this is 'not an argument that concerns morality'.

191. See later, pp. 62–3, 134.

the idea of the impassibility of God, which belongs to the traditional meaning of 'God'; or perhaps she feels that the association between God and suffering is *validating* suffering and contributing to an evasion of death. However, modern theologians who affirm the possibility of God have not *replaced* death by suffering. Taking the hint from Luther's finding of the 'hidden God' (*deus absconditus*) in the cross of Jesus,[192] and his use of the dramatic expression 'the death of God',[193] recent theology has asserted that in the cross God has exposed God's very being to the onslaught of death and nothingness. The resurrection of Christ is not then to be understood as a mere cancelling out of the cross, avoiding the impact of death or weakening the element of tragedy in the Christian story. It is a sign that God has overcome death by taking it into God's self and making it God's own experience. As Eberhard Jüngel puts it, after the cross, death can only be understood as 'a phenomenon of God' or the 'death of the living God';[194] death belongs to God, and yet God is not dead. By identifying God's self with the dead Jesus, God has used death to define the very nature of divinity, absorbing death into life. To such reflections we may well be led by Murdoch's placing the phrase 'death is one of my names' on the lips of Christ, though she herself thinks this would be undercut both by resurrection and by the objective existence of a personal God.

Another theological perspective: Dietrich Bonhoeffer and facing death

Just as Murdoch asserts that a religious attitude can try to 'cheat death by suffering instead', so in *Letters and Papers* Bonhoeffer criticizes the kind of piety in which 'our thoughts are more about dying than about death'. It seems a parallel thought to Murdoch when Bonhoeffer writes that 'being able to face dying doesn't yet mean we can face death'.[195] So Murdoch's Christ announces to Anne Cavidge that his wounds are not 'the point', whereas 'death is a teaching'.[196] However, there is a fundamental difference in Bonhoeffer's account. His reflection arises from

---

192. E.g. *D. Martin Luthers Werke: Kritische Gesamtausgabe* (Weimar: H. Bohlaus Nachfolger, 1883–1929), WA (Weimarer Ausgabe) 1.362, 14: 'Vere absconditus tu es Deus' (quoting Isaiah 45:15); WA 1.613, 23–8: 'the crucified and hidden God'. See Alister E. McGrath, *Luther's Theology of the Cross* (Oxford: Blackwell, 1985), pp. 149–68.

193. E.g. Martin Luther, WA 50.590, 11–33; *Confession Concerning Christ's Supper* (ed. H. T. Lehmann) (American Edition of Luther's Works 37; St Louis: Concordia, [1528] 1961), pp. 210–11. Luther's concern to go beyond a merely verbal *communicatio*, or exchange of human and divine properties, in the person of Christ has been stressed by recent 'theology of the cross': e.g. Moltmann, *The Crucified God*, pp. 233–4, Eberhard Jüngel, 'Von Tod des lebendigen Gottes', *Zeitschrift für Theologie und Kirche* 65 (1968), pp. 93–116 (113–14).

194. Jüngel, *God as the Mystery of the World*, pp. 363–4.

195. Bonhoeffer, *Letters and Papers*, DBW 8, p. 333; *Letters and Papers* (1966), p. 85.

196. Bonhoeffer, *Letters and Papers*, DBW 8, p. 291.

the celebration of Easter, and for him 'facing death' does not mean a denial of resurrection, but an assertion of it:

> We're more concerned about how we shall face dying than about conquering death. Socrates mastered the art of dying, Christ overcame death ... It's possible for a human being to manage dying, but overcoming death means resurrection. It is not through the *ars moriendi* but through Christ's resurrection that that a new and cleansing wind can blow through our present world.

Bonhoeffer's point is that, when we face the finality of death seriously, as the end to all human potentiality and as a shock to our being, we are thrown upon something 'new' that is not in our competence, the sheer gift of God's life in resurrection. Resurrection is, he admits, 'mythological' language, but it cannot be totally 'demythologized'; it must be interpreted in a way that 'does not make religion the condition for faith' in a 'world come of age'.[197] What this *might* mean is at least partially worked out in other letters from prison, and he is anxious – no less than Murdoch – that neither the concepts of resurrection or redemption should undermine the significance of a life lived under the horizon of death. He criticizes the 'redemption myth' to which Christianity has often been reduced, which 'looks for eternity outside of history beyond death'; it is an error to place the emphasis on 'that which is beyond death's boundary'. Rather:

> Redemption is ... within history, that is, this side of the bounds of death, whereas everywhere else the aim of all the other myths of redemption is precisely to overcome death's boundary ... The Christian hope of resurrection is different from the mythological in that it refers people to their life on earth in a wholly new way ... Unlike believers in redemption myths, Christians do not have an ultimate escape route out of their earthly tasks and difficulties into eternity.[198]

In her copy of *Letters and Papers*, Murdoch has placed a side-line against this passage and has added a terse and enigmatic query in the margin – 'redemption?'[199] This seems at least to indicate that she is interested in what Bonhoeffer thinks redemption might be. Bonhoeffer does not deny that the image of 'resurrection' has some reference beyond death, but this should not be our concern: 'This-worldliness should not be abolished ahead of its time ... Redemption myths arise from the human experience of boundaries. But Christ takes hold of human beings in the midst of their lives.' This assertion echoes what Bonhoeffer has said elsewhere about God's being present and hidden in the midst of life, not at its edges: 'Belief in the resurrection is not the "solution" to the problem of death.

---

197. Ibid., pp. 430–1.
198. Ibid., pp. 447–8.
199. Bonhoeffer, *Letters and Papers* (1966), p. 112. The handwriting appears to be Murdoch's at this point.

God's "beyond" is not what is beyond our cognition! ... God is the beyond in the midst of our lives.'[200]

In this letter to Eberhard Bethge, Bonhoeffer confesses that 'I'd like to speak of God not at the boundaries but in the center', and he ends by saying that 'I am thinking a great deal about what this religionless Christianity looks like.' One is compelled to say, however, that what it 'looks like' remains fragmentary in these letters. There are clues about what it 'looks like' to face the reality of a life lived under the horizon of death, experiencing the resurrection here and now and finding oneself 'taken hold of' by Christ as redeemer. But Bonhoeffer's agenda to relate the great doctrines of the Christian faith – such as creation, fall, atonement and resurrection – to a secularized world 'in such a way that their essence in worldly life can be immediately seen'[201] is scarcely worked out. Bonhoeffer knows that Christ 'takes form' in a world that lives 'as if there were no God', but the shape of the form remains shadowy and evanescent.[202] Of course, Bonhoeffer, dying as a martyr on 9 April 1945, was to have too little time for this task. But there are indications that he thought that the vocabulary and concepts were actually not yet available to carry the programme through successfully, and until the church could learn how to do this kind of relating to a world come of age, he advised that it was better to preserve the Christian mysteries in a 'secret discipline'.[203] Perhaps the most vivid forms of 'religionless Christianity' are not in the vehicle of theology but in the poems Bonhoeffer wrote in his last year. There he discerns that 'people go to God when God's in need', and there he asks the question, 'Who am I?', answering 'Whoever I am, thou knowest me: O God, I am thine!'[204] Looking to God for our identity like this strikes a blow at all attempts to build a world around ourselves and exactly breaks into the machine-made worlds that Murdoch wants to disturb.

When we recognize, in Bonhoeffer's letters, that we only have an incomplete view of what it 'looks like' to live *etsi non deus daretur*, we are the more likely to find the same incompleteness in Murdoch's imaginative world of living within the same horizon. While appreciating her critique of relying upon the consolation of false saviours, of indulging in suffering and of avoiding the facticity of death, we may still ask how well her own ministers of grace (traces of the Good) open the characters beyond themselves. When we ask 'what it looks like', we notice that her 'good' characters tend to be isolated. The way of truth, 'doing it all yourself', is

---

200. Bonhoeffer, *Letters and Papers*, DBW 8, p. 367.

201. Eberhard Bethge, 'The Challenge of Dietrich Bonhoeffer's Life and Theology', in Smith, *World Come of Age*, pp. 22–88 (82).

202. Although, in his earlier *Ethics*, pp. 98–102, Bonhoeffer writes of Christ 'taking form in a segment of human history', his ethics essentially concern the church as the place where this taking form 'happens' (p. 102). Keith Clements, *Dietrich Bonhoeffer's Ecumenical Quest* (Geneva: WCC, 2015), pp. 260–5, maintains that the 'religionless Christianity' of *Letters and Papers* is actually only about the nature of the church, but this seems to be too restrictive.

203. Bonhoeffer, *Letters and Papers*, DBW 8, pp. 364–5, 373, 390.

204. Ibid., pp. 459–60.

meant to be warning against making others into saviours, not an assertion of sheer autonomy; but there is the danger that it will turn out to be a stoical, privatized discipline which is only meaningful from within the perspective of the sole participant. Ann does not tell her love to the 'Count', and Gertrude draws him into her own circle of love and warmth by granting him an intimate affection without actually becoming lovers. Gertrude structures the world around herself and wants to keep Ann as part of it, demanding 'you call it little to be loved by me?'[205] But Ann goes to America to work with a lay religious order among deprived young people, alone and misunderstood, serving the God who does not exist. It is hard for us to see why Ann's decision should be the way of integrity for her; is it serving the truth to let Gertrude's circle have the 'soldier' they want (the Count), even if she denies them the 'nun' (herself)? As Gertrude's husband, a philosopher, is dying he reaches beyond the 'dance of bloodless categories' in an intensified quest for truth and is reduced to a few fragments of speech that encapsulate meaning for him: 'hey hey the white swan', 'she shouldn't have sold the ring', 'logical space'. In his disciplined search for reality he is alone in a cage of his own language game. But is Ann any less enclosed in her private space? She is presented as making her great sacrifice, not to save her friends but to remain in the truth of herself; yet we simply have to believe this is so.

Other characters in quest of the Good appear similarly as cut off from communication with others and from their sympathy; Stuart appears to be 'a corpse, a dead man'; Kathleen seems to her husband to possess 'unlife'; Tallis is regarded as an 'unperson'; and his friends 'made nothing of Jenkin'.[206] While some who quest for the good (and notably the 'saints' of religious traditions) are going to appear as outsiders to society,[207] if they are always marginalized they may cease to be the disturbers they need to be. Moreover, despite breaking the shells of their worlds, they may still appear to be trapped within their own self-enclosed space; in terms of the novel, this raises the question as to whether the portrayal of character is consistent with the underlying idea.

In fact, the perplexing character of Crimond (in *The Book and the Brotherhood*) appears to embody Murdoch's own questioning about this and seems to me to be her most radical testing of her own ideas. Early on he denies the ability of the ego to break its self-made world: 'The individual cannot overcome egoism, only society can aspire to do that.'[208] But the value of this thesis about the need for others to impinge on the self is thrown into doubt by Gerard's comment that Crimond's Marxism shows the same masochism and desire for instant salvation

205. Murdoch, *Nuns and Soldiers*, p. 465.
206. Murdoch, *Good Apprentice*, p. 292; Murdoch, *The Red and the Green* (London: Chatto & Windus, 1965), p. 189; Murdoch, *Fairly Honourable Defeat*, p. 127; Murdoch, *Book and the Brotherhood*, p. 252.
207. See Murdoch, 'Existentialists and Mystics', pp. 225–7; cf. Conradi, *The Saint and the Artist*, pp. 56–7, 84–7, 309.
208. Murdoch, *Book and the Brotherhood*, p. 174.

as Calvinism[209] and by Jean's judgement that anyway he enjoys 'being an incarnate individual'. Through Crimond, Murdoch has raised a questioning note, and this also extends to the value of facing death as a means of encountering reality. Crimond, aptly named after a popular tune for the setting of Psalm 24, twice passes through 'the valley of the shadow of death'. But the suicide pact with Jean and the duel with Duncan seem less a facing of reality than an imposing of his own will upon others, and so a reinforcing of his own world.

Iris Murdoch's novels call the reader to give 'attention' to the truth, living within the tension between the self and the particularities of the world. If the perspective of the Christian story of a hidden God alerts us to strains within her presentation of plot, character and idea, it would surely be the kind of testing that she herself would welcome as a disciple of the Truth and the Good.

---

209. Ibid., pp. 245, 339.

Chapter 2

IRIS MURDOCH ON 'GOD' AND 'GOOD': A DIALOGUE WITH MODERN THEOLOGY

In the twenty years or so between her novels *The Time of the Angels* (1966) and *The Good Apprentice* (1985), Iris Murdoch read a good deal of modern theology. It seems that during this period she gave herself a sort of 'crash course', including works by Paul Tillich, Donald MacKinnon, Karl Barth, Dietrich Bonhoeffer, Don Cupitt, John Robinson, Martin Buber and John Hick. She also had copies of books by John Caputo, John Macquarrie, James Mackey, Hans Küng, Geoffrey Lampe, C. F. D. Moule and Thomas Merton, but we do not have the same evidence from annotations that she had read them.[1] Her earlier reading, before 1966, included

---

1. Her Oxford library, archived in Kingston University, includes underlined and/or annotated copies of Karl Barth, *The Epistle to the Romans* (1968); Dietrich Bonhoeffer, *Letters and Papers from Prison* (1966); Paul Tillich, *Systematic Theology*, 3 vols (repr., London: SCM Press, 1978); John A. T. Robinson, *The New Reformation* (repr., London: SCM Press, 1965), Don Cupitt, *Taking Leave of God* (London: SCM, 1980); Don Cupitt, *Radicals and the Future of the Church* (London: SCM, 1989); Martin Buber, *Eclipse of God* (Sussex: Harvester, 1969); Maurice Wiles, *The Remaking of Christian Doctrine* (London: SCM, 1974); Donald MacKinnon, *Borderlands of Theology and Other Essays* (London: Lutterworth, 1968) and *The Problem of Metaphysics* (Cambridge: Cambridge University Press, 1974). The dates of publication (and occasionally inscriptions) of these editions demonstrate that Murdoch must have read them after the writing of *The Time of the Angels*. For her reading of John Hick (ed.), *The Myth of God Incarnate* (London: SCM, 1977), see her letter to Scott Dunbar, 19 October 1977, in Horner and Rowe, *Living on Paper*, p. 451. Among other theological books, she also had un-annotated copies of John Caputo, *The Mystical Element in Heidegger's Thought* (Athens: Ohio University Press, 1978); Hans Küng, *On Being a Christian* (London: Collins, 1978) and *Does God Exist?* (London: Collins/Fount, 1983); Geoffrey Lampe, *God as Spirit* (Oxford: Oxford University Press, 1977) and Lampe, *Explorations in Theology*, vol. 8 (London: SCM Press, 1981); James Mackey, *The Christian Experience of God as Trinity* (London: SCM, 1983); Donald Mackinnon, *Explorations in Theology*, vol. 5 (London: SCM Press, 1979); John Macquarrie, *Principles of Christian Theology* (1966); Thomas Merton, *Contemplation in a World of Action* (London: Allen and Unwin, 1971); and C. F. D. Moule, *The Origin of Christology* (Cambridge: Cambridge University Press, 1977).

theology by MacKinnon, Rudolph Bultmann, Ian Ramsey and Simone Weil.[2] One might say of her, as of the amateur philosopher Marcus in *The Time of the Angels*, that although he did not believe in God 'his favourite reading was theology'.[3] Both that novel and *The Good Apprentice* feature discussions about the relation of 'God' and the 'Good', and the aim of this chapter is to discern the difference that her reading in theology made to her writing in moving from the one novel to the other.

Notoriously, Murdoch insisted that she was not writing philosophical novels but was simply featuring characters who happened to be interested in philosophical ideas – and, we may add, theological ideas. She is right about her own work, in so far as the novels, taken as whole units, do not advocate any philosophical positions. But her own ideas and concerns are scattered among the cast of characters, who will from time to time voice her convictions while undermining these through *also* holding contrasting opinions which she would certainly oppose, or through failing to live up to their ideals. She presents us then with a glittering variety of characters, engaged in a constant conversation we are invited to enter and make our own decisions about, rather than spokesmen for an ideology. We notice that the plots and the fates of the characters may, however, implicitly exhibit Murdoch's moral philosophy.

What Murdoch's ideas *are* may be gleaned from two pieces of philosophical writing which she was engaged upon respectively at about the time of the two novels we are exploring. Alongside *The Time of the Angels* (1966) we may place *The Sovereignty of Good*, published in 1970, with the major central essay, '"God" and "Good"', first appearing in 1969. Alongside *The Good Apprentice* (1985) we may place *Metaphysics as a Guide to Morals*, which was published in 1992, but which is based on her Gifford Lectures of 1982. Respecting her own viewpoint on her work, I shall be asking about the effect of her reading of modern theology on the imaginative development of character and plot and trying to avoid treating them as mere illustrations of her philosophy. So let us turn first to the two novels in question.

Hans Küng, *Credo: The Apostles Creed Explained for Today* (London: SCM Press, 1993) was added to her collection after 1985.

2. Murdoch's library contains annotated copies of Ian Ramsey, *Religious Language: An Empirical Placing of Theological Phrases* (London: SCM Press, 1957) and Rudolph Bultmann, *Jesus Christ and Mythology* (London: SCM Press, 1963), as well as Donald MacKinnon's inaugural lecture, *The Borderlands of Theology* (Cambridge: Cambridge University Press, 1961). It also contains nineteen volumes by Simone Weil, in French and in English translations, with publication dates from 1949 to 1977, nine of them annotated; they are, however, scarcely classifiable as 'modern' theology, and I refer to many of them in Chapter 6.

3. Murdoch, *Time of the Angels*, p. 21.

From The Time of the Angels *to* The Good Apprentice

Both novels feature the scenario, familiar to readers of Murdoch, of an unusual house in which people are either literarily imprisoned or are held prisoner by emotional constraints.[4] In *Angels* the house is a gloomy and cold rectory standing in a sea of mud in the City of London, on what was originally a bomb-site and is now a deserted building site. The church was destroyed in the war, all that remains being the tower, designed by Christopher Wren, and due for demolition. The priest posted here, to a situation in which there is no church and no parish, is Carel Fisher, a man who has, appropriately, lost any faith in God. Through the force of his powerful personality and emotional domination, he is holding three women confined in this house: his daughter Muriel, his ward and supposed niece Elizabeth, who is a semi-invalid, and his maid Pattie, who is half-Irish and half-Jamaican. Pattie has been his mistress since his wife was alive, though until a point near the end of the novel he no longer has an active sexual relationship with her. Also inhabiting this Gothic rectory is an elderly caretaker, Eugene, who is a Russian refugee who fled Nazi violence, and his feckless son Leo. The son, aptly, has fantasies of finding 'a girl that's hidden in a country house ... kept behind locked doors'. 'She'd be a sort of sleeping beauty,' he muses, 'and I'd have the task of setting her free.'[5]

In *The Good Apprentice*, the house, called *Seegard*, is a rambling architectural experiment, built again in a muddy environment – this time in the middle of woods and marshland near the sea – by a quite-famous painter, Jesse Baltram. Some years before the novel begins, Jesse had retreated there from his artistic London life, accompanied by his wife May and two daughters – Bettina and Ilona – with the aim of creating an ideal, mostly self-sufficient community. It appears at first that the women are held within the constraints of the daily timetable, lifestyle and dream-world *he* has mandated, while he is travelling away somewhere. Later it transpires that he is in the grip of mental degeneration and is being effectively confined there in a Gothic tower by the three women, who continue to live according to the rhythms and cycles of life that he originally ordained. As they put it, 'he was a god and has cheated us by becoming a child'.[6] The scene of a house and its prisoners is an image repeated a number of times in Murdoch's novels and acts as an image for the world which characters build around themselves as, by implication, we all do. Instead of giving *attention* to people and things as they really are, noticing their reality and through them attending to the Good, the greedy self imposes and projects itself on others and traps them within a web of its own devising.

The scenario in *The Good Apprentice* is, however, not entirely parallel with *The Time of the Angels*, since the Seegard story occupies only the middle of three sections in the book, although being intermeshed with the rest of the action. The

---

4. For example, there is Hannah in *The Unicorn*, and Hartley in *The Sea, The Sea*.
5. Murdoch, *Time of the Angels*, p. 72.
6. Murdoch, *Good Apprentice*, pp. 238–9.

plot actually begins somewhere else, and this brings us to a second linking feature, the parable of the Prodigal Son. The first section of *The Good Apprentice* is called 'The Prodigal Son' and features Edward, who has been plunged into a nightmare world of guilt and remorse. He had administered a drug to his best friend, Mark, without Mark's knowledge and consent and then left Mark lying on his bed in the middle of an ecstatic 'high', in order to visit a girl and have sex with her. Returning after just half an hour, he had discovered that Mark, in the middle of a drug-induced vision, had thrown himself out of a window and killed himself. Life is now meaningless to Edward, who is plunged into the blackest of despair. While Edward has been brought up by a stepfather, Harry Cumo, his actual father was the artist Jesse Baltram, and he goes to stay at Seegard (at the invitation of the women there) with the hope that he can find peace and forgiveness by confessing to his natural father – who to this point has shown no interest in him. The novel thus begins with the words, which we are told that Edward repeated often, 'I will arise and go to my father, and will say to him, Father I have sinned against heaven and before thee, and am no more worthy to be called thy son.'

When Edward does finally meet the half-mad and infantile Jesse at Seegard, he discovers that his absolution cannot cure him; thereby Edward joins all the other characters in Murdoch's novels who vainly try to make saviour-figures of others, thereby trying to force them into the world of their own ego and evading their own responsibility. He is not alone in these two novels in this attempt. The futility of such a salvation, whether sought from heavenly or earthly father-figures, is shown in *The Time of the Angels*. Leo has stolen and sold a precious icon of the Holy Trinity belonging to his father, the only remnant of his early life in Russia. The totally amoral Leo refers jokingly to doing a 'prodigal son act' in confessing to his father,[7] and only does so, not to gain real absolution but to satisfy Muriel who had made this a condition of introducing Leo to the sleeping beauty of the house, Elizabeth.

Muriel's intention here is another parallel between the novels. She decides to bring Leo and Elizabeth together in order to administer a shock. Throughout Murdoch's novels, the question is how we can be freed from the false world we build around ourselves, so that we can attend to people as they really are and so serve the Good. One way of being pulled out of oneself is to be confronted with the unexpected, the contingent. But while accidental events and unlikely relationships can shock people into noticing the truth, it is a mark of self-centredness to want to *procure* shocks for others. In *The Time of the Angels*, Muriel seeks to arrange an accidental event to dispel what she believes to be the stifling atmosphere of the rectory, and in particular the unhealthy sleep of apathy into which her cousin Elizabeth has sunk. Leo will be the accident:

> It was time for something noisy and unexpected, for something a little unpredictable and entirely new. Leo was noisy, unexpected, unpredictable and

---

7. Murdoch, *Time of the Angels*, p. 118.

new ... A shake, a shock would do them all good ... With Leo she would procure Elizabeth an experience. She would procure herself an experience.⁸

But instead of being shaken out of themselves, this plot results in a deeper fall into self, symbolized by Muriel's falling out of the linen cupboard with Leo, after spying on Elizabeth through a crack in the wall. She has seen what Carel and Elizabeth are doing together in secret; though Carel knows that Elizabeth is actually his daughter, not the niece whom everyone else supposes, he is having sex with her. This is the decisive point of moral decline for Muriel. To look into the world of others from a spyhole of one's own, as well as to 'procure' an experience for another, is to deny that they have a world of their own at all.

There is a similar driver of the plot in *The Good Apprentice*. Mother May, Jesse's wife, invites Edward to come and stay with them in Seegard because 'we needed a disturbance, a catalyst, we came to feel that any change was better'.⁹ To increase the disturbance, she also invites his half-brother Stuart, a young man who has made it his aim to serve the good;¹⁰ he is the 'apprentice of the Good' in the title of the book, and though he only partly apprehends what this means, he knows that it involves observing the difference between good and evil, noticing the particulars of the world, paying attention to others and telling the truth. Though he *does* very little, in his very being he acts as a catalyst for others, causing them to question themselves, puncturing their self-enclosed worlds as do all signs and emissaries of the Good (art, for Murdoch, works in the same way). Edward comments that 'he's just an external impulse, a sort of jolt, a solid entity, something you bump into', and 'like a monument, he just exists, and that's a good thing, he's an unmoved mover'.¹¹ One of those he bumps into is 'Midge', Edward's aunt, wife to an eminent psychiatrist, Thomas, who has been having a two year affair with Edward's and Stuart's father, Harry. Her reaction to Stuart is to admit the truth of her affair to Thomas, telling Stuart that 'you were just an external impulse, like a bump or a jolt ... a *negative presence*, a sort of catalyst'.¹² Harry's verdict on Stuart, not surprisingly, is that he is 'dangerous'.¹³ In the Seegard community, Stuart does not stay long enough to cause many waves.¹⁴ The result of Mother May's attempted manipulation, however, is as disastrous as Muriel's in the Rectory: the small community breaks up and Jesse

8. Ibid., p. 114.
9. Murdoch, *Good Apprentice*, p. 240.
10. Ibid., p. 140.
11. Ibid., pp. 469, 520.
12. Ibid., p. 508, my emphasis.
13. Ibid., p. 442.
14. He does, however, effectively break up the affair between Midge and Harry when they accidentally arrive at Seegard one evening after a breakdown of Harry's car on the way back from a clandestine weekend, and at first try to disguise their identity. Midge is deeply affected simply by his silent presence, his sheer 'being', in the car on the way home (pp. 396–7).

wanders out of the house and is drowned in a nearby river, which he once crossed in a manner that seemed to Edward to be a walking on water (actually on hidden stepping stones).

Other parallels between the novels will emerge as this chapter continues. The most obvious link, however, and the most relevant here is theological. Characters in both novels debate the question: can morality survive the loss of belief in God, or what was being called 'the death of God' in the theology of the time? More exactly, the question about which characters disagree is this: can Good replace God as the foundation of morality? There is no doubt where Murdoch herself stands on this issue. The argument of her essay 'On "God" and "Good"', the centrepiece of *The Sovereignty of Good*, is that what *used* to be affirmed of a personal God can *now* be attributed to the Good. This she summarizes as: a *single perfect transcendent non-representable and necessarily real object of attention*.[15]

In *The Time of the Angels*, the authority of Good is originally affirmed by Carel's brother Marcus, who is writing a book on the subject called *Morality in a World without God*. His intention is to rescue the idea of an Absolute in morals by 'showing it to be implied in the unavoidable human activity of moral evaluation', thereby 'avoiding the theological metaphor'.[16] The draft of his first chapter asserts that the idea of the Good cannot survive the death of God by attaching it merely to the exercise of the human will; rather, Good must not be 'severed from perfection' and so must involve some kind of transcendence.[17] This is the substance of the book that Murdoch herself shortly publishes as *The Sovereignty of Good* and the Gifford Lectures that she publishes over twenty years later. The latter even fulfils the intended programme of Marcus in containing a chapter on the Ontological Argument for the Good.[18] Marcus abandons his project, doubting that it is any longer possible after a bruising talk with Carel; if we ask why, it seems that he lacks elements that Murdoch includes in her own project, as we shall see shortly. In this novel, Carel represents the chief opposition to the sovereignty of good, rejecting the Good along with God.

Twenty years later, in *The Good Apprentice*, the argument for the Good as a replacement for God is carried by Stuart, the Apprentice. While asserting that 'I don't want any God at all, even a modified modernised one',[19] he agrees with Thomas that he is afraid of 'Spirit without absolute', which is 'lost, bad spirit'.[20] Thomas himself does not *deny* the sovereignty of the Good, as Carel does, but neither does he argue *for* it. Having no belief in God himself, he nevertheless wants to go on using the word 'God' as a cipher for something deeply human: he

---

15. Murdoch, *Sovereignty of Good*, p. 55, original emphasis.
16. Murdoch, *Time of the Angels*, pp. 77–8. Murdoch, *Sovereignty of Good*, p. 57, similarly argues that placing values in hierarchy demonstrates there is a unity of the Good.
17. Murdoch, *Time of the Angels*, p. 128.
18. Ibid., p. 100; Murdoch, *Metaphysics*, pp. 391–430.
19. Murdoch, *Good Apprentice*, p. 140.
20. Ibid., pp. 30, 53.

echoes Murdoch's key sentence about the Good, but avoids actually *attributing* it either to God or to the Good, asking Stuart to 'imagine' that God is 'a permanent, non-degradable love object', to which Stuart later adds in his mind, 'automatically purifying desire.'[21]

In his approach to goodness, Stuart stands closest to Murdoch, though he is not simply her mouthpiece. While trying to give attention to others, he can be immature and clumsy (after all he is only an Apprentice), and he has decided that he can only concentrate on serving the good if he abandons the 'messy' business of sexual love, taking a vow of celibacy that helps to alienate him from his friends and family. By contrast, Murdoch, we know, finds that eros – including and perhaps especially sexual eros – can be a means of drawing us towards the Good. The character who overtly rejects the authority of a transcendent Good in this novel is the worldly Harry. Having abandoned belief in God, he sits light to all moral values; when Stuart insists on the difference between good and evil, he retorts: 'These extremes are fictions ... false opposites which invent each other, decent people don't know about either.'[22] Notably, he strikes his son Stuart hard in the face after an argument about the Good, just as Carel strikes his brother Marcus.

God is not a person

Through this cast of characters, Murdoch thus explores, in an open way, various aspects of the relation between 'God' and 'Good'. The foundational point is that it is no longer possible to believe in God as some kind of supernatural person, existing 'elsewhere', and here Murdoch draws upon her theological reading and enters a dialogue with modern theology which develops over the period between the two novels.

The Time of the Angels already shows a recognition that theologians are 'demythologizing' the notion of a personal God, and it seems likely that Murdoch has gleaned this knowledge from her reading of Rudolph Bultmann's *Jesus Christ and Mythology*, Ian Ramsey's study of *Religious Language* and from a general awareness of John Robinson's popularization of such ideas in his recent and notorious book *Honest to God*.[23] No copy of *Honest to God* is extant in the remains of Murdoch's library in the Kingston University archives, but the collection is sadly incomplete. An article by Robinson in the *Observer*[24] was widely read at the time, and Murdoch's library does contain a copy of Robinson's *The New Reformation*[25]

---

21. Ibid., pp. 140, 245.
22. Ibid., p. 442.
23. John A. T. Robinson, *Honest to God* (London: SCM Press, 1963).
24. John A. T. Robinson, 'Our Image of God Must Go', *Observer*, 17 March 1963, p. 21.
25. Murdoch's copy is the eighth impression of March 1965; reading *The New Reformation* could thus have had some impact on the writing of *The Time of the Angels*, drafted between April and August 1965, but the timetable is tight.

with underlining and notes; a personal inscription by 'John Woolwich' indicates some existing contact. Murdoch comments on Robinson's theology and mentions *Honest to God* in her later *Metaphysics as a Guide to Morals*.[26] Robinson at the time was usually referred to not by his name but simply as 'the Bishop of Woolwich', and it must be more than a coincidence that it is an unnamed *bishop* who appears at Marcus's dinner table, relishing the food on offer and defending Carel's apparent loss of faith as symptomatic of a necessary demythologizing.

Murdoch's bishop reports that theologians are finding that the particular *historical* nature of Christianity poses intellectual problems, that 'the outward mythology changes, the inward truth remains the same' and that he is not speaking about 'God as a person'. He insists that 'our symbolism must change',[27] which seems to echo the resonant headline of Bishop Robinson's article in the *Observer*: 'Our image of God must go.' The bishop is, however, a composite figure. When he goes on to argue for a relativism in morality, asserting that 'what measures man as a spiritual being is not his conventional goodness and badness but the genuineness of his hunger for God', he seems to be drifting away from the theological demythologizers such as Robinson. The *actual* bishop does call for a reformation in morality, moving away from adherence to a set of moral rules, but his criterion is not human desire for God but – like Dietrich Bonhoeffer – an encounter with Christ in the midst of life in the world and obedience to his demands. Robinson calls for 'an exit from the morasses of relativism' through an 'encounter with the unconditional as the Christ of our lives'.[28]

Murdoch's bishop in fact seems to show just a touch of the neo-Hegelian F. H. Bradley, who argued that, in human desire for communion with Absolute Spirit, evil was in a necessary dialectic with the good[29] and with whom Murdoch contends in her *Metaphysics as a Guide to Morals*.[30] In both this and her earlier book *The Sovereignty of Good*, Murdoch sets herself against the moral relativism her character Harry exemplifies, and she is evidently concerned that this might be a result of the loss of a personal God. She comments ironically that Muriel and Elizabeth in *The Time of the Angels*, having discarded belief in God, pride themselves on being 'theoretical immoralists of some degree of refinement'.[31]

Murdoch's familiarity with the theological demythologizing of God has evidently been strengthened by her theological reading between writing the two novels. Thomas in *The Good Apprentice* assures Stuart that theologians are

---

26. Murdoch, *Metaphysics*, pp. 452, 455.

27. Murdoch, *Time of the Angels*, p. 101.

28. Robinson, *Honest to God*, p. 121; cf. Bonhoeffer, *Letters and Papers from Prison* (the 1966 edition used by Murdoch), pp. 123–5.

29. F. H. Bradley, *Appearance and Reality: A Metaphysical Essay* (London: Oxford University Press, 2nd edn, 1897), pp. 408–35. This is the edition, heavily annotated, in Murdoch's library (IML 1051).

30. Murdoch, *Metaphysics*, pp. 488–91.

31. Murdoch, *Time of the Angels*, p. 45.

'working as fast as they can precisely to reach people like you'.[32] Murdoch also shows herself aware that there is a sense among some theologians – such as Bonhoeffer[33] – that they are in a kind of interim period, when it is not possible to speak meaningfully of God outside the Christian community, but that there is hope for speech and reference to return. The bishop of *The Time of the Angels* reflects that 'we must think of this time as an interregnum. It is a time when, as one might put it, mankind is growing up'.[34] The actual bishop, Robinson, had similarly written in his *Observer* article: 'I can understand those who urge that we must give up using the word "God" for a generation', and had quoted Bonhoeffer as saying that 'man is growing out of [religion]; he is coming of age'.[35] In *Metaphysics as a Guide to Morals*, Murdoch reports that the Jewish theologian Martin Buber views the present age as a period of darkness or silence which awaits a new revelation – a period of 'interregnum' when we confront the 'silence of the Transcendent'.[36] Thomas, in *The Good Apprentice*, remarks that 'some say that God has gone away to a vast distance, that for a time the transcendent is silent'. But Stuart regards this as still being some kind of mythology: 'That's an act in a play,' he retorts, 'There is no play'.[37]

For her part, Murdoch considers it essential to demythologize God thoroughly. In her two mature philosophical works, she regards it as an advance for theologians who want to speak about God in the present age to abandon a *personal* image of God, as this brings them closer to her convictions about a transcendent Good. Apparently drawing on her theological reading, she writes that there is a feeling among many religious believers and 'fellow travellers' that it is time to say goodbye to the old literal personal 'elsewhere' God.[38] Theologians, she had reported earlier, 'are busy at their desks at this very moment trying to undo the results of [the] degeneration' of the personal image of God into fake 'consolation'.[39] But she herself thinks it more consistent for demythologizing theologians to give up using the word God altogether. This is surely partly why, in *The Sovereignty of Good*, she is critical of Bonhoeffer, commenting that when he says 'that *God wants* us to live as though there *were no God* [my emphasis] I suspect he is misusing words'.[40] In

---

32. Murdoch, *Good Apprentice*, p. 140.
33. See Bonhoeffer, *Letters and Papers* (1966), pp. 91–2.
34. Murdoch, *Time of the Angels*, p. 101. In urging the need for 'obedience' in a time of 'emptiness' and 'blackness', the Bishop is blending echoes of Simone Weil on the 'void' with allusions to John Robinson and Bonhoeffer. See Weil, *Waiting on God*, pp. 66, 139, and later, pp. 159–61.
35. Robinson, 'Our Image of God', p. 21.
36. Murdoch, *Metaphysics*, p. 465; she is citing Buber, *Eclipse of God*, p. 30 (IML 1083).
37. Murdoch, *Good Apprentice*, p. 140.
38. Murdoch, *Metaphysics*, p. 420.
39. Murdoch, *Sovereignty of Good*, p. 59.
40. Ibid., p. 79. See earlier, pp. 29–31.

Metaphysics as a Guide to Morals, she is critical of both Buber and Don Cupitt[41] for retaining the word 'God',[42] remarking of the first that she does not believe in his 'I-Thou God' or in his fundamental idea of a dialogue between human beings and transcendent reality.[43] While saying that she has been writing as a 'neo-Christian or Buddhist Christian or Christian fellow traveller',[44] she thinks that useless confusion arises from attempts to extend the meaning of our word 'God' to cover *any* conception of spiritual reality; 'God,' she asserts, 'is the name of a supernatural person.'[45] Buber, she notes, insists that though no word has become 'so soiled, so mutilated' as 'God', he 'may not abandon it'. God for him is 'the word of appeal'; when we can no longer say 'he', we implore 'Thou'.[46] Murdoch replies that the 'Thou' is still 'an external supernatural person' – the 'really existing elsewhere father figure'.[47] We hear her voice in Stuart's reflection: 'There was no God ... He had never looked for a Him or a Thou, or tried to reconceptualise the old deity into some kind of nebulous quasi-personal spirit. "God" was the proper name of a supernatural Person in whom Stuart did not believe.'[48]

In her definition of the Good, Murdoch includes the element of transcendence and therefore claims to be offering a metaphysics.[49] We recall that the Good is, for her, *a single perfect transcendent non-representable and necessarily real object of attention*. Her mentor Plato, she asserts, places the Absolute outside the existing cosmos, but not in the supernatural sense familiar in traditional Christianity.[50] As she explains in *The Sovereignty of Good*, respecting transcendence means directing attention outward, away from the self, to something real that is indestructible and incorruptible – what her character Thomas calls 'a non-degradable love object'. We can *experience* the transcendence of what is beautiful; the beautiful object fades, yet we sense that '*something* has not suffered from decay and mortality'.[51] However, we cannot *experience* the transcendence of the Good to which beauty and all contingent good things point. Beautiful things contain beauty, whereas good acts do not exactly 'contain' good, because beauty is partly a matter of the senses, and in that distinction lies the sovereignty of good over all other ideas. If we speak of

---

41. She has his books *Taking Leave of God* and *Radicals and the Future of the Church*: see note 1.

42. Murdoch, *Good Apprentice*, p. 455.

43. Murdoch, *Metaphysics*, p. 464.

44. Ibid., pp. 419–21.

45. Ibid., p. 419. For a critique of her assumption, see William Schweiker, 'The Sovereignty of God's Goodness', in Antonaccio and Schweiker, *Iris Murdoch*, pp. 209–35 (224–7).

46. Buber, *Eclipse of God*, pp. 17–18.

47. Murdoch, *Metaphysics*, p. 421.

48. Murdoch, *Good Apprentice*, p. 445.

49. Here she differs from her character Marcus, who argues that holding Good to be an Absolute need not be a metaphysics: Murdoch, *Time of the Angels*, pp. 77–8.

50. Murdoch, *Metaphysics*, p. 511.

51. Murdoch, *Sovereignty of Good*, p. 59, my emphasis.

the Good as a transcendent reality, Murdoch admits that she is tempted to call this 'faith', but it is an act of faith supported by the ontological argument: that is, the Good carries within its very concept the implications of perfection, certainty and necessary existence.[52]

In order not to confuse this transcendent Good with a personal God, Murdoch often writes about 'good' or 'Good' rather than '*the* Good' with a definite article, though she also widely employs the latter expression.[53] Good is the supreme object of attention and love and can be meditated upon like a kind of prayer,[54] as can beautiful things such as artworks which are signs of the Good. In their reality or 'thinginess', contingent things in the world have the power to draw the self out of its self-constructed world. Stuart constantly engages in a practice of attention which is a kind of prayer. The Good supremely has this magnetic power to pull the human ego out of self-centredness, but it is not possible to have a personal relation with the Good. We must be 'good for nothing', for no reward, even the compensation of a mutual relation with the divine. Pattie, in *Time of the Angels*, believes for a while that she not only loves God but that God loves her, yet the sense of God as a person has become 'veiled'.[55] Eugene once prayed to 'the bearded Russian God', but now the 'building was empty' and there is 'nothing but the darkness'. He loves his icon of the Trinity, but as 'the blank image of goodness from which all personality had been withdrawn'.[56] Indeed, nobody in the two novels has a vital belief in a personal God any longer.

We can nevertheless trace a development in the portrayal of characters' demythologizing of God between the two novels. In the *Metaphysics* of the 1980s Murdoch now distinguishes between a weaker and a stronger form of demythologizing. She refers to 'the mild tinkerings of Ramsey and Robinson'[57] such as she had reviewed earlier and observes that they were essentially looking for the most appropriate form of religious speech, which still referred to an objectively existing God. Ramsey, for example, maintains that the question 'did the resurrection occur?' does not have the same kind of logic as 'did the empty tomb occur?'[58] By contrast, others have taken up a 'more ruthless radical position', such as Don Cupitt. She applauds Cupitt as a brave thinker, who (reusing a phrase of Meister Eckhart) has 'taken leave of God' altogether.[59] He stands closer to her replacement of God by another spiritual reality than Robinson or Bultmann do, but she does take exception in two ways to the result of his thinking,

---

52. Ibid., p. 60.
53. See, e.g., Murdoch, *Sovereignty of Good*, pp. 64, 66, 68, 70, 71, 74, 75 for 'the Good'.
54. Murdoch, *Good Apprentice*, pp. 47, 153.
55. Murdoch, *Time of the Angels*, p. 34.
56. Ibid., p. 62; cf. Murdoch, *Sovereignty of Good*, p. 71: 'the non-representable blankness of the idea of Good itself'.
57. Murdoch, *Metaphysics*, p. 455.
58. Ibid., 452, citing Ramsey, *Religious Language*, p. 127 (IML 386).
59. Murdoch, *Metaphysics*, pp. 452, 455–7.

judging that he is 'unnecessarily extreme'. First, he has replaced a transcendent object of attention with human subjectivity, making religion a matter of 'private existentialist choice', asserting a 'self-defining self' as a 'fully achieved, conscious and autonomous spiritual subject'; this she finds to be a programme reminiscent of Feuerbach and Sartre. Second, he has made a distinction between fact and value, a disjunction Murdoch always opposes.[60] For Cupitt, she judges, religious language is not *descriptive* of a true state of affairs but merely 'expressive'; the myths are not 'somehow' vehicles of truth (as they are, for instance, to Robinson), while religion is certainly a 'cluster of values'. Cupitt thus utterly discards a view of a world which is 'full of images of God and hierarchies pointing to God'.[61]

For Murdoch, of course, this is exactly what the world *is* like, with the substitution of the 'Good' for God. Denial of God, she insists, need not involve a surrender of a 'spiritually informed understanding of "all the world"'.[62] Demythologization need not mean a total disappearance of myths and icons, as long as we understand the truth they carry.[63] 'We are not cut off from St Paul'[64] who affirms in Romans 1:20 that we find God everywhere in the world, seeing in material things the spirituality reality which is beyond them. For the spiritual and the holy we are to look toward all the world, not toward our isolated self-will. Rather oddly she presses into service here the commentary of Karl Barth on Romans 1:20, underplaying his verdict that human beings *fail* to see God in the world and overemphasizing his critique that they *should* be seeing God there, adducing the reference he makes to 'Plato in his wisdom [who] recognised that behind the visible there lies the invisible universe which is the Origin of all concrete things'.[65] Having virtually turned Barth into a natural theologian for her purposes, she adds Tillich's quotation of Psalm 139 in

60. See as early as 1957: 'Metaphysics and Ethics' in Murdoch, *Existentialists and Mystics*, pp. 59–75 (62–3).

61. Murdoch, *Metaphysics*, p. 453, citing Cupitt, *Taking Leave of God*, p. 51 (IML 1105). A. N. Wilson, *Iris Murdoch as I Knew Her* (London: Hutchinson, 2003), pp. 237–9, criticizes Murdoch for inconsistency in nevertheless commending Cupitt in *Metaphysics* and calls in Fergus Kerr for support, who stresses Murdoch's critique of Cupitt's dichotomy between fact and value: see Fergus Kerr, 'Back to Plato with Iris Murdoch', in Kerr, *Immortal Longings: Versions of Transcending Humanity* (London: SPCK, 1997), pp. 68–88 (73–8). Murdoch's criticism of Cupitt is much stronger in annotations to her own copy of Cupitt's *Taking Leave of God*: on fact and value, see her copy, pp. 126 and 167 (twice, 'No!'). Cupitt himself wistfully believes that he and Murdoch were 'very close' in thought about 'non-realism' in 1980, but had drifted apart by 1990 due to a move by her to a harder Platonism: see Don Cupitt, 'Iris Murdoch: A Case of Star-Friendship', in Anne Rowe and Avril Horner (eds), *Iris Murdoch: Texts and Contexts* (New York: Palgrave Macmillan, 2012), pp. 11–16 (13–14).

62. Murdoch, *Metaphysics*, p. 454.

63. Ibid., pp. 459–60.

64. Ibid., p. 455, cf. p. 460.

65. Ibid., pp. 397, 410. In *Metaphysics*, p. 254, Murdoch places alongside Romans 1:20 Barth's comments on Romans 8:21–4 (Barth, *Epistle to the Romans*, pp. 308–14), which she has marked with a marginal line in her own copy of Barth's commentary (IML 350). Her

his *Systematic Theology*: 'Whither shall I flee from thy presence?' While Tillich has in mind the continual presence of God as the Ground of Being, she comments that 'our general awareness of good, or goodness, is with us unreflectively all the time, as a sense of God's presence *used* to be to believers'.[66]

The more 'radical' kind of demythologizing represented by Cupitt, along with his insistence on continuing to use the word 'God' for the unconditional claim that human values make on us, gives Murdoch the basis for a kind of character who did not appear in *The Time of the Angels*. This is Thomas the psychiatrist in *The Good Apprentice*, who wants to help Edward out of his black misery and who is genuinely interested by Stuart's state of mind in wanting to serve the good. The power to choose a renewal of life comes, in Thomas's view, entirely from spiritual forces within a person: the therapist 'must find and release that force in the deep mind of his patient' (78) since 'there is no end to [the soul's] power to create new being' (359). The therapist, he explains, 'is not God ... and must prompt the sufferer to heal himself through his own deities, and this involves finding ... good powers'. Thomas's family has strong religious traditions, Catholic on his father's side and Jewish on his mother's, but he is 'psychologically disabled from adherence' to either faith (80). Affirming that 'God is a belief that at our deepest level we are known and loved' (77), like Cupitt, Thomas continues to use God-language while reducing ultimate reality to the self's own self-creation. Thomas is a highly complex character, and Murdoch creates an ambivalence in the reader's response to him which I suggest may reflect her own ambivalence to the work of Don Cupitt.

At the same time Thomas fails Murdoch's test of giving proper attention to others, especially to his wife Midge, preferring to impose his theories on them. Telling him about her affair with Harry, she exclaims, 'You have never really seen me at all' (407). What he finds unbearable is that she has been living her own life with Harry outside his knowledge and control: 'the whole full-blooded flow of another life happening in the interstices of his presence to her' (422); he 'wants his dear wife back as she once was, tender and true' (423), that is, not as she actually is. Earlier he reflects that he was lucky to 'possess' her (82).

The unity and necessity of Good

The key philosophical/theological argument in *The Time of the Angels* is whether, with the loss of One God, there is a unity of the Good. For Murdoch, the Good cannot be sovereign over all ideas and values, and so cannot replace God, unless it

---

character Stuart cites Romans 8:21, 'the whole of creation groaning' as an expression of his own sense of affliction in *Good Apprentice*, p. 246.

66. Murdoch, *Metaphysics*, pp. 511–12, my emphasis: see Tillich, *Systematic Theology, Volume 1, Reason and Revelation; Being and God* (repr.; London: SCM Press, 1978), p. 11, and Murdoch's note on her copy at page 290 (IML 1106).

is unitary. Returning to her definition of the Good in her philosophical writing, it is '*a single* [my emphasis] perfect transcendent non-representable and necessarily real object of attention'. Murdoch admits that seeking unity ('all is one') can be a false means of consolation, but she thinks that reflecting on the virtues must lead us to consider their relation to each other – for example, we cannot answer the question 'what is just?' without relating justice to the other virtues – and the idea of an 'order' or hierarchy of virtues then suggests itself, leading to the idea of a single supreme virtue.[67] It is a shortcoming of moral philosophy, she thinks, to proceed to some sovereign concept other than a virtue, such as sincerity or authenticity or freedom. This is an empty idea of unity, which is properly filled by the idea of the Good.

This is exactly what Carel denies. His reaction to the loss of God is to surrender to evil; he believes that the single Good has been scattered into many powers, and these he regards as forces of chance which are inevitably hostile to human life. He tells Marcus:

> The death of God has set the angels free. And they are terrible … There are principalities and powers. Angels are the thoughts of God. Now he has been dissolved into his thoughts which are beyond our conception in their nature and their multiplicity and their power. God was at least the name of something which we thought was good. Now even the name has gone and the spiritual world is scattered. There is nothing any more to prevent the magnetism of many spirits … We are the prey of the angels. (185, 186)

Carel realizes that 'good is only good if one is *good for nothing*' (my emphasis, i.e. good for no hope of 'reward') (186), but he believes such a stance to be totally impossible. If there is no single, universal Good to be grasped, then there is no goodness at all. Instead, Carel creates his own universe around himself and so imprisons himself in a hellish underworld, of which the underground railway that rumbles away beneath the rectory is a constant reminder. 'When I celebrate mass I am God,' he declares (187). Eugene's icon of the Trinity, which is evidently painted ('written') in imitation of Rublev's famous work, depicts three angels sitting in unity, the many in one. When Marcus shows it to him, after buying it back from the dealer to whom Leo had sold it, Carel's comment is: 'How can those three be one?' (188). This is not a conventional objection to the arithmetic of the Trinity but a denial that the many faces or fragments of the Good can be unified in one Sovereign Good. At first Marcus protests to Carel, 'But there is goodness, whatever you say, there is morality, it's just there, it makes a difference, our concern for others' (185). But he comes to doubt the unity of the Good as well as the value of his own intended book which appears to be close in content to Murdoch's own *The Sovereignty of Good*. Unlike Murdoch, he is in fact baffled by the plural forces in the world represented by the image of angels, concluding that they 'get in the

---

67. Murdoch, *Sovereignty of Good*, p. 57.

way' of his argument (210). Murdoch herself is more successful than Marcus in giving place to contingency and accident; she holds together the many particulars of the world with the one Good, regarding them – as does her character Stuart – as 'signs' of the Good.[68] Among them are Eugene's icon and the mouse that Stuart sees living in the dark cavern under the railway lines. They are accidental, pointing to the Good which alone is necessary.

Moreover, Murdoch, like Stuart, recognizes that the many contingencies of the world can present a face which has the overwhelming aspect of the negative sublime.[69] As he recalls the plaited hair cut from Jewish girls at Auschwitz and now on exhibition there, Stuart reflects that 'it was the details that were so unendurable' (248). The angels can indeed be terrible, but at the same time 'the world is full of signs' of the Good (522). Murdoch shares Stuart's suspicion of talk about 'Spirit without the Absolute', or a spirituality that breaks away from 'religion', religion being understood as being 'about good and evil and the distance between them' (245). As Murdoch expresses it in her *Metaphysics*, Spirit without Absolute would indeed be 'the time of the Angels'[70] – a period in which the angels were allowed unchecked sovereignty.

The key argument in *The Good Apprentice* is not in fact whether the Good is unitary, as it was in the former novel. Murdoch's focus has shifted. It is about whether the energies of the many scattered forces of the Good, when internalized as 'angels' within the self, are sufficient to bring about renewal of the human person when enough willpower is applied. Unlike Carel, Thomas believes that it is possible to make what he calls 'alliances' with the principalities and powers. He does not regard the 'angels' as simply malevolent, but as both good and evil. The 'dark powers', he reflects, 'were essentially ambiguous'. He 'recognised them … daily trying to make benignant allies out of the most dangerous things in the world. When … rational morals seem to fail, can not they, vehicles after all of spirit, be invoked and charmed into friendliness?' He concludes that 'I have to play this dangerous game, because I am that sort of healer' (149–50). These forces are, for Thomas, entirely within the psyche. When he speaks to Stuart about the unconscious mind as both an 'abode of monsters' and 'a reservoir of spiritual power' (141), Stuart dislikes the idea instinctively: 'Spirits. Magic. No, I don't like what you've just said. It's a misleading bad idea.' Thomas indeed reflects that there is within him 'the conflict between holiness and magic' (364) and admits to himself, 'I'm a calculator, a manipulator' (430).[71]

For Thomas, one of the ambiguous forces within the unconscious mind is, as Freud diagnosed, a death-wish (258). His great theory, on which he has come to base all his practice, is that people must use all their negative experiences and

---

68. Murdoch, *Good Apprentice*, pp. 55, 245, 445, 508.
69. On Murdoch and the negative sublime, see Chapter 3.
70. Murdoch, *Metaphysics*, p. 460.
71. Edward meets Thomas's talk about 'dying to live' with the reaction 'it was all magic': Murdoch, *Good Apprentice*, p. 511.

feelings to produce a 'fruitful death of the self', making an ally of the death-wish. Speaking to Edward in his state of black misery, Thomas urges that 'Your picture of yourself, your self-illusion is in process of being broken ... Your unconscious mind rejoices in the defeat of your proud ego ... Your endless talk of dying is a substitute for the real needful death, the death of your illusions ... here a religious believer would pray, and you must try to find your own equivalent of prayer.'[72] This is a 'fruitful death' because it is not the end of the self but only of the egotistic self: 'That self is dying, but another self is watching it die.'

Murdoch's portrayal of Thomas is complex, embodying both her own convictions and views which she resists. She certainly accepts the Freudian description of psychological forces, such as the death-wish, and Freud's exposure of illusions that need to be destroyed. She relies on Simone Weil for the idea of the 'decreation' of the self, as well as for another version of rejecting illusions,[73] and she cites Karl Barth for the claim that 'faith sees death and non-existence where [the man of the world] beholds full-blooded life ... The living must die in order that the dead may be made alive.'[74] Thomas employs her *own* favourite visual image of the needful death of the ego – the painting of the flaying of Marsyas by Domenichino: he echoes her in reflecting that 'the entranced face of the tortured Marsyas, as Apollo kneels lovingly to tear his skin off, prefigures the death and resurrection of the soul.'[75] But Murdoch does not accept Thomas's theory that the self is enabled to choose a rightful death and so is renewed, *only* by its own efforts or simply by tapping into inner spiritual powers such as the death-wish. Rather, the Good is objective and 'magnetic',[76] prompting the self to attend to other persons and things in the world and finally drawing the self to desire Good itself. Healing by what Thomas names one's 'own deities' is like the existential or romantic hero she condemns in Sartre's account. Edward puts his finger on the defect in Thomas's theory: 'One thing's missing from your awfully poetic picture, and that's the motive. I haven't got the *motive*, that's what's missing from your plan for my salvation.'[77] Creating a new being from inner spiritual forces alone lacks the motivation that can only come from some external attraction, from the 'transcendent magnetic centre' of the Good.[78] As Murdoch writes, 'What is needed is a re-orientation which will provide an energy of a different kind, from a different source.'[79] Thomas's theory, however, becomes an important mechanism of the plot: the reader is kept in suspense as to whether he

---

72. Murdoch, *Good Apprentice*, p. 71.

73. On Murdoch and Weil, see later, pp. 159–60.

74. Murdoch, *Metaphysics*, pp. 509–10, citing Barth's commentary on the *Epistle to the Romans* at 4:17, and noting the parallel Barth adduces there with Plato.

75. Murdoch, *Good Apprentice*, p. 78; for the image, see the interview of Murdoch with Eric Robson, in Lello, *Revelations*, pp. 89–90.

76. Murdoch, *Sovereignty of Good*, pp. 63, 75.

77. Murdoch, *Good Apprentice*, p. 73.

78. Murdoch, *Sovereignty of Good*, p. 75, see also p. 71.

79. Ibid., p. 55.

will himself be able to use the negative experience of discovering Midge's adultery in order to put his own ego to death. At first he fails the test, 'physician, heal thyself', but he is allowed to recover by the author.

This shift in focus from the earlier to the later novel, from the question of the unity of the Good to the question of the source of energy for turning the self towards the Good, appears to be assisted by Murdoch's theological reading in the interim. Negatively, she reacts strongly against the 'voluntarism' she finds in some modern theology, exemplified by what she calls Don Cupitt's 'subjectivist non-cognitive philosophy of will'.[80] Positively there is the impact of her assiduous reading of Paul Tillich's *Systematic Theology*. Twice in her *Metaphysics* she heads chapters by quoting from his version of the ontological argument for the reality of Being Itself, in order to support her *own* argument for the necessary existence of the Good.[81]

Murdoch relies on two forms of the Ontological Argument, logical and experiential. First, she considers that the very idea of the Good or Absolute Perfection implies a certainty of its existence since, following Plato, 'when we really think we must be thinking of a real object'; this is not dependent on Anselm's formulation that what exists in reality must be 'greater' than what exists in thought alone. Second, we recognize and identify degrees of goodness in life, and such experience both makes the idea of a greatest good conceivable and enables us to intuit that a hierarchy of value must lead to a necessarily supreme value.[82]

Murdoch thus approves of Tillich's approach in rejecting the idea of God as a person while at the same time affirming that 'nothing is more important for philosophy and theology than the truth [the ontological argument] contains, the acknowledgement of the unconditional element in the structure of reason and reality'.[83] He continues that loss of this grasp of the unconditional element has led to an imposing of 'the idea of God' on the mind as a 'strange body', which has resulted first in 'heteronomous subjection' and then 'autonomous rejection'.[84] Clearly, Murdoch views some modern theology as 'autonomous rejection' not only of a personal God but also of the Good. The voluntarism she detects in Cupitt 'seeks autonomy, human potential, freedom'. She comments: 'These are good things, but isolated and in a religious context the programme may remind us more of Feuerbach and Sartre.'[85] Sartre, she thinks, has erred in stressing the autonomous will over attention to the Good, and the Cupitt-type of theologian is being placed in the same camp.

---

80. Murdoch, *Metaphysics*, p. 454.

81. Ibid., pp. 391–2, 431.

82. Murdoch, *Sovereignty of Good*, pp. 62–6, and *Metaphysics*, pp. 392–402. Marije Altorf, *Iris Murdoch and the Art of Imagining* (London: Continuum 2008), pp. 104–7, stresses that for Murdoch the proof arises from, and yet exceeds, consciousness and imagination.

83. Tillich, *Systematic Theology*, vol. 1, p. 208, cited by Murdoch, *Metaphysics*, p. 391.

84. This assertion is cited three times by Murdoch, *Metaphysics*, pp. 381, 392, 431.

85. Murdoch, *Metaphysics*, p. 454.

Examination of her heavily annotated copies of the first two volumes of Tillich's *Systematic Theology* reveals the alternative she has found in Tillich to the 'autonomous rejection' of the Good. Her notes show she is interested in Tillich's idea of the 'New Being' which is possible for human persons.[86] For Tillich this comes from a participation in Being Itself which is continuously overcoming the threat of non-being. Admittedly, Murdoch shows suspicion of the notion of 'Being', especially as it is found in Heidegger, fearing that it may become a sinister and wanton cosmic force without any moral content or relation to love,[87] but she certainly ascribes to the idea that 'new being' is possible through participation in the energy of the transcendent Good. Mention of 'new being' appears five times in *The Good Apprentice*,[88] once in inverted commas as if referring to a technical term to be found elsewhere: Midge, for instance, thinks that Stuart would be able to discern the grain of truth in her confused and darkened 'new being' (in quotation marks).[89] While Thomas believes that 'there is no end to the power of the soul to create new being',[90] this is evidently in opposition to Murdoch's own belief that new being depends finally on the Good and not on one's inner spiritual energies. It is objective truth, she writes in *Metaphysics*, that 'can bring about "new being"'[91] – again the phrase is placed in quotation marks.

In her annotations to his *Systematic Theology*, she also shows herself interested in Tillich's idea of the 'demonic'.[92] His argument is that when we make things ultimate which are not our final concern (as is Being itself), these lesser concerns become demonic, gaining power over us. So for Murdoch the 'angels', the scattered fragments of the Good, can become evil when appropriated by the self. Reading Tillich seems then to have helped the shift of Murdoch's focus to discuss the origin of person-renewing energy. References in *The Good Apprentice* to the courage that

---

86. See Murdoch's underlining and marginal crosses in her copy of Tillich, *Systematic Theology*, vol. 1, pp. 38, 49–55, 136; vol. 2, pp. 87, 89, 115–16, and her notes on vol. 1, p. 70 and vol. 2, p. 181. On vol. 2, p. 87, she objects in a marginal note that Tillich is drawing 'too sharp distn. [distinction]' between the form of New Being in historical and non-historical religions.

87. Murdoch, *Metaphysics*, pp. 414–15. Murdoch raises questions about the validity or meaning of language of being, especially in dialectic with non-being, in Tillich: see her copy of Tillich, *Systematic Theology*, vol. 1, pp. 210, 211, end-papers 1, 3.

88. Murdoch, *The Good Apprentice*, pp. 72, 254, 359, 460, 517. Also Stuart is 'full of being', as Eugene is 'full of himself': Murdoch, *Time of the Angels*, p. 90; *Good Apprentice*, p. 144. The phrase 'his new being' does appear in *Time of the Angels*, p. 206, which must precede her reading of Tillich, but it is used casually and without the technical implications where it appears in *Good Apprentice*.

89. Murdoch, *Good Apprentice*, p. 460.

90. Ibid., p. 359.

91. Murdoch, *Metaphysics*, p. 143.

92. See her underlinings in Tillich, *Systematic Theology*, vol. 1, pp. 133–5, 140, 208, 216; see her notes on vol. 1, pp. 159, 160 and vol. 2, end-paper 2.

comes from openness to the Good ('our courage and our desire to be good'),[93] rather than just from existential decisions, are perhaps echoes of Tillich's 'courage' which is grounded in being, and of which Murdoch takes some notice.[94]

Demythologizing and Christology

So far we have explored Murdoch's version of the demythologizing of a personal God, but she was evidently aware of modern theologians whose demythologizing included – and was even centred on – the history and meaning of Jesus Christ. She read and annotated Rudolph Bultmann's *Jesus Christ and Mythology*, and since her copy was published in 1963, it is likely that she was familiar with Bultmann's approach to demythologizing before writing *The Time of the Angels*. Given that she makes her bishop the spokesman for theological demythologizing, it is also likely that she was alerted to this particular work of Bultmann by Robinson's extensive discussion of it in *Honest to God* (1963).[95] She appears to have acquired the second of Robinson's acknowledged major sources, Bonhoeffer's *Letters and Papers from Prison*, some time later in the 1960s (her edition was published in 1966), although his third source – Tillich – does not appear to have entered her reading until over a decade later.[96]

John Robinson integrates and popularizes three insights from his sources: that we should abandon images of God as a personal subject 'out there' and adopt images of God at the 'depth' of human existence, such as 'Ground of Being' (Tillich); that we should replace the mythological meaning of the person of Christ with a more existential meaning, relevant to our human experience (Bultmann); and that we should find a 'Christ for us today' who is not constructed to fill a supposed religious need or a 'God-shaped blank' (Bonhoeffer). The modernizing bishop of *The Time of the Angels* notes that there are historical problems about the event of Christ, hinting that demythologizing also means dehistoricizing, or a good dose of doubt about the historical Jesus in favour of the Christ people know in faith in their own time. This is certainly Bultmann's approach, though not Robinson's. He approves of Bultmann's stripping out of the 'spatial' myths that are used in the Gospels to give significance to the event of Christ (such as a 'descent' from heaven and an 'ascent' to sit on the right hand of God) and their replacement by forms of thought which express Christ's significance in a way more appropriate

---

93. Murdoch, *Good Apprentice*, p. 248. There are fifteen references to courage in Murdoch, *Good Apprentice*, e.g., pp. 144, 172, 473.

94. See underlining in Murdoch's copy of *Systematic Theology*, vol. 1, pp. 209, 273. But already in *Time of the Angels*, Muriel knows she needs courage: p. 125.

95. Robinson, *Honest to God*, pp. 23–5, 34–5, 44.

96. We are, however, reliant for knowing this on the particular collection of books preserved in the section of her library conserved at the University of Kingston, which is incomplete.

for today. However, Robinson points out that this demythologizing does not in itself entail dehistoricizing, and that Bultmann's historical scepticism 'is not necessarily implied in his critique of mythology'.[97] Robinson agrees that Jesus had a mythological world view (including eschatology in mythological form) and that we can abandon these conceptions for a deeper meaning,[98] but Robinson himself has a greater confidence in the Gospel records as they attest to history.

Murdoch appears to sit closer than Robinson to Bultmann, whose insistence that the 'real' Christ is the figure we encounter 'here and now' emerges in Murdoch's thought in her writings after the 1960s, although in a form that does without Bultmann's Christian emphasis that Christ is met in the proclamation of the Word in the context of the church. Murdoch's attachment to the 'mystical Christ' or 'my Christ', as her thought develops, is thus consistent with at least a partial demythologizing and dehistoricizing.[99] It also attempts to answer Bonhoeffer's question, 'who is Christ for us today?', as repeated many times by Robinson.

However, there is no trace of such a mystical Christ in *The Time of the Angels* or in the philosophical essays most closely associated with the novel, which are collected in *The Sovereignty of Good*. Christ does receive mention in the latter work as someone whom Christians find a source of energy for transforming the 'selfish empirical psyche': believers feel they can receive extra help, praying 'not I, but Christ'. 'Prayer,' Murdoch writes, 'can actually induce a better quality of consciousness and provide an energy for good action which would not otherwise be available.'[100] Christ seems to function here like all good things and people, 'altering consciousness' to give attention to others beyond the self.[101] This idea of Christ persists throughout Murdoch's writing, culminating in her comment in *Metaphysics* that 'Christ seems to be a unique case, a personal Ontological Proof.'[102] As yet, however, there is no indication of what Murdoch goes on to say in this passage in *Metaphysics*, that 'the Christ who saves is the mystical Christ whom we make our own'.

For Murdoch, a negative aspect of belief in Christ lies in making a religion out of suffering, thus avoiding the crisis of the death of the selfish ego. Murdoch repeats this criticism a number of times in the novels and in her philosophy. A central idea of Christianity, she complains in *Metaphysics*, is 'the transformation of sin into purifying pain', so that the crucified Christ becomes 'the image of suffering without death'.[103] Christ upon the cross, 'that ultimate picture of human suffering',

---

97. Robinson, *Honest to God*, p. 35.

98. Ibid., pp. 24, 34.

99. See Iris Murdoch to Scott Dunbar, 19 October, 1977, about reading Hick's *The Myth of God Incarnate*, p. 322: 'As far as I can see, I believe what they (Maurice Wiles, John Hick etc.) believe about Christ' (Horner and Rowe, *Living on Paper*, p. 451).

100. Murdoch, *Sovereignty of Good*, p. 83.

101. Ibid., p. 84.

102. Murdoch, *Metaphysics*, p. 429.

103. Ibid., pp. 82-3, 128-9.

has become, she judges, 'probably the greatest single consolation in western history'.[104] She means that because this figure is believed to have been resurrected from death, meditation upon his suffering produces a feeling of solace in all who suffer. Thus, in the vision Anne Cavidge has of Christ in *Nuns and Soldiers*, she makes the suffering of Christ the archetype of universal human suffering:

> They pierced your hands and your feet with nails and your side with a spear. They shot your kneecaps off, they drove a red-hot needle into your liver, they blinded you with ammonia and gave you electric shocks.

Christ responds, 'You are getting mixed up, Anne', and gently assures her that 'I have no wounds. My wounds are imaginary ... You do not need to see my wounds. If there were wounds they have healed. If there was suffering it has gone and is nothing.'[105] Already, in *The Time of the Angels*, Pattie appeals to the example of Christ in her romantic and unrealistic view of wanting to suffer for others; she pictures herself as 'giving her life a meaning by devotion to those who suffered', reflecting, 'Must one, to help the sufferer, suffer oneself? A purely good person would do so automatically just like Jesus Christ did'.[106] Correspondingly, Carel imagines himself to be saved by Pattie's suffering in the mode of Christ's crucifixion: 'Your faith matters to me Pattie ... will you be crucified for me, Pattie? ... I want to bind you in chains you can never break.'[107]

Later, Murdoch associates this religion of suffering with Jung's refusal to demythologize Christ, so making 'the eclipse of death by creative suffering' a matter of psychoanalytic therapy.[108] Rather than discarding the eschatological myths and the god-man language used in the Gospels to interpret Christ, Jung has transferred them to the interior forces of the psyche. In Murdoch's account, Jung intends to 'preserve and develop [the] religious mythology' associated with Christ 'no longer by reference to any traditional "good" or "absolute", but by fostering in our own souls a natural harmony of opposites, good and evil, masculine and feminine, dark and light'.[109] Jungian therapy is thus, in Murdoch's mind, a fusion of the retaining of myth, the redemptive power of suffering and the cultivation of moral relativism. She protests against this account of the consciousness by asserting the sovereignty of the Good or 'the struggle with an alien reality which engenders and imposes and develops absolute distinctions between good and evil'.[110] The 'mystic Christ', suitably demythologized, can be an 'image' of the Good providing energy for the conflict.[111] Her character Thomas in *The Good Apprentice* shows many of the

---

104. Ibid., p. 83.
105. Murdoch, *Nuns and Soldiers*, pp. 290–1.
106. Murdoch, *Time of the Angels*, p. 90.
107. Ibid., p. 168.
108. Murdoch, *Metaphysics*, p. 132.
109. Ibid., p. 135.
110. Ibid.
111. Ibid., p. 505, but without specific reference to Christ here.

characteristics of a Jungian psychotherapist (in addition to what I have identified as Cupitt-like aspects), especially in his attempt to harmonize conflicting forces in the psyche from within itself, but he does take seriously the need to face the death of the ego-self.

Present-day demythologization may, Murdoch thinks, be seen as part of 'the long mythical story of Christian theology, growing and changing with the "growing-up" of the human race'.[112] The 'beautifying of suffering' that Jung fosters with his remythologizing is 'the traditional and persisting picture upon which the light of modern theology attempts to fall with a difference'.[113] Perhaps, in aligning herself with 'modern theology' here, Murdoch has in mind not only its demythologizing approach but the kind of refusal to defuse the cross of Christ of its unevadable reality of death and nothingness that we find in Donald MacKinnon's writing which she read with appreciation.[114] In *The Good Apprentice*, Stuart assents when Thomas asks about Christ, 'Isn't he one of your signals … One of those non-degradable love-objects you say are everywhere?', but Stuart adds that 'resurrection spoils everything that has gone before … I have to think of [Christ] in a certain way, not resurrected … he has to mean utter loss, pointless suffering, the deep and irremediable things that happen to people.'[115] In the word 'irremediable' we can perhaps hear the echo of MacKinnon's discernment of an 'intractable' element of evil and suffering in human existence in which Christ was deeply implicated, insisting in essays heavily annotated by Murdoch that there can be no easy metaphysical 'consolations' for this phenomenon to be met in the contingencies of everyday life;[116] for MacKinnon this 'intractable' suffering is disclosed in the cross of Jesus, which shows the sheer 'waste' of Christ's failure.[117] We hear a reference to McKinnon's classification of the cross of Jesus as a 'tragedy' in Murdoch's words that 'we cannot regard Christ's passion as tragic unless we regard his death as real death, which [traditional] theology and art discourage us from doing'.[118] For MacKinnon, however – but not for Murdoch – there is still the hope of resurrection, which does not alleviate, trivialize or 'reverse'[119] the death on the cross. While the cross belonged in a journey that 'moved from life

---

112. Ibid., p. 136.

113. Ibid., p. 129.

114. See MacKinnon, *Problem of Metaphysics*, pp. 124–6, and Murdoch's notes in her copy (IML 1049) on the front blank pages, especially on the nature of tragedy.

115. Murdoch, *Good Apprentice*, p. 147.

116. Mackinnon, *Borderlands*, p. 102 (IML 55).

117. Ibid., p. 103; also MacKinnon, *Explorations in Theology*, pp. 185–7 (IML 379). For a strong critique of Mackinnon's insistence on Christian tragedy, see David Bentley Hart, *The Beauty of the Infinite: The Aesthetics of Christian Truth* (Grand Rapids: Eerdmans, 2003), pp. 380–3.

118. Murdoch, *Metaphysics*, p. 141.

119. Mackinnon, *Borderlands*, p. 96; cf. p. 64.

to death' in all its finality, the resurrection life 'no longer moves to the horizon of death'.[120]

Carel in *The Time of the Angels* attempts to find salvation through the willingness of another – Pattie – to suffer for him, making her a substitute figure for Christ. In *Nuns and Soldiers*, Anne is told that Christ himself cannot function as this kind of saviour: in response to her plea that she wants to be saved, 'to be made good', he gently insists that 'I am not a magician'.[121] Without explicit reference to Christ, characters in both our novels continually attempt to evade their own responsibility for putting the ego to death by making 'saviours' of others – which is at least an implicit critique of salvation by Christ. Like Mary Magdalen (apparently) attempting to touch Christ in her encounter with him in the garden on Easter morning, this desire to be saved by another is often accompanied by wanting to touch him or her. In *The Time of the Angels*, Muriel wants Eugene to be her saviour, thinking 'I will go to [Eugene] now … I will lay my head against him. All will be well,'[122] and 'now she would fly straight to Eugene as to her salvation'. Similar thoughts are harboured by Marcus about both Elizabeth and Marcus ('I must touch you for a moment'[123]) and by Eugene about Pattie. In *The Good Apprentice*, Edward first thinks that Jesse will save him by granting him absolution, and he then transfers this salvific power to Mark's sister, Brownie, crying 'You're the only person who can save me … just love me and give me life' (230, 284). Midge makes Stuart into her saviour, pleading, 'Save me, comfort me, touch me … Your touch can heal' (372), and she 'yearns' for Stuart, 'that saving image' (462). Similarly Harry makes his saviour out of Midge: 'If I lose you, I'll drown' (399). In *Nuns and Soldiers*, Christ has to rebuke Ann: 'Love me if you must, my dear, but don't touch me.'[124] Stuart, in *The Good Apprentice*, resists all attempts to make a saviour figure – 'to imagine that somewhere at the end of the world in a cave there's a wise man – that's sentimentality, that's magic' (140).

Murdoch thus develops over the two decades between the two novels a critique of a 'suffering saviour', or – taken separately – the critique of a religion of suffering and a fixation on a saviour. The ideas are already appearing in *The Time of the Angels*, and I argue in a later chapter that they are her transmutation of the thought of Simone Weil.[125] By the time of *The Good Apprentice*, the critique has become much more obvious than in the earlier novel, and what is completely new compared with the novels of the 1960s is the notion of the 'mystical Christ' or 'one's own

---

120. D. M. Mackinnon, 'The Resurrection: A Meditation', in William Purcell (ed.), *The Resurrection: A Dialogue between Two Cambridge Professors in a Secular Age* (London: A. R. Mowbray, 1966), pp. 61-70 (64-5). Further on the resurrection, see the 'Conclusion' to this chapter.

121. Murdoch, *Nuns and Soldiers*, p. 292.

122. Murdoch, *Time of the Angels*, p. 144.

123. Ibid., p. 86.

124. Murdoch, *Nuns and Soldiers*, p. 294.

125. See later, pp. 175-81.

Christ' present in the here and now. This idea begins to appear from about 1976. In *Henry and Cato*, Brendan advises Cato to 'hold onto the Christ that the Church cannot take away from you',[126] and after Anne Cavidge meets Christ she reflects that 'he was *her own* Christ, the Christ that belonged only to her, laser-beamed to her alone from infinitely far away'.[127] Then in *The Good Apprentice* Stuart identifies with Christ as 'a sort of presence, not quite a mystic person':

> Christ was a pure essence, something which, as it were, he might have kissed, as one might kiss a holy stone, or the soil of a holy land, or the trunk of a holy tree: something which was everywhere, yet simply separate and alone. Something alive; and he himself was Christ. The identification was unanalysed and instinctive, where 'not I but Christ' was interchangeable with 'not Christ but I', experienced sometimes as a transparency and lightness, the closeness, even the easiness, of good. (52)

This inner reflection continues the idea in *The Sovereignty of Good* that Christ is one of those particular things or persons in the world, like a stone, that can awaken attention to the Good and can be a focus of meditation, but now this is combined with the idea of presence – 'something alive', 'the closeness of good'; and the Christian (Pauline) submission 'not I but Christ' cited in the earlier text is now reversed into 'not Christ but I'. As Stuart says to Thomas, 'Of course he's *there*. But he's not God' (144, original emphasis). In this passage Stuart takes only a cautious view of Christ as a 'mystic person' but in a later reflection, recalling Thomas's quotation (from 'a Christian mystic')[128] about God as a 'vast dark boiling' sea of 'perpetually self-creating being', he envisages 'the mystical Christ walking upon the boiling sea' (246).

That Stuart is voicing Murdoch's own convictions is likely when we read her as wondering, in *Metaphysics*, to what the demythologizing of Christ might lead:

> Can the figure of Christ remain religiously significant without the old god-man mythology somehow understood? Can Christ, soon enough, become like Buddha, both real and mystical, but no longer the divine all-in-one man of traditional Christianity? ... We must stop thinking of 'God' as the name of a super-person, and indeed as a name at all. Can we then be saved by a mystical Christ who is the Buddha of the west? A Buddhist-style survival of Christianity could preserve tradition, renewing religious inspiration and observance in a vision of Christ as a live spiritual symbol.[129]

---

126. Murdoch, *Henry and Cato*, p. 338.
127. Murdoch, *Nuns and Soldiers*, p. 304.
128. Meister Eckhart; see later, pp. 75–6.
129. Murdoch, *Metaphysics*, pp. 136–7.

Such a mystical Christ can 'save', not in the sense of taking away human responsibility in a substitution for the death of our own ego-selves, but – through a mysterious presence, both distinct from and yet identified with ourselves – in prompting us to attend to the Good. Murdoch goes on in *Metaphysics* to endorse such a Christ: 'The Christ who saves is the mystical Christ whom we make our own, whose figure is a mixture of essence and accident, partly a creation of art as well as being compact of everything we know about goodness. We look through this Christ into the mystery of good.'[130] Murdoch also writes that this Christ is 'the perfect mystical non-individual',[131] that 'the mystical Christ too can be "met" with'[132] and that 'the mystic Christ who is an image of Good is lovable'.[133] It is because such a Christ can turn us to the Good that we know he lives, not because he is resurrected; as characters in two later novels put it: 'If Christ saves, he lives,'[134] and conversely, in an anti-Pauline text, 'if Christ be risen our faith is vain'.[135]

Murdoch's developing idea of the mystical presence of Christ is, no doubt, partly due to her interest in Buddhism which begins in the early 1970s.[136] In her *Metaphysics* she draws an analogy between 'the mysterious Buddha in the soul' and 'Eckhart's God and Christ in the soul'.[137] But her reference at the same time to modern theologians who might 'invent new modes of speech'[138] also alerts us to the results of her theological reading in this period. I have already suggested that one early influence here might be Bultmann's demythologized 'Christ of faith' who is to be encountered in the preaching of the Word in the present moment.[139] This, I suggest, is reinforced by her careful reading of Tillich and by her apparent approval of Tillich's view that the Gospel writers give us only impressionistic 'pictures' of Christ and that the original does not have to be identical with a historical 'Jesus of Nazareth'.[140] Tillich writes of an *analogia imaginis* as 'an analogy between the picture and the actual personal life from which it has arisen'; he adds that 'it was, and still is, this picture which mediates the transforming power of the New Being' and compares the word-portraits of Jesus with expressionist artistic style.[141] In her copy of Tillich's *Systematic Theology*, Murdoch has almost totally

130. Ibid., p. 429.
131. Ibid., p. 352.
132. Ibid., p. 487.
133. Ibid., p. 507.
134. Murdoch, *The Book and the Brotherhood*, p. 490.
135. Murdoch, *Philosopher's Pupil*, p. 188.
136. See Conradi, *Iris Murdoch*, pp. 544–6.
137. Murdoch, *Metaphysics*, p. 487.
138. There is a curious echo here of John Macquarrie's expression 'modes of theological discourse', in a discussion of demythologizing in his *Principles of Christian Theology*, pp. 118–25, a copy of which Murdoch possessed (IML 397).
139. In her copy of Bultmann's *Jesus Christ and Mythology* (IML 65), she circles the term *kerygma* on page 36.
140. Tillich, *Systematic Theology*, vol. 2, p. 114.
141. Ibid., pp. 115–16.

underlined the page on which this account appears, noting in the margin '*analogia imaginis*'. In her notes on the end pages of the book she aptly summarizes Tillich's argument in her own words as 'our pic[ture] of Xt in faith is [she underlines "is"] the divine power'.[142] Further, in notes on the front pages of the same volume she refers to the phrase 'Thou Art the Christ' which appears at the opening of the chapter in which the *analogia imaginis* is discussed. She notes Tillich's point that 'Christianity will live as long as there are people who make this assertion' and so receive the power of the New Being,[143] and she adds 'cf DC's view of Xty proved by saving efficaciousness'.[144] DC is of course Don Cupitt. Perhaps the kind of assertion by Cupitt she has in mind is that enjoyment of 'the maximal degree of liberation from the power of evil and of ... creativity' through Jesus 'is, by definition, faith in his resurrection',[145] a passage from *Taking Leave of God* that she takes particular care to summarize in her annotations to his book.[146] In the process of 'getting to know her Christ', Murdoch's character Tamar reflects on the words of her Cupitt-like teacher Father MacAlister: 'If Christ saves he lives ... *That* is the resurrection and the life.'[147]

Tillich's insight that we receive the power of New Being through an impressionistic portrait of Christ is reflected in several places in Murdoch's work. Echoing his *analogia imaginis*, she writes that 'the art object is an analogy of the person-object, we intuit our best selves in its mirror', and that 'we see in God in a magnified form the analogy between work of art and person; and Christ as God provides both personality and story'.[148] While she thinks that St Paul's Christ 'seems more like a personal creation and a work of art than does the calmer figure of the Gospels', she celebrates the four evangelists with Paul as 'five artists of genius' and concludes that 'Christianity, providing us with a mythology, a story, images, pictures, a dominant and attractive central character, is itself like a vast work of art.'[149] To be sure, she distinguishes between the Christ whom we meet through the Gospel picture from the Christ of much western art, which presents the picture of the 'suffering saviour' that she rejects.[150] But she seems to have the Gospel picture in mind when she characterizes 'the mystical Christ' who saves as a figure which is 'a mixture of essence and accident, partly a creation of art'[151] and acknowledges the impact through the centuries of the image of Christ.

---

142. Murdoch's copy (IML 1107) of Tillich, *Systematic Theology*, vol. 2, blank end-page, facing index.
143. Tillich, *Systematic Theology*, vol. 2, p. 97.
144. Murdoch's copy, notes on front page xii.
145. Cupitt, *Taking Leave of God*, p. 45.
146. Murdoch's copy (IML 1105), rear page 178, facing inner back cover.
147. Murdoch, *Book and the Brotherhood*, p. 490, original emphasis.
148. Murdoch, *Metaphysics*, p. 81.
149. Ibid., p. 82.
150. Ibid., p. 83.
151. Ibid., p. 429.

Other theological reading which has strengthened Murdoch's sense of the 'mystical Christ' who has a kind of contemporary presence is probably that of Donald MacKinnon, whom I have already cited. While he does not use the exact phrase, his book *The Problem of Metaphysics* culminates with an essay on 'The Notion of Presence', heavily annotated by Murdoch. By presence here he means 'the way in which we can significantly speak of the transcendent as impinging upon our experience, as being present in stretches of that experience',[152] and he finds it to be a 'nearness ... an involvement' which is 'not a spatial inclusion'.[153] Here we might compare Stuart's reflections on the presence of Christ as 'transparency, lightness ... closeness'.[154] MacKinnon concludes that 'Jesus is received by those who read the tale of his life as a means of coming to see the world in a particular way as one who does not merely illustrate a principle but ... achieves it and brings it into being.'[155] Murdoch's interesting summary in her notes on this section is that 'Life of Jesus achieves [underlined] what it narrates. Not choice of viewpoint but assertion of what is. Substance',[156] thereby picking up MacKinnon's final words that 'we are immediately aware that we are concerned with what is not a matter of our choice but what is thrust upon us'. Murdoch, like MacKinnon, thus associates the moral imperative of the Good with the presence (in some way) of Christ.

Beyond the void

A steady theme throughout the two novels and two works of philosophy we have been considering is the 'death' of God *as a person*. For Murdoch, this is exactly the same as the rejection of a *personal God*. Like her character Stuart she rejects 'quasi-personal' views of deity.[157] In her notes written in her copy of Tillich's *Systematic Theology*, she dissents even from his formulation that Being is *'not less than a person, although it can and must be more than personality'*.[158] He writes: ' "Personal God" does not mean that God is *a* person. It means that God is the ground of everything personal and that he carries within himself the ontological ground of personality. He is not a person, but he is not less than personal.'[159] In the margin, Murdoch writes 'boring stuff' and then comments elsewhere: ' "God not a person" – OK – but "personal" as part of ground of being (156) – can this make any sense?'[160]

152. Mackinnon, *Problem of Metaphysics*, p. 151.
153. Ibid., p. 154.
154. Murdoch, *Good Apprentice*, p. 52.
155. Mackinnon, *Problem of Metaphysics*, p. 163.
156. Murdoch's copy of Mackinnon, *Problem of Metaphysics*, second front page, facing title page.
157. Murdoch, *Good Apprentice*, p. 445; here she seems to be alluding to the 'Thou' of Martin Buber. See *Metaphysics*, pp. 467–9, 472.
158. Tillich, *Systematic Theology*, vol. 1, p. 156, my emphasis.
159. Ibid., p. 245.
160. See Murdoch's copy of *Systematic Theology*, vol. 1, end-paper 2.

In her *Metaphysics* she dismisses any attempt to 'get around' the outdated notion of God as a person 'by saying that since we are persons God must be *at least a person*'.[161]

Murdoch appears to waver, however, between regarding formerly personal language about God as being symbolic of an impersonal Good and admitting that *all* language about unconditional reality is symbolic, *including* the Good. While, on the one hand, she writes that 'the Good ... is what the old God symbolised',[162] on the other, she calls for terminology which 'shows how our natural psychology can be altered by conceptions which lie beyond its range' and suggests that 'the Platonic *metaphor* of the idea of the Good provides a suitable *picture*'.[163] Again, she urges that with regard to the existence of the Good, 'we can only appeal to certain areas of experience, and use suitable metaphors'.[164] There is a fascinating parallel here with Tillich's oscillation between taking the language of 'person' to be a symbol of Being and affirming that *all* religious language – including Being – must be symbolic.[165] Now, if all language about our ultimate concern is symbolic or metaphorical, whether 'Being' (Tillich) or 'Good' (Murdoch), then there is surely still a place for personal symbols, while not for 'a person' in the sense of 'a being'.

Murdoch's theological reading does not, it seems, cover a renaissance in theological interest in the symbol of the Trinity, which may be dated from the 1980s,[166] later than most of Murdoch's reading, and which envisages the personal relations of the triune God as a 'space' or 'room' in which all created beings are invited to dwell. I myself have been advocating a radical form of this vision of God, in which talk of 'persons' (*hypostases*) in God must be deobjectified and understood as infinite movements or 'flows' of relationship in which all finite beings can find themselves participating.[167] These relations, I suggest, cannot be known apart from relations in the created world, whether between persons or more extensively throughout organic life, and yet are 'transcendent' in never being exhausted into the empirical relations of everyday. 'Personal relations' must, of course, remain an analogy for God, since God as ultimate reality cannot be

---

161. Murdoch, *Metaphysics*, p. 472, my emphasis; Murdoch is referring here in the first place to Buber's divine 'Thou', but she evidently echoes Tillich as well.

162. Ibid., p. 428.

163. Murdoch, *Sovereignty of Good*, p. 71, my emphasis.

164. Ibid., p. 74.

165. See Tillich, *Systematic Theology*, vol. 2, pp. 9–11.

166. See Moltmann, *Trinity and the Kingdom of God* (1981); Robert Jenson, *The Triune Identity* (Philadelphia: Fortress Press, 1982); Alasdair I. C. Heron (ed.), *The Forgotten Trinity* (London: BCC/CCBI, 1989); Elizabeth Johnson, *She Who Is* (New York: Crossroad, 1992). Much of this writing popularized the work of Karl Barth and Hans Urs von Balthasar.

167. See, e.g., Paul S. Fiddes, 'Relational Trinity: Radical Perspective', in Jason Sexton (ed.), *Two Views on the Doctrine of the Trinity* (Grand Rapids: Zondervan, 2014), pp. 159–85; Fiddes, *Participating in God: A Pastoral Doctrine of the Trinity* (London: Darton, Longman and Todd, 2000), pp. 34–46.

described literally, but such language is – I have urged – the most appropriate we have. It makes sense to speak of being immersed into currents of love and justice which are felt – in traditional terms – to be like a father sending out a son on mission, a son responding in obedience to a father and a spirit opening out relations to new depths and a new future. Since we are talking of divine relationships and not beings, these should of course be gendered in diverse ways, complementing (but not replacing) the traditional language of father, son and spirit with metaphors such as mother, daughter and friend. Other symbols such as 'Being Itself', as employed by Tillich and John Macquarrie, are also appropriate in attempting to speak about the final mystery of God, but cannot be awarded a precedence over the personal, as happens when both these theologians declare the personal to be a symbol 'for' another reality, Being;[168] indeed, a case can be made that personal metaphors are *most* appropriate for a religion which has its grounding in a particular personal life and experience, that of Jesus of Nazareth.

Murdoch is unaware of this kind of use of personal symbols, but does nevertheless appeal several times to a passage from Meister Eckhart which works in a similar manner, using personal language in a mode of participation rather than objectification. Twice in *The Good Apprentice* and twice in her *Metaphysics* she cites Eckhart's account of 'seething' depths of being. On the first occasion in her *Metaphysics*, she quotes at some length:

> A certain turning-back and reversion of [God's] being into and upon itself and its indwelling and inherence in itself: not only this, but a boiling-up, as it were, or a process of giving birth to itself – inwardly seething, melting and boiling in itself and into itself, light in light and into light wholly interpenetrating itself … monad begets, or begat, monad and reflected its love and ardour upon itself. For this reason it is said in the first chapter of St. John's Gospel: 'In Him was life.' For life denotes a sort of outpouring whereby a thing, swelling up inwardly, completely floods itself, each part of it interpenetrating the rest, until at last it spills and boils over.[169]

Thomas, quoting this passage to Stuart in *Apprentice*, refers it to the unconscious mind with its inner forces and movements.[170] For Murdoch, it is a 'deep abyss' which is 'not Jung's or Freud's unconscious mind'[171] but is 'more like the dark

168. Tillich, *Systematic Theology*, vol. 1, pp. 244–5; Macquarrie, *Principles of Christian Theology*, pp. 83–6.

169. Murdoch, *Metaphysics*, pp. 464–5; see also *Good Apprentice*, pp. 145, 246; *Metaphysics*, p. 501. The passage is from Eckhart's *Commentary on the Book of Exodus*; it can be found in the selections of Bernard McGinn (ed.), *Meister Eckhart. Teacher and Preacher* (New York: Paulist Press, 1986), p. 218. Unfortunately, Murdoch does not reference the source of the English translation she quotes.

170. Murdoch, *Good Apprentice*, p. 145.

171. Murdoch, *Metaphysics*, p. 464. She adds that it might be seen as some kind of unconscious mind or 'deep soul'.

realm of Plato's *anamnesis*, or St John of the Cross's abyss of faith into which we fall when we have discarded all images of God; or the seething bubbling cauldron in terms of which Eckhart once described God'.[172] The words of Eckhart, however, combine the positive with the negative way of speaking about God, as he goes on to write (and Murdoch to quote): 'This explains the fact that the emanation of the Persons of the Deity is the reason for the creation.'[173] This is certainly not an account of a supernatural person or the three personal beings of Eugene's icon of the Trinity. But it *is* a kind of personal language of 'begetting' in 'love and ardour', so inviting us to fall, or be immersed, into flowing currents of loving relations. We notice, however, that Eckhart envisions this 'interpenetration' as happening 'before' or outside creation, rather than being *inconceivable* without the participation of created things. I am suggesting, by contrast, that it is not possible to conceive of this 'indwelling' and 'interpenetration' without such relations in everyday life, and it is there – I propose – that we encounter transcendent relations.

The term 'abyss' which Murdoch uses appears in Eckhart in the form *Abgrund* and it reappears in the *Ungrund* of Jacob Boehme[174] as the self-generating aspect of the divine Ground of Being. From Boehme it passes into use by Tillich, for whom similarly the 'abyss' is the 'divine depth' or 'the unapproachable intensity' of Being in which everything has its origin; it is also the power of Being, 'infinitely resisting' the non-being which is a dynamic element within God, energizing Being and 'forcing it out' into the open.[175] In the finite creature, this same non-being, however, is 'a threat and a potential disruption'.[176] The 'abyss' appears in the penultimate chapter of Murdoch's *Metaphysics* that is devoted to the phenomenology of 'The Void', but it is by no means a synonym for the void. The chapter follows closely Simone Weil's account of the experience of the void, or *malheur*,[177] which Murdoch also names as 'despair', 'affliction', 'desolation', 'emptiness', 'absence of good' and 'non-being'. While in Tillich, 'abyss' stands for a deep-laid energy which overcomes non-being, Murdoch's 'void' is non-being itself, altogether an experience to be placed 'in opposition to transcendence'.[178] This is a philosophical account of the black state depicted as befalling Edward in *The Good Apprentice* in his extreme remorse after the death of Mark, which he variously describes as not having 'any real being left', 'everything … coming to an end', a feeling of 'nowhere to go', and the soul as 'dead'.[179]

---

172. Ibid., p. 464. Cf. Murdoch, *Henry and Cato*, p. 337, 'fall into the abyss'.

173. Murdoch, *Metaphysics*, p. 465.

174. Jacob Boehme, *Clavis Specialis*, in G. Ward and T. Langcake (eds), *The Works of Jacob Behmen*, 4 vols (London: Richardson, 1764–81), vol. 1, p. 58.

175. Tillich, *Systematic Theology*, vol. 1, pp. 246–67, 250–1.

176. Ibid., p. 246.

177. See Murdoch, 'Knowing the Void', pp. 157–61. See below, pp. 158–9, 170–2.

178. Murdoch, *Metaphysics*, p. 498.

179. Murdoch, *Good Apprentice*, pp. 45, 56–7, 68.

Murdoch again follows Weil in her tentative advice to those who have descended into the void: 'Live close to the painful reality and try to relate it to what is good'; it is possible, even in the most severe affliction, to 'orientate' oneself towards 'good and love'.[180] Her counsel is extraordinarily like that which is offered to Edward by Thomas and Stuart respectively – use the desolation creatively to put to death the greedy ego and remain *attentive* to 'any person, any pure or innocent thing that could attract love and revive hope'.[181] This, for Murdoch herself, is not just a matter of sheer willpower since 'the sovereign Good ... is something we all experience as a creative force',[182] although Murdoch also admits, somewhat grudgingly, that 'there may be a place here for the idea of an effort of will'.[183] This is where the reference to the 'abyss' fits in: it is possible to experience the 'void' *as* 'abyss'. She writes that 'the emptiness ... is also, potentially, the dark night spoken of by St John of the Cross, wherein, beyond all images, lies the abyss of faith into which one falls (perhaps as into Eckhart's seething cauldron).'[184]

Murdoch knows of the meaning given to 'abyss' by Tillich, as 'the infinite potentiality of being and meaning'.[185] In her copy of his *Systematic Theology*, she draws attention several times to Tillich's use of 'abyss'.[186] Her references to the abyss in her *Metaphysics* recognizes this dynamic character, finding it to be a transcendent 'mystery' and fecund source of images of the Good. Here she seems affected by the sense of 'abyss' in Martin Buber's book *The Eclipse of God*, despite her definite rejection of his personalist identification of God as a 'Thou'; she commends his statement that 'the ground of human existence in which it' (i.e. encountered reality, for Buber, God) 'gathers and becomes whole is also the deep abyss out of which images arise. Symbols of God come into being, some of which allow themselves to be fixed in lasting visibility.'[187] There is a significant shift of thought happening here, during the period of Murdoch's reading of theology. In a Weilian perspective, the void can become a place where, *despite* emptiness, nothingness and absence of the Good, the human personality can be orientated towards good and love. Now, influenced by Tillich, Buber and MacKinnon's 'notion of presence', the void can become a place where the good is actually *present* and encountered, in short – abyss. Murdoch sums up in her concluding chapter that 'the "dead" void can become "live" or "magnetic" '.[188]

It may seem a small change to say that the void can *become* abyss, but it is a symbol of something more far-reaching – that the Good is not only to be served

180. Murdoch, *Metaphysics*, p. 503.
181. Ibid.
182. Ibid., p. 507.
183. Ibid., p. 503.
184. Ibid., p. 501.
185. Tillich, *Systematic Theology*, vol. 1, p. 79, underlined by Murdoch in her copy.
186. Ibid., vol. 1, markings in Murdoch's copy at pp. 79, 157, 229.
187. Murdoch, *Metaphysics*, p. 464, quoting Buber, *Eclipse of God*, p. 45.
188. Murdoch, *Metaphysics*, p. 504.

for nothing, as an absolute only to be known indirectly through signs, but is in some way also close and at hand, though never subject to being possessed. This nearness can give confidence that the contingent details of the world, sometimes felt as threatening, can be experienced as sacraments of the Good.[189] Edward, beginning to recover at the end of *The Good Apprentice*, reflects on his period of 'blackness'; he had felt it to be associated with the sheer contingency of life, 'all sorts of things which happened by pure chance', but now it could also be experienced as something of promise: 'It's a whole complex thing, like a dark globe, a dark world, as if we were all parts of a single drama, living inside a work of art'.[190] Once more Murdoch finds an apt reference in her theological reading for this shift of mood, from Barth's commentary on the Epistle to the Romans 4:17 which she owned and read: 'God, who quickeneth the dead and calleth the things that are not as though they were.' Murdoch cites Barth's comment that 'the living must die in order that the dead may be made alive. The things which are must be seen as if they were not in order that the things which are not may be called as though they were ... a similar faith appears on the borderland of Plato... and of the religion of Luther'.[191] Barth no doubt has in mind Luther's comment that 'God brings everything to nothing in order to put us in the right'.[192]

In the final chapter of her *Metaphysics as a Guide to Morals*, Murdoch reflects on 'presence', perhaps echoing MacKinnon's words in his essay on 'The Notion of Presence' that 'we are concerned with what is not a matter of our choice but what is *thrust* upon us'.[193] Murdoch asserts that the notion of the Good is 'forced upon us', that 'our general awareness of good, or goodness, is with us unreflectively all the time, as a sense of God's presence ... used to be to all sorts of believers'.[194] Good is something 'clearly seen and indubitably discovered in our ordinary unmysterious experience of transcendence, the progressive illuminating and inspiring discovery of *other*'.[195] Murdoch ends the chapter by deliberately following Tillich in quoting Psalm 139, 'whither shall I flee from thy presence?', which – like Tillich – she refers to 'matters of "ultimate concern", our experience of the unconditioned, and our continued sense of what is holy'.[196]

---

189. See further below, pp. 86–9, 94–5.

190. Murdoch, *Good Apprentice*, pp. 517–18.

191. Murdoch, *Metaphysics*, pp. 509–10, citing Barth, *Epistle to the Romans*, p. 141.

192. Martin Luther, *Die zweite Disputation gegen die Antinomer* (WA 39.1, 470), cited and discussed by Eberhard Jüngel, 'The World as Possibility and Actuality', in J. B. Webster (ed. and trans.), *Theological Essays* (Edinburgh: T&T Clark, 1989), pp. 95–123 (107).

193. Mackinnon, *Problem of Metaphysics*, p. 163, my emphasis.

194. Murdoch, *Metaphysics*, p. 509.

195. Murdoch, *Metaphysics*, p. 508, original emphasis.

196. Ibid., p. 513. Tillich cites the Psalm in *Systematic Theology*, vol. 1, p. 12, referring to a 'religious concern' which is 'ultimate, unconditional, total and infinite'. Murdoch takes special note of this citation in her notes on page 68 of her own copy.

Other of Murdoch's concluding words in her *Metaphysics* might stand as a summary of her dialogue with modern theologians:

> We may see how close to religion certain parts of philosophy may come ... The mythology of religion does not necessarily vanish but finds a new and different place ... We need a theology which can continue without God. Why not call such a reflection a form of moral philosophy?[197]

In this 'new and different place', Murdoch finds ambiguously, with A. N. Wilson, that 'Jesus has survived'.[198] The dialogue with modern theology, I aim to have shown, throws a good deal of light on Murdoch's development both as a thinker and a novelist between *The Time of the Angels* (1966) and *The Good Apprentice* (1985). In entering conversation with her, a theologian today may point out that Murdoch's attachment to Eckhart's images, which include those of 'self-begetting', 'indwelling' and 'love', opens up the possibility of using personal symbolism for our 'ultimate concern', despite demythologizing God as 'a person'. At the same time her phenomenology of the void should surely mark theology and prompt theology to make a proper place in itself for the tragedies of life.

---

197. Murdoch, *Metaphysics*, pp. 510, 512.
198. Ibid., p. 510, citing A. N. Wilson, *Jesus* (London: Sinclair-Stevenson, 1992), p. 253.

Chapter 3

THE SUBLIME AND THE BEAUTIFUL: BRINGING MURDOCH AND GERARD MANLEY HOPKINS INTO CONVERSATION

'I'm rather overwhelmed by it. I hadn't expected such an extreme landscape. It takes getting used to. Sublime rather than beautiful isn't it?'[1] These words of Marian in Iris Murdoch's novel *The Unicorn* point to a contrast between the 'sublime' and the 'beautiful' which was at the heart of Kant's analysis of aesthetics, and which has been carried through into our late modern period. With John Milbank,[2] we can identify a pervasive discourse today of not only *contrasting* the sublime with the beautiful but also *opposing* the one to the other, a way of speaking which acknowledges a strong debt to Kant (in fact, virtually canonizes him) and which characterizes many forms of the movement often called 'postmodern'. While beauty is seen as a matter of form, determination and individual essences, the sublime is conceived as an irruptive event, overturning all attempts at representation of the world with what is unrepresentable, whether this be called infinity, difference, chaos or the sheer fact of existence itself. In turn, a number of theologians have attempted to reaffirm the reality and truth of beauty, and to reintegrate the sublime with the beautiful, in the interests of portraying a world which is 'charged with the grandeur of God'[3] and of conceiving a God whose infinity is beautiful.

Oddly, this discussion about the relation between aesthetics and theology has usually proceeded in an abstract way, without close reference to any specific form of art. My aim in this chapter, as flagged up by its opening sentence, is to locate the philosophical and theological issues in the particular forms of the novel and the poem and to see how far literature might help in the construction of a theology of the sublime. Iris Murdoch will provide us with the novel. As a philosopher in

---

1. Murdoch, *The Unicorn*, p. 99.

2. John Milbank, *Theology and Social Theory: Beyond Secular Reason* (Oxford: Blackwell, 1993), pp. 100-10; Milbank, 'Sublimity: The Modern Transcendent', in Regina Schwarz (ed.), *Transcendence* (London: Routledge, 2004), pp. 211-34; cf. Frederick Christian Bauerschmidt, 'The Theological Sublime', in John Milbank, Catherine Pickstock and Graham Ward (eds), *Radical Orthodoxy: A New Theology* (London: Routledge, 1999), pp. 201-19.

3. Gerard Manley Hopkins, 'God's Grandeur', in *Poems*, p. 66.

dialogue with Kant, she has made a notable contribution to understanding the relation between the sublime and the beautiful, and she has exemplified her theory practically in the writing of novels. Giving special attention to her novel *The Unicorn*, we will see that her practice does, in fact, offer an interesting variation on her theory as expressed elsewhere. Then I want to compare Murdoch's approach to the sublime and the beautiful with that of some modern theologians, and most notably David Bentley Hart. This discussion will leave some theological issues unresolved, and I intend to see whether they can be clarified by a reflection on the relation between the sublime and the beautiful in the poetry of Gerard Manley Hopkins. Bringing us back full-circle, we shall find some similarities as well as differences between Hopkins and Murdoch which are of significance for our theological project.

This will be the first of two chapters in the book where I, as author, bring Murdoch into conversation with 'others' with whom she held no actual dialogue herself. Murdoch owned an edition of the collected poems of Gerard Manley Hopkins,[4] but the copy in her Oxford library carries no annotations, and I have been able to discover no comments written by her directly about his poetry. There is a remarkable affinity between Murdoch's attention to 'thinginess'[5] and Hopkins's attention to 'inscape' that one might wish stemmed from a reading of Hopkins, but of this there is little firm evidence.[6]

Iris Murdoch and revising Kant

In two key essays, 'The Sublime and the Good' and 'The Sublime and the Beautiful Revisited', Murdoch analyses the relation between the beautiful and the sublime in the thought of Kant and offers a striking revision of his theory. Kant followed the lead of Edmund Burke (1757)[7] in overturning a long tradition of conceiving the sublime as an intensification of the beautiful[8] and in replacing it by the opposition of one to the other. For Kant, the sense of the beautiful is a result of harmony between the imagination and the understanding, while the feeling of sublimity is the result of a conflict between the imagination and the reason.

First, Kant considers what he calls 'free beauty', or beauty properly speaking, arising from the free play of the imagination and the understanding. In finding something to be beautiful, the imagination works harmoniously with the

---

4. *Poems of Gerard Manley Hopkins* (ed. Robert Bridges) (London: Oxford University Press, 2nd edn, 1930), IML 191.

5. See earlier, p. 17.

6. However, for Hopkins's and Murdoch's image of Christ as a kestrel (Windhover), see later, p. 104. For the bell in Murdoch and Hopkins, see earlier p. 24.

7. Edmund Burke, *A Philosophical Enquiry into the Origin of Our Ideas of the Sublime and Beautiful* (ed. Adam Phillips) (Oxford: Oxford University Press, 1990).

8. From at least the time of Longinus, *On the Sublime*, 8.4, 9.9.

understanding to apprehend a sensuous object which is not being brought under any particular concept.⁹ In an objective perception of the world around us, the understanding is assisted by the imagination (recalling and combining previous sense impressions) in applying pre-existing concepts and categories in the mind to what is received through the senses. But in the judgement of taste, there is no such application. There is no rule we can formulate to categorize an object which appears beautiful. Beauty is a matter of form only. It is 'independent' of any interest or 'messiness of emotion'¹⁰ shown by the observer, and it must not be conceptualized in any way that brings it into the sphere of moral judgement about what is 'good'.¹¹ We claim that it will be found beautiful by everyone but, since we cannot formulate a rule according to which the object is constructed, we can never be proved right.¹² It seems to have been composed with a purpose in mind, but we cannot name any purpose it has.¹³ In short, as Murdoch perceives it, the judgement of taste about beauty is the freedom of mere playfulness over against moral freedom.¹⁴

By contrast, Kant considers the sublime to be connected with both emotion and morality. Sublimity results from a conflict between imagination and reason (as distinct from understanding) and is occasioned by what is vast, limitless and formless in nature or by what is immensely powerful. Reason demands that we place what we see in the world within a totality or systematic wholeness. Reason imposes the law that things must make a whole. But confronted with lofty mountains, a sky full of stars, a great waterfall or a stormy sea imagination strives to its utmost to satisfy the requirement of reason for wholeness, and fails.¹⁵ Murdoch points out that the result is a mixture of feelings: 'On the one hand we experienced distress at this failure of imagination to compass what is before us, and on the other hand we feel exhilaration in our consciousness of the absolute nature of reason's requirement and the way in which it goes beyond what mere sensible imagination can achieve.'¹⁶ So the experience of the sublime is a 'negative pleasure',¹⁷ shocking us into realizing that we are not trapped in the senses, that we have a 'supersensible faculty'¹⁸ and a supersensible destiny. This mixed experience, Kant remarks, is very like the experience of respect for the moral law, which he calls

---

9. Immanuel Kant, *The Critique of Judgement* (trans. James Creed Meredith) (repr., Oxford: Oxford University Press, 1973), part I, paras 1, 6, 7 (pp. 41–2, 50–3).

10. Murdoch, 'Sublime and the Beautiful Revisited', p. 262; see Kant, *Critique of Judgement*, para. 13 (p. 64).

11. Kant, *Critique of Judgement*, part I, para. 7 (pp. 51–3).

12. Ibid., paras 8, 22 (pp. 53–6, 84–5).

13. Ibid., para. 16 (pp. 72–4).

14. Murdoch, 'Sublime and the Good', pp. 207–9.

15. Kant, *Critique of Judgement*, part I, para. 26 (pp. 98–109).

16. Murdoch, 'Sublime and the Good', p. 208.

17. Kant, *Critique of Judgement*, part I, paras 23, 29 (pp. 91, 120).

18. Ibid., para. 25 (p. 97).

Achtung.[19] In *Achtung* we feel frustrated at the thwarting of our sensuous nature by a moral requirement, but at the same time, we are elated by the consciousness of our rational nature. We are exhilarated by a sense that we have freedom to conform to the absolute requirements of reason. So Murdoch draws the conclusion that for Kant the experience of the sublime, resembling as it does the exercise of the will in moral judgement, is actually an experience of moral freedom: 'The freedom of sublimity does not symbolize, but *is* moral freedom, only moral freedom not practically active but only, as it were, intuiting itself in an exultant manner.'[20]

The stage is now set for Murdoch to make a highly creative revision of Kant. As Murdoch expresses it, 'I cannot help brooding on the relation of sublimity to *Achtung* and feeling that it must be pregnant with something marvellous.'[21] The marvel is to transfer to the experience of beauty all the features that Kant discerns in the sublime. In this, there is to be found the true sublime, rather than 'an uplifting emotion experienced in the Alps'.[22] The 'independence' of beauty to which Kant draws attention, whether in objects and persons found in the world or in deliberately constructed works of art, is not a separation from emotion and morality but a witness to the *particularity* of the beautiful. 'Independence' is to be reinterpreted as distinct, contingent and individual form.[23] The vastness of the world which prompts a sense of the sublime is thus the sheer multiplicity and abundance of particular things with which the mind is confronted and which occasion aesthetic judgement. This means that the essence of both art and ethics is the same, namely love, or a respect for the other and a genuine noticing of the other for what it – or he, or she – is: 'Love is the perception of individuals. Love is the extremely difficult realization that something other than oneself is real. Love, and so art and morals, is the discovery of reality'.[24] The sublime shocks and amazes us, but 'what stuns us into a realization of our supersensible destiny is not, as Kant imagined, the formlessness of nature, but rather its unutterable particularity.'[25] To know the world as a reality other than ourselves is to love it. And this love is truly moral, since for Murdoch virtue is apprehending that other persons exist and letting them be as others.

The experience of the sublime-in-the-beautiful is a moral one, since we are being turned away from ourselves towards the other and finally towards the Good. The enemies of art and morals, which are enemies of love, are things that prevent us noticing the particular and the individual: notably, these are convention or neurosis.[26] The first means being sunk in a social totality (such as we find in

19. Ibid., paras 25, 29 (pp. 96, 123).
20. Murdoch, 'Sublime and the Good', p. 209, original emphasis.
21. Ibid., p. 213.
22. Ibid., p. 212. Murdoch makes a similar move in her *Sovereignty of Good*, pp. 81–4.
23. Murdoch, 'Sublime and the Good', p. 219; Murdoch, 'Sublime and the Beautiful Revisited', pp. 282–3.
24. Murdoch, 'Sublime and the Good', p. 215.
25. Ibid., p. 215.
26. Ibid., pp. 216–17.

Hegel), and the second means enclosing ourselves in a world of our own into which we try to draw all things from outside. The latter Murdoch identifies as the Romantic ideal of the self, which has influenced a great deal of both literary and political activity since Kant.[27] But 'the exercise of overcoming one's self, or the expulsion of fantasy and convention ... is indeed exhilarating ... it is very like *Achtung*. Kant was marvellously near the mark'.[28] Love, then, is an exercise of the imagination.[29] The sense of the sublime is not, as in Kant, the exhilarating freedom of intuiting the moral reason but the freedom to notice others and to turn to the Good which is beyond us. However, this will be a tragic sense of beauty and sublimity, since we can never attain the wholeness to which freedom aspires. Love implies a tragic freedom: we all have an indefinitely extended capacity to imagine the being of others, but they remain infinitely different from ourselves. There is no totality available, but only the situation of the confrontation of the one by another in which freedom is to be exercised.[30] As Murdoch stresses over and over again in her philosophy and novels, the good cannot be possessed as a whole; we must serve the good for no reward, being 'good for nothing'.[31]

Murdoch's reenvisaging of the sublime *in* the beautiful, or in the unutterable particularity of things, applies to the work of art as much as to things and people in the world, and thus to the novel itself. She thinks that the independence or self-containedness of a work of art, which she finds to be an attractive aspect of Kant's theory, derives from the intensity with which artists go through the exercise of attending to something quite particular, other than themselves. 'With what exhilaration do we experience the absence of self in the work of Tolstoy, in the work of Shakespeare. That is the true sublime.'[32] Because it is an attempt, though ultimately unsuccessful, at making a complete statement among lives that are accidental and incomplete, the artwork has a reality which is felt to exist objectively over against us. It is a quasi-sensuous object,[33] and by its intense 'otherness', it diverts our attention from ourselves and prompts a quest for the true and the good. Her modified theory of the sublime and the beautiful thus offers Murdoch a critical perspective on the writing of novels. In her judgement, the nineteenth-century novel tended to succumb to convention, whereas the modern novel succumbs to neurosis: in a heritage from Romanticism, the modern novel presents a subject locked in struggle with itself, externalizing a personal conflict, where other characters are not really separate or contingent but mere extensions

---

27. Murdoch, 'Sublime and the Beautiful Revisited', pp. 270–2.
28. Murdoch, 'Sublime and the Good', p. 216.
29. Altorf, *Iris Murdoch*, pp. 79–80, finds that Murdoch not only transforms Kant's view of the sublime but his view of imagination.
30. Murdoch, 'Sublime and the Good', pp. 216, 219.
31. See Murdoch, 'Existentialists and Mystics', p. 233: the mystical novelist has grasped the need to be good 'for nothing ... because somebody is hungry or somebody is crying'.
32. Murdoch, 'Sublime and the Good', pp. 218, 219.
33. Ibid., p. 219; also Murdoch, 'Salvation by Words', p. 239.

of the consciousness of the central self.[34] A novel which is a true work of art allows characters within it to exist as free and separate beings. It is tolerant of diversity and resists a subjection of the characters to the will of their author.[35] Murdoch comments: 'The novel has to face the special problem of the individual within the work: it will fail if it denies freedom to the fictional individual either by making him merely a part of his creator's mind or treating him as a conventional social unit.'[36]

It is a reasonable deduction that Murdoch's own aim in writing her novels is to present a plurality of characters, existing in their own right and in continuous interaction with each other; this she regards as a tragic form of art, in her special definition of tragedy. Kant contrasted the sublime with the beautiful: for him, only the sublime, as an upsetting glimpse of the boundlessness of nature, was a moral and spiritual experience and had nothing to do with art. Murdoch believes that experience of art, and especially the novel, is a spiritual experience so that 'the theory of the sublime can be transformed into a theory of art'.[37] For Kant, the sublime is a renewal of spiritual power arising from observing the vast formless strength of the natural world; Murdoch aims to replace the spectacle of the Alps with 'the spectacle of human life' in its boundless individuality and manifold relationships. This can be found in observing the world around and can be embodied in intense form in a novel.

As is well known, Murdoch herself denied firmly in various interviews that she was writing 'philosophical novels' and asserted that she kept her philosophy and novel writing in separate spheres. We can perceive, however, that her theory of the sublime and the beautiful has an effect on her writing beyond attention to diversity of character. The plots of the stories and attitudes of the characters inevitably reflect her theory of art. Respect for contingency and particularity, or failure to notice it by being absorbed in the self, drives her plots and is exemplified in the approach of her characters to others. In fact, we may judge that in her novel writing she has extended a brief critique she makes of Kant's view of a beautiful work of art, that 'we should take a more liberal view on the extent to which it may incarnate, use or express concepts'.[38]

Visions of the sublime in Murdoch's novels

Visions of the sublime-in-the-beautiful, impressing us with the endless particularity of particular things and people and drawing us out of our enclosed selves, abound in Murdoch's novels. We may call these an experience of the 'positive sublime',

---

34. Murdoch, 'Sublime and the Beautiful Revisited', pp. 279–80.
35. Ibid., p. 271.
36. Ibid., p. 280.
37. Ibid., p. 282.
38. Murdoch, 'Sublime and the Good', p. 210.

and we find them variously in everyday life, in other people and in art-objects. When Marian kisses Denis in *The Unicorn*, it seems to her that 'this at last, after an interval of ... simply looking at herself in the mirror was the real other, the real unknown', and that 'they were two unique things meeting each other'.[39] Art-objects have a particular 'otherness' and reality of their own: for Henry Marshalson, the colours of Titian's *Diana and Actaeon* are 'so intense and frightening' that the picture produces a 'piercing joy' which was 'surely as real as the gods'.[40] Often in Murdoch's novels, stones, in their hard 'thinginess' and multiplicity, become symbols of the sublime; as Rose looks at her brother's collection of stones, with 'so much dense individuality, so much to notice' in each one, she muses, 'How accidental everything was, and how spirit was scattered everywhere, beautiful, and awful.'[41]

James Arrowby, in *The Sea, The Sea*, calls his cousin Charles to look at the force of the water in the maelstrom of Minn's Cauldron: 'Isn't it fantastic, isn't it terrifying? ... It's sublime, yes, in the strict sense sublime. Kant would love it.' But unlike Kant, James immediately turns his attention to what seems equal sublime to him, the sheer diversity of natural life: '*And* the birds...' – naming shags, choughs, oyster-catchers, curlews.[42] When Charles visits James in his flat, he finds a huge collection of diverse objects from nature and human culture with which his mystical cousin, a disciple of Tibetan Buddhism, has crammed his rooms. Among paintings, precious jade carvings and Chinese porcelain are 'oddly shaped stones, sticks, shells, to which other things such as feathers have been (why, by whom?) tied or stuck, uneven bits of wood carved with crude faces, large teeth and even bones with strange marks (writing?) upon them'. What strikes Charles is the sheer accidental nature of the collection: 'He seems to have no conception of how to sort or arrange his possessions, they are dumped and piled rather than arranged, and elegant objets d'art are juxtaposed with the merest oddments of the bazaar.'[43] Charles is irritated to detect in James a look 'as if he were voyaging elsewhere'. James is not trapped in his collection, but it enables him to travel out of himself, out of the 'cavern' of Plato's myth to which he refers.[44]

In *Bruno's Dream*, the Bruno of the title, an old man lying in bed and gradually dying full of fear and guilt, has made a specialist study of spiders and remembers that '[God] was those spiders ... There was a wonderfulness, a separateness, it was divine to see those spiders living their extraordinary lives.'[45] Bruno's son, Miles, trying to be a poet, has made three 'Notebooks of Particulars', in which he has recorded the intense detail of the world, aiming 'to take in the marvels that

---

39. Murdoch, *The Unicorn*, pp. 238–9.
40. Murdoch, *Henry and Cato*, p. 96.
41. Murdoch, *Book and the Brotherhood*, p. 533.
42. Murdoch, *Sea, The Sea*, p. 242, my emphasis.
43. Ibid., p. 172.
44. Ibid., pp. 174, 175.
45. Murdoch, *Bruno's Dream* (London: Chatto & Windus, 1969), p. 96.

surrounded him. The ecstatic flight of a pigeon, the communion of two discarded shoes, the pattern on a piece of processed cheese.' But he reflects, 'How hard it was to see things'; in fact, we know as readers that the sublime of the particular – the 'ecstasy' and the 'communion' – is passing him by because he is refusing to see his father, and cannot be reconciled with him.

If we venture to name this positive sublime as a distinctively 'Murdochian' sublime, this does not mean that Murdoch fails to portray Kant's negative sublime, the moment which for Kant arouses awe and fear without actually making us afraid, but which in the Gothic and Romantic moods evolves into feelings of sheer terror. We notice that this may be of two kinds in Murdoch's fiction. In the first place, it is one aspect of the beautiful sublime itself, transferring a sense of dread from the blank *vastness* of nature to the fascinating *multiplicity* of persons and things. This superabundant contingency may seem terrible at first encounter – as Rose reflects, 'beautiful, and aweful'. The myriad and multicoloured stones upon the beach that Murdoch's characters collect in sheer delight at the variety of the world can also be horrific tokens of the merely random,[46] but in this first mood of the negative sublime, the experience of sublimity results in the strengthening of human confidence, as Kant himself suggests. Or, as Murdoch puts it, 'the realization of a vast and varied reality outside ourselves brings initially a sense of terror, and then of exhilaration and spiritual power'.[47] Morgan experiences this transformation of sublime horror in a secret valley made by a disused railway cutting, which she explores with the young Peter Foster. As she stares up at the sloping walls of grass and flowers, 'she began to see more and more detail, more and different flowers hidden in the grassy jungle ... How extraordinary flowers are, she thought.' With this vision of the sublime there comes what she names as 'panic': 'She lay there prone and struggled with giddiness and nausea and unconsciousness.' The 'expanse of green floor between the high flowering banks ... was alive with movement and huge forms':

> Was it giddiness she was feeling now, a dazzled sensation of spinning drunkenness, or was it something else, disgust, fear, horror as at some dreadfulness, some unspeakable filth of the universe? Saliva was dripping from her mouth. The loathsomeness as the centre of it all. She let herself fall forward again and the stones pressed into her face.[48]

The very stones – so often symbolic of the beautiful diversity of the world – have become hostile. Morgan on *this* occasion is allowed to recover from the negative sublime, as infinite horror transitions into infinite beauty:

---

46. See earlier, p. 12 above.
47. Murdoch, 'Sublime and the Beautiful Revisited', p. 282.
48. Murdoch, *Fairly Honourable Defeat*, p. 165.

> The hot air was thick with flowery scents and subtle dry emanations. The insects were hissing and murmuring in the honeyed grass of the forest. But now it was suddenly more beautiful to her, more intensely coloured and more absolutely here, under a sky which had resumed its blue … 'How beautiful it all is,' she said, 'How infinitely beautiful. I worship it … I mean the world, the universe, everything that is. All is good, all is beautiful.'[49]

Her sense of the positive sublime has, nevertheless, an element of the illusory in it. She immediately proposes to Peter, who has fallen in love with her, that they should practise 'a free, innocent love', a 'doing each other good' without the sex he desperately wants, a 'happy love' which will preserve her freedom and fulfil her own needs rather than his: 'You're perfect,' she exclaims, 'you just fit, you see, you fit the rôle, you're exactly what I need.' The reader is being warned that the negative sublime may yet return to Morgan without its positive dimension. Miles likewise experiences the negative side in his positive sublime of 'particulars'. Trying to record the details of anemones and their reflection in the polished wood of a table, 'it suddenly seemed pointless'; the anemones 'now seemed to him just a bunch of rather vulgar flowers, pert faces with frilly collars'.[50] At this point he is not only unreconciled to his father; he is consumed with jealousy, having fallen in love with his wife's sister, Lisa, while correctly suspecting that she is also loved by his brother-in-law, Danby. However, he will be allowed to recover his vision, and we leave him at the end of the book, uneasily restored to his wife and at peace with his – now dead – father, writing down his 'particulars' with a 'strange angelic smile on his face'.[51]

The sea frequently appears in Murdoch's novels as an image of the boundlessness and multiplicity of the world,[52] and some will drown in it. Others, however, take courage to immerse themselves bravely in the manifold details of the world and survive, such as Jake at the end of *Under the Net*, for whom 'the tempest subsided' so that he feels 'like a fish which swims calmly in deep waters'.[53] Murdoch is offering a revision of the positive element in Kant's negative sublime; for Kant the terror can simply lead to an affirmation of the superior nature of human reason which lays such demands on the imagination, while for Murdoch it can lead to a deeper appreciation of beauty. The reuse of the negative sublime in postmodern philosophy is thus closer to Kant than Murdoch is in finding the event of the sublime to stand in contrast to all representations, all forms of beauty in the world, although it exceeds Kant in finding an actual *opposition* between the sublime and the beautiful.

49. Ibid., p. 166.
50. Murdoch, *Bruno's Dream*, p. 144.
51. Ibid., p. 283.
52. Conradi, *Saint and the Artist*, p. 337.
53. Murdoch, *Under the Net*, p. 282.

However, we find a second account of the negative sublime in Murdoch's novels which mirrors more closely the experience of the Kantian sublime. In this experience the negative stands on its own and does not obviously seem to lead to a new appreciation of the multiplicity of particular things.[54] Occasioned by a sense of the vastness of the world which is indeterminate, it swamps the sense of the beautiful and blanks out all particulars. This Kantian sublime, which reappears in the Romantic movement, is discounted in the philosophical essays as of little significance: Who, enquires Murdoch sarcastically, is interested in Kant's emotions in the Alps?[55] But Murdoch *depicts* this kind of negative sublime from to time to time in the novels. Morgan, for instance, in the last days of her relationship with Julius King, believed she had a 'mystical vision into the heart of reality' in which she was 'promised the secret of the universe' and then felt it was like being 'shown a few mouldering chicken bones lying in a dark corner covered with dust and filth'.[56] Much later in the novel, she tries, unsuccessfully, to rescue a pigeon trapped in the Underground and falls into a negative state in which 'the huge cast iron vaults were not glowing with light, they were obscure and yellow as if filled with steamy mist, and below them it was as dim and murky as a winter afternoon'. There bursts upon her 'the horror of the world'.[57]

When Charles Arrowby imprisons his childhood love, Hartley, in his house by the sea – supposedly for her own protection from a violent husband – the stones which he has delighted to collect for his garden become sinister, part of a black 'void': he reports that 'I could hear the splash of the sea and the very faint rattle of the stones that the waves were gently clawing as they withdrew from the Cauldron ... I could hear also, or sense, a vast void, a dome of silence ... I felt suffocated ... The void dark house was ominously quiet.'[58] Later he is to be pushed into Minn's Cauldron and will suffer 'a complete fall into the void', from which James miraculously rescues him.[59] The experience of the 'void' in life was one with which Murdoch's mentor, Simone Weil, was well acquainted, as we shall see later.[60] Similarly, Barney Drumm, trapped in an unhappy marriage and racked with guilt about the loss of his priestly vocation, gazes at the stormy water from Kingston Pier, wondering 'which was more horrible, the huge savage sea or the piled rocks with their shapeless crannies'. The word 'shapeless' picks up the sense of terrible contingency, the roaring of the sea into 'mountainous *random* rocks ... to howl in chambers far below'.[61]

---

54. Conradi, in his chapter on the sublime in *Saint and the Artist*, pp. 133–66, fails to notice this double aspect of the negative sublime in Murdoch, reducing it all to the same experience.
55. Murdoch, 'Sublime and the Beautiful Revisited', p. 264.
56. Murdoch, *Fairly Honourable Defeat*, pp. 131–2.
57. Ibid., p. 295.
58. Murdoch, *Sea, The Sea*, p. 308.
59. Ibid., p. 365.
60. See later, pp. 159–61.
61. Murdoch, *Red and the Green*, p. 218, my emphasis.

This kind of negative sublime, standing on its own without alleviation, has a central place in *The Unicorn* as a mood evoked by the landscape. This is much closer in feeling to the postmodern sublime, but closer still to the Gothic which is a predecessor first to Romanticism and then to the postmodern mood. When Marian Taylor arrives for her new job as a companion to a lonely woman in her country house in a remote part of western Ireland, she discovers 'an appalling landscape':

> Marian had read about the great cliffs of black sandstone. In the hazy light they seemed brownish now, receding in a series of huge buttresses as far as eye could see, striated, perpendicular, immensely lofty, descending sheer into a boiling white surge. It was the sea here which seemed black, mingling with the foam like ink with cream.
> 'They are wonderful,' said Marian. She found the vast dark coastline repellent and frightening. She had never seen a land so out of sympathy with man. (16)

Gerald Scottow immediately comments, 'they are said to be sublime', and as Marian looks inland to an apparently boundless expanse of limestone, heather and bog, she was 'overcome by an appalling crippling panic' and was 'almost faint with terror' (20). Significantly, Gerald comments, 'no one swims in this sea'. At the very end of the novel, as Effingham Cooper leaves the area by train, 'he closed his eyes upon the appalling land' (319). Marian's assessment, with which I began this chapter, is that the landscape is 'extreme ... sublime rather than beautiful'.

In her essays Murdoch notes that the Kantian sublime results in the self-exaltation of the subject, in admiration of its power of reason, and she also identifies the Romantic subject, sucking the world into itself as an enemy of art and morals. The implication is that the negative sublime *prompts* a Romantic absorption in the self, leading to the moral danger of fantasy. While the postmodern sublime runs contrary to Kant in aiming to make an attack on the dominant consciousness of the subject, theologians such as David Bentley Hart suggest that, ironically, its end point is a turn back to the self since the sublime finally denotes only a 'nothingness' which challenges all representation of the external world.[62] In *The Unicorn* the Gothic setting of the landscape and gloomy house fosters fantasy in its inhabitants. All are absorbed in the myth which the beautiful lady of the house, Hannah Crean-Smith, weaves around herself as a prisoner for seven years in a dark castle, held by an ambiguous mixture of constraint and voluntary self-sacrifice. While she is apparently being incarcerated by a violent, absent husband as a punishment for trying to kill him, she seems to have embraced her situation as a spiritual project. Hannah herself draws the connection between the landscape and what she finally comes to regard as an illusion: 'You have made me unreal ... Just like this landscape I have made it unreal by endlessly looking at it instead of entering it.' Marian immediately asks herself, 'What *was* [original emphasis] there,

---

62. Hart, *Beauty of the Infinite*, pp. 70–1, 82.

in that strange desolate landscape?', and makes the link between the sublime and Hannah's preoccupation with the cultivation of the self: 'In desperation, but quietly, she said, "Hannah, you are the most sublime egoist that I have ever met"' (259).

One of Hannah's devotees, Effingham Cooper, who serves her with an unrequited courtly love, takes an ambiguous view of Hannah's situation: 'What kind of surrender, what kind of resignation, he could never quite come to decide ... whether it was a great virtue in her or a remarkable vice' (88). Murdoch presents us with the question as to whether Hannah is suffering her seclusion and reduced life in obedience to the Good, or whether she is merely indulging a romantic sense of suffering. On the side of Effingham's 'great virtue', two theories are advanced that treat her semi-voluntary imprisonment as a redemptive suffering, one Platonist and the other theistic, the first voiced by a neighbour, Max Lejour, and the second by one of Hannah's attendants, the gentle Denis. Max, a philosopher, thinks that Hannah may be offering (he is not sure) an image of the supreme Good by being a good person who is guilty like the rest of humankind, but who suffers without trying to inflict suffering on others. Like the 'Good', she is 'non-powerful', and 'in the good' the transmission of suffering (symbolized as *Até*) 'is finally quenched when it encounters a pure being who only suffers and does not attempt to pass the suffering on' (116). Thus, suggests Max, 'she is our image of the significance of suffering' (115). Her spiritual practice involves love of the Good, and Denis interprets this theistically. For him, she makes suffering redemptive by seeking and achieving a 'peace with God' and 'obedience' to God in the midst of suffering (76–7). Hannah herself tells Marian that '[God] desires our love so much, and a great desire for love can call love into being'; despite the apparent absence of God, 'if you really love, then something is there' (63–4). Max pronounces that 'the only being she can afford to love now is God', though he goes on immediately to gloss 'God' as 'Good ... the unimaginable object of our desire' (117). Byatt points out that both these interpretations of Hannah's suffering, those of Max and Denis, can be found in Simone Weil.[63] On the one hand, Weil urges that, in the intense suffering of what she names the 'void', one must resist the consolation of transferring one's suffering to others, the 'desire to see somebody else suffering exactly what one is suffering oneself'.[64] On the other hand, one must persist in the *surnaturel* love of the God who is absent in the void,[65] a bidding echoed in Denis's phrase 'what is spiritual is unnatural' (76).

On the other side of Effingham's ambivalence, Murdoch offers hints that there are doubts about the redemptive nature of Hannah's plight. As Byatt again has pointed out, her behaviour looks remarkably like the kind of obsessional neurosis described by Freud.[66] Moreover, there are strong indications that the myth of redemptive suffering is a fantasy, imposed on herself by Hannah and fostered

---

63. Byatt, *Degrees of Freedom*, pp. 182, 184.
64. Weil, *Notebooks*, p. 158; Weil, *Gravity and Grace*, p. 5.
65. Weil, *Gravity and Grace*, pp. 55, 99–102.
66. Byatt, *Degrees of Freedom*, pp. 173–5.

by those who attend her, in order to meet both her and their emotional needs.[67] Towards the end of the novel, Hannah herself concludes:

> The false God is a tyrant. Or rather he is a tyrannical dream, and that is what I was. I have lived on my audience, on my worshippers. I have lived by their thoughts, by your thoughts – just as you have lived by what you thought were mine. And we have deceived each other. (258)

The word 'dream' is a powerful clue here: it is one of Murdoch's favourite descriptors for the world that the ego builds around itself. Marian, drawn as she is into the myth and Hannah's controlling consciousness, finally concludes that 'no one should be a prisoner of other people's thoughts, no one's destiny should be an object of fascination to others' (237). Fearing her husband's imminent return,[68] Hannah is to take her own life, after first killing Gerald Scottow to whom she has finally submitted sexually. After her death, Max diagnoses her failure to notice and love others as they really are:

> Hannah was like the rest of us. She loved what wasn't there, what was absent. This can be dangerous. Only she did not dare to love what was present too. Perhaps it would have been better if she had. She could not really love the people she saw, she could not afford to, it would have made the limitations of her life too painful. She could not, for them, transform the idea of love into something manageable: it remained something destructive and fearful and she simply avoided it. (301)

Hannah's suffering is associated in the novel with the sense of the negative sublime aroused by the landscape. It is a kind of manifestation of it. In other novels, Murdoch uses Weil's term 'the void' to express this overwhelmingly negative experience,[69] and in this novel, Hannah's suffering parallels Weil's 'void', as Byatt has maintained.[70] But in it Hannah cannot find the positive sublime. Driven into herself, she fails to give attention to the others who are present to her. In Murdoch's later philosophy and novels she is to warn against the delusion of suffering for its own sake, avoiding the real pain of the death of the egoistic self which opens up attentiveness and which is symbolized and embodied in the event of physical

---

67. Avril Horner, 'The "wondrous necessary man": Canetti, *The Unicorn* and *The Changeling*', in Rowe and Horner, *Iris Murdoch: Texts and Contexts*, pp. 163–76 (168), finds that the illusion stems from Hannah's mistaking her admirers' desire for her with love.

68. In fact, he is killed by Denis on his way to the Castle, through what is generally believed to be an accidental drowning in a flash flood.

69. E.g. *Sea, The Sea*, pp. 308, 365; *Henry and Cato*, p. 274; *Good Apprentice*, p. 375; *Message to the Plan*et, pp. 54, 88.

70. Byatt, *Degrees of Freedom*, p. 185. The actual word 'void' does not however appear in *The Unicorn*.

death.[71] In this novel there is no clear contrast as yet between suffering and death, which is to become a later theme. Rather, the two are elided with regard to Hannah, so that when she dies Effingham can comment that she has become 'that death which she had so much striven to emulate in life, which she had studied and practised and loved' (303).

However, there *is* a true death of the self depicted in the novel, in the vision granted to Effingham as he struggles and nearly drowns in the bog.[72] Firstly the narrator evokes a sense of a Kantian or Gothic negative sublime delivered by the forbidding landscape; epithets multiply such as 'a vivid, incomprehensible, menacing presence', 'a great force, a great dark positive force', 'empty now, utterly empty', 'the centre of a black globe', 'a very dark central blackness', 'an endless dark' (194–5, 227). He loses his way because he cannot find any distinguishing features in the vast and blank landscape, and significantly, as he wanders into the bog, he cannot find the stones, typical for Murdoch of particularity: 'He tried the earth round about him … there didn't seem to be any stones any more. He missed those stones. They were at least things solid like himself' (195). It is, then, in this situation, sinking into the all-embracing bog, that he has his moment of vision, and the negative becomes a positive sublime:

> Why did it seem now that the dark ball at which he was staring was full of light? Something had been withdrawn, had slipped away from him in the moment of his attention and that something was simply himself … It came to him with the simplicity of a simple sum. What was left was everything else, all that was not himself, that object which he had never before seen and upon which he now gazed with the passion of a lover … since he was nothing all that was not himself was filled to the brim with being and it was from this that the light streamed … this then was love, to look and look until one exists no more, *this* was the love which was the same as death. He looked, and knew with a clarity which was one with the increasing light, that with the death of the self the world becomes quite automatically the object of a perfect love. (198)

Murdoch portrays even *this* experience of the negative sublime as turning the subject towards the Good. The horrifying 'sublime' of the vastness of nature (Kantian, Gothic or Romantic) is a negative sublime, the incomprehensible challenging the rationality and representative power of the mind. By contrast, the diversity of things and persons provides a positive sublime. The first encourages a romantic centring of the universe in the self, whereas the second turns the self outwards. However, it seems that both *can* shock the self into noticing the otherness of the world. If the negative sublime leads to an *enforced* death of the self, then nothing remains except what is not the self, and so this can 'automatically' turn the self to 'look' at the other. This attention is love, and the world itself becomes

---

71. See, e.g., Murdoch, *Sovereignty of Good*, pp. 82–3; *Henry and Cato*, p. 336.
72. See also earlier, p. 9.

'the object of perfect love'. We are left to assume, however, that a better way is the *voluntary* death of the self encouraged by the positive sublime.

Out of this experience (regrettably short-lived for the pompous and selfish Effingham) comes a new awareness of beauty of the contingent particularities of the world. Stumbling away from his near death he reflects: 'How beautiful the bog looks in the sun. So many colours, reds and blues and yellows. I never knew it had so many colours' (201). As the three women, Hannah, Marian and Alice, lean over him in their concern and love, they appear like the three angels in the Orthodox icon of the Trinity (an image Murdoch is to use again in *The Time of the Angels*): it seems to Effingham that 'the three Angels were a radiant globe out of which light streamed forth. He had seen this before. The globe was the world, the universe. He said, "I think it is love which happens automatically when love is death"' (201). The three, manifold in their own particular identities, are the occasion for seeing the true sublime and so appear as a world of light.

While the Gothic is not a setting that Murdoch often draws on in her novels, she seems in this novel to be using it to suggest that panic and terror might strike a person not only because the universe overflows with contingent details but because at times it seems to face us with an alien force of overwhelming power which speaks of nothingness and threatens all beauty. This negative experience emerges in the novels in the process of depicting the variety of her characters. It appears, that is, in the course of taking seriously her mandate that characters should be allowed to be themselves. Perhaps it also belongs to the idiosyncrasy of character that Effingham interprets this negative force as essentially evil, whereas in a postmodern view what deconstructs representation is life-enhancing, making us face the sheer givenness of existence or being.

Theological reflection on the sublime

Murdoch's portrayal of characters in her novels as facing a crisis of the negative sublime is not a world with which a recent theologian, David Bentley Hart, is working in his book *The Beauty of the Infinite*. For him, we might say, there is only the positive sublime. The glory of God is shining out in the beauty of the world, and he is highly critical of the postmodern notion of the sublime as the 'thrill of the void', an event of nothingness and absence that overturns the realm of representation, presence and stability. Following Jean-François Lyotard, he finds 'narratives of the unrepresentable' everywhere in the philosophy of our age.[73] His diagnosis of this late modern era is that the 'unrepresentable', whether it be called 'difference' (Jacques Derrida), 'chaos' (Gilles Deleuze), 'being' (Martin Heidegger), 'otherness' (Emmanuel Levinas) or infinity, is thought to be truer than

---

73. Jean-François Lyotard, *Lessons on the Analytic of the Sublime: Kant's Critique of Judgment* (trans. Elizabeth Rottenberg) (Stanford: Stanford University Press, 1994), pp. 50–8. See Hart, *Beauty*, pp. 43–52.

the representable.⁷⁴ There is a mood proposing that what is true and good lies beyond the surface of things and enters to break up the surface; because beauty calls attention to the surface it seems that it must be illusory. By contrast, Hart insists that theology *should* remain at the surface, since it is the fabric of the world in which the glory of God finds wonderful expression.⁷⁵

For Hart, the infinite is not a *negation* of finitude. He has learnt from Gregory of Nyssa that it is a positive concept: God's transcendence is an actual excessiveness. The finite participates in the infinite in an endless display of beauty surpassing beauty, and God thus draws us into the life of the world.⁷⁶ The infinite horizon of beauty is not an orientation towards a formless, infinite absolute or towards a sublime that surpasses the aesthetic; rather, an object of attention and of love is open to an infinity of perspectives, allowing for ceaseless supplementation, expansion of meaning and recomposition. Here he is implicitly in accord with Murdoch in finding beauty to lie in the boundless particularities of the world. The question we must pose to Hart, however, is whether theology might be able to incorporate the negative sublime as more than an aberration of our late modern age. This is a challenge that Murdoch's writing brings to the theologian; while she is equally critical of the 'postmodern', we have seen that she finds a place for the negative sublime in drawing a picture of the whole of life.

While Hart's main aim is to *replace* the negative sublime with attention to the beautiful, he clearly agrees with Murdoch that a 'true sublime' lies in the manifold and particular appearance of beauty and says this overtly at least once, urging a theological account of 'beauty in which a truer sublime (the inexhaustible glory of being) is contained'.⁷⁷ He also agrees that beauty involves emotion, love and ethics, consisting as it does in attention to the other. However, for Murdoch the sublime points us away from ourselves towards a Good which is unnameable and beyond our experience, while for Hart a sharing in the beautiful means *participation* in the Good which is the divine life of the Trinity. Contingency need not be negated in order to participate in the infinite God. The vision of God entails, in the distance and difference between the persons of the Trinity, an analogical expression of the multiplicity of the world.⁷⁸

John Betz takes a similar view, arguing that engagement with the truly sublime means sharing in an analogy of being: in fact, he maintains that the modern attack on the doctrine of *analogia entis* is exactly correlative with the attack on beauty in the interests of the negative sublime.⁷⁹ When any concept of analogy between

---

74. Hart, *Beauty*, pp. 44–5, 52–90.

75. Ibid., pp. 24, 90–1.

76. Ibid., pp. 231–60; cf. pp. 18–19 on beauty.

77. Ibid., p. 72.

78. Ibid., pp. 18–19, 55; for 'difference at the origin', see also Milbank, *Theology and Social Theory*, pp. 308–9.

79. John R. Betz, 'Beyond the Sublime: The Aesthetics of the Analogy of Being', part one in *Modern Theology* 21.3 (2005), pp. 367–411; part two in *Modern Theology* 22.1 (2006), pp. 1–50.

created beings and uncreated being is lost, he urges, then the link between the beautiful and the sublime is snapped. Like Hart,[80] he is convinced by Jean-Luc Nancy's contention that Heidegger's thought has aesthetic implications. Nancy urges that just as 'being' stands over against 'beings' in Heidegger, and just as being does not appear until the stability and everydayness of beings is undone by the experience of anxiety, so it is not until representation is unlimited by an experience of the sublime that the sheer givenness of the form of beauty appears.[81] Betz notes that there is a total absence of form in Heidegger's ascribing *es gibt* to being. So, while the beautiful is understood in terms of form, contour and limitation according to an economy of representation, the sublime is understood as an event of unlimitation.

What is needed by contrast, urges Betz, is to understand the relation between the beautiful and the sublime as being analogical. In theological terms this is the relation between the world and God. Here Betz discerns an unholy alliance between Karl Barth and Heidegger, since Barth (suggests Betz) polarizes the self-disclosure of God with the material of the world through his attack on the analogy of being; the glory or sublimity of God always comes into confrontation with the world and undermines all attempts at representation.[82] The Word of God strikes into life and destroys all bridges between human experience of existence and participation in God. There is thus, in his view, a curious affinity between Barth and Heidegger, even though one presents a sublime God and the other a sublime Abyss. We shall shortly question whether this is an entirely accurate understanding of Barth.

Returning to Murdoch, we may observe that while she similarly dispenses with an analogy of being, this does not mean for her an assault by the sublime on the forms of beauty in the world. She thus provides a counterexample to the assertion that loss of an analogy of being means a sundering of the beautiful from the sublime. However, despite finding the sublime *in* the beauty of the world, she can only conceive of beauty as *awakening* us to the supremely Good rather than giving us a personal relation with the Good. Murdoch follows Kant in demanding a performance of the good only for the sake of the good, without any consideration of happiness or reward. From the point of view of theology, there is a deficiency here, since Hart is right to affirm that love should involve reciprocity, an expectation of return from the other; otherwise it is problematic to speak of love of the Good. Hart reserves his most withering scorn for those, like Levinas, who use theological language about the sublimity of the 'absolute other', and yet who think that to be 'for-another' requires an 'ingratitude of the other', human or divine, and even a

---

80. Hart, *Beauty*, pp. 73–5.

81. Jean-Luc Nancy, 'The Sublime Offering', in Jean-François Courtine, Michel Deguy, Eliane Escoubas, Philippe Lacoue-Labarthe, Jean-Francois Lyotard, Louis Marin, Jean-Luc Nancy and Jacob Rogozinski (eds), *Of the Sublime: Presence in Question* (trans. Jeffrey S. Librett) (Albany: State University New York Press, 1993), pp. 31–45. See Betz, 'Beyond the Sublime', part 1, pp. 387–99.

82. Betz, 'Beyond the Sublime', part 1, pp. 369–72.

'persecuting hatred'.[83] By expecting nothing of the other, wanting nothing, Hart judges that: 'I leave the other behind ... stripped of the dignity of being desirable.'[84] The other is not really 'other' at all, he maintains, but the infinite orientation of 'my ethical adventure'. While Murdoch does not use the extreme language of Levinas, her understanding of a non-reciprocal love of the Good may be subject to a similar critique of moral heroism.

A further theological question arises about the notion of form. In finding the true sublime *in* the beautiful, Murdoch perceives a kind of 'formlessness' in the beauty (the contingent details) of everyday life, in contrast with the deliberate form of a work of art. In conversation Murdoch declared that 'a deep motive for making literature or art of any sort is the desire to defeat the formlessness of the world and cheer oneself up by constructing forms out of what might otherwise seem a mass of senseless rubble'.[85] Again, she writes that 'what differentiates art from life [is] the question of form'.[86] Nevertheless, she suggests that the work of art contains a tension between the 'consolation' of its self-contained patterns and the inchoate relationships between particular people that strike against it.[87] Art has a form that loves and includes the contingent,[88] and the *effect* of an art-object is thus a mixture of form and the formless.

For Hart, beauty which prompts our participation in the divine is never formless, and so neither is the true sublime, despite its presentation in this way in postmodern thought. Here Murdoch is being just as nuanced in writing of 'formless' nature as she is of the 'form' of art. We notice that in her conversation about art, Murdoch carefully refers to 'what might ... *seem* [my emphasis] a mass of senseless rubble' in the everyday. The beauty of the world consists in the manifold of *particular* things and persons, so that Murdoch can contrast the Kantian sublime of a 'formlessness of nature' with her view of an 'unutterable particularity' of nature.[89] It is a matter of emphasis: 'Tragic art is disturbing because the self-contained form comes into conflict with something which defies form – the individual being and the destiny of human persons.'[90] She might well agree with Hart that all beauty involves form in the sense that the world is made up of determinate, bounded objects, like the stones with which she litters her landscapes. However, the point she is making is

---

83. Emmanuel Levinas, 'Meaning and Sense', in Adrian T. Peperzak, Simon Critchley and Robert Bernasconi (eds), *Basic Philosophical Writings* (Bloomington: Indiana University Press, 1996), pp. 33–64 (49); Levinas, *Otherwise than Being, Or Beyond Essence* (trans. Alphonso Lingis) (Pittsburgh: Duquesne University Press, 1998), p. 111.

84. Hart, *Beauty*, p. 82.

85. Murdoch in conversation with Bryan Magee, in Murdoch, *Existentialists and Mystics*, p. 7.

86. Murdoch, 'Sublime and the Beautiful Revisited', p. 285.

87. Murdoch, 'Sublime and the Good', pp. 219–20.

88. Byatt, *Degrees of Freedom*, p. 145.

89. Murdoch, 'Sublime and the Good', p. 215.

90. Ibid., p. 219.

that these entities are also formless in the sense that they do not make up a whole, nor are part of a whole. Art *does* consciously attempt to construct a whole, though it never entirely succeeds. Indeed, beauty in itself does not constitute a wholeness.

Murdoch perhaps best expresses this balance between form and the formless not in her philosophical essays but in the characters of a novel. In *An Unofficial Rose*, Randall Lindsay explains that he cannot live any longer with his wife, Ann, because he seeks form in life while she does not, putting his frustration into the image of the roses that they cultivate in their nursery business:

'I need a different world, a formal world. I need form. Christ, how I fade!' …
'Form?'
'Yes, yes, form, structure, will, something to encounter, something to make me *be*. Form as this rose has it. That's what Ann hasn't got. She's as messy and flabby and open as a bloody dogrose. That's what gets me down. That's what destroys all my imagination.'[91]

Ann is the 'unofficial rose' of Rupert Brooke's poem, the wild rose blowing 'unkempt among those hedges'.[92] To her sententious rector she says of herself, 'All that one *sees* [original emphasis] is shapeless and awkward,' and he replies eagerly, 'Precisely. We must not expect our lives to have a visible shape. They are invisibly shaped by God. Goodness accepts the contingent. Love accepts the contingent.' Sadly she responds, 'Randall wants everything to have form … But then he's an artist.'[93] We recall Murdoch's critique of the Romantics that they had 'a fear of contingency, a yearning to pierce through the messy phenomenal world to some perfect and necessary form and order … what is feared is history, real beings and real change, whatever is contingent, messy, boundless, infinitely particular, and endlessly still to be explained.'[94] But an over-exaggeration towards either form or the formless is dangerous. Randall finds his form by allowing himself to be dominated by another woman, Lindsay: 'Like a complex rose, her polychrome being fell into an authoritative pattern which proclaimed her free.' Ominously, he continues that accepting her authority leads him into 'the world above the mess of morality'.[95] On the other hand, in her 'openness' Ann accepts everything that happens to her in a condition that she recognizes as 'unconsciousness'.[96] While the rector assures her that 'being good is a state of unconsciousness', we have Simone Weil's assertion that 'we want to possess good consciously, not unconsciously', that

---

91. Iris Murdoch, *An Unofficial Rose* (London: Chatto & Windus, 1962), p. 39, original emphasis.
92. Brooke, 'The Old Vicarage, Grantchester'.
93. Murdoch, *Unofficial Rose*, p. 133.
94. Murdoch, 'Sublime and the Beautiful Revisited', pp. 273–4.
95. Murdoch, *Unofficial Rose*, p. 75.
96. Ibid., p. 273.

deliberate attention to others overcomes the weight of gravity, and that 'anyone who works unconsciously does not imitate the Crucifixion'.[97]

For Murdoch, multiplicity and contingency in the world may *present* itself to us as chaos (here there is a touch of Deleuze), but we have to summon up the courage to immerse ourselves in it like swimmers in wild water. For Hart beauty is rooted in the unity of being, as in the theology of Hans Urs von Balthasar, and this by analogy is rooted in the unity of God. This leads him to be highly critical of any notion of the sublime as chaotic and conflictive. Multiplicity and profusion is always the excessiveness of being which is as one in itself as God. Murdoch agrees with other philosophers of modernity and postmodernity that the unity of being has been scattered into diversity and cannot be recovered. As Carel expresses it mythically in *The Time of the Angels*, 'Angels are the thoughts of God. Now he has been dissolved into his thoughts which are beyond our conception in their nature and their multiplicity and their power.'[98] But, unlike Carel, Murdoch still thinks there is a unity of the Good which is beyond being, and that it is possible to serve it, though not for the reward of relating personally to it. Beauty, however, is not a unity and will be experienced in the 'messy' and 'boundless' phenomenal world.

A trinitarian theology must find that the beauty of the world is finally grounded in the wholeness of God, though the conceptualizing of God as triune means that this wholeness will be a complex unity characterized by relation and difference.[99] Since the persons in God are nothing less than relationships, not beings who 'have' relationships, it also means that this wholeness cannot be objectified or envisaged in the mind's eye.[100] With both Murdoch and with Hart, the Christian theologian will maintain that there is a wholeness in existence, and with Hart that this wholeness is personal (though not a person). With Murdoch and against Hart, however, I suggest that this wholeness will be expressed in fragmented and even chaotic phenomena. God (as the Good) is not a simple unity and remains deeply mysterious. Since this unity is complex and differentiated, we may expect the phenomenon of beauty in the world to be similarly complex. Here Murdoch expresses something valid about human experience. When beauty, in the limitless and boundless details of the world, shocks and disturbs us, the sublime may sometimes be experienced in the negative way that Murdoch describes in her novels – either as a baffling and disturbing multiplicity of representations which may seem at times to be chaotic, or as a challenge to representation altogether (i.e. a form of the Kantian sublime). In this way Christian theology can find something authentic in the descriptions of the negative sublime offered in postmodern philosophy. It may be that the transcendence of God can be experienced as a shock to representation, while God is also present immanently in the forms of beauty of the world.

---

97. Weil, *Notebooks*, pp. 528, 592.
98. Murdoch, *Time of the Angels*, p. 164.
99. For the argument of this at greater length, see Fiddes, *Seeing the World*, pp. 149–60.
100. Fiddes, *Participating in God*, pp. 36–7.

This brings us back to the charge of Betz against Barth that, by opposing the *analogia entis*, he has also opposed the glory of God to created reality. In fact, Barth complements the idea of the glory of God with the idea of beauty: beauty is the form of glory and the dimension of glory which is enjoyable, attractive, lovable, welcoming and creative of response from the recipient.[101] His presentation of the relation between beauty and glory is a theological version of the beautiful and the sublime. Balthasar, who defines beauty as the composition of glory and form, compliments Barth for recognizing the importance of form, where other Protestant theologians have neglected form in favour of glory, or the impact upon human life of the self-revelation of God. He nevertheless criticizes Barth for confining form 'theologically' – that is, to the being of the triune God, to the form of a servant which God assumes in the incarnation in the world and to aspects of life in the church. Barth, he insists, neglects the analogy between the beauty of the world and the beauty of God.[102]

Now, it is certainly true that Barth misunderstands the idea of *analogia entis* in Catholic theology; he errs badly in suggesting that it presents God and the world as two exemplifications of a common principle of being. It is also true that Barth makes no *explicit* link between beauty in the world and theological beauty. However, there is much in Barth's thought that can be constructed by a sympathetic reader into an analogy between secular and divine beauty, even without a formal analogy of being. Barth recognizes, for instance, that as creatures glorify the creator, the glory of God shines out in all the world and not only in the sphere of the church.[103] He also recognizes that the Word or self-expression of God can take secular form in the world outside the walls of the church.[104] Although in the early volumes of the *Church Dogmatics* he insists that it is the task of the Christian disciple only to pay attention to the secular forms of the Word in the church and the Bible, in later volumes he calls Christians to listen to the voice of the Good Shepherd speaking in strange contexts.[105] The conclusion may be drawn that God's glory takes form in all the beauty of the world, and in this case we have theology that can affirm *both* the sublimity of everyday forms in the world and a kind of 'negative sublime' that deconstructs these forms and brings all human representations to nothing.

Can we make sense theologically of this duality? It is such a duality, I suggest, that is anticipated in the poetry of Gerard Manley Hopkins, to which we now turn.

---

101. Barth, *Church Dogmatics*, 2.1, pp. 649–66.

102. Hans Urs von Balthasar, *The Glory of the Lord: A Theological Aesthetics. Vol. I: Seeing the Form* (trans. E. Leiva-Marikakis, ed. J. Fessio and J. Riches) (Edinburgh: T&T Clark, 1982), pp. 53–7.

103. Barth, *Church Dogmatics*, 2.1, pp. 647–8, 667–8; 3.1, pp. 369–71.

104. Ibid., 1.1, p. 55; cf. pp. 175–6.

105. Ibid., 4.3, pp. 101–2, 116–17.

The beautiful and the sublime in Gerard Manley Hopkins

The theme of beauty is pervasive throughout Hopkins's poetry, not only in those poems which explicitly address the subject but also in the sonnets which explore the natural world as a place of sharply delineated forms. Like Iris Murdoch much later – and indeed like the theologians Balthasar and Hart – Hopkins understands the beauty of the world to consist of the vast multiplicity of particular things and persons. For Hopkins, everything has a unique 'self' or its own characteristic form, which (he notes) Duns Scotus called *haecceitas* or 'thisness'.[106] In contrast to other scholastic thought which aims to extract *universal* ideas from individual forms, it is in the particular that objects and persons touch reality and from which the universal can be constructed. So Hopkins rejoices in the particularity of things, none exactly like another. While everything has its distinct identity, Hopkins gains particular pleasure from dappled and freckled things that combine shapes and colours in odd combinations:

> All things counter, original, spare, strange;
>   Whatever is fickle, freckled (who knows how?)
>   With swift, slow; sweet, sour; adazzle, dim…[107]

Hopkins had anticipated this idea in the Platonic dialogue 'On the Origin of Beauty' he wrote as an undergraduate, in which one of the characters argues that beauty is to be considered as 'regularity or likeness tempered by irregularity or difference'.[108] His character (a professor of aesthetics) further argues that the same principle relates to metre in poetry, and later Hopkins was to develop what he calls 'sprung rhythm' where the regularity consists in the same number of stresses in each line while the number of unstressed syllables is quite irregular.[109] His extraordinary poetic vocabulary shows the same kind of combination of the regular and irregular, interweaving standard speech with dialect expressions, neologisms and surprising compounds of words. The early dialogue claims that this principle can also be seen in poetic rhyme and assonance,[110] and Hopkins once again exemplifies this in his own poetry, rhyming and half-rhyming within the line as well as at the end and breaking words in pieces in order to rhyme with a fragment of them. Hopkins thus

---

106. Gerard Manley Hopkins, *The Sermons and Devotional Writings* (ed. Christopher Devlin, S.J.) (London: Oxford University Press, 1959), pp. 151, 341–3.

107. Hopkins, 'Pied Beauty', *Poems*, p. 69.

108. Gerard Manley Hopkins, 'On the Origin of Beauty: A Platonic Dialogue', in Lesley Higgins (ed.), *Oxford Essays and Notes*, The Collected Works of Gerard Manley Hopkins, 9 vols (vol. 4, Oxford: Oxford University Press, 2006), pp. 136–73 (152).

109. See Walter J. Ong, 'Sprung Rhythm and English Tradition', in Geoffrey Hartman (ed.), *Hopkins. A Collection of Critical Essays* (Englewood Cliffs: Prentice Hall, 1966), 151–9: 'rhythmic units of … equal weight while retaining great variety' (158).

110. Hopkins, 'Origin of Beauty', *Oxford Essays*, pp. 153–5.

not only *observes* the particularity of 'pied beauty' in the world, but also *creates* beauty in an art-object which has its own distinct and 'pied' character. In every way he fulfils the requirement of Murdoch that an artist should give sustained attention to the contingent details of the world.

For Hopkins, the universe is full of individual forms like notes in a musical scale or separate fractions in scales of light. Hopkins calls the form of these myriad selves their 'inscape', denoting that they have an outer shape (scape) which expresses an inner nature:

> Each mortal thing does one thing and the same:
> > Deals out that being indoors each one dwells;
> > Selves – goes itself; *myself* it speaks and spells,
> Crying *What I do is me: for that I came*.[111]

So, for instance, creatures reflect sunlight in different ways – 'as kingfishers catch fire, dragonflies draw flame'. Each stone makes its own kind of splash when thrown into a well; each bell makes its own ring, 'finds tongue to fling out broad its name'.

Now, it appears from his poetry that Hopkins finds inscapes to be sustained by a charge of energy which he calls 'stress', and this also makes a bridge of communication between them. One inscape delivers a surge of stress out of itself to another, and linked to the inscape, this energy becomes 'instress'. Stress, then, is the medium of sensation through which a human consciousness meets the world. When persons observe something in the natural world, they receive stress from it, accepting it ('instressing' it) within their own inscape. Thus, stress upholds each individual thing and unifies the whole of nature.[112] God has made all things with their own self, in order that they may exist in communion with him, for when an inscape 'stresses itself' or speaks itself out, it is in fact responding to God. It is opening itself to God by riding upon the surge of energy that comes from God's own presence in his world; the stress of grace, which is the work of the Holy Spirit, unites the created inscape with the divine lovescape. The presence of God finds the focus in the dwelling of Christ within all inscapes as the incarnate God, so there is a eucharistic presence of Christ in the world from the very moment of creation:

> . . . For Christ plays in ten thousand places,
> > Lovely in limbs and lovely in eyes not his
> > > To the Father through the features of men's faces.[113]

Hopkins makes no explicit resort to a doctrine of *analogia entis*. Nor does he have a metaphysic such as Balthasar's, in which all forms in the world (*essentia*) are

---

111. Hopkins, 'As kingfishers catch fire', *Poems*, p. 90, original emphases.
112. See W. A. M. Peters, *Gerard Manley Hopkins. A Critical Essay towards the Understanding of His Poetry* (London: Oxford University Press, 1948), pp. 13–15.
113. Hopkins, 'As kingfishers catch fire', *Poems*, p. 90.

rooted in a common created being (*esse* or existence) which itself is analogous to the pure uncreated being of God.[114] His ideas of inscape and instress enable him to conceive of things of beauty in the world as participating directly in Christ and so in the divine life. In Balthasar's own commentary on Hopkins, 'all natures and selves are fashioned and determined for Christ, who is both their ultimate inscape and instress ... and out of the glory of the Incarnate God there breaks forth the truest and most inward glory of the forms both of natures and persons'.[115] It is no mere allegory to discern the eucharistic Christ in the gathering together of stooks in harvest.[116] In the provoking phrase of Daniel Harris, 'the incarnation has made metaphor superfluous'.[117] Likewise the sacrifice of Christ can be discerned in the sudden drop earthwards of the 'windhover' – or kestrel – which has been hovering in the currents of air.[118] Murdoch is perhaps alluding to this image when she portrays Cato, who has just given up his priesthood and buried his cassock, as watching a kestrel: 'hovering, a still portent', vibrating with colour and light, it suddenly swoops to the ground, and Cato exclaims aloud, 'my Lord and my God'.[119] Hopkins has subtitled his poem 'To Christ Our Lord'.

There is a parallel in Hopkins's poems to Murdoch's sense of the 'positive sublime' received through beauty, though of course Hopkins has in mind a direct participation in the transcendent Good that she does not envisage. Indeed, Hopkins (in 'To what serves Mortal Beauty?') warns us that unless we *do* find 'God's better beauty, grace' *through* the 'mortal beauty' where 'self flashes off frame and face', then beauty becomes an occasion for 'dangerous' and idolatrous absorption in the world. Hopkin's vision of the sublime at the heart of beauty is summarized in a stanza from the 'Wreck of the Deutschland':[120]

> I kiss my hand
> To the stars, lovely-asunder
>   Starlight, wafting him out of it; and
>   Glow, glory in thunder;
> Kiss my hand to the dappled-with-damson west;
> Since, tho' he is under the world's splendour and wonder,

---

114. Balthasar, *Glory of the Lord*, vol. I, pp. 118–20.

115. Hans Urs von Balthasar, *The Glory of the Lord: A Theological Aesthetics. Volume III, Studies in Theological Style: Lay Styles* (trans. Andrew Louth, Ohn Saward, Martin Simon and Rowan Williams) (Edinburgh: T&T Clark, 1986), p. 390.

116. Hopkins, 'Hurrahing in Harvest', *Poems*, p. 70.

117. Daniel A. Harris, *Inspirations Unbidden: The 'Terrible Sonnets' of Gerard Manley Hopkins* (Berkeley: University of California Press, 1982), p. 46.

118. Hopkins, 'The Windhover', *Poems*, p. 69.

119. Murdoch, *Henry and Cato*, p. 186. Earlier, Cato has referred to the kestrel as a 'symbol of the Holy Ghost' (p. 64). Murdoch writes of giving attention to a hovering kestrel as an occasion for 'unselfing' in her *Sovereignty of Good*, p. 84.

120. Hopkins, *Poems*, p. 53.

> His mystery must be instressed, stressed
> For I greet him the days I meet him, and bless when I understand.

So we meet the grace of God in Christ as indwelling the beauty of nature ('wafting him out of it', 'under the world's splendour') and respond ('kiss my hand to the stars'), stressing the mystery, linking it to our inscapes through the instress of grace.

However, in this poem we also find the 'negative sublime', a mood which, as Jerome Bump shows,[121] has been influenced by a literary tradition of the sublime stemming from Kant and passing through the Romantic poets such as Byron, Shelley and Wordsworth. This is not a delight in the contingent details of nature, but a sense of horror and dread when faced by the vastness, massive forces and overwhelming power of nature. In discussing the 'dynamic sublime' under the heading 'Of Nature as a Power', Kant gives as examples storms and 'the ocean rising with rebellious force';[122] and among the Romantic poets, for instance, Shelley exults in the destructive power of the stormy sea,[123] as does Hopkins in his own poem. The setting of the scene of the wreck in the second half of the poem is darkness in which shapes can hardly be discerned, very far removed from the light, colour and varied forms of his nature sonnets, and even from the 'lovely-asunder starlight' and the 'dappled-with-damson west' of the first part. In his portrayal of the scene, the prevailing tone is the 'black-about air' and the 'black-backed sea'.[124] Hopkins summons us to see the coming of Christ to the nun in the darkness, but can only cry 'look at it loom there'; in calling on Christ, the nun has had to read the 'unshapeable shock night'.[125] Darkness is a typical component of the romantic sublime, as Bump shows in his reference to the 'Shadows but half-distinguished' of Tennyson's ode 'On Sublimity'.[126] As we have already seen, in her depiction of the Gothic sublime, Murdoch makes Effingham Cooper have his experience in the bog in darkest night. In the first part of the poem, Hopkins recounts his own experience of the negative sublime in the story of his vocation to priesthood; like the nun in the wreck, his is the experience of a 'mastering me/God', who knows the 'terror' he felt under the 'lightning and lashed rod', significantly in the hours of night.

That this experience is the Kantian or Romantic kind of 'negative sublime', rather than the negative side of a positive sublime (as in Murdoch's sense of terror at the contingency of particulars in the world), is shown by the fact that *this* sublime swallows up all distinct shapes and colourful details in the nothingness of night and darkness. There are, of course, shifting boundaries that I have already

---

121. Jerome Bump, '"The Wreck of the Deutschland" and the Dynamic Sublime', *English Literary History* 41.1 (1974), pp. 106–29.
122. Kant, *Critique of Judgement*, part 1, para. 28 (p. 110).
123. See, e.g., his 'Lines Written among the Euganean Hills'.
124. Hopkins, 'Wreck', stanzas 13, 24, *Poems*, pp. 55, 59.
125. Ibid., stanzas 28–9, *Poems*, pp. 60–1.
126. Bump, 'Wreck', pp. 124–5.

identified in Murdoch's novels between the positive sublime and the two modes of the negative. Hopkins in this poem, for instance, speaks of the moment of 'election' in Ignatian spirituality; he recalls that 'I did say yes / O at lightning and lashed rod' and describes the nun as effectively saying yes in crying 'O Christ, Christ, come quickly', but he also recounts saying 'yes' to the grace of God in the beauty of the world: 'I kiss my hand / to the stars … wafting him out of it.' The opening octet of the sonnet 'God's Grandeur' is similarly ambiguous:

> The world is charged with the grandeur of God.
>   It will flame out, like shining from shook foil;
>   It gathers to greatness, like the ooze of oil
> Crushed. Why do men then now not reck his rod?[127]

On the one hand, this speaks of the beauty of the world, in all its particular details, as witnessing to God's glory – a positive sublime. But the mood is also negative: the world is charged not with glory but with 'grandeur', and there is reference to crushing and the imposing of the divine rod. Since the light of morning in the final sestet succeeds the night of the 'black west', we might conclude that the poem opens with the experience of a negative sublime and then moves into the positive. However, matters cannot be so easily divided up: the opening line of the sonnet does seem to sum up Hopkins's vision of a world whose particular and 'pied' beauty is grounded in the presence of God in Christ. Some of this ambiguity may be due to Hopkins's conviction that the world has been created as an act of divine sacrifice,[128] and that Christ is present in it in the mode of Eucharist. But he may also be witnessing to the truth that to participate in the life of the triune God is to have a diversity of experiences of the sublime, which cannot easily be separated out.

In the 'Wreck of the Deutschland', Hopkins is employing the literary tradition of the negative sublime in order to assert the presence of God at the darkest moments, a use which seems to derive from the identification of God with the dynamic sublime in the literary tradition. Even Kant associated the sublimity of feeling aroused in us by nature with the sublimity of God,[129] although this was finally in aid of exalting the god-like reason within us. It was a convention of the negative sublime in the Romantics to see sublime scenes in nature as an image of an infinite Presence, 'boundless, endless, and sublime / The image of eternity, the throne / Of the Invisible' (Byron).[130] However, in the final 'dark-night sonnets' we find a different experience of the negative sublime, where darkness becomes an image for absence, an image for the failure of Hopkins to find Christ any longer at

---

127. Hopkins, *Poems*, p. 66.
128. Hopkins, *Sermons*, p. 197.
129. Kant, *Critique of Judgement*, para. 28 (p. 113).
130. Lord Byron, *Childe Harold's Pilgrimage*, Canto IV, lines 1643–5.

the centre of the inscapes and of the world, so that his prayers are like 'dead letters sent / To dearest him that lives alas! Away'.[131]

The sonnet 'Spelt from Sybil's Leaves',[132] for instance, offers both a parallel and a striking contrast to the use of night in 'The Wreck of the Deutschland'. As the sonnet begins, night is drawing in, first in the scene external to the poet and then within the poet's own consciousness. Both evening and the night which it 'strains' to become are described in terms which are typical of the Kantian and Romantic dynamic sublime. Evening is 'vaulty, voluminous, stupendous', issuing in the 'vast womb-of-all … hearse-of-all night' whose stars are a sheer wasteland. The details of the world have become 'unbound' and gone 'astray', so that all the 'dapple' of its particular things, with their own uniqueness ('self in self steeped'), are being lost to memory and disembodied – 'Disremembering, dismembering'. As W. H. Gardiner puts it, 'objects are stripped of both colour and individual form'.[133] Though the technical language is not used, the sublime is displacing the beautiful. The night has reduced the diversity and variety of the world, in which the poet once delighted, to the two tones of black and white. Black boughs can just be discerned against the blackness of the night, black on black ('ever so black on it'), like damask material. The cloth of the world, which used to be a 'stained, veined variety', is now being woven off just two spools, black and white. The effect is awesome, vast, overwhelming: it 'whelms, whelms, and will end us'. The remaining of only two shades, black and white, is a kind of last judgement in nature where all created things are assigned to one of two groups ('two flocks, two folds') as the Gospel parable of Jesus divides humanity at the last into either sheep and goats.

This experience of the sublime in the world also acts as a final judgement on the consciousness (a *Dies Irae* to which the prophetic Sibyl testifies), putting an end to all power of representation, and stifling creativity.[134] In Kant's sublime, the result of initial frustration is an exaltation of the power of the moral reason. In the 'sacrificial sublime'[135] of 'The Wreck of the Deutschland', the result of admiration of the supreme Judge revealed in the power of the storm is exaltation of the soul. Yet here the mind turns in on itself, 'selfwrung, selfstrung', so that it can no longer rejoice in the 'selves' of other things: 'thoughts against thoughts in groans grind'. Elsewhere in this period, Hopkins takes another symbol of the sublime, lofty mountains, and complains:

---

131. Hopkins, 'I Wake and Feel the Fell of Dark', *Poems*, p. 101.

132. Hopkins, *Poems*, pp. 97–8.

133. W. H. Gardner, *Gerard Manley Hopkins: A Study of Poetic Idiosyncrasy in Relation to Poetic Tradition*, 2 vols (vol. 2, London: Oxford University Press, 1961), p. 315.

134. Though often read as a 'meditation on hell' (so Paul Mariani, *Gerard Manley Hopkins: A Life* [New York: Viking, 2008], p. 331), John Robinson is correct to judge that the conflict is 'happening inside his own mind' in the present: Robinson, *In Extremity: A Study of Gerard Manley Hopkins* (Cambridge: Cambridge University Press, 1978), p. 136.

135. Jerome Bump's term, in 'Wreck', p. 129.

> O the mind, mind has mountains; cliffs of fall
> Frightful, sheer, no-man-fathomed.[136]

In postmodern thought, the sublime is often similarly envisaged as absence rather than presence, but there this shocking event is conceived as bringing the experient to realize the sheer fact and the goodness of existence.[137] There is no such outcome for Hopkins. Since he *expects* to find the presence of God in the sublime, and fails to do so, nothing good can come. We need, then, to listen to the religious and poetic witness of Hopkins to a variety of experience of the sublime; it cannot all be neatly categorized as an analogy of the beautiful.

A theological place for the negative sublime

The relation between the sublime and the beautiful is a pervasive topic in late-modern philosophy and has become an important part of commentary on this thought by theology. Theologians (such as Milbank, Hart and Betz) have tended to deny the validity of a postmodern sense of the negative sublime in favour of a sublime of superabundance which positively inheres in beauty. This discussion, I have suggested, needs to be brought into conjunction with the presentation of the sublime and the beautiful in creative literature. Doing so will lead us to a more varied understanding of the theological sublime, as we find that a novelist such as Murdoch and a poet such as Gerard Manley Hopkins both make room for an experience of the negative sublime as described by Kant, the Romantic poets and their 'successors' in postmodern philosophy. While Murdoch appears to do so in order to take seriously the particularity of her characters, Hopkins does so in order to express a whole range of experience of participating in the triune God: 'Thou art lightning and love, I found it, a winter and warm.'[138] Barth's understanding of beauty as an aspect both of the sovereign self-glorification of God and of the glorification of God by creatures, though it may not be entirely consistent, has the same kind of openness of experience about it.

Theology, against much of the drift of postmodern thinking, must affirm the reality of truth and goodness in the beauty of the world. But it may also find validity in the experience of the sublime which arises on the outer borders of representation, when human words and images fail and fall to nothing.

---

136. Hopkins, 'No worst, there is none', *Poems*, p. 100.
137. On the general unsettling of presence by absence, see Jacques Derrida, *Speech and Phenomena* (Evanston: Northwestern University Press, 1973), pp. 88–93; on the absence of God, see Levinas, 'Meaning and Sense', *Basic Philosophical Writings*, pp. 59–64. Cf. Hart, *Beauty*, pp. 53–5, 79, 90–1.
138. Hopkins, 'Wreck of the Deutschland', stanza 9, *Poems*, p. 54.

Chapter 4

THE SUBLIME, THE CONFLICTED SELF AND ATTENTION TO THE OTHER: BRINGING IRIS MURDOCH AND JULIA KRISTEVA INTO CONVERSATION

The idea of the 'sublime' is widespread in aesthetics and philosophy today, as my previous chapter has shown. Indeed, it may – as Jean-Luc Nancy suggests – have maintained its popularity for several centuries, as 'a fashion that that has persisted uninterruptedly into our own time from the beginnings of modernity'.[1] The sublime, as modified by Kant and the Romantics, has become a cipher in our late modern period for what brings thought, reason or beauty into question. It goes under such other names as 'the void' (Jacques Lacan), 'difference' (Jacques Derrida), 'chaos' (Gilles Deleuze), 'otherness' (Emmanuel Levinas), infinity or even death (Freud). The 'sublime' in recent thought is the thrilling event of nothingness and absence that overturns the realm of representation, presence and stability, so that Jean-François Lyotard finds narratives of the *unrepresentable* everywhere in the philosophy of our age.[2]

Everywhere too are *studies* of the sublime, and here the names of Iris Murdoch and Julia Kristeva are surprisingly absent or very infrequent.[3] This is a pity, because both Murdoch and Kristeva have important insights to make to understanding the phenomenon of the sublime and offer significant modifications to a prevailing

---

1. Nancy, 'Sublime Offering', p. 25.
2. See Lyotard, *Lessons on the Analytic of the Sublime*, pp. 50–8.
3. Neither appear in Lyotard, *Lessons on the Analytic of the Sublime*; Courtine et al., *Of the Sublime*; Slavoj Žižek, *The Sublime Object of Ideology* (London: Verso, 2008); Clayton Crockett, *A Theology of the Sublime* (London: Routledge, 2001); Philip Shaw, *The Sublime* (London: Routledge, 2006). Passing references to Kristeva appear in Neil Hertz, *The End of the Line: Essays on Psychoanalysis and the Sublime* (New York: Columbia University Press, 1985), pp. 231–3, and Christine Battersby, *The Sublime, Terror and Human Difference* (London: Routledge, 2007), p. 116. More attention is given to Kristeva in some articles: see Charles I. Armstrong, 'Echo: Reading the Unnamable through Kant and Kristeva', *Nordic Journal of English Studies* 1.1 (June 2002), pp. 173–87; Judy Lochhead, 'The Sublime, the Ineffable, and Other Dangerous Aesthetics', *Women and Music: A Journal of Gender and Culture* 12 (2008), pp. 63–74.

tendency of thought. A great deal has been said about Kristeva's psychoanalytical explorations of the second term in the title of this chapter, the conflict in the self, but very little about the place of the *sublime* in this experience of fragmentation. Again, much has been written about Murdoch's concern with the third term of the title – 'attention to the other'. Commentators have rightly focused on the insistence of this philosopher and novelist that we should notice the 'other' as he or she really is, and that we should look attentively at the world around us; but there is little comment about Murdoch's connection of 'attending to the other' with the experience of the *sublime*.

With the last chapter I made a start on tracing Murdoch's appeal to the sublime, but here I want to take a different direction and explore the three-way interactions between the sublime, 'attention' and the conflict within the self, placing these in a staged dialogue between Murdoch and Kristeva. I realize that Murdoch might have had little sympathy, at least initially, with my project of bringing her and Kristeva into conversation on these issues. In May 1988 she wrote dismissively to an American friend and professor of English, Naomi Lebowitz:

> Have you read Julia Kristeva? And is it true that she is anti-Semitic? She is endlessly quoted by poor wretches who are entangled in revolting women's studies. Oxford now has a ghastly (optional) women's studies paper in final exam.[4]

The worry about Kristeva's being anti-Semitic, mainly arising from her study of the poet Louis Ferdinand Céline, who was certainly an anti-Semite, may quickly be put to rest (it also troubled Murdoch about Simone Weil);[5] Kristeva clearly condemns anti-Semitism as a symptom of a 'psychic instability' arising from fear of the other who is consequently made into a 'non-object'.[6] Murdoch would almost certainly have counted Kristeva among those French philosophers whom she indiscriminately bundled together as 'structuralists', a tendency I comment upon in the next chapter. It may be that Murdoch's antipathy towards Kristeva is due in large part to her violent reaction against women's studies, but it is of interest that Murdoch witnesses to the popularity of reading Kristeva in Oxford at that time, relatively early in her reception outside France. However, there is no better dialogue-companion for Murdoch than Kristeva if we are to consider the relation

---

4. From IM to Naomi Lebowitz, 21 May 1988, in Horner and Rowe, *Living on Paper*, p. 548.

5. See Murdoch, 'Knowing the Void', p. 160.

6. See Kristeva, commenting on Céline's anti-Semitism in Toril Moi (ed.), *The Kristeva Reader* (Oxford: Blackwell, 1986), pp. 318–19, and Kristeva, *Powers of Horror: An Essay on Abjection* (trans. Leon S. Roudiez) (New York: Columbia University Press, 1982), 136–7, 174–78. While she (unwisely) allows that 'the anti-Semite is not mistaken' in finding Jewish monotheism to be the most rigorous application of the 'Unicity of the Law', she adds immediately that it is also the religion that 'wears with the greatest assurance, but like a lining, the mark of maternal, feminine … substance' (*Powers of Horror*, p. 186).

between the conflict in the self and its relation to the sublime.[7] It is illuminating to consider *three versions* of the conflicted self – Murdoch's, Kristeva's and, to begin with, the version to which all writers on the topic of the sublime appeal, Immanuel Kant. We may thus review Kant's account of the sublime, considered generally in the last chapter, more specifically now as a drama of struggle, with the main actors as imagination and reason, and with understanding as a kind of understudy.

The Kantian and the Murdochian sublime: Nuns and Soldiers

For Kant, *reason* always demands that we make a whole of our experience: reason always works towards totality, though it can never achieve it. *Imagination* seems to have an inner compulsion to seek out those situations in which it *cannot* answer these demands of reason. Though it works in a happy harmony with the *understanding* in the realm of cognition, in another realm – the aesthetic – it comes into conflict with reason.[8] It finds what Kant calls experiences of the 'sublime' where it struggles and fails to make a whole out of things. Imagination strives after infinity and has some apprehension or intuition of what it is – whether it is an infinite series of things in human cognition (the 'mathematical sublime') or whether it is prompted by awesome and terrible objects in nature which seem to have no limits – seas, mountains, skies full of stars, deep ravines, waterfalls (the 'dynamical' sublime). Imagination has an *apprehension* of the infinite, but cannot *comprehend* it. Faced by the sheer boundlessness of things, the imagination feels terror, and yet it also feels a kind of 'negative pleasure',[9] because finally it will enjoy the sense of the superiority of reason which makes such demands upon it, and which is therefore greater than any phenomena in the world. Here is Kant's brief summary of this mental conflict according to his *Critique of Judgement*:

> Precisely because there is a striving in our imagination towards progress *ad infinitum*, while reason demands absolute totality as a real idea, that same inability on the part of our faculty for the estimation of the magnitude of the things of the world of sense to attain to this idea, is the awakening of a feeling of a supersensible faculty [i.e. reason] within us.[10]

---

7. Wendy Vaizey, 'Language, Memory and Loss: Kristevan Psychoanalytical Perspectives on Intertextual Connections in the Work of Murdoch and Banville', in Browning, *Iris Murdoch on Truth and Love*, pp. 192–206 (195–7), compares Murdoch and Kristeva on the way that deep-laid drives in the psyche surface into language, but does not consider the relevance of this to the sublime.

8. Kant, *Critique of Judgement*, part I, para. 26 (pp. 98–109).

9. Ibid., paras 23, 29 (pp. 91, 120).

10. Ibid., para. 25 (p. 97); cf. para. 29 (p. 119).

For Kant, this is quite unlike the sense of the 'beautiful', where the imagination works in harmonious free play with the *understanding*. The same imagination that assists the understanding to see and grasp objects in the world that come to us through our senses (phenomena) also runs free – without concepts – in fields of taste or aesthetic judgement.[11] There is no rule we can formulate to categorize an object which appears beautiful: we cannot identify it as either 'good' or 'purposeful'.[12] Beauty is a matter of form only. It is 'independent' of any moral judgement or even any emotion. Our sense of the beautiful, for Kant, is the freedom of mere playfulness, over against moral freedom.

A second version of the conflicted self is to be found in one of Kant's most profound interpreters and modifiers, Iris Murdoch. In Kant, the self is in conflict with *itself*, the imagination struggling with the demands of human reason, a situation very like the experience of respect (*Achtung*) for the inner moral law.[13] For Murdoch the self is in conflict with something *outside* itself, nothing less than the moral demands of a transcendent and sovereign Good. As in Kant, the demands are mediated through phenomena in the world that evoke a sense of the sublime.[14] But, as a Platonist, she is clear that the Good exists beyond the self; we cannot commune with it, and it is certainly not a *personal* God, but we must *serve* it for hope of no reward, being 'good, for nothing'.[15]

It is here that Murdoch makes her leap of originality. The sublime is not to be contrasted with the forms of the beautiful, as in Kant, but is to be found precisely *in* them. The sense of the sublime is marked by the boundless, the endless, the being without limit, before which we feel awe and even terror. This, Murdoch claims, is exactly the sense evoked by the boundlessness of forms in the world, by the multiplicity of contingent things and by the diversity of people who fill the world. The sublime shocks and amazes us, but (as she puts it) 'what stuns us into a realization of our supersensible destiny is not, as Kant imagined, the formlessness of nature, but rather its unutterable particularity'.[16] Kant, she thinks, was afraid of the messy details of the world and all the bodies in it. To know the world as a reality other than ourselves is to love it. And this love is truly moral, since for Murdoch virtue is apprehending that other persons exist and letting them be as others.[17] Through the sublimity of the many contingent details of the world, focused especially but not exclusively in works of art,[18] the self is brought into

11. Ibid., paras 1, 6, 7 (pp. 41–2, 50–3).
12. Ibid., paras 7–8 (51–6), para. 16 (pp. 72–4), para. 22 (pp. 84–5).
13. Ibid., paras 25, 29 (pp. 96, 123).
14. Murdoch, *Sovereignty of Good*, pp. 81–2.
15. Murdoch, 'Existentialists and Mystics', p. 233; cf. Murdoch, *Sovereignty of Good*, pp. 58–61; *Nice and the Good*, p. 350; *Good Apprentice*, p. 245.
16. Murdoch, 'Sublime and the Good', p. 215.
17. Carla Bagnoli, 'Constrained by Reason, Transformed by Love: Murdoch on the Standard of Proof', in Browning, *Murdoch on Truth and Love*, pp. 63–88, explores the way that Murdoch replaces Kant's practical reason by love as a moral authority.
18. Murdoch, *Sovereignty of Good*, pp. 64–6, 69.

conflict with the Good, and we can break out of an artificial world we construct around ourselves.

The sense of excess here has some resonances with the way that Lyotard reconstructs the sublime in Kant. He suggests that 'the sublime can be thought of as an extreme case of the beautiful' in which there occurs 'the proliferation of forms by an imagination gone wild'.[19] But unlike Murdoch, for Lyotard this excess of form-giving results in the *overwhelming* of forms. Conflict is introduced into the relation between the beautiful and the sublime. Personifying the Kantian faculties of Imagination, Reason and Understanding, Lyotard tells the story of the birth of the sublime in his own myth: Reason (male) rapes/violates Imagination (female), and the sublime is conceived. Imagination dies giving birth to the sublime.[20] Apart from the persistence of a patriarchal violence here,[21] the myth is intended to express the fact that postmodern art 'denies itself the solace of form'. Murdoch certainly perceives the dangers of consolation in art: when a particular object is regarded as containing the whole of reality, we are discouraged from dying to the self.[22] But for her, the self is turned towards the Good and stripped of its self-centredness by paying attention to a multiplicity of forms that remain in their own integrity. They deliver the shock of the negative sublime, but this is intended to lead to love of others and finally to the 'supersensible destiny' of the Good.

In Murdoch's novel *Nuns and Soldiers*, Anne Cavidge is a former nun who has lost belief in a personal God and left her convent to serve the Good in the world, though she scarcely knows how. Like many of Murdoch's characters, she comes up against the contingency of the world in the form of the many small stones that litter its beaches and landscapes, and her ability to swim is symbolic of her willingness to plunge into the boundless ocean of the world. At first she is appalled by the stones on the beach, reflecting:

> Each one, if carefully examined, revealed some tiny significant individuating mark ... What do their details matter, what does it matter whether Christ redeemed the world or not, it doesn't matter, our minds can't grasp such things, it's all too obscure, too vague ... We can see so little of the great game. Look at these stones. My Lord and My God ... There they are.[23]

While she remains under a negative impression of the sublime she is preoccupied by her self and nearly drowns in the sea, but coming up out of it 'she saw, close to her now, the sloe of dark, shifting stones ... [and] Anne's feet were *again upon the stones*' (111–12, my emphasis). Later she has a vision of her own, personal

---

19. Lyotard, *Lessons on the Analytic of the Sublime*, p. 75.
20. Ibid., p. 180.
21. See the critique by Lochhead, 'The Sublime, the Ineffable', pp. 66–8.
22. Murdoch, *Metaphysics*, pp. 81–8.
23. Murdoch, *Nuns and Soldiers*, pp. 107–8.

Christ and he shows her a symbol of the world – not a hazel-nut as in the similar visions of Julian of Norwich – but a small, elliptical, grey stone (292). It is a little chipped stone from the beach of her near fatality that he holds out to her, inviting her to accept its 'thereness' and so to experience the sign of her negative vision as a positive instance of a world full of particular things. Towards the end of the novel she feels that she can now 'call upon the name of the non-existent God' as she touches 'the dense ... stone in whose small compass her Visitor had made her see the Universe, everything that is' (500).

For most of the story Anne is staying with an old school friend, Gertrude, and the novel begins with Gertrude's husband, Guy, facing an imminent death by cancer. Before he dies he urges Gertrude to find happiness by marrying again, and much of the plot of the novel is generated by the question of whom she might marry in the close circle of her friends and admirers. Might it be, for instance, a work colleague of Guy's, an upright, well-mannered Polish man who carries the nickname of 'The Count' and who has long secretly and honourably loved her? The successful candidate turns out to be the most unlikely one of all – a feckless and penniless painter called Tim Reede, who has been living for years in an on-off relationship with his punkish girlfriend Daisy. Guy has been a father-figure to Tim, and so Daisy persuades Tim to go and see Gertrude after his death to try and borrow some money. Gertrude, however, wants to help him without injuring his pride and so lends him her cottage in France to live and paint in over the summer. There, in the enchanting countryside, Tim and Gertrude fall in love.

Two locations in the country around become occasions for prompting their love – a great face of rock with a crystal-clear pool at its base and a fast-running canal that disappears underground. Both are described in ways that seem to recall the Kantian dynamical sublime, but which quickly modulate into what one might call the Murdochian sublime: that is, they have the aspect of the boundless and unlimited that evokes awe and even terror, but they also have the beauty of fine detail. We read of the Great Face, for instance, that 'he looked upon it with awe ... he fled' (152); 'the numinous power of the rock shook him' (271). But he also draws its multiple lines and shifting contrasts of light, a profile which is full of diversity and plurality, and observes the floor of the rock basin as 'covered with small crystalline pebbles' (154). It is this contingent detail that actually makes him frightened and brings on a sense of panic. In a period of separation and misunderstanding between Gertrude and Tim before they finally come together in marriage, Tim reflects on the Great Face, that 'there was absolute truth in the thing, something of wholeness and goodness which called to him from outside the dark tangle of himself ... That it should have been accidental [i.e. contingent] did not dismay him' (272). We notice that this is a 'thing' in the phenomenal world embodying 'absolute truth': later, we shall draw a contrast with the Lacanian Thing, which inhabits the Void.

Again, during the miserable time of separation, the breach in their love, Tim moves from a Kantian mood of the negative sublime to a Murdochian sublime. Here is a description of his feeling of the first, echoing Kant:

Sometimes the void gleamed like the sea ... Everything seemed to vanish, including his own personality. He was a tiny scrap of being, a particle, and yet also he was the surrounding area which seemed infinite. He was an atom, an electron, a proton, a point in empty space ... The sense of emptiness was occasionally almost pleasurable. It was always awful. It's a condition of pure freedom ... the cosmos itself, gentle, terrible final. It was also a vision of death. (385)

After taking a decisive step of leaving Daisy, the mood changes. The detail of the world impinges on him again: 'The white light seemed to be with him again but was different now ... He found that he could see through it. He could *see* the trees ... he could *see* in the distance the line of the lake' (388, my emphasis). He could *see* the Autumn leaves, and in a period he calls 'the time of the leaves' he begins to make collages of them: 'little works of art lay around – masterpieces which were lying about free of charge ... though he was still afraid to go back to the National Gallery' (400–3). Finding the sublime in the detail of the world, he will soon be ready not only to see the art in the Gallery (474) but also to see Gertrude as she really is and to recognize her love for him. The story makes clear how, for Murdoch, the essence of both art and ethics is the same, namely love, or a respect for the other and a genuine noticing of the other: as she puts it in her essay on 'the Sublime and the Good': 'Love, and so art and morals, is the discovery of reality.'[24]

For all that, there is always the danger of mere consolation in art, a temptation that Murdoch is always ready to admit. There is just a hint of truth in Daisy's view of the paintings in the National Gallery, that they constitute 'a fantasy world where everything's easy and pretty', echoing Plato's judgement that 'art is a lie' (129). But when used as a pathway to the Good, the sublime-in-the-beautiful is truth. As the newly married Tim returns to work, his drawings were 'coming to him out of a faintly discernible background of relentless form which he could apprehend as taking shape behind them' (475). The sublime for Murdoch does not destroy form, but clarifies it, allowing for the element of the contingent and accidental within it. Here Murdoch differs both from Kant and from the postmodern appeal to the sublime. The postmodern mood follows Kant in placing the sublime in opposition to the beautiful, although the recent appeal to the sublime breaks down not only art and forms in the world but also – unlike Kant – reason itself. Murdoch, however, wants to affirm sublimity *in* the beautiful.

The Kristevan sublime

Turning now to Julia Kristeva, we find our third version of the conflicted self. Here it seems we are back more firmly in the world of Kant, with the sublime as a symptom of a conflict only within the self itself, rather than between the self and an external and transcendent Good. The self is riven by many conflicts,

---

24. Murdoch, 'Sublime and the Good', p. 215.

as Kristeva perceives it. But this is Kant psychoanalysed, or perhaps a drawing out of the already incipient psychological character of Kant's thought. Here, for Kristeva, Freud is mediated through Jacques Lacan. The phenomenal level, the consciousness, is a world of language, a symbolic realm in which the self holds only a fragmented identity. For Lacan, therapy is centred on getting the individual to come to terms with his or her alienated identity. The infant, growing into a sense of individual identity, has had to exchange its preconscious sense of wholeness for a kind of being which is inscripted by language and by a society shaped by language.[25] Entry into the symbolic, into the world of words, comes at a price: this phenomenal world fails to satisfy, and we long for the 'real Thing' lost in the world of the preconscious. We have a desire for the 'lost object', and yet this can never be possessed.[26] There is a central impossibility, a Void or Thing, at the heart of the symbolic realm which can never be represented, but which must be recognized if meaning is to be generated by signifiers.[27] And those signifiers, according to Lacan, are essential male in orientation; the symbolic realm unavoidably privileges male symbols and is inevitably patriarchal.

Now, Kristeva has taken on much of Lacan's analysis but wants to draw attention to the role of the woman in all this. For Freud and Lacan, the key point of entry into the symbolic is the Oedipal moment, which is all about the relation of father and son. Daughters and mothers are side-lined, given walk-on parts in this psychodrama. For Kristeva, the key moment for the growing infant is the necessary separation from the mother, or what she calls the 'abjection' of the mother, taking up a term from Bataille and a load of theory from Melanie Klein. In the development of human subjectivity the child must break from the mother: to attain a sense of self-identity the mother must be abjected, sacrificed, violently rejected. This point of separation is the boundary which the growing subject has to pass over to reach the realm of language and meaning, where subject is separated from object.[28] According to Kristeva, a person moves from deep, precognitive immersion in the life of the body to a social life.

---

25. Jacques Lacan, *Écrits: A Selection* (trans. A. Sheridan) (repr., London: Tavistock/Routledge, 1977), pp. 104–5, 218.

26. Leeson, *Iris Murdoch: Philosophical Novelist*, pp. 58–61, argues for the influence of Lacan on Murdoch's novel *A Severed Head*, and particularly on Lacan's 'existential (and unconscious) linkage between the self and other', a connection that Kristeva inherits. A passing reference by Murdoch to Lacan, *Metaphysics*, p. 49, dismisses him as another 'structuralist'.

27. Jacques Lacan, *The Four Fundamental Concepts of Psychoanalysis* (trans. A. Sheridan) (Harmondsworth: Penguin, 1979), pp. 54–5; Lacan, *The Ethics of Psychoanalysis: The Seminar of Jacque Lacan: Book VII* (trans. Dennis Porter) (London: Routledge, 2008), pp. 65–8, 130–1, 160.

28. E.g. Kristeva, *Powers of Horror*, pp. 5–6; *Black Sun: Depression and Melancholia* (New York: Columbia, 1989), pp. 9–30.

Yet that preconscious realm remains as a living factor in symbolic life, capable of disturbing the patriarchal realm of symbols. A primary maternal body cannot be entirely suppressed, and this is associated with the realm that Kristeva calls the 'semiotic'.[29] As distinct from the symbolic, the semiotic is pre-discursive, expressing an original libidinal multiplicity over against the monolithic tendencies of culture; it has the capacity to irritate and subvert the symbolic. Poetic language, for instance, relies upon multiple meanings and so challenges the law of unity. For Kristeva there is something 'in play' beyond or outside rational discourse, something which goes 'beyond the theatre of linguistic representations'.[30]

Where the semiotic breaks into the symbolic, there is a resurgence of infantile drives arising from the *jouissance* of the subconscious. This moment of extreme, disruptive pleasure includes sexual pleasure, but can also be experienced through art and literature. Kristeva suggests that the language of poetry recovers the maternal body, a field of impulse, full of diversity. Poetic speech is characterized by rhythm, sound play and repetition, movements which reflect primal movements of love and energy. Here Kristeva envisages the semiotic as flowing from a realm that she denotes as the 'chora', taking the concept from Plato's *Timaeus* where it refers to an unnameable space which exists between Being and Becoming. She develops the concept of *chora* as a womb-like, nurturing space of origin, as the prelinguistic receptacle of subconscious drives and archetypal relations with the mother *and* the father. The *chora*, she writes, 'precedes and underlies figuration and … is analogous only to vocal or kinetic rhythm'. Poetry, in its rhythms of sound and idea, reflects the *chora* which is a place 'constituted by movements'.[31] To this idea of a primal movement I want to return, as it is full of potential for theology.

The essential conflict in the self for Kristeva is thus between the symbolic and the semiotic, at the hinge of which is abjection, a moment of horror and terror. So we come to the place of the sublime, the experience of terror and pleasure, in this psychoanalytic rewriting of Kant. At the very beginning of her book *Powers of Horror*, Kristeva tells us that 'the abject is *edged by the sublime*'.[32] This perception colours everything that follows, but what can it mean? First, it means that abjection is nameless, just as Kant thinks that the sublime cannot be comprehended by the imagination. Anything that is abject is felt as a threat to be repelled, and yet (Kristeva confesses) 'I feel that it belongs to me'; it cannot then be objectified over against me, given a name or even imagined. It is not object but 'abject'. It is, says

---

29. Julia Kristeva, *Desire in Language: A Semiotic Approach to Literature and Art* (trans. T. Gora, A. Jardine and L. Roudiez) (Oxford: Blackwell, 1980), pp. 133-6.

30. Julia Kristeva, *In the Beginning Was Love: Psychoanalysis and Faith* (trans. Arthur Goldhammer) (New York: Columbia University Press, 1987), p. 5.

31. Julia Kristeva, *Revolution in Poetic Language* (trans. M. Waller) (repr., New York: Columbia University Press, 1984), pp. 25-30.

32. Kristeva, *Powers of Horror*, pp. 11-12, my emphasis.

Kristeva, 'a "something" that I do not imagine as a thing', and 'respects no borders'. It simultaneously 'beseeches and pulverizes the self'.[33] The prime instance of the abject is the rejected mother, as we have described her: she is no longer an object of our knowing, but coded as an 'abject'.

Second, the abject is 'edged by the sublime' because it is the source of excessiveness. Confronted by something felt as sublime, writes Kristeva, 'the object dissolves in raptures of bottomless memory'.[34] The sublime triggers a boundless expansion of memories; echoing Derrida's notion of a *parergon* (an 'addition' or a 'frame'),[35] she says that it is 'something added that expands into an impossible bounding'. The time of the abject is one of 'veiled infinity from which revelation bursts forth'.[36] It is a mark of psychosis, and particular of the 'dark sun' of melancholia, to try to regress behind the moment of abjection, to attempt a recovery of undisturbed unity with self and mother. Facing up to the fact of abjection is to shatter the wall of repression, and so one can – in a certain sense – take 'joy' in the abject while not knowing it or desiring it. There is what Kristeva calls a 'sublime alienation', which *can* take perverse forms such as taboos in religion, or the attempt to 'purify' what is felt to be unclean. Excessiveness, then, is a highly ambiguous state, tending to life or death.

Third, the abject is sublime because it leads to *sublimation*. As Kristeva puts it, confronted by the abject, there is an attempt to name it, to keep it under control[37] and so to sublimate it. The sublime triggers *sublimation*. This insight is perhaps the most significant for our discussion, and it is here I believe that Kristeva makes the greatest, but most neglected, contribution to the theme of the sublime. 'Sublimation' has a double meaning. First, it is about elevation: to sublimate something is to raise it to the level of the sublime, as the reason is raised (*erheben*) by Kant above the sublimity of nature. Second, sublimation has the Freudian sense of transfer, the sublation of deep, primal impulses of the libido by redirecting them into other pursuits, such as artistic efforts and poetry.[38] In particular, the unconscious drive towards death is sublimated in objects of art and love. Kristeva merges the two meanings, elevation with transfer, following Lacan's concept of the 'ideal'.

---

33. Ibid., pp. 2, 4–5.

34. Ibid., p. 12.

35. Jacques Derrida, *The Truth in Painting* (trans. Geoff Bennington and Ian Macleod) (Chicago: Chicago University Press, 1987), pp. 58–63. Derrida takes up the term 'parergon' from a passing use by Kant.

36. Kristeva, *Powers of Horror*, p. 9.

37. Ibid., p. 11.

38. This relies on the Hegelian sense of sublation (*aufhebung*) which takes its point of departure from the Kantian *erhebung*. In Hegelian idealism, two antitheses are sublated and the resulting synthesis takes place at a higher level. Freud, however, denies both Kant and Hegel: he disallows the raising of an individual or group onto some spiritual plane above the material.

The sublime and sublimation: Kristeva's Murder in Byzantium

For Lacan, the mind sublimates its sense of the Void, or the loss of the 'Thing' which is buried deep in the unconsciousness. An object or person acquires a sublime quality when it is raised to the dignity of the 'Thing', or stands in for the 'Thing'.[39] As sublime, it becomes an ideal, pointing to the Void at the heart of the symbolic world. The ideal object might be an artwork, or it could be a person – and here Lacan takes as a key example the sublime figure of Antigone in Sophocles's tragic drama. For Lacan, the self-willed victim Antigone possesses 'unbearable splendour ... a quality that attracts and disturbs us' and which captivates the chorus.[40]

He has, to be sure, come under a good deal of feminist criticism for using the myth of Antigone to describe the 'other' that threatens the identity of a masculinized self, the only 'I'; he appears to use the idealized woman simply to support the delusion of male autonomy.[41] Indeed, let us admit that Kristeva has fallen under the same criticism, for agreeing with Lacan that the lost Thing is to be located in the pre-Oedipal state, before the separation of the child from the mother so that the mother takes on the role of a threat to identity. I should anticipate my later argument by acknowledging that there are all kinds of problems with her notion of abjection, not least what seems to be a feminist capitulation to violence and a patriarchal society,[42] but I want to suggest that Kristeva's real contribution lies beyond this critique.

Meanwhile, I want to introduce Kristeva's novel *Murder in Byzantium*[43] in which we can explore themes of abjection and sublimation in an imaginative way. Her detective novels feature Stephanie Delacour, a Parisian journalist and amateur detective whom Kristeva describes as her alter ego. She is sent as a reporter to the imaginary country of Santa Varva, a corrupt sea-board state which appears to be in Eastern Europe but which is presented as the global village. Everything that happens in the world – terrorism, rampant capitalism, mass media distortions, the drug culture – happens in Santa Varva. In one strand of the plot there is a murderer at large who calls himself the Purifier and who is killing members of a cult called 'The New Pantheon' which mixes religion, drugs and the mafia. The police-chief, Rilsky, reflects that the murderer 'is the purifier of abjection ... not only does he measure the horror, but this figure confronts it with a certain jubilation' (32). Later, Stephanie reflects that the murderer is in quest of his 'immemorial premasculine

---

39. Lacan, *Ethics of Psychoanalysis*, pp. 122–3, 136–67.
40. Ibid., pp. 305, 310.
41. See Christine Battersby, *The Phenomenal Woman* (Cambridge: Polity Press, 1998), pp. 88–9.
42. Judith Butler, *Gender Trouble: Feminism and the Subversion of Identity* (London: Routledge, 1990), p. 93.
43. Julia Kristeva, *Murder in Byzantium* (trans. C. Jon Delagu) (New York: Columbia University Press, 2006).

embryo', an 'imaginary infinite' which is the 'secret abyss, his joy, his love'. He wants to return to the preabjective, pregendered time which is 'the mathematics of the infinite' (208–11) and so becomes a murderer without limitation of victims, signing his work with the sign of infinity in their own blood.

In another strand of the plot, a professor named Sebastian Chrest Jones disappears while researching the Byzantine Princess Anna Commena, a brilliant intellectual who wrote a history of the reign of her emperor father, Alexias. Sebastian is obsessed by two ideals who attain the state of the sublime for him: Anna and a Crusader called Ebrard whom he believes to be his ancestor and Anna's lover. Sebastian has disappeared from his university post in order to retrace their steps through his home country – and Kristeva's – namely Bulgaria. Stephanie reflects that 'Sebastian is in love with Anna. He is a dangerous man ... he's pursuing a dream' (136) and later the narrator adds, 'Stephanie was right, Sebastian was in love with Anna Commena; but he loved her as though he were Ebrard ... the transfusion into his presumed ancestor had become such a strong hallucination and so intoxicating that he hardly took notice of real living people' (157–8). Ebrard is 'the ghost or ideal Sebastian, who went back in time' (205), in fact back not just in history but to the pretemporal state of the psyche.

The two plots are linked romantically, since Stephanie's lover and co-sleuth is the police-chief Rilsky who also happens to be Sebastian's uncle. They are linked psychologically, as both Sebastian and the murderer are prompted to their violence and their idealization by loss of their fathers and 'the illusory hope of returning to the authentic origin where the mother is awaiting ... that unknown mother squashed by the Powers-that-Be' (67), a state known especially by exiles in society – among whom Kristeva includes herself (68). Like the murderer, Sebastian 'projects himself into the black sun' of melancholia (116) – 'ah, the sweetness of Byzantine sorrow' with which Stephanie herself toys: 'My own Byzantium is the colour of time ... Byzantium is nowhere; it is no place' (83). The plots are also linked dramatically, as Sebastian has killed his lover Fa, who turns out to be the sister of the murderer, and he is killed in the dénouement by the murderous brother, in the ruins of the Bulgarian church where he locates his ancestor. Sebastian, we learn, has killed Fa because in becoming pregnant without his knowledge or consent, she has 'dared to become an origin without him' (100), supplanting the authentic origin he seeks.

The novel is a lot of fun, but one can see immediately how it is a vehicle for Kristeva's psychoanalytic philosophy, and particular of the sublime and sublimation. Indeed, Kristeva sees the writing of novels as a form of sublimation in itself. In addition, we see Sebastian and Stephanie in different ways trying to overcome the oppression of the symbolic order, so that she feels an odd sympathy with him: both, as exiles in society, speak a 'language of silence' (51). Stephanie reflects that in times of 'emptiness' she feels the conflict between the symbolic and the semiotic that I have suggested is characteristic of Kristeva's sublime:

> I do not express myself in either words or sentences, even though I like to trace out rhythms and visions ... More and less than words and sentences, it's the underside of a language that I sense flowing in my mouth. (63)

This novel may seem very different from Murdoch's. But in *Nuns and Soldiers* there is the same sense of the ambiguity of the ideal – of the artwork or the person raised to the level of the sublime. In the face of the loss of the father-figure, Guy, both the Count and Tim idealize Gertrude: to the Count she is a 'sudden, radiant source' (45), and Tim believes that 'Gertrude would save him' (214). Murdoch is always suspicious of consolation, and especially the making of others into saviour-figures who will relieve us of the burden of our own dying to self. So Anne asks Christ in her vision, 'What shall I do to be saved?', and her 'nomadic' Christ replies: 'You must do it all yourself, you know' (290–1). As we have already seen, even the things of beauty in the National Gallery can become false consolation, reflecting Kristeva's statement that, while beauty never disappoints the libido, if it is used to *deny* loss then it is perishable and mere artifice.[44]

For all the similarity, Murdoch finds the sublime experience of the ambiguous ideal to be pointing towards a Good which exists objectively, beyond the individual. For Kristeva, the sublime ideal points to a preconscious experience of separation and splitting in the psyche which has to be faced and dealt with. There is, however, a further dimension of sublimation, beyond idealization, that Kristeva perceives, and which I believe to be highly significant for the healing of the person – that is, *forgiveness*. On the way to this, we should think a little more about the third term in our title, 'attending to the other'.

Attending to the other and the sublime

Kant, so Murdoch claims, is not much concerned with the other.[45] For him, the sublime reinforces the self and especially reason. By contrast, Murdoch is concerned with the sublime as the occasion for giving attention to the *particular other* and so for embracing a death of the self. 'Love,' writes Murdoch, 'is the extremely difficult realization that something other than oneself is real.'[46] As Guy expresses it, lying on his deathbed in *Nuns and Soldiers*, 'death and dying are enemies', and the problem with Christianity is that it 'changes death into suffering' (69–70). That is, religion can get so absorbed in the glorifying of suffering, even the act of dying, that it neglects actual *death*, which is putting an end to the self, or a life built around the self. In the appearance of Christ to Anne Cavidge, he tells her that 'my wounds are imaginary … if there was suffering it has gone and is nothing … though it has proved so interesting to you all' (290–1). Instead, 'death is a teaching. It is one of my names.' So the 'little bit of safety' of Tim's self has to be smashed open by exposure to the details of the world (419). Emerging from the underground tunnel into which he has been swept as in a kind of death, he sees the grass and trees around him 'with a clarity that remained with him ever after'

---

44. Kristeva, *Black Sun*, pp. 98–100.
45. Murdoch, 'Sublime and the Good', pp. 213–14.
46. Ibid., p. 215.

(424). For Murdoch, the sublime is the beauty of particular things and persons in all their diversity, which we are to *see* and love.

Julia Kristeva, on the other hand, seems to inherit a Kantian assertion of the self. She accepts the Lacanian analytical theory that in phobic or depressive regression, the mother is felt to *threaten* the self, which must struggle into its identity through abjection. But the violence of this act (criticized by other feminists) is softened by attention to an 'Another' who appears deep within the psyche. At the moment of dawning consciousness, on the verge of language and so of separating from the mother, the self imagines an image of a *father*, a father who belongs to the earliest, prelinguistic life of the individual.[47] This is indeed the pre-Oedipal 'father of pre-history' in Freud's theory and so not yet a gendered figure. But the key move that Kristeva makes is to privilege *this* kind of 'father' or 'mother-father' over the definitely *male* father who appears subsequently in Freud's famous Oedipal triangle. Unlike Lacan, *this* is the decisive moment evoked by the experience of the sublime, not the Oedipal pact which seems to concern only fathers and sons.

The image of the father that arises in the growth of subjectivity is not the demanding Freudian super-ego but a self-giving father. The subject, says Kristeva, enters the realm of 'trinitary logic'.[48] As the subject has to face separation from the mother, it shares in an exchange of gifts of love which is symbolized in the mutual self-giving of the Trinity – Father, Son and Holy Spirit. In later life, then, the self can become aware of others and share imaginatively in an interchange with them.[49]

The sublimation prompted by the terrors of the sublime is thus a transfer to the imaginary Father-Mother, not an Oedipal pact but a tale of love. Most important, this entails forgiveness. In an essay on Dostoyevsky's *Crime and Punishment*, Kristeva stresses that forgiveness is a form of sublimation, substituting the pair eros/forgiveness for eros/death.[50] Like Murdoch, Kristeva stresses that a preoccupation with suffering is unhealthy, a sign of dependence on the symbolic realm of divine law.[51] Rather, the sublimation of forgiveness 'opens up a strange space in time' which is a counterpart of the unconscious, so that the unconscious may 'inscribe itself in a new narrative that will not be the eternal return of the death drive'.[52] Against Lacan she insists that the unconscious is not structured as a language, not

---

47. Julia Kristeva, *Tales of Love* (trans. Leon S. Roudiez) (New York: Columbia University Press, 1987), pp. 23–30, 42–50.

48. Kristeva, *Black Sun*, p. 135. This must be a reference to the 'trinitarian self-giving', in Hans Urs von Balthasar, *The Glory of the Lord: A Theological Aesthetics: Vol. VII, Theology: The New Covenant* (trans. Brian McNeil, CRV) (Edinburgh: T&T Clark, 1989), pp. 391–8; see Kristeva's reference to the French version of this volume (*La Gloire et La Croix* [1975] 3:2), *Black Sun*, p. 272 n28.

49. Kristeva, *Tales of Love*, p. 140.

50. Kristeva, *Black Sun*, p. 184, cf. pp. 97–8.

51. Ibid., p. 185.

52. Ibid., p. 204.

part of the symbolic order. Instead it is semiotic, marked by identification with the other.

Forgiveness renews the unconscious and rebuilds the personality, affirms Kristeva, because it is empathetic. She writes: 'Whoever is in the realm of forgiveness, giving and receiving, is capable of *identifying* with a loving father, an imaginary father, with whom he is willing to be reconciled, with a new symbolic law in mind.'[53] This is not just a matter for the inner life of the psyche, but for relation with others in society: forgiveness, she writes, gives 'shape to relations between insulted and humiliated individuals … [so] giving shape to signs'. Thus, the sublime experience of facing up to abjection can lead to forgiveness, which in turn challenges the old law of the Father. Kristeva writes: 'There is no beauty outside the forgiveness that remembers abjection'; so, she continues, 'forgiveness … is essential to *sublimation*'. Identification with the other is always 'unstable and unfinished' so that the 'suffering body of the forgiver (and the artist) undergoes a "transubstantiation"'.[54] The language of 'unstable identity' and 'transubstantiation' betokens, I suggest, empathy. This empathic forgiveness, she proposes, is symbolized by the Orthodox doctrine of the Trinity in which there is 'a permanent instability of identity between the persons … each person of the Trinity identified with the others in an erotic fusion'.[55]

In *Murder in Byzantium*, as in Murdoch's novel, attending to others involves 'seeing' them as they are. Sebastian kills Fa because 'he no longer saw her' (14); we are not surprised to learn that when he was a child he liked to crush the eyes of butterflies. Yet Sebastian knows that the culture of Byzantium, based on icons, was all about seeing: 'the eyes, this is the key to Byzantium … so many debates about the visible and invisible' (121). Viewing Byzantine art at Boyana in Bulgaria, he reflects that 'for the people of Boyana the *image* [my emphasis] of someone or something meant nothing less than being in a living relationship with that person or thing', and he understands the roots of this in the Orthodox Trinity: he thinks 'there is a whole history of love between the Father and the Son no less than between model and image … the walls of Boyana impressed on Sebastian the economy of love of another age, another way of seeing' (172).

There is not much, at least explicitly, about forgiveness in this novel, but there is a great deal about the empathy as well as the seeing involved in love. Love happens in the 'silence' that belongs to the inner Byzantium, not in much speaking (69, 72, 74). Love is the 'intense sensation of proximity, this osmosis between two bodies' (119). Towards the end, Stephanie reflects on her love affair with Rilsky that:

> The silence that we love and in which we love each other … preserves my lucidity and yours, incommensurable will and yet not shut off: you're me and I'm you, but we remain quite different inside this reciprocal echo chamber … what name

---

53. Ibid., p. 207, my emphasis.
54. Ibid., pp. 206–7, my emphasis.
55. Ibid., p. 211.

shall we give "it"? Nothingness is too melancholic ... silence is a humble term that doesn't rule out language ... all the while remaining attentive to my body and yours. (182)

Such a love is one of empathy ('you're me and I'm you'), but this very process is one in which the self or the 'incommensurable will' is not lost, for 'we remain quite different inside this reciprocal echo chamber'. For both Murdoch and Kristeva, eros is a force which can lead us to notice each other as well as some primordial power. As Stephanie reflects, it is hard to name the place of silence, yet 'all the while remaining attentive to my body and yours'.

For Murdoch, sexual love is a form of the energy of eros, which can sink towards a degraded state or be purified and point towards a higher eros of loving the Good for no reward.[56] Unlike Kristeva, eros always falls under the suspicion of becoming a false ascesis or an illusory stripping of the self, driven by the fantasy of 'being in love'. The contingency of all that is not the self is *for a moment* unveiled with a sublime radiance, but it does not last. It must lead on to true ascesis, a flaying away of the self for the sake of the Good. But even this 'refined' eros, as a 'force that joins us to Good', is not empathetic: there is no question of reciprocal response of the Good. Consequently, as Peter Conradi puts it, being 'unselfed by the sublime' is a falling out of 'intense' love into 'love with the separate world and the separate people it contains', and this is 'a darker, colder, more impersonal commodity'.[57] Murdoch does raise the issue of forgiveness in *Nuns and Soldiers*, but it seems a mechanical process of adjustment: Daisy forgives Tim, but there is nothing empathetic about it: she remarks 'one bit of wood doesn't ask another bit of wood to forgive it' (381), and Murdoch comments that they forgave each other 'out of a kind of hopelessness' (368).

Glen Pettigrove suggests that forgiveness for Murdoch simply takes the form of giving more accurate attention to those who have harmed us, such as being able to see them as consisting in more than the injuries they have caused.[58] In this connection he mentions in passing Hilary Burde in *A Word Child*, who has caused a great deal of havoc, but does not elaborate on his case. Falling in love successively with the first and second wives of Gunnar Jopling, Hilary is a factor in causing the death of both of them (Anne by a road crash, and Kitty by drowning), and in the second infatuation also betrays his lover, Tommy. She herself has contributed to the death of Kitty by sending a revealing letter to Jopling, though she does not realize its fatal impact. In the ambivalent ending of the book, she asks for Hilary's forgiveness for writing the letter. In black despair, he had earlier made the great discovery that 'perhaps being forgiven was just forgiving',[59] but he also seems to

---

56. Murdoch, *Sovereignty of Good*, pp. 75, 102–3; Murdoch, *Metaphysics*, pp. 494–6.
57. Conradi, *Saint and the Artist*, p. 142.
58. Glen Pettigrove, 'Forgiveness without God?', *Journal of Religious Ethics* 40.3 (2012), pp. 518–44.
59. Iris Murdoch, *A Word Child* (London: Chatto & Windus, 1975), p. 298.

exemplify the view of Bradley Pearson in *The Black Prince* that 'forgiveness is often thought of as an emotion. It is not that. It is rather a certain kind of cessation of emotion.'[60] When Tommy asks him 'can you forgive me?' he replies 'I expect so. As I said, time will show.' When she responds in turn, 'You sound very cold about it. Perhaps you don't care much what I do', he can only say 'perhaps not'. Yet the narrator seems to find this exchange satisfactory: Christmas bells ring out in the snow 'with wild cascades of joy' (recalling the connection of bells with the sublime in other novels),[61] and Thomas declares, 'I'm going to marry you.'[62]

What then can we conclude from the connection of 'attending to the other' with the sublime? For Murdoch, the experience of the sublime prompts an attention which is a cold, dispassionate kind of love and forgiveness, but which includes attending to a Supreme Good that is not confined to the human self. For Kristeva there *is* no transcendent Good except what lies in individuals and in society, although trinitarian symbolism is a powerful means of evoking it. Any kind of God, even the Platonist nameless Good, is an illusion.[63] But the sublime provokes an attention which is a highly empathetic form of love and forgiveness.

Internal and external conflict: The Bell

In making this contrast between Murdoch and Kristeva, we must of course acknowledge that Murdoch is as familiar with the conflict *within* the self as Kristeva is, and that she also associates these tensions with the sublime. The point is that the internal psychological conflict is always connected with the external reality of the Good, a scenario that we can see being played out in Murdoch's novel *The Bell*. It is this novel that Conradi selects, alongside *The Unicorn*, as exemplifying 'the sublime', which he understands as having a visionary experience of 'the world's particulars' in which 'the box-like enclosure of the self is attenuated and opened out'.[64]

The story is set in a country mansion, Imber Court, which houses a lay religious community. In the grounds of the mansion, across a lake is an enclosed religious community, an abbey of (Anglican) Benedictine nuns. The two houses are linked by a causeway across the lake. Lost somewhere in the depths of the lake is an ancient medieval bell once belonging to the Abbey church, carrying the inscription *Ego Vox Amoris Sum* ('I Am the Voice of Love'), while the walls of Imber Court display the worldly motto *Amor Vita Mea* ('Love Is My Life'). The theme is thus set up, that there is a route, a causeway from earthly love to divine love, from the lower eros to the higher eros. The way is that of giving attention to others as they

---

60. Murdoch, *Black Prince*, p. 331.
61. See Murdoch, *Severed Head*, p. 120; Murdoch, *The Bell*, p. 268.
62. Murdoch, *Word Child*, pp. 390–1.
63. Cf. Kristeva, *Murder in Byzantium*, p. 224.
64. Conradi, *Saint and the Artist*, pp. 138–9.

are and to the world as it is, but the spiritual enquirers in the lay community fail lamentably in following this way. One of the leaders, Michael Meade, is unable to see the disturbed young man Nick Fawley as he really is, with his actual needs; this is mostly because of continuing guilt over a disastrous homosexual encounter between them years before when he was a teacher at Nick's school. Failure to communicate with him and to show him accepting love appears to be one prompt for Nick's suicide towards the end of the story. The art historian, Paul, fails to see his wife Dora as she is in her own right with her gifts and needs and simply bullies her with his own world view; early in the story, Dora looks at herself in the mirror before going obediently to Paul's bed: 'Dora looked with astonishment at the person that confronted her ... she continued to look at the person who was there, unknown to Paul. How every much, after all, she existed.'[65]

Works of art, and especially the medieval bell engraved with Gospel stories, are external summoners to serve the Good, as the stones on the beach and the great cliff face function similarly in *Nuns and Soldiers*. Dora seeks to raise the medieval bell from the lake to serve her own ends, enlisting a young volunteer at the community, Toby Gashe, to assist her with a mechanical digger and his knowledge of engineering. Just as her favourite pictures in the National Gallery call her imperiously from 'dreary solipsisms', so, confronting the bell she is jolted by an experience for which Murdoch uses her accustomed vocabulary of the negative sublime: the bell is 'immense', 'huge', 'terrible', 'monstrous', a 'black hole' and 'a thing from another world', and it creates 'panic' within her (220). Yielding to her response, she rings the bell to summon everyone to see it, rather than manipulating it for her own purposes as she had intended. Again, we read the grammar of the sublime: the darkness, the 'great shape', the terror, the amazement:[66]

> She stood a moment longer in the darkness feeling with her hand how the great thing was shuddering quietly before her. Then suddenly with all her might she hurled herself against it ... the clapper met the side with a roar that made her cry out, it was so close and so terrible. ... It returned, its great shape scarcely visible, a huge moving piece of darkness ... bellowing out in a voice that had been silent for centuries that some great thing was newly returned to the world. the clamour arose, distinctive, piercing, amazing. (268)

She is shocked into the self-knowledge which Michael has urged in his sermon to the community (205), feeling now the capacity to 'become what she had never been, an independent grown-up person' (305); though she nurses an unrequited love for Michael, 'she had survived' (320). She also learns to swim, mastering the waters that – for Murdoch – represent the multifarious accidents and contingencies

---

65. Murdoch, *The Bell*, p. 45.

66. Johnson, *Iris Murdoch*, p. 85, suggests that Dora finds the bell threatening because it evokes unexplored (and unexpressed) female sexuality deriving from its historic location in the abbey, but she misses the vocabulary of the sublime.

of life. Catherine, Nick's sister, is not so fortunate; on the day when it was planned for her to enter the Abbey as a postulant, she admits to herself that she has lost her vocation, tries to drown herself and is carried away to hospital in a drugged and unconscious state. On that same day the new bell which was being installed in the Abbey falls into the lake from the causeway, and Nick takes his life. A press report of the sensational events, written by Dora's former lover, puts an end to the community, and Imber Court is leased permanently to the Abbey.

Dora has inner conflicts, especially doubts over whether she owes loyalty to Paul, but the narrative about her focuses on the sublime impact on her consciousness of an external object, the bell. With Michael, his inner conflicts play a central role in his facing of the demands of the Good, and outer events, some experienced as sublime, are objectifications of his subjective state. There is a deep confusion in his mind between religion and sex, but the first is not just a sublimation of the second. Murdoch is modifying Freud's analysis of the libidinal drives of the ego, but not in the same way as Kristeva does with her theory of abjection. Murdoch agrees with Freud that eros – sexual love and desire – is a kind of spiritual energy that may be either constructive or destructive for the self,[67] but she does not treat Michael's love for God simply as an obsessional neurosis, or as an illusory projection of a father-complex in the manner of Freud.[68] One critic thinks that Murdoch intends us to dismiss Michael's religious vocation as a projection of self-importance and a sublimation of homosexual impulses,[69] but Conradi rightly perceives that Murdoch 'everywhere displays the roots of virtue in sex'. Thus, as Conradi judges, 'Murdoch's Platonic use of Eros undercuts Freud.' What Michael exemplifies is not the bogus nature of his religion, but 'the dangers of too swift or unsceptical ascent' from the lower to the higher regions of eros.[70] Eros is the ambiguous common root of both sexual desire and an orientation towards not (for Murdoch) a personal God but virtue and the Good. When Michael, having drunk too much Devon cider, impulsively kisses Toby and sets in motion a fatal mechanism which has its mainspring in the original incident with Nick, Murdoch subtly evokes both his yielding to illusion and an underlying reality about love. Just before the catastrophic kiss, Michael muses: 'He was conscious of such a fund of love and goodwill for the creature beside him. It could not be that God intended such a spring of love to be quenched utterly. There must be a way in which it could be made a power for good' (158). Later, in the Abbey chapel he reflects similarly that he had been too quick to take fright, 'how unready to seek for that real goodwill towards Toby which should be his guide' (168). Later still, after Nick's

---

67. Murdoch, *Fire and the Sun*, pp. 37–9; Murdoch, *Metaphysics*, p. 24.

68. Sigmund Freud, *Totem and Taboo: Some Points of Agreement between the Mental Lives of Savages and Neurotics* (trans. James Strachey) (repr., Oxford: Routledge Classics, 2001), p. 171.

69. G. S. Fraser, 'Iris Murdoch and the Solidity of the Normal', in John Wain (ed.), *International Literary Annual*, vol. 11 (London: John Calder, 1959), pp. 37–54.

70. Conradi, *Saint and the Artist*, p. 146.

suicide, he bitterly regrets his failure to answer his appeals for help, thinking 'so great a love must have contained some grain of good, something at least that might have attached Nick to this world' (311).

A typical inner conflict in Murdoch which is explored here is thus a confrontation with the good in the ambiguous mixture of the lower and higher states of eros.[71] In *The Bell* this is externalized in mixed experiences of the negative and positive sublime, or the Kantian and Murdochian sublime. Resolving to find an opportunity to talk to Toby about the kiss, to apologize and put his mind at ease, Michael takes Toby in the twilight to see the flocking together of the nightjars in preparation for migration. The scene is described in the vocabulary of the negative sublime: it is 'quite obscure' in the wood, the trees 'generate their own darkness', the two are lulled 'in a kind of coma' in 'the darkening wood', and the birds make a 'hollow clapping sound' with their wings. Suddenly the birds are present with them, and the observers are immersed into a sense of vastness and uncountability characteristic of the sublime: 'It was impossible to see how many there were, but it seemed like a multitude as they fluttered and poised in the granular darkness.' It seems that the negative will turn into the positive sublime, as 'Michael now felt an extraordinary peace in which he felt sure that Toby shared,' and 'it was as if they had been present together at some esoteric and liberating rite' (170). But even as he makes his apology, negative elements are stressed in the environment: 'It was almost completely dark now ... and the trees were almost invisible, opaque presences of deeper black on either side.' Toby accepts his apology, but 'looking at his darkened countenance', Michael recalls a similar 'fading light' in his final conversation at school with Nick. Fatally, Michael grips Toby's hand for a long while, and they 'stood silently together in the darkness' (171). It is that handclasp that Toby, now unsure of his sexuality, recalls in the Abbey chapel, prompting his own experience of the negative sublime as he listens to the chanting of the nuns: the presence of the women is 'monstrous', 'the hideous purity and austerity of the song became intolerable to him', and, as he stumbles out into the daylight, he feels 'unutterably sick and disconsolate' (176).

In the days following the suicide of Nick, the breakdown of Catherine and the dispersal of the community, Michael experiences intense inner conflict which is described like an interior negative sublime: his love for Nick 'seemed to grow, in almost devilish way, to the most colossal dimensions ... like a great tree growing out of him', and 'he was tormented by strange dreams of cancerous growths' (310). However, an experience in the Abbey chapel, where Toby suffered a negative vision, gives just a hint of the positive or Murdochian sublime. The celebration of the Mass is not 'consoling' in his present state of unbelief, but it is 'in some way factual'; it offers him an object which is real in its particularity: 'It simply existed as a kind of pure reality separate from the weaving of his own thoughts,' and observing it

---

71. Leeson, *Iris Murdoch: Philosophical Novelist*, pp. 89–91, finds the whole novel to be structured after the Platonic myth of the cave, with the members of the community as 'prisoners' in the darkness of Imber Court.

enables him to give 'attention' to others whom he has offended. Murdoch injects a note of doubt, however, even at this point about Michael's capacity for attention, as it is described not only as 'endless' but also 'perhaps meaningless' (313–14).

The story makes clear how, for Murdoch, the essence of both art and ethics is the same, namely love, or a respect for the other and a genuine noticing of the other. Love can lead to a true ascesis, a flaying away of the self for the sake of the Good, and the sublime has its part to play here. But for Murdoch this eros is not empathetic: there is no question of reciprocal response of the Good, which is elusive, 'above being, non-personal, non-contingent, and not a particular thing among other things'.[72] She is adamant that the 'traditional' God, whom she understands to be an 'answering judging rewarding Intelligence and a comforting flow of love', does not exist.[73] She does not therefore associate empathy, with either the Good or others, with that moment of the sublime in which Good makes its demand on the experiencer. All she can say of Michael is that 'one day too he would experience again, responding with his heart, that indefinitely extended requirement that one human being makes on another' (313). For Kristeva too there is no personal God, but the sublime is precisely the discovery of the other *within* one's own psyche, and so it is inseparable from the act of forgiveness.

The sublime: A theological dialogue

It may come as no surprise that I want to combine *Murdoch's* kind of sublime, where attention to the multiple details of the world prompts attention to the Good, with *Kristeva's* sense of the sublime, where sublimation means empathetic identification and forgiveness. I aim to integrate two kinds of attending to the 'other', two kinds of spiritual practice. But how shall we achieve this combination? First, it will be by living in the narrative world created by the three novels I have been describing. As works of art they do not simply *illustrate* philosophical ideas, as if they are optional extras to the argument. As we inhabit the lives and the thoughts of the characters, as we read the novels alongside each other, there begins to stir within us an inkling of how their worlds *might* connect. We begin to see the possibilities of a spiritual practice that is embodied in taking the narratives together, and that cannot be totally contained in any theory.

But we can also begin to think theologically and to create a dialogue. In so doing, I must resist theological projects that fail to combine the two modes of the sublime that Murdoch and Kristeva together show us. Slavoj Žižek, for instance, adopts a Lacanian reading of the sublime, as an indicator of the traumatic emptiness or lack at the heart of the symbolic realm.[74] Desire for the other (woman, or God, for instance) is the result of this primary deprivation; an object of love becomes

---

72. Murdoch, *Metaphysics*, p. 37.
73. Ibid., p. 344.
74. Žižek, *Sublime Object of Ideology*, pp. 227–34.

sublime when it is raised to the place of the inaccessible Thing, as in courtly love. But, Lacan argues, as soon as woman is encountered in her body, she changes from a sacred object to a transgressive *abject*, and sublimation is brought to an end.[75] Following Lacan, Žižek thus maintains that religious discourse, claiming that God is love, has to avoid the fleshly associations of love, to enable sublimation to continue. Divine love, the totally self-giving love of *agape*, frees us from the realm of the law and must be distinguished from *eros*, the love which satisfies the body and the self.[76] Above all for Žižek, *Christ* is *agape*; he is sublime because his mortality stands in place of the overwhelming glory of God. His abjection in the cross does not contradict the logic of sublimation, since he is not (according to Žižek) presented here as an object of beauty; it is his consequent transformation through resurrection into a sublime object of desire that enables his follows to enter into the inexhaustible dimensions of the sacred Thing.[77]

We detect some echoes of Kristeva here, but her stress on love and forgiveness as empathy means that, for her, an *agape*-love cannot be separated out from *eros* in the experience of the sublime. Moreover, she finds (building on the trinitarian thought of Hans Urs von Balthasar)[78] that abjection is to be found in the erotic fusion of the Trinity itself, as separation or splitting (a 'hiatus') enters into the very relations of the Father and the Son. Anyway, the old distinction between *eros* and *agape* has long been rejected by many theologians, who stress the eros of God for the world;[79] God opens God's own self in desire for creation and in dependence on it, though not as an external necessity but as a free choice, as one who desires to be in need.[80] As the theologian Eberhard Jüngel expresses it, *eros* and *agape* belong together in the being of God as love, as an event of 'a still greater selflessness within a very great self-relatedness', since in giving himself away to the beloved, any lover is related to himself anew.[81] Žižek, an atheist arguing for the indispensability of Christian symbolism, unfortunately misreads the symbols here. His project also fails Murdoch's analysis of the sublime, since for him sublime

---

75. Lacan, *Ethics of Psychoanalysis*, pp. 158–9, 185–97.

76. Slavoj Žižek, *The Fragile Absolute: Or Why Is the Christian Legacy Worth Fighting For?* (London: Verso, 2008), pp. 91–2, 132–4, 136–7.

77. Žižek, *Fragile Absolute*, pp. 147–9; cf. Žižek, *Sublime Object of Ideology*, pp. 227–9.

78. Kristeva, *Black Sun*, p. 132: 'a caesura, which *some have called* a "hiatus"' (my emphasis); see Balthasar, *Glory of the Lord*, vol. VII, p. 190, 'the hiatus of the cross', and note 48, for Kristeva's referencing of Balthasar.

79. For instance, Daniel D. Williams, *The Spirit and the Forms of Love* (London: Nisbet, 1968), pp. 52–90; Tillich, *Systematic Theology: Combined Volume* (Welwyn: James Nisbet, 1968), vol. 1, pp. 310–16; vol. 3, pp. 143–7.

80. Paul S. Fiddes, *The Creative Suffering of God* (Oxford: Oxford University Press, 1988), pp. 66–8; so, in agreement, Vincent Brümmer, *The Model of Love* (Cambridge: Cambridge University Press, 1993), p. 237.

81. Jüngel, *God as the Mystery of the World*, pp. 317–18.

objects do not represent any transcendent 'thing in itself' such as the Good, but only a human lack.

We are brought, I suggest, to what might be called a 'theopoetics',[82] a vision of God as the poet-maker of the universe, creating all its particular details in an excess of divine generosity and love and relating to them in compassionate imagination. Indeed, just as a poem is generated within what Kristeva identifies as the inner space of the person, her very own 'Byzantium', we may think of the whole of created reality (this universe and probably many others) as existing within God. It exists not in a mind but in the space made by the interweaving of the divine persons which – as Augustine and Aquinas hinted[83] – are nothing other than movements of relationship. As Leibniz proposed, and as is increasingly affirmed by modern science, relations do not exist in a Newtonian receptacle of space and time, but space is what is created *by relations* themselves.[84] So, we may say, finite beings share in the movements of love and justice that are happening within God, like movements of relationship between a father and a son.[85] And because these are movements of giving and receiving in love, it is *also* appropriate to say that they are like relations between a mother and a daughter, deepened and opened to the future by the rhythm of a shared love.

This triune imagery of space *within* God picks up what Kristeva calls 'trinitarian logic' in the preconscious state and relates it to her description of immersion in the deep rhythmic movements of the *chora*. This rhythm, she affirms, is a constant semiotic challenge to the old law of the symbolic realm of society; it is embodied in the revolutionary power of poetry. So, I suggest, we can only think of God in terms of our participation in rhythmic, triune movements of love and justice which are greater than we are: like the *chora*, the movements that open the space for us to dwell cannot be objectified or conceived as a supreme subject – and certainly not three subjects. The idea of God as an interweaving of relations is of course kataphatic, but it is also apophatic, since we are not thinking of personal subjects who *have* relations, but only movements of relation themselves which defeat all attempts at observation and objectification. This is a participatory kind of thinking, not a subject–object relationship. God as sublime disrupts all human, objectifying speech; thus far, there is a truth in the postmodern experience of the negative sublime, and we should be wary of theologies that dismiss it as inauthentic.[86] Yet this sublime also makes possible an *analogy of beauty* with relations in the created

---

82. For the term, see, e.g., Amos Wilder, *Theopoetics: Theology and the Religious Imagination* (Philadelphia: Fortress Press, 1976); Roland Faber, *God as Poet of the World* (Louisville: Westminster/John Knox, 2008), pp. 14–15.

83. Augustine, *De Trinitate*, 5.6: 'the names ... refer to relations'; Aquinas, *Summa Theologiae*, 1a.29.4: 'person signifies relation'.

84. G. W. Leibniz, *Die Philosophischen Schriften* (ed. G. J. Gerhardt), 7 vols (vol. 7, Hildesheim: G. Olms, 1875–90), pp. 389–420.

85. See Fiddes, *Participating in God*, pp. 28–55.

86. For example, Hart, *Beauty*, pp. 43–92; cf. Milbank, 'Sublimity', pp. 223–31.

world – analogy, that is, with various kinds of relations but not with created *beings* who have relations.

This kind of theopoetics takes up Kristeva's emphasis that the sublime means *sublimation* in empathetic forgiveness. For Kristeva, of course, 'trinitary logic' is only useful symbolism for exploring the psyche. Here I am combining her insights on *sublimation* with Murdoch's insistence that the experience of the *sublime* turns our attention towards a Good which is a reality beyond the individual self. For Murdoch this Good is not a person; but then, I am myself only using the metaphor of personal relations to enable us to *engage* in the rhythms of a God who cannot be objectified as a Person or Supreme Subject. As in both Murdoch and Kristeva, spiritual growth involves increasing attention to the other, and a theologian will understand this to be both the created and the uncreated Other. Experiencing the sublime, rejoicing in the beautiful and participating in movements of unconditional forgiveness, we who are the creations of the divine poet of the world can become poets too.

Chapter 5

LANGUAGE AND WRITING: MURDOCH IN DIALOGUE WITH JACQUES DERRIDA

Why Murdoch and Derrida?

In this chapter I intend to place a piece of Iris Murdoch's philosophical writing alongside one of her novels, juxtaposing her chapter on 'Derrida and Structuralism' from her book *Metaphysics as a Guide to Morals* with her novel *The Black Prince*. Though *Metaphysics* was published in 1992, some nineteen years after her novel (1973), Murdoch tells us that she read Derrida's early book *Writing and Difference* when it was published in 1967 and was 'impressed and disturbed by it'.[1] As will become clear, after that time she continually reflected on his works, which she calls 'brilliant and difficult', and so it is not an anachronism to suggest that there is some echo of Derrida's thought in her 1973 novel.

Let me make clear right at the beginning, however, that I have not proposed this exercise because I think that the protagonist of *The Black Prince* is a Derridean figure in any *exact* way. I do not suggest for one moment that Murdoch has portrayed the central character Bradley Pearson simply as a Derrida in disguise. Rather, my point is this. The 'Derrida' of her philosophical chapter is a kind of composite figure or a cipher. For those who know the work of Derrida he hardly seems like Derrida at all; in fact, he has become the target for all that she dislikes about recent philosophy. Similarly, Bradley Pearson, the narrator of *The Black Prince*, is a composite figure, incorporating several of the philosophical opponents that Murdoch later identifies in her book on metaphysics, including touches of the *kind of thought* that she is later explicitly to identify as 'Derridean'. It is not impossible that she actually has Derrida in mind for aspects of Bradley's personality at the time of writing the novel,[2] but this is not essential for my argument. My

---

1. Murdoch, *Metaphysics*, p. 91.

2. In her Romanes Lecture of 1976, *The Fire and the Sun*, pp. 31-2, Murdoch discusses Derrida in relation to the issue of voice and writing, which (later) I suggest is illuminated by *The Black Prince* (1973). References to structuralism, which Murdoch later oddly attributes to Derrida, are also to be found in her writing of the 1970s: see Murdoch, in conversation with Bryan Magee (1977), in *Existentialists and Mystics*, p. 22, and 'Art Is the Imitation of Nature' (1978), in *Existentialists and Mystics*, pp. 243-58 (249).

proposal is that Bradley exhibits traits of thought that worry her and which she later extensively attributes – not altogether accurately – to Derrida himself.

Like many of her characters, both the 'Derrida' of the chapter and the 'Bradley' of the novel disregard the truth that comes from engaging with a reality that lies beyond us, and this means failing both to struggle with the contingencies of everyday life and to serve the Good. Murdoch thus satirizes Bradley in the same way as she later attacks Derrida. As is well known, Murdoch had an ambiguous relationship with mid- and late twentieth-century French philosophy, beginning with her early work on Sartre in 1953. She is fascinated by the moves to give attention to 'ordinary life' in the phenomenological tradition and to make it the stuff of philosophy, but she finds a lack of moral seriousness in Sartre's particular emphasis on a mere act of the human will.[3] Derrida represents for her a climax in the loss of the moral self, and so her critical account of Derrida is central to her vision of the world, not merely passing comment. By 1992 he appears as a major opponent, making an appearance in nearly every chapter of her book, but especially in 'Derrida and Structuralism'. Exploring her account of Derrida makes clear the kind of philosophical thinking she is rejecting, though we shall see that her earlier novel not only exemplifies the nature of her opposition but ironically tends to undermine one aspect of it. Moreover, working through this interaction between Murdoch and Derrida will finally lead us to a theological horizon within which both of their concerns can be seen to have a proper place.

A curious account of Derrida

Let us start with the chapter of philosophy. The first surprise for those who know Derrida at all well is the very title, 'Derrida and *Structuralism*'. Murdoch classifies Derrida as a *structuralist*; indeed she regards him as its leading advocate. Further, it transpires that she regards post-structuralism, deconstruction and postmodernism (even at times modernism) as all varieties of structuralism. There is a grain of truth in this, since they all do rely on the view of Ferdinand de Saussure that the 'individual is submerged in language, rather than [being] an autonomous user of language'.[4] Put another way, the common element is the belief that language constructs the world. After that, however, there are profound differences between these intellectual movements and structuralism.

To take a key instance, Murdoch regards Derridean 'deconstruction' as a kind of intensification of structuralism. Those like Derrida who seek to 'deconstruct' a text do so, she maintains, in order to seek 'the hidden-deep … meaning of the text'.[5] They are searching for the deep structure of language and meaning that

---

3. Murdoch, *Sartre*, pp. 68–72; Murdoch, *Metaphysics*, pp. 52–3.

4. Murdoch, *Metaphysics*, p. 185. Cf. Ferdinand de Saussure, *Course in General Linguistics* (trans. Roy Harris) (repr., London: Duckworth: 1995), pp. 65–70.

5. Murdoch, *Metaphysics*, p. 189.

lies beneath the surface; they are on a quest for the universal system of language that pre-exists the use of words by a particular writer, who is quite unaware of being used *by* this system or structure of signs. Murdoch parodies this theory in the figure of Marcus Vallar in *The Message to the Planet*, who is searching for 'deep foundations, pure cognition' and 'a universal language',[6] but who ends up speaking a *glossolalia* that the psychiatrist treating him notes was regarded with suspicion by St Paul: this 'speaking with tongues', he judges, is 'the voice of the spirit not of the reason, and [Paul] warned the Corinthians against this sort of private language. Magic besieges the religious life.'[7] Actually, Derrida is reacting against such a magical claim for 'deep meaning'; for him, meaning multiplies and proliferates endlessly in the difference between the surface signs.[8] Here he is turning structuralism against itself. He agrees with Saussure that the meaning of a word is to be found in its relation to, and difference from, other words; meaning belongs within the network of signs, but this, for Derrida, means precisely that meaning cannot be trapped in any pre-existing structure.

How is that Murdoch appears so wilfully to misunderstand Derrida? He has given a hostage to fortune (or at least to this implacable critic) by his concept of *archi-écriture*, or primal language, to which he constantly appeals. Here Murdoch quotes (in French) an important passage from *Of Grammatology* (1967) – in fact, it is the only direct quotation from Derrida in her chapter.[9] In this paragraph Derrida is placing what he calls *archi-écriture* over against particular types of experience and comments that 'the putting into brackets of regions of experience, or of the totality of natural experience, must uncover a transcendental field of experience'. The task of deconstruction, he says, is to reach this 'deep foundation' (*son dernier fond*) of experience. Murdoch takes this to mean that the experience of individual people, in particular times and places, is being subjected to a metaphysical totality, an overarching transcendent reality which exists behind all readings of a text. Her conclusion is that the notion of *archi-écriture*

> obliterates a necessary recognition of the contingent. What is left out of the picture, magically blotted out by a persuasive knitting-together of ideas and terminology, is that statements are made, propositions are uttered, by individual incarnate persons in particular extra-linguistic situations, and it is in the whole of this larger context that our familiar and essential concepts of *truth*

---

6. Murdoch, *Message to the Planet*, p. 13.
7. Ibid., p. 509.
8. Jacques Derrida, 'La Différance', in Derrida, *Margins of Philosophy* (trans. Alan Bass) (Chicago: University of Chicago Press, 1982), pp. 1–28 (6–15); cf. Derrida, *Speech and Phenomena* (trans. David Allison) (Evanston: Northwestern University Press, 1973), pp. 135–41.
9. Murdoch, *Metaphysics*, pp. 190–1; there is a corresponding English translation in Jacques Derrida, *Of Grammatology* (trans. G. C. Spivak) (repr., Baltimore: Johns Hopkins University Press, 1976), pp. 60–1.

and *truthfulness* live and work. 'Truth' is inseparable from individual contextual human *responsibilities*.[10]

The notion of 'primal language' she finds to be an assault not only on contingency but also on individual responsibility and on any distinction between what is true and false. She sees Derrida as having a totalizing metaphysics which also issues in a rigid determinism; the freedom of the individual and the reality of the contingent is lost 'by equating reality with integration in system'.[11] Derrida's theory of language is guilty of 'siding with the system against the individual'. He loses the experience of the individual, the contingent, truth, freedom and all moral values. The theory of *archi-écriture* is, she concludes, 'linguistic monism'.[12] It is a sea of language in which most people are simply submerged, and in which the favoured elite (i.e. deconstructionists) can splash around making their playful readings.[13]

Murdoch is adopting an aggressive strategy against Derrida because she regards him as highly dangerous, in his avowed determination to bring metaphysics to an end. She herself, of course, considers metaphysics – and especially that of a Platonist kind – to be a guide to morals. Moral values are shaped by giving attention to the transcendent Good, serving the Good for no hope of reward since it can never be possessed.[14] And the path to serving the Good is in giving attention to others outside one's own self – noticing other people and contingent details of the world.[15] In fact, love of others has the power to turn us outwards from mere absorption in ourselves and so set us on the track to love of the Good; so the lower eros can serve the higher eros.[16] This is her understanding of spirituality;[17] this is what she sees as being under attack in a whole range of modern philosophies, and Derrida serves here as a cipher for them all. Her strategy is ingenious – to accuse the very one who sets out to be anti-metaphysical of actually founding his thought on a strong metaphysic, an *archi-écriture*, a linguistic idealism which suppresses truth. Ironically, she insinuates, Derrida *is* offering a metaphysic as a guide to morals, but his is a morality that fails to recognize the difference between truth and falsehood, good and evil. Murdoch had already used the same strategy against Sartre, maintaining that his emphasis on the existential freedom of the individual self was a kind of metaphysics, issuing in a valueless morality.[18] To mention *The*

---

10. Murdoch, *Metaphysics*, p. 194, original emphases.
11. Ibid., p. 196.
12. Ibid., p. 197.
13. Ibid., pp. 202, 216.
14. Ibid., pp. 506–10; cf. Murdoch, *Sovereignty of Good*, pp. 68–72.
15. Murdoch, *Metaphysics*, pp. 195–6; cf. Murdoch, 'Sublime and the Good', pp. 215–16, 219.
16. Murdoch, *Metaphysics*, pp. 496–7; cf. Murdoch, *Fire and the Sun*, pp. 35–8.
17. Murdoch, *Sovereignty of Good*, pp. 55–7, 83.
18. Murdoch, *Metaphysics*, pp. 154–6; cf. Murdoch, 'The Novelist as Metaphysician', in *Existentialists and Mystics*, pp. 101–7 (104–6).

Black Prince for a moment, we shall find echoes of both opponents, Sartre and Derrida, in Bradley's personality.

Much of Murdoch's attack on a linguistic system is valid for structuralism, though not for Derrida. Later in *Metaphysics* Murdoch mentions that she read Derrida's book *Writing and Difference* in 1967 with considerable admiration, yet this book is a prolonged assault on structuralism. There is no time here to explore in detail her misunderstanding (or at least misrepresentation) of Derrida. Suffice it to say that Derrida does not only place individual experience 'under erasure', for which she attacks him implacably; he also puts 'primal writing' itself 'under erasure': that is, it can only be referred to by crossing it out at the same time. As Derrida writes: 'The value of the transcendental arche must make its necessity felt before letting itself be erased. The concept of arche-trace must comply with both that necessity and that erasure.'[19] For Derrida, 'nothing is ... anywhere simply present or absent. There are only, everywhere, differences and traces of traces.'[20] The dictum that 'an unerasable trace is not a trace'[21] applies even to primal writing. *Archi-écriture* is thus a 'deep foundation' for all speech, but not a 'deep meaning'; as the 'movement of différance, irreducible arche-synthesis',[22] it is the basis for an infinite multiplication of meaning and deconstruction of 'vulgar writing', but is not a pre-existent system of meaning in itself which somehow shapes the meaning of a text.[23] Nor is Derrida's assertion of the endless deferral of meaning a mere relativism, as both critics and North American disciples have assumed; he is concerned for the 'little truths' of particular situations, and certain values – such as concern for otherness, difference and justice – are carefully preserved.[24] Above all, Derrida is opposed to any principle or reality that can float free of the signs that indicate it, that can escape the text and the internal differentiation of signs from each other. In his essay 'White Mythology' he pursues this principle thoroughly, making clear that meaning can

---

19. Derrida, *Of Grammatology*, p. 61, cf. pp. 65–7. Derrida is indebted to Heidegger for the notion of effacement: see Derrida, *Speech and Phenomena*, pp. 155–7.

20. Jacques Derrida, *Positions* (trans. Alan Bass) (Chicago: University of Chicago Press, 1971), p. 26.

21. Jacques Derrida, *Writing and Difference* (trans. A. Bass) (London: Routledge, 1978), p. 230.

22. Derrida, *Of Grammatology*, p. 60.

23. Tony Milligan, 'Murdoch and Derrida: Holding Hands under the Table', in Rowe and Horner, *Iris Murdoch: Texts and Contexts*, pp. 77–90 (85), similarly judges that Murdoch goes astray in her reading of Derrida's *archi-écriture* in assuming that it is a fusion of Saussure's structuralism and Heideggerian determinism.

24. E.g. Jacques Derrida, *On the Name* (trans. Thomas Dutoit) (Stanford: Stanford University Press, 1995), pp. 80–4; Jacques Derrida, *Rogues: Two Essays on Reason* (trans. Pascale-Anne Brault and Michael Naas) (Stanford: Stanford University Press, 2005), pp. 80–90.

never displace the medium of signs that are always rooted in the contingencies of time and place.[25] He resists therefore the exalting of 'pure experiences' for which Edmund Husserl argues, which are a direct and unmediated awareness of the present moment.[26]

In her own critique of Husserl, Murdoch should therefore have found an ally in Derrida. In his phenomenology Husserl had insisted that objects in the world 'appear' in the consciousness as they are thought about, hoped for or desired. The attitude taken towards the object is inseparable from it, so that consciousness is always 'consciousness of', and the object is always 'perceived as'.[27] This inseparability is what Husserl calls 'intentionality', so that observation is always 'intentional' and things are 'intentional objects'. While this approach reduces the gap between subject and object, and certainly does not deny the existence of objects in the world beyond the consciousness, the actuality of the world is placed in parenthesis or 'bracketed' out.[28] By a special process of reflection or 'reduction', judgement is suspended about the external reality of the 'intentional object' in order to grasp its essence intuitively as pure phenomenon, or as an appearance in the consciousness uncontaminated by any prior assumptions or intellectual schemes. Murdoch detects here an escape from the variety of phenomena as they are in themselves in the world and urges that we should be attending to these rather than to the 'pure essences' and 'deep structure' of our own mental activity.[29] Again, Marcus Vallar, in *The Message to the Planet*, is made the bearer of the thought she is opposing, in conversation with Ludens:

'One can only understand what one identifies with. A pure experience.'
'Experience of what?'
Marcus hesitated, as if fearing to unveil a mystery. 'Of suffering.'
'What kind of suffering?'
'The most extreme.'
'You mean compassion?'
'Deeper than compassion.'
'What is deeper?'
'I cannot name it.'
'Marcus, try, say something – '
'The world must be saved.'[30]

---

25. Jacques Derrida, 'White Mythology', in Derrida, *Margins of Philosophy*, pp. 207–72 (236–9).

26. Derrida, *Speech and Phenomena*, pp. 52–9.

27. Edmund Husserl, *Ideas Pertaining to a Pure Phenomenology and to a Phenomenological Philosophy* (trans. F. Kersetn) (Dordrecht: Kluwer Academic, 1983), p. 214.

28. Husserl, *Ideas Pertaining*, p. 215.

29. Murdoch, *Metaphysics*, pp. 232–42.

30. Murdoch, *Message to the Planet*, p. 98.

Another character, Gildas, has much earlier dismissed this kind of thinking with a Murdochian brusqueness: 'As for deep foundations, what a hope! Our lives rest upon contingency, rubble, rubbish.' Later, Ludens recalls Vallar as asserting that 'there will be no writing … A pure experience will save the world. The suffering will be the message.'[31] Knowing Murdoch's suspicion of devotion to suffering as a way of salvation, we can be fairly confident where her sympathies lie.

Yet they do not extend to Derrida, despite the fact that he is just as opposed to 'pure experiences' as Murdoch and suspects that Husserl's way will lead to a 'transcendental ego'[32] which ignores the 'writing' or the textuality of a world. Derrida stresses – unlike Vallar – there always *will* be writing. It is this emphasis on the necessity of the sign that will, however, lead us to discern a real difference between Derrida and Murdoch.

Real differences between Derrida and Murdoch

Murdoch has certainly put her finger, unerringly, on a contradiction in Derrida's thought. He does have a sort of metaphysic. She has also detected a danger: that his notion of *archi-écriture* might become in some hands the *kind* of metaphysical system which suppresses the individualities and the contingencies of the world. It seems unfair to propose that this is how Derrida himself is using it. However, in positively presenting her own philosophy and theory of art, she takes issue with two other aspects in Derrida's thought where I suggest there is more substance for doing so. She connects them with his supposedly 'totalizing system', but they can be looked at in their own right, and they will lead us to *The Black Prince*.

First, she insists on the need to test all attempts at finding coherence against the contingencies of everyday life. We work, she writes, 'at a meeting point where we deal with a world which is other than ourselves'.[33] This does not, despite what Murdoch thinks, put her at a distance from Derrida. What does distance her is the fact that she envisages this encounter as a meeting between language and a *non-linguistic* external world, and here she certainly differs from Derrida, who thinks that we can never know anything without the mediation of signs or language.

Murdoch asserts in this chapter that philosophy and art both involve searching for coherence, or making sense of things. Philosophers like F. H. Bradley, Hegel and Kant work hard at finding a 'sort of ideal moral situation where partial truths emerge into an ideal harmony which alone is entirely true'.[34] But this quest for coherence has to be constantly checked against contingencies in the world which 'impede or inspire the search'. Murdoch thus holds a view of truth which includes both coherence and correspondence. The quest for coherence is conducted in

---

31. Ibid., p. 543.
32. Derrida, *Speech and Phenomena*, p. 78.
33. Murdoch, *Metaphysics*, p. 215.
34. Ibid., p. 195.

language, and this must correspond to an external reality which is *not* language and so which constantly challenges it.[35] She judges that Kant succeeds in meeting the challenge, but that Hegel does not. He looks for coherence without testing it against the individual and the particular[36]– what cause initially a 'sense of terror',[37] or what at the very beginning of *The Black Prince* is called the 'fear and horror' of the world.[38] Derrida in her view fails under the same test (though I think she is wrong in suggesting that Derrida is searching for such a coherence at all). Her view on Bradley, one in the group called 'British idealists', is left ambiguous here, though elsewhere she dubs him a 'smaller more confused copy' of Hegel.[39] We notice that her view of Bradley takes concrete form in some aspects of the personality of Bradley Pearson, who – we notice – refuses to be called 'Brad'. To himself he is always 'Bradley'. Murdoch *might* be making a jocular reference to the philosopher here, though (as with Derrida) what matters is not an exact identification but the use of the figure of Pearson to criticize certain trends of thought.

Murdoch herself is on the quest for a Platonic coherence in the transcendent Good, but she believes it can only be reached through attending to the reality of others in the world. She criticizes Derrida for divorcing language from the world, since (in her interpretation of his thought) words for him do not signify anything except the self-referential nature of language. This is not quite correct, as Derrida's point is that what is signified always becomes a signifier in turn, and so meaning is dispersed down an endless chain of signs.[40] For Derrida, language and world cannot be torn apart; the world itself or 'all the structures called real' are a text or system of signs.[41] By contrast, she herself *does separate* language from the world, the linguistic from the non-linguistic, in order to achieve their reunification in art and philosophy. She writes that 'we are truth-seekers on that familiar everyday (transcendental) edge where language continually struggles with an encountered world. In this activity we are like, or are, artists.'[42] This struggle also implies that the individual person is a 'presence' in the world, and this leads to a second point of difference from Derrida.

---

35. Niklas Forsberg, '"Taking the Linguistic Method Seriously". On Iris Murdoch on Language and Linguistic Philosophy', in Browning, *Murdoch on Truth and Love*, pp. 109–32 (127–9), points out that Murdoch also tests against concrete particulars the concepts to which words direct us.

36. Murdoch, *Metaphysics*, p. 490

37. Murdoch, 'Sublime and the Beautiful Revisited', p. 282.

38. Murdoch, *Black Prince*, p. xviii.

39. See Murdoch, *Metaphysics*, pp. 489–91.

40. Derrida, *Of Grammatology*, p. 7.

41. Jacques Derrida, 'Afterward: Toward an Ethic of Discussion', in *Limited Inc.* (trans. Samuel Weber) (Evanston: Northwestern University Press, 1988), pp. 111–54 (148). Cf. Derrida, *Speech and Phenomena*, p. 36: following Husserl, no clear boundary can be drawn between the linguistic and non-linguistic.

42. Murdoch, *Metaphysics*, p. 211.

Second, then, Murdoch rightly discerns that Derrida regards writing – or the network of signs – as prior to speaking. This is because Derrida is reacting against the view that 'being' consists in 'being present', or 'presence', and that the fuller the presence the more beingful something or someone is.[43] This seems to him to lead to the attempt of the self to *assert* its presence and so to dominate the world and others, and a key way of imposing presence is by our direct speech.[44] He does not, as Murdoch implies, deny the presence of the subject altogether, but rather the pretension of achieving 'full presence'; there can only be a flickering of presence and absence. Murdoch understands him to be attempting to suppress the 'localized talk of individual speakers' by making writing prior, and so she insists with Plato on the priority of living speech. This seems to her to preserve the freedom of the individual, what she calls the centrality of the 'moral and rational mastery of our individual being' as well as the primacy of presence to a 'non-linguistic world'.[45]

She writes, ' "Speech" here must be extended to cover, not only audible utterance but all our awareness and reflections. They are primary. We speak to ourselves. "Writing" codifies and makes available what originates in and what returns to individual minds and voices. The original bases of our life are in spoken encounter.'[46] This observation may explain why a large amount of Murdoch's novels consists of conversation, sometimes without naming the speakers, leaving us to guess who they are just as we might listen in on a conversation across a crowded room. Soliloquy or 'speaking to ourselves' also plays a large part in the novels. Derrida's point, of course, is that all speech – even internalized speech – depends on signs, and these belong to a vast network that might be called 'primal writing'. What he is opposing is the idea that human subjects can exist before or beyond the sign, and imagine that they are merely using words as tools or counters at their complete disposal. In his work *Plato's Pharmacy* he thus identifies Plato's attack on writing as the source of western 'logocentrism', in which a transcendent Good, a transcendental signified, legitimizes in turn a human speaking subject who stands behind the sign and manipulates it.[47]

While Derrida should not therefore be seen as altogether dispensing with the subject, there is admittedly a difference of *emphasis* here between Murdoch and Derrida – the one stressing individual freedom, and the other the involvement of the self in a system of signs that transcends the individual. *The Black Prince*, as we shall see, mocks Bradley as the kind of artist who cannot bear direct face-to-face encounter and personal speaking and who is comfortable only with writing. However, it does also show up the problems with conversation as well.

43. Derrida, *Positions*, p. 26. Cf. Derrida, *Grammatology*, pp. 9–10, 143.
44. See Derrida, *Speech and Phenomena*, pp. 50–2.
45. Murdoch, *Metaphysics*, p. 213. On Plato and speech, see *Metaphysics*, pp. 18–24.
46. Ibid., p. 213.
47. Jacques Derrida, 'Plato's Pharmacy', in Derrida, *Dissemination* (trans. Barbara Johnson) (Chicago: University of Chicago Press, 1981), pp. 61–171 (75–80). Murdoch comments on this in *Fire and the Sun*, pp. 31–2; see note 2.

Before we move on to set the novel alongside Murdoch's philosophical writing, we should take note once more of Murdoch's own reluctance to consider that she was writing 'philosophical novels'.[48] Indeed, one of her complaints against Derrida is that he brings the style of creative literature into philosophy. She admires the brilliance of his writings as works of literature, but complains that he should not try to present this as philosophy.[49] However, we cannot quite follow Murdoch in the separation she is setting up. In this very chapter, when discussing (and dismissing) the view that nothing lies beneath the network of meaning set up by words, she remarks: 'See a philosophical discussion of these matters in my first novel, *Under the Net*.'[50] The chapter on Derrida discusses structuralism both as a philosophical idea *and* as a form of art. Thus, in this chapter Murdoch complains that philosophical systems in their 'totalities' fail to recognize contingency, while the plots of most of her novels precisely turn at some key point on the failure to respect contingency, or on the successful attention to some contingent detail of life.[51] This looks remarkably like dramatizing a philosophical idea.[52]

The Black Prince: *Contingency and coherence*

Turning to *The Black Prince*, we find precisely the encounter between language and contingency, the testing of the quest for coherence against everyday things and accidental events that Murdoch outlines in her chapter in *Metaphysics as a Guide to Morals*.

The novel is the story of a frustrated novelist, Bradley Pearce, who published two novels in his earlier years but has now suffered a writer's block for two decades. At the age of fifty-eight he is still in search of the great ideal, the work of art that will perfectly present truth and beauty. He declares himself to be a 'Puritan', working in a highly disciplined way at creating art which comes from 'endless restraint and silence' (26). He prides himself on the fact that 'I have never tried to please

---

48. E.g. see Murdoch's conversation with John Haffenden, *Novelists in Interview*, pp. 191–209.

49. Murdoch, *Metaphysics*, pp. 197, 290–1.

50. Ibid., p. 187.

51. See Nicol, 'Philosophy's Dangerous Pupil', p. 591. Like me, Nicol brings Murdoch's account of Derrida into interaction with a novel (in his case *The Philosopher's Pupil*), but his purpose is different from mine; he aims to examine the relation between philosophy and literature in Murdoch's writings. See further above, p. 4.

52. Patricia Waugh, 'Iris Murdoch and the Two Cultures: Science, Philosophy and the Novel', in Rowe and Horner, *Iris Murdoch: Texts and Contexts*, pp. 33–58 (48), argues that Murdoch wanted the novel to 'contribute to the picture of the fully human', as part of an idealist aesthetics. Altorf, *Iris Murdoch*, p. 117, claims that Murdoch writes her novels as a philosopher, expressing metaphysical regret about the discrepancy between the messiness of contingency and the structuring of thought by a novelist.

at the expense of truth'; he admires the 'saints of art' who 'have simply waited mutely all their lives rather than profane the purity of a single page with anything less than what is perfectly appropriate and beautiful' (xii). Thus he shows aspects of F. H. *Bradley*, perhaps his namesake, in his painstaking effort at finding the coherence that will draw all the pieces together. He also shows touches of *Sartre* in regarding the consciousness as the exercise of the freedom of the will (154–5),[53] in finding that the accidents of life create anxiety and a sense of absurdity (149), and in feeling keenly that how we are regarded by others is unbearable (156–7). When Bradley throws away a remark with the tag 'some clever person (probably a Frenchman) has said', this is instantly recognizable as Sartre (127). Finally, Bradley shows echoes of *Derrida* in exalting writing above direct speech. He is not good at personal conversation with others, as becomes painfully clear in the love scenes in which he engage. He reflects:

> I am, I must confess, an obsessive and superstitious letter-writer. When I am troubled I will write any long letter rather than make a telephone call. This is perhaps because I invest letters with magical power ... A letter is a barrier, a reprieve, a charm against the world, an almost infallible method of acting at a distance (And, it must be admitted, of passing the buck.) (37–8)

He is proud of his skill in letter writing, but a recipient of one of these letters, Arnold Baffin, dismisses it as 'that funny letter you wrote me'.

What is common to all these three strands in Bradley's persona is that they are about avoidance of the contingent world, insulation from the messy details of everyday life. Bradley is holding language, his written words, at a great distance from what he calls the 'horror' of the world (xviii, 80, 187, 298). He is not checking the quest for the ideal against external reality. He falls under the condemnation that Murdoch levels against Derrida, Sartre and F. H. Bradley. On the other hand, there is his fellow writer and rival, Arnold Baffin, who is an enormously popular novelist. Once Bradley's protégé, he is now the one who is famous, finding it easy to write, pouring out a torrent of novels that Bradley considers, fastidiously, to be mediocre and untruthful. He shows the opposite tendency to Bradley; he embraces the contingency of the world, being fascinated by all its details and particularly by the details of other people's lives to whom he listens avidly, but has little sense of the ideal of truth which language is meant to embody. When he tells Bradley that 'what makes a writer' is 'knowing the details', Bradley rebukes him: 'Why pile up a jumble of details? Art isn't the reproduction of oddments out of life' (26). Bradley knows that it is the power of imagination to bring together the ideal and the details, but cannot achieve this himself. Later Bradley reflects:

---

53. See Jean-Paul Sartre, *Being and Nothingness* (trans. H. Barnes) (London: Methuen, 1959), p. 461; Murdoch, *Metaphysics*, pp. 154–5.

> I think I objected to [Arnold] most because he was such a gabbler. He wrote very carelessly of course. But the gabble was not just casual and slipshod, it was an aspect of what one might call his 'metaphysic'. Arnold was always trying, as it were, to take over the world by emptying himself over it like scented bath water. This wide Catholic imperialism was quite alien to my own much more exacting idea of art as the condensing and refining of a conception almost to nothing. (152)

Against this contrast, the plot of the novel unfolds, as told by the narrator, Bradley. It begins with Arnold in a panic summoning Bradley to come to his house, because he thinks he might have killed his wife Rachel in a marital fight. He hasn't. Later Bradley toys with the idea of an affair with Rachel as a way of releasing his trapped creative urges, but this comes to nothing much, though she seems willing. He does fall, desperately and obsessively, in love with the Baffins' twenty-year-old daughter, Julian, for which the catalyst is a tutorial on Shakespeare's *Hamlet*. Fleeing together to a seaside cottage, Bradley succeeds in consummating his passion only when Julian dresses up as the prince. Shortly afterwards they are quickly discovered by Arnold who is of course implacably hostile to the match between them. Julian returns to London during the night, for a reason we will come to in a moment. Bradley follows and fails to find her, but in a matching end-piece to the beginning he is summoned by Rachel to come to her house because she thinks she may have killed *Arnold* in a fight. She has (at least in Bradley's version of the event). Bradley is accused of the crime, stands trial and ends in prison where he dies. Other strands in the plot involve Bradley's sister Priscilla, who has fallen apart mentally and physically in the middle of a messy divorce and whom he fails to support. There is also his former wife Christian, who has returned to London after the death of her second husband and who is still showing interest in Bradley; it is her affair with Arnold Baffin that prompts the murderous attack on him by Rachel. The rich tapestry of the novel is also woven through by threads from *Hamlet*.

Love, art and the detail of the world

If the novel dramatizes the tension between the search for coherence and the test of contingency, it also dramatizes Murdoch's conviction that love can be a means of releasing the person from the self-enclosed cage of the self, and of turning the person outwards to notice the details of the world and the reality of others. Love is thus the essence of art: 'They were, I knew, from the same source,' reflects Bradley (172). Art in its 'thinginess' as an object of attention[54] can, like love, liberate the self. This duality between love and art, which can also be experienced as a dark and imperious force threatening the self (the 'Black Prince'), is summed

---

54. See Murdoch, 'Salvation by Words', pp. 237–8; Murdoch, 'Sublime and the Good', pp. 215–16, 219.

up mythologically in the god Apollo, who appears in the mysterious persona of the supposed editor of the book, P. Loxias. Loxias-Apollo is presented as the companion who comes to know and comfort Bradley in his last days in prison and whom he addresses as his dearest friend. In a rare burst of self-interpretation, Murdoch has said that Bradley at the end can be seen as a minor artist whom the god rewards and comforts for his patient zeal and longing.[55] Love, the novel tells us, produces loss of the self in both life and art, and so the lower eros sets the devotee on the road to the higher eros, or the Good. So Bradley reflects:

> Love brings with it a vision of selflessness. How right Plato was to think that, embracing a lovely boy, he was on the road to the Good ... Ah, even once, to will another rather than oneself! Why should we not make of this revelation a lever by which to lift the world? (174)

Bradley however, as he confesses in his narrative, did not get far enough on the road to the Good. Struck by the lightning bolt of eros, he makes a beginning in trying to be kind to others, and especially to notice the needs of Priscilla. But he recognizes that this was a *false* loss of self in contemplation of the image of the beloved, a kind of fantasy love-religion (205). He comes quickly to a more Sartrean regret ('some Frenchman said...') that 'in love part of oneself has been ... stolen' and to an anxiety about the power of the loved one over him (207). Similarly, he dislikes music because 'it can get at me, it can torment' (216), and it is ironic that he makes his declaration of love to Julian after being sick during a performance of a Strauss opera. (In his last days in prison Loxias teaches him to love music.) The critical exchange between Bradley and Julian, after Bradley has vomited over the Covent Garden strawberries, can be read as making clear that Bradley cannot talk about his love in the real world, to a real person. Nor can he truly move outside himself to notice the other, for all his efforts. It is the agony of *his* love, the love he owns and possesses that he expresses, not a reciprocal self-giving. Julian protests 'I'm an equal partner in this game' (223) and observes acutely that 'you don't seem to know me at all. Are you sure it's *me* you love? ... You say you love me, but you aren't *interested* in me in the least' (224–5, original emphases).

This painful and hilarious exchange is evidently modelled on the interview between Hamlet and Ophelia, which Julian again points out, quoting 'to a nunnery go and quickly too. Farewell' (227). It is summed up in an amusing moment when Bradley tells her: 'I feel a lot of things. Some of them were expressed by Marvell' (234). Once again writing trumps speaking. Another way of reading the interview is that Bradley is manipulating Julian, protesting that *she* cannot truly love *him* as a way of getting her to declare that she does. But on any reading, there is no true loss of self, no real encounter with the challenge of contingency.

---

55. Murdoch in personal conversation with Peter Conradi, as reported in Conradi, *Saint and the Artist*, p. 239.

This same failure lies at the heart of Bradley's final loss of Julian. She does all she can to get him to bring his ideal of love into contact with the mundane details of life. She shows him tokens of contingency – the bread, toothpaste and dustpan she has bought for their stay in the cottage. She throws herself from the moving car to jolt him out of abstract flights of speculation about their love; as he reflects later, it was the 'demons of abstraction in protest against which she had hurled herself' (268). But he still fails. He receives a telephone call from London informing him that his sister Priscilla has committed suicide and omits to tell Julian in case she insists (as she would) on returning to London immediately, and their union would not be consummated. He reflects that:

> Of course I was stricken with guilt and horror at my unforgivable failure to keep my dear sister alive. But as I drove along I was also employed in minute calculations about the immediate future. I was perhaps absurdly influenced by the idea that it was a pure accident, a mere contingent by-product of my carelessness, that Francis had known where to find me. And if that terrible telephone call had been so little determined, so casually caused, it made it seem that less real, that much easier to obliterate from history. I was scarcely distorting the real course of events at all. It had, because it so absolutely needn't and shouldn't have occurred, but a very shadowy existence. (278)

In an attempt to be what he calls 'faithful to the visitation' of the god of love, this contingent event has no reality at all. There are other solid tokens of contingency in the novel whose impact he also fails to acknowledge: there is the little brass buffalo-lady figurine which keeps appearing at critical moments, the gilt snuff box and especially the stones on the beach by the holiday cottage that Bradley and Julian collect and lay out carefully on the lawn: the stones 'varied immensely in colour [...] it was like being in a huge art gallery and being told to help oneself' (268). Stones, we have noticed, appear constantly on the landscapes of Murdoch's novels, as instances of contingency, hard and separate things in their own right which share a 'thinginess' or quasi-sensuous objectivity with works of art. Characters often marvel at the myriad of pebbles upon the beach, each different from the other; Charles Arrowby, in *The Sea, The Sea*, is a compulsive collector of stones from the shore: 'The stones, so close-textured, so variously decorated, so individual, so handy, pleased me as if they were a small harmless tribe which I had discovered.'[56] For Bradley, the telephone call is the contingent event that brings the most critical challenge, among all others, to his enclosed self. Dismissing it as a detail with 'very shadowy existence', he loses Julian who is horrified by this evidence of his lack of care for his sister. She is also, we should say, shocked by another detail he has suppressed: he is fifty-eight rather than the forty-six years he had confessed to her.

---

56. Murdoch, *The Sea, The Sea*, p. 242.

Voice and writing: Undermining Murdoch's own thesis

Let us return finally to the differences between Murdoch and Derrida. Are they illuminated by this novel? I will not delay long here on pointing out the Derridean style of 'deconstruction' which she herself indulges in here, by giving us a narrative with a foreword and postscript by the supposed editor, Loxias; a foreword and postscript by Bradley; and then postscripts by four of the characters in the story who give us their own perspective on the events and speculate on the identity of Loxias. Bradley in his narrative has finally produced the book he has been labouring all his life to create, but it is open to endless reinterpretation as, he admits, are his favourite kind of writings, letters; he reflects, as Derrida does on all texts, 'What dangerous machines letters are ... a letter can be endlessly re-read and reinterpreted, it stirs imagination and fantasy, it persists' (150).[57] We might also say generally that the novel supports the Derridean integration of philosophy and literature; Murdoch is herself engaged here in the mixing of genres that she overtly rejects. But my greater interest is in the relation between writing and speech and whether one can be prior to the other. This connects with the other issue I identified earlier, about whether the contingent reality that language encounters is non-linguistic.

I suggest, tentatively, that despite Murdoch's own philosophical statements, the novel itself shows the danger of giving either writing or speech priority over the other. Whether or not the novel directly has Derrida in mind, it tends to support the Derridean conviction that the world is inseparable from signs and so undermines Murdoch's own later critique of Derrida. This, in fact, seems to be the implication of Bradley's exegesis of Hamlet in the ill-fated tutorial with Julian, which comes across with force and conviction. He declares that:

> [Shakespeare] has performed a supreme creative feat, a work endlessly reflecting on itself, not discursively but in its very substance, a Chinese box of words as high as the tower of Babel, a meditation upon the bottomless trickery of consciousness and the redemptive role of words in the lives of those without identity, that is human beings. *Hamlet* is words, and so is Hamlet. He is as witty as Jesus Christ, but whereas Christ speaks Hamlet is speech. He is the tormented empty sinful consciousness of man seared by the bright light of art, the god's flayed victim dancing the dance of creation. The cry of anguish is obscure because it is overheard. It is the eloquence of direct speech, it is *oratio recta* not *oratio obliqua*. But it is not addressed to us. Shakespeare is passionately exposing himself to the ground and author of his being ... *Hamlet* is a wild act of audacity, a self-purging, a complete self-castigation in the presence of the god. Is Shakespeare a masochist? Of course ... [but] because love has here invented

---

57. Pamela Osborn, 'Minding the Gap: Mourning in the Work of Murdoch and Derrida', in Rowe and Horner, *Iris Murdoch: Texts and Contexts*, pp. 110–28, argues that Murdoch uses deconstructionist techniques in several novels to deal with the issue of mourning.

language as if for the first time, he can change pain into poetry ... What redeems us is that speech is ultimately divine. What part does every actor want to play? Hamlet. (164)

In this rhapsodical speech, Murdoch presents tragedy as *speech* or *speaking*, the direct speech of the victim being flayed by the god, caught within the complexities of particular relationships and confronted by the horrors of a contingent world: as Bradley says, 'It is the eloquence of direct speech, it is *oratio recta*.' And yet Hamlet's speech is, stresses Bradley, not addressed to us. So it is not the 'local speech', the making present of one individual self to another that Murdoch celebrates in her *Metaphysics*.[58] It is finally 'divine speech' and is rooted in 'the author of being'. And it comes to us as written text, vulnerable to endless reinterpretation, as (Bradley says) 'a work endlessly reflecting on itself ... a Chinese box of words'. This is also how we receive Bradley's speech, in a written work which also has the form of a Chinese box. Neither writing nor speaking seems to have simple priority here. Murdoch's description of what she calls 'speaking' in this passage is not after all far from Derrida's actual understanding of *archi-écriture*.

Hamlet is central to the novel, though Murdoch warns us herself that Hamlet is not the 'Black Prince' of the title.[59] Earlier on Bradley has accepted a Freudian psychoanalysis of the play, that Hamlet wanted to kill his father to possess his mother sexually, and that all his sense of guilt and hesitation flows from this situation.[60] Variations are played on this Oedipal triangle throughout the novel, echoed in the relations between Julian and her father and (in recollection) between Bradley and his parents. In an absurdly self-advertising postscript, Francis Marloe even applies it to the relation between Bradley and Arnold ('Of course,' he pontificates, 'Arnold Baffin is a father-figure' [348]). But Bradley mentions and accepts the Freudian exposition of Hamlet only to dismiss it as of little significance, preferring a neo-platonic reading. 'Did Shakespeare hate his father?' asks Bradley, replying, 'Of course. Was he in love with his mother? Of course. But this is only the beginning of what he is telling us about himself' (163). The tangles of the lower eros that Freud discloses lead us on to the higher eros of desire for the Good, which requires a painful loss of the self, or 'unselfing'. This *ascesis* is the agonizing experience of Hamlet and, at the same time, of Shakespeare himself.

Here Murdoch has been powerfully affected by the Greek myth of the flaying alive of the musician Marsyas by the god Apollo, and by the neoplatonist use of the image as portraying a divinely inspired *ascesis*, the opening of the soul beyond the

---

58. Murdoch, *Metaphysics*, pp. 192–3.

59. Michael Bellamy, 'An Interview with Iris Murdoch', *Contemporary Literature* 18 (1977), pp. 129–40.

60. This interpretation was first promoted by Freud's disciple, Ernest Jones, in *Hamlet and Oedipus* (London: Gollancz, 1949). However, Richard Todd, in 'The Plausibility of the Black Prince', *Dutch Quarterly* (1978), pp. 82–93, maintains that it is difficult to identify Bradley with Hamlet on the grounds of an Oedipal theme.

shadows of the outer bodily self to the One or the Good beyond Being.[61] Hamlet, and Shakespeare with him, is (Bradley comments) the 'flayed victim ... exposing himself to the author of his being'. Apollo, the Black Prince[62] who presides over love and the arts, appears in the novel as the mysterious P. Loxias, editor of Bradley's book and his final friend. In *her* postscript, Rachel makes the reference clear, writing: 'The name conceals the identity of a notorious rapist and murderer, a well-known musical virtuoso, whose murder, by a peculiarly horrible method, of a successful fellow-musician made the headlines some considerable time ago' (355). Like Hamlet and Shakespeare, Bradley undergoes a purging and a flaying and finally opens himself to the Good. Everyone, as he comments, wants to play Hamlet and he certainly gets the chance to do so.

In her earlier essays on the relation between the beautiful and the good, Murdoch finds a convergence between beauty, art, love and morality; what unites them is paying attention to what is other than the self, in an attentiveness which is shaped by noticing the contingent details of the world.[63] Shakespearean tragedy, she suggests, gives us a sense of the 'sublime' – the boundless – because it presents us with the multiplicity of contingent things in the world and sets us in the midst of a host of differing relationships, without any hope that we can encompass the whole or bring it into harmony.[64] Tragic art is disturbing because its self-contained form comes into conflict with something which defies form – the particularity of individual beings and things. This tragic incompleteness does, however, have the power to turn us away from self and towards the good. What Bradley calls 'divine speech' in his rhapsody on Shakespeare contains includes both speaking and writing, both direct address and text which is endlessly open to meaning, a kind of speech which – despite Murdoch's rejection of Derrida – actually reflects his *archi-écriture*. If Murdoch were closely following her *Metaphysics* chapter, she would presumably envisage Shakespeare as testing out his search for the Good against a *non-linguistic* 'real world'; but in fact the sense we receive from her portrayal of Hamlet's changing pain into poetry is of a self in a world which is never devoid of language. In this portrayal of the self in the agonizing 'dance' (164) of creation, there is no hint of a non-linguistic reality.

---

61. So also in *Fairly Honourable Defeat*, 41; cf. Murdoch, *Severed Head*, p. 42.

62. Murdoch identifies Apollo both as the God of Art and the Black Eros in Jean-Louis Chevalier (ed.), *Recontres avec Iris Murdoch* (Centre de Recherches de Littérature et Linguistique des Pays de Langue Anglaise, Université de Caen, 1978), pp. 73–93; see Conradi, *Saint and the Artist*, p. 238. On the relation between erotic love and attending to the other, see Martha Nussbaum, '"Faint with Secret Knowledge": Love and Vision in Murdoch's *The Black Prince*', in Justin Broackes (ed.), *Iris Murdoch, Philosopher* (Oxford: Oxford University Press, 2011), pp. 135–54.

63. Murdoch, 'Sublime and the Good', pp. 215–16; 'Sublime and the Beautiful Revisited', pp. 282–3.

64. Murdoch, 'Sublime and the Good', pp. 217–20.

Attending to the other: A theological horizon

The point is thus not to contrast the 'verbal sign' with the 'thing', to test language against a world without signs, but to detect the way that signs *in* the world, in all their particularity, open us to 'the god' (Good) who comes (Murdoch) or, as Derrida says, to 'what comes in'.

In his essay 'Of an Apocalyptic Tone Newly Adopted in Philosophy' (1983), available to Murdoch when writing her chapter on Derrida, though not mentioned by her, Derrida reflects on the appeal to 'come' which resonates through the *Revelation* of St John the Divine. At the beginning of the book, he notes, we are presented with the one who 'comes' (Revelation 1:8); Christ warns that he will come unexpectedly (3:3); and the book ends with the invitation 'Come' issued by the Spirit and the bride, to which the visionary responds 'Come, Lord Jesus' (22:17–20).[65] We may add that the invitation to 'come' accompanies the opening of the first four of the seven seals (Revelation 6:1–8), the showing of the judgement of the Great Harlot (17:1) and the showing of the bride of the Lamb in the heavenly Jerusalem (21:9). The very repetition underlines that this is a coming that 'is always to come'.[66] The text shows the multivalency of meaning that a deconstructive critic finds in all texts, since – according to Derrida's exegesis – it is unclear to the reader who the speaker or author of the invitation is. Throughout the text Derrida finds a 'differential multiplication of messages', a complex interaction of narrative voices and narrating voice so that one is often not clear who speaks or writes or who addresses what to whom.[67] There is an interlacing of 'narrative sending', which Derrida evidently identifies as an open series of signifiers and signified. 'Come' cannot be made into an object to be examined or categorized: it points to an absent place which is not described, and it is addressed to recipients who are not identified in advance. 'Come' is the apocalyptic tone itself, 'the apocalypse of the apocalypse', without message, without messengers, without senders or destinations.[68]

It points, Derrida suggests, to an event of 'coming' (*venir*) which is an 'event of the other', a 'breaking out' into the open in which the cry 'come' (*viens*) is for something new that shatters the horizon of sameness and challenges us with the need for justice. Far from the supremacy of a linguistic monism, the apocalyptic plea 'come' points to a place and a time which cannot be contained by philosophy, metaphysics or dogmatic theology. This coming is an *in-venir*, an in-coming or an 'invention of the other' which cannot be objectified and possessed and which is always 'yet to come'.[69] In *Psyche: Inventions of the Other*, to which Murdoch *does*

---

65. Jacques Derrida, 'Of an Apocalyptic Tone Newly Adopted in Philosophy' (trans. J. Leavey), in Harold Coward and Toby Foshay (eds), *Derrida and Negative Theology* (Albany: State University of New York Press, 1992), pp. 25–72 (54, 64).

66. Ibid., p. 54.

67. Ibid., pp. 54–6.

68. Ibid., pp. 65–7.

69. See also Jacques Derrida, *Parages* (Paris: Galilée, 1987), p. 66.

briefly refer as 'a headlong commentary on everything and everybody',[70] Derrida affirms that deconstruction is prompted by the arrival (*venue*) of what is coming (*à-venir*) as the 'altogether other' (*tout autre*),[71] and that 'in the language of the same, the other can come'.[72]

John Caputo, in a book on Derrida aptly subtitled *Religion without Religion*, identifies this coming of the other as a 'quasi-transcendence'. For Derrida, he asserts, *différance* does a 'quasi-transcendental work' in ensuring that no beliefs, practices or institutions 'effect closure', keeping them open 'so that something new or different may happen'.[73] Derrida denies he is doing 'negative theology', since he thinks that even that kind of theology finally affirms a 'super-essential being' floating free from the world of signs.[74] The advent of the other is to be distinguished, Derrida says, from a 'theological order', by which he means an 'ontotheology'[75] in which God establishes a pregiven order of things where the only 'invention' (*in-venir*) is for us to 'discover' it, where we can only fill in the details to a predetermined scheme and where 'nothing comes to the other or from the other'.[76] That is the kind of transcendence he rejects, as I suggested at the beginning of this chapter. However, theology should not, I suggest, be interested in such a God either, but in a creator who enables what is created to be itself genuinely creative. Reading both Derrida and Murdoch on the many contingent things which alert us to the Good (Murdoch) or to 'what comes in' (Derrida) should prompt a theology in which God is eternally committed to the particularity of a world of signs, and – as I have already suggested – the symbol of the Trinity can express the holding of such a world within the space generated by the interweaving of divine relations of love.[77] Indeed, a theologian may say that signs are shaped by participation of matter within the triune movement of self-giving relations which mutually signify and are signified.[78] Derrida himself regards the symbol of the Trinity as a circular, harmonious rhythm of 'suffocating closure', but – as Robert

---

70. Murdoch, *Metaphysics*, p. 291.

71. Jacques Derrida, *Psyché: L'Inventions de L'Autre* (Paris: Galilée, 1987), p. 55.

72. Ibid., pp. 35, 160–1.

73. John D. Caputo. *The Prayers and Tears of Jacques Derrida: Religion without Religion* (Bloomington: Indiana University Press, 1997), p. 12.

74. Derrida, 'How to Avoid Speaking. Denials', in Coward and Foshay, *Derrida and Negative Theology*, pp. 73–142 (120).

75. As used by Derrida, following Heidegger, 'ontotheology' means equating god as a Supreme Being (a projection of existent beings) with Being itself, or with the first principle and ground of all reality. See Derrida, 'Différance', p. 6; Martin Heidegger, 'The Onto-theo-logical Constitution of Metaphysics', in Heidegger, *Identity and Difference* (trans. J. Stambaugh) (Chicago: Chicago University Press, 2002), pp. 42–76 (58).

76. Derrida, 'Psyché', p. 60.

77. See earlier, pp. 74–5.

78. For a more detailed account, see Fiddes, *Seeing the World*, pp. 164–5.

Magliola argues – Derrida could take more seriously the symbol of the Trinity as expressing 'différence' – differentiated relations which are always open to others.[79]

Reading Derrida and Murdoch should then bring the Christian theologian to conceive of an immanent transcendence which does not point to another reality altogether, but to an inexhaustibility within the reality in which we live, where the divine 'altogether other' can only be known *within* finite others while not being constricted by them. This actualizes the language of the theologian Hans Urs von Balthasar that with God there is 'excess' or 'always more'.[80] In an alternating movement of dialogue, this then can offer a theological horizon within which we can see that Murdoch and Derrida are closer to each other than Murdoch imagines. Both conceive of actually *encountering* a transcendent (or 'quasi-transcendent') other through attending to the many contingent 'others' which operate as signs. Certainly, Derrida has no place for Murdoch's Platonic form of the Good, but for Murdoch this unity of the Good can only be known through its scattered fragments.[81] It is thus possible to serve the Good, and while there can be no reward of relating to it personally, there is a kind of Derridean event of a 'coming', or encounter, because the Good is known through beauty, and we 'can *experience* the transcendence of the beautiful'.[82] Thus the many beautiful objects in the world can become entrances to the one Good.

It has, to be sure, been suggested that Derrida's orientation to the 'event of the other' is an assault of the negative sublime on the beautiful, a total overthrowing of the plenitude of particularities which appear in the world in favour of a primordial 'difference' that does not itself appear.[83] I considered this critique in a previous chapter and observed that such an assault would indeed be different from Murdoch's concern for an attention to otherness in mundane things and persons which direct our attention to the Good (though we can never possess it), so that the sublime is *in* the beautiful.[84] It would also have to be opposed by Christian theology which asserts that it is possible to participate in the infinite through the excessive and overflowing beauty of the world.[85] However, this judgement misses a tension in Derrida. The unrepresentable which unsettles all representations can never be *separated* from the contingent signs of the world.

For Derrida, the 'other which comes' cannot be simply classified as either inside language or outside it,[86] but comes 'as the other in the language of the same'. So,

---

79. Robert Magliola, *Derrida on the Mend* (West Lafayette: Purdue University Press, 1984), pp. 134–5.

80. Hans Urs vonBalthasar, *Theo-Logic: Theological Logical Theory, Vol. I: The Truth of the World* (trans. Adrian J. Walker) (San Francisco: Ignatius Press, 2000), p. 142.

81. See earlier, pp. 59–61.

82. Murdoch, *Sovereignty of Good*, p. 60 (original emphasis).

83. Hart, *Beauty*, pp. 52–6; cf. Milbank, *Theology and Social Theory*, pp. 100–10, 306–13.

84. See earlier, pp. 84–5, 112–13.

85. Hart, *Beauty*, pp. 17–20, 90–2.

86. See Derrida, *Limited Inc.*, pp. 152–3; Derrida, 'Of an Apocalyptic Tone', p. 67.

while 'the coming is always to come', Derrida maintains in his exegesis of the *Book of Revelation* that this coming is also 'the *present* of a to-come' and is 'in the process of coming'.[87] He concludes with a flourish, 'I tell you this, that's what's happening.'[88] A theological perspective helps us to perceive this coming of the transcendent other in both Murdoch and Derrida, while at the same time the attention to the many others in both Derrida and Murdoch disturbs any dogmatic complacency within theology itself.

---

87. Derrida, 'Of an Apocalyptic Tone', pp. 54–5.
88. Ibid., p. 67.

Chapter 6

THE VOID AND THE PASSION: A DIALOGUE WITH SIMONE WEIL

Iris Murdoch and Simone Weil: An enigma

Yes, Simone Weil helped me very much. I can't recall just when I discovered her – probably in the late 1950s. My copy of *La source grecque* is dated by me January 1961. She came to me somehow through France. I have almost all her works in French.

So Iris Murdoch wrote in a letter of 13 January 1992 to her future biographer, Peter Conradi.[1] It is a curious recollection and not one that he himself refers to in his subsequent *Iris Murdoch: A Life*. The curiosity is that Murdoch was evidently familiar with the work of Iris Murdoch much earlier than 'the late 1950s'. Conradi himself *appears* to imply that Murdoch read Weil's *The Need for Roots* and *Gravity and Grace* during her period in Cambridge in 1947–8, since he mentions her reading both of these books in the middle of his passages about her life in Cambridge, but his location of the reference to them at that point in the biography is probably misleading.[2] The editors of Murdoch's *Letters 1934–1995* explicitly state (without giving evidence) that Murdoch 'first came across Weil's work at Cambridge in 1947',[3] but this is unlikely to be the case. *The Need for Roots* (*L'Enracinement*) was not published in French until 1949,[4] and *Waiting on God* (*Attente de Dieu*) in 1950.[5] *Gravity and Grace* (*La Pesanteur et la Grâce*) was, it

---

1. Horner and Rowe, *Living on Paper*, p. 572. Murdoch's Oxford library contains her annotated copy of *La Source Grecque* (Paris: Gallimard, 1953; IML 943).

2. Conradi, *Iris Murdoch*, p. 260, writes that 'she before long found in Simone Weil's *Need for Roots* and *Gravity and Grace* ... a way of thinking that put decentring and displacement at the centre'.

3. Horner and Rowe, *Living on Paper*, p. 625.

4. Paris: Éditions Gallimard. This is the edition owned and annotated by Murdoch (IML 942).

5. Paris: Éditions Gallimard. The unannotated French edition present in Murdoch's Oxford library (IML 468) is dated 1957, published by Éditions La Colombe. Her annotated copy of the English translation, IML 1102, is the first edition, Simone Weil, *Waiting on God* (trans. Emma Craufurd) (London: Routledge and Kegan Paul, 1951).

is true, first published in French in 1947, but her own copy is missing from her library which is now preserved at Kingston University.

Murdoch does record in 1951 that she had read *La Pesanteur et la Grâce* in a library copy,[6] and so it is not impossible she read it this way on first publication in 1947. However, it is more likely that Murdoch began reading Weil in 1950–1. She notes in her journal for 23 September 1951 that she would not call Weil 'romantic', as she would Sartre.[7] On 18 October 1951 she gave a BBC Third Programme radio talk on Simone Weil, essentially a review of *Waiting on God* which had just been published in its first English edition; in the talk she shows not only a detailed knowledge of the book under review but also of *Gravity and Grace*, and an awareness of *The Need for Roots*, which she calls 'a really thrilling piece of political thinking'.[8] One of her pupils, Jennifer Dawson, recalls that she urged her students to read *Waiting on God* in 1951.[9] Moreover, when A. S. Byatt sent her a typescript of her book on Murdoch's early novels, *Degrees of Freedom*, asking for comment in about 1964, Murdoch 'pointed out that I should have read Simone Weil'.[10] The first three novels, in which Byatt subsequently noted strong affinities with Weil, were published between 1954 and 1957, and of course in each case were written somewhat earlier.

All this is at odds with Murdoch's statement in 1992 that she 'probably' discovered Weil in 'the late 50s'. Perhaps even more startling was a letter she wrote as early as 1968 to an American student of her work, in which she informs him: 'About Simone Weil: I don't myself think that *The Bell* is deeply influenced by her and I'm not even quite sure that I had read her at that time. I had certainly not studied her, as I did later. (And later novels *are* influenced by her.)'[11] *The Bell* was published in 1958, presumably written during 1957, and in *The Spectator* for November 1956, Murdoch had written a highly perceptive review article – 'Knowing the Void' – which greets with enthusiasm the appearance of Weil's *Notebooks* in English and in which she refers to her knowledge of the 'previously published selection' from the complete *Notebooks*, which were in fact the pieces in *Gravity and Grace*.[12] It seems odd, to say the least, that Murdoch was not sure whether she had 'read' Weil at the time she was writing *The Bell*.

---

6. Iris Murdoch, '"Waiting on God": A Radio Talk on Simone Weil (1951), with a Prefatory Note by Justin Broackes', *Iris Murdoch Review* (2017), pp. 9–16 (16).

7. According to Conradi, *Iris Murdoch*, p. 270. Conradi (p. 270) also notes that she wrote in her copy of Weil's *Intuitions Pré-Chrétiennes* (Paris: Editions La Colombe, 1951; IML 941) the highly significant note 'Virtue is knowledge/ is attention', but her actual possession of the volume cannot be dated to 1951.

8. Murdoch, 'Waiting on God', p. 16.

9. Conradi, *Iris Murdoch*, p. 299.

10. Byatt, *Degrees of Freedom*, p. x.

11. Horner and Rowe, *Living on Paper*, p. 372.

12. Murdoch, 'Knowing the Void', p. 157.

There is an enigma here, in which we cannot discount an element of sheer forgetfulness. It is understandable how, in a busy professional and artistic life, Murdoch could have forgotten a radio broadcast nearly two decades earlier. In advising Byatt about her 'early' novels, Murdoch may have had in her own mind novels after *The Bell*, as, for example, *The Unicorn* (1963), while Byatt subsequently applied the advice to the earliest novels as well. Further, Justin Broackes draws attention to the exact wording of her comment in the letter of 1968, that she had not 'studied' Weil until after writing *The Bell*, and suggests that the concentrated attention she gave to Weil after 1957 might have left her with the impression that this was the period when she first became acquainted with her; it would, after all, have been easy to be confused about the date of her review of the *Notebooks* – late 1956, 1957 or early 1958? Broackes points out that from the late 1950s she was supervising a graduate student, Miklós Vetö, who finally produced a DPhil thesis (1964) on 'The Ethics of Simone Weil', and that she would have engaged in intense work on Weil with him.[13]

Perhaps most perceptively, Broackes suggests that there is a difference between Murdoch's first reception of Weil in the early 1950s and the way that she 'reworked and transformed' ideas of Weil in the 1960s, especially in *The Sovereignty of Good*. He thus proposes that the change, equivalent to a new discovery, was not so much in her 'understanding' of Weil 'but in what she could do with that understanding'.[14] It may be significant, I suggest, that the copy of *Attente de Dieu* (French) in Murdoch's Oxford library carries the publication date of 1957,[15] whereas her annotated copy of the English translation, *Waiting on God*, is the first edition of 1951; it is from the English edition that she quotes in her broadcast talk of October 1951, while she quotes directly from the French text of *Gravity and Grace* (*La Pesanteur et la Grâce*). It might be that she only acquired the French edition of *Attente de Dieu* when she began to give Weil more sustained study from 1957.[16]

I want to comment later on Broackes's own proposal about what Murdoch 'did' later with Weil. I will have my own suggestion about what Murdoch found she could 'do' with Weil, and these shifts of approach to Weil may go a long way towards explaining why Murdoch thought she had not become familiar with Weil until the 'late 1950s'. To this, I think that we must add another factor: there may have been such a deep absorption of Weil's general ideas in Murdoch's mind – notably the need to give 'attention' to others and to the world, to which I have constantly referred in the preceding chapters of this present book – that Murdoch simply counted them as her own and no longer recognized them as

---

13. Justin Broackes, 'Iris Murdoch's First Encounters with Simone Weil', *Iris Murdoch Review* (2017), pp. 17–20 (18).

14. Ibid., p. 19; for Murdoch's adaptation of Weil, see also Justin Broackes, 'Introduction', in Broackes (ed.), *Iris Murdoch, Philosopher*, pp. 1–89 (19–20).

15. Éditions La Colombe; IML 468.

16. However, she could have possessed an earlier copy which has gone astray; oddly the 1957 French volume bears no annotations.

being in (and from) Weil at all. This is, unfortunately, a common phenomenon among authors accused of incorporating the ideas and vocabulary of others into their work. She indeed seems to have had the hazy feeling, even in denying a reading of Weil before the 'late 1950s', that her acquaintance with her goes back much further; in a journal entry in 1968 she asks herself, 'Have I come to the end of the path which started many years ago when I first read Simone Weil and saw a far off light in the forest?'[17] The expression 'many years ago' hardly fits a mere decade.

It is appropriate, then, to explore Murdoch's dialogue with Weil from 1951 to 1958, despite her own (mis-)recollections, as well as her later well-acknowledged dialogue from 1958 onwards, and to seek to identify the shifts in her use of Weil. I intend to reflect on Weilian themes as they appear in an early novel, during that period which later seems to have been a Weilian-shaped blank in Murdoch's mind, and as they reappear in a late novel. I have chosen Murdoch's second published novel (perhaps written before the first), *The Flight from the Enchanter* (1956), and her penultimate novel, *The Green Knight* (1993). As the penultimate chapter in my own book, this study will enhance some of the themes I have already considered and steer discussion of 'Murdoch and the Others' to a conclusion.

Affliction, gravity and attention: An early talk

In her broadcast talk on Simone Weil in 1951, Murdoch acutely summarizes Weil's thought about human life as being an integration between the three elements of 'affliction', 'gravity' and 'attention'. The first, *Malheur*, is – as Murdoch discerns it in Weil – 'the main fact of human life, and the fact from which we must not flinch if we are to find out any truth about it.'[18] For Weil, 'affliction' is a more severe state than suffering in its intensity and extent, while it never occurs without suffering and pain. It is an 'uprooting of life' and affects a person's life in all its dimensions:

> There is not real affliction unless the event which has seized and uprooted a life attacks it, directly and indirectly, in all its parts, psychological and physical. The social factor is essential. There is not really affliction where there is not social degradation or the fear of its in some form or another.[19]

Weil thus associates affliction particularly with the displacement of people by war from the environment where they have their 'roots', in a situation where 'the innocent, are killed, tortured, driven from their country, made destitute or reduced to slavery, imprisoned in camps or cells'.[20] She surveys this kind of affliction in

---

17. According to Conradi, *Iris Murdoch*, p. 501.
18. Murdoch, 'Waiting on God', p. 11.
19. Weil, *Waiting on God*, p. 64
20. Ibid., p. 65.

The Need for Roots (*L'Enracinement*), written in 1943 in response to a request by the Free French in London to write about the possibilities of bringing about the regeneration of France, and the circumstances of forced migration can be seen reflected in Murdoch's first two novels. However, affliction is a universal human state and is promoted by what Weil identifies as 'gravity'. As Murdoch summarizes in her broadcast: 'The dualism is between *La Pesanteur* and *La Grâce* – gravity, this is gravitational force, and grace. All natural phenomena, including psychological phenomena are subject to "gravity".'[21] Weil explains that 'we must always expect things to happen in conformity with the laws of gravity unless there is supernatural intervention'.[22]

Weil is diagnosing a force composed of social conditions, human sin, the negative reaction of others to a person's suffering and the self-regarding ego which drags a person down into an experience of 'emptiness' or 'the void': 'Grace fills empty spaces but it can only enter where there is a void to receive it … Void: the dark night.'[23] In her 1951 broadcast, Murdoch does not use the precise term 'the void', though the word is to occupy a key place in her thinking from at least 1956 onwards. In giving an account of Weil here she speaks only of 'the realm of gravity', which is felt as the 'purposeless' nature of things. For Weil, no human will or action can counteract this gravity and release from the void. Vainly we try to fill the void with acts of imagination, especially looking for imaginary compensations or rewards for our suffering and affliction; we even 'invent a God who smiles on us'.[24] As Murdoch comments, we indulge in 'the unreal life of soothing expectation, in which are to be included the so called "consolations of religion"'.[25] Weil sees this as the continual work of the ego, in which each person constructs an illusionary world around themselves, a phenomenon which is universal, whether or not somebody is afflicted:

> Just as God, being outside the universe, is at the same time the centre, so each man imagines he is situated in the centre of the world. The illusion of perspective places him at the centre of space; an illusion of the same kind falsifies his idea of time; and yet another kindred illusion arranges a whole hierarchy of values around him … We relegate the spatial form of this illusion to the place where it belongs, the realm of the imagination.[26]

---

21. Murdoch, 'Waiting on God', p. 11.
22. Weil, *Gravity and Grace*, p. 1; cf. Simone Weil, *The Need for Roots: Prelude to a Declaration of Duties towards Mankind* (trans. Arthur Wills) (repr., London: Routledge, 2002), pp. 289–90. Only the French edition of *The Need for Roots* is present in Murdoch's Oxford library as preserved at Kingston University (IML 942).
23. Weil, *Gravity and Grace*, p. 10.
24. Ibid., p. 9.
25. Murdoch, 'Waiting on God', p. 11. On consolation, see above p. 25.
26. Weil, *Waiting on God*, p. 98. For world-creation in Murdoch, see above pp. 9–10.

We can only escape our imaginary world, which is in fact 'emptiness', when the void is filled by grace, the counterpoint to gravity. The soul has to go on simply enduring the void, loving in the emptiness, or at least wanting to love, maintaining an orientation to the God who is apparently absent. In Murdoch's summary, 'In the very act of our loving acceptance of the realm of gravity, we have left it for the realm of grace.' It is, Murdoch explains, to 'accept the reign of necessity obediently, as being itself a manifestation of obedience to God, and attempt to love God even here'.[27] We should add that, for Weil, it is *possible* to love in the void because a supernatural love has already been implanted in human beings by the creator. This is an intrinsically 'selfless' love, and the self-regarding love of the ego is just another 'illusion'; in fact, a longing for the absolute Good is always there at the centre of the human heart.[28] The ego must thus be 'decreated' – a term later adopted by Murdoch[29] – allowing it to pass into the divine realm of the 'uncreated',[30] in order to remove the blockage to this inherent power of love.

This love is nothing other than giving 'attention'. In Weil's words, 'attention is bound up with desire. Not with the will but with desire ... the attention turned with love towards God'.[31] In Murdoch's summary again, 'To open ourselves to the operation of grace requires an exercise of attention. This image of *waiting* is a favourite one of Simone Weil's.'[32] In the void, rejecting illusions, we are to attend to God and to others, waiting for and noticing them. Murdoch here compares Weil's view of academic studies, in which – in Murdoch's paraphrase – 'one has to learn a certain way of not being too active, a way of concentrating which consists, not of pushing and straining, but of waiting upon the truth'. Murdoch then cites Weil's conclusion: 'That is why every time we really concentrate our attention we destroy the evil in ourselves.'[33] This destruction, notes Murdoch, 'is not brought about by any violence of the will'.

In her study of *Sartre: Romantic Realist*, published in 1953, Murdoch will shortly reject as solipsistic his notion of the individual as a free agent, determining his or her self-development by acts of the will, and (while she does not mention Weil), this is in tune with what she discerns in Weil here. In her later work, Murdoch is to stress that will should always be modified by 'a sustained attention to reality'.[34] Already in *Sartre*, Murdoch recalls that the hero of his novel *La Nausée*, Roquentin, discovers, as he picks up a pebble on the seashore, that 'the world is contingent', and

27. Murdoch, 'Waiting on God', p. 11.
28. Weil, *Gravity and Grace*, p. 53; cf. Weil, 'Draft for a Statement of Human Obligations' (1943), in Siân Miles (ed.), *Simone Weil: An Anthology* (London: Penguin, 2005), pp. 221–30 (222).
29. Murdoch, *Metaphysics*, pp. 140, 352, 354.
30. Weil, *Gravity and Grace*, p. 28.
31. Ibid., p. 107.
32. Murdoch, 'Waiting on God', p. 11, original emphasis.
33. Ibid.; Weil, *Waiting on God*, p. 56. Later, see Murdoch, *Metaphysics*, p. 505.
34. Murdoch, *Sovereignty of Good*, p. 40.

she quotes the question of Gabriel Marcel, 'Why ... does Sartre find the contingent over-abundance of the world nauseating rather than glorious?'[35] Her answer is that Roquentin has no sense of being *pour autrui*, for the other,[36] but, in accord with Sartre's philosophy, is attempting to achieve a wilful 'self-contemplative stability' (*being en-soi*) over against the other, especially the other who has consciousness of oneself.[37] In a later new preface to her *Sartre* (1987), she pictures 'knowledge as an attentive truthful patience with the contingent, where the latter is not a hostile Other to be overcome, but more like an ordinary world-round-about-us.'[38] While she credits Theodor Adorno for this perception about 'attentive truthful patience', she might as well have referenced Weil.

Continuing her account of affliction and the void, which is an acute instance of Weil's more general psychology of the human being, Weil finds that to an attentive spirit, God will reveal the beauty of the world. The spirit will be given objects of attention, things of beauty in creation to contemplate, which will increase a hesitant love and enable an escape from the void, releasing the imprisoned person from the dark shadows of Plato's cave into light:

> What is terrible is that if, in this darkness where there is nothing to love, the soul ceases to love, God's absence becomes final. The soul has to go on loving in the emptiness ... Then one day, God will come to show himself to this soul, and to reveal the beauty of the world to it.

Following Plato, Weil associates the beautiful with the good. Paying attention to contingent things of beauty in the world and in art is a kind of obedience to the 'order' in creation, and so by this means is obedience to God. She writes that 'the subject of art is sensible and contingent beauty discerned through the network of chance and evil'; that the beautiful in nature 'captivates the flesh in order to obtain permission to pass right to the soul'; that 'the beautiful is that which we can contemplate ... something on which we can fix our attention'; and that 'the attitude of looking and waiting is the attitude which corresponds with the beautiful'.[39] Murdoch comments that for Weil the attempt to love God in the void 'will extend our apprehension of the order of the world as something which is in itself beautiful'[40] and portrays Weil as thinking that 'religion ... is essentially a matter of looking'. She draws the conclusion that 'this is also why good, like the object of artistic inspiration, always surprises us'.[41] This seems to be the first perception by

---

35. Murdoch, *Sartre* (1953, repr. 1967), p. 21.
36. Ibid., p. 16.
37. Ibid., pp. 88, 92.
38. Iris Murdoch, *Sartre, Romantic Rationalist* (London: Chatto & Windus, 2nd edn, 1987), p. 36. She repeats this criticism of Sartre in *Metaphysics*, p. 186.
39. Weil, *Gravity and Grace*, pp. 135–6.
40. Murdoch, 'Waiting on God', p. 11. On Plato's cave in Murdoch, see above p. 10.
41. Ibid., p. 12.

Murdoch that, as she puts it in the later lecture 'Knowing the Void' (1956), 'There is a theory of art implicit here,' going on to quote Weil the effect that 'all art is religious'.[42] This is quite a long time before her famous dictum that attending to good art 'can be like praying'.[43] Weil, indeed, had declared that 'absolutely unmixed attention is prayer'.[44]

In this broadcast talk we can thus already find a bundle of ideas from Weil that will play a prominent part in Murdoch's writings, and quite early on – as we shall see – in the novel *The Flight from the Enchanter*: affliction, illusion, attention. Murdoch commends Weil at the moment where her own earlier enchantment by Sartre's philosophy was fading: 'No existentialist could excel her in picturing the pointlessness of the natural world – and yet, how she has transformed this idea! She makes of it a picture of obedience, a form of beauty, something which can command our love.'[45] In this perceptive account, there are, nevertheless, elements of Weil that make her 'uneasy' and from which she wants to part company, as she will throughout her writing career.

First of all, Murdoch finds that Weil undermines the particularity of the human person. She charges Weil with 'seem[ing] to be attaching a supreme degree of reality to an order which is … completely independent of the particular mind', so that 'the higher part of the soul appears to be impersonal'. Weil, she complains, in her desire for self-effacement before God 'seems to offer a picture which is austere to the point of deleting the human person altogether'. This is characterized by a view of love in which the human person simply becomes an impersonal conduit for selfless divine love ('the only real actor here is God')[46] and in which the counter-movements of gravity and grace are simply what Murdoch calls an 'automatic operation'.[47] As well as 'automatic',[48] Weil even more frequently uses the word 'mechanical' or 'mechanism' for these necessary processes[49] and shows that human persons are caught in the mechanism; she evidently feels that both

---

42. Murdoch, 'Knowing the Void', p. 158. Weil, *Gravity and Grace*, p. 137, writes 'all art of the highest order is religious in essence'.

43. Murdoch, *Fire and the Sun*, pp. 76–7; cf. Murdoch, *Sovereignty of Good*, p. 75.

44. Weil, *Gravity and Grace*, p. 106.

45. Murdoch, 'Waiting on God', p. 13.

46. Weil, *Waiting on God*, p. 92. The same view of love is urged by Søren Kierkegaard, *Works of Love* (trans. H. V. Hong and E. H. Hong) (Princeton: Princeton University Press, 1955), pp. 303–4, and more strongly by Anders Nygren, *Agape and Eros* (trans. Philip Watson) (London: SPCK, 1982), pp. 129, 735.

47. For these quotations, see Murdoch, 'Waiting on God', pp. 13–14.

48. See Weil, *Roots*, pp. 28, 43, 240, 267, for 'automatic' social, psychological and spiritual processes; also Weil, *Waiting on God*, pp. 67 ('as automatic as gravity'), 88, 95, 107, 123, 134.

49. See, e.g., Weil, *Roots*, pp. 11, 29, 94, 112, 123, 124, 187, 208, 210, 230, 261, 264, 286, for social, psychological and spiritual mechanisms; also Weil, *Waiting on God*, pp. 69, 71, 72, 73, 85, 99. Murdoch draws attention to Weil's imagery of the mechanical in her *Metaphysics*, p. 503, and the image is widespread in her novels.

'automatic' and 'mechanical' are suitable metaphors for the industrial age of the machine. Murdoch lists Weil's 'notion of the hardness of truth and its automatic operation upon the mind' among features that are 'both repellent and attractive about her, but concludes in the end that 'her idea of the operation of truth is too simple'.[50] For instance, while recognizing that the imagination busily manufactures illusory compensations to avoid admitting the blackness of affliction, Murdoch protests that 'one simply cannot say that the realm of imagination is the realm of delusion' and that the contemplation of beauty is 'untouched by the imagination'. Murdoch thus judges that 'her model for the spiritual life is not the particular human bond, it is the life of the intellect'.[51] Yet Weil, Murdoch suggests, was also 'too impatient with what one might call the intellectual state of soul'.[52] Weil sees the person as an individual thinker, but in Murdoch's view she restricts the work of the intellect to 'waiting upon truth in order to accept it'. For Murdoch 'intellectual work is not only attention – it is also setting the stage for attention'.[53] In these ways Murdoch wants to enhance our apprehension of the human person.[54]

Despite her critique, as Murdoch develops her own thought, it appears to absorb some of Weil's impersonality. God (who is, for Weil, both personal and impersonal)[55] is to be replaced by the impersonal Good; the 'fat, relentless ego' must be suppressed;[56] and the self must be 'decreated'[57] and stripped for attention to others. As her character Effingham Cooper faces physical death in a bog, he learns that 'with the death of the self the world becomes quite automatically the object of a perfect love'.[58] The word 'automatically' seems odd, until we recall that this was Murdoch's characterization of Weil's 'impersonal' operation of truth on the mind, echoing Weil's own use, such as in the following statement:

> Supernatural love, which is obedience, is that which in us answers to the will of God. We have to be indifferent both to good and evil; but whilst remaining indifferent, that is to say, whilst bringing the light of the attention to bear equally on the one and on the other good prevails as a result of an *automatic* mechanism. This represents the essential form of grace.[59]

---

50. Murdoch, 'Waiting on God', p. 15.
51. For these quotations, see ibid., pp. 14–15.
52. Murdoch, 'Waiting on God', p. 16
53. Ibid., p. 15.
54. Later, see Murdoch, *Metaphysics*, p. 439: 'What is absolute and unconditional is what each man clearly and distinctly know in his own soul.'
55. Weil, *Notebooks*, p. 173
56. Murdoch, *Sovereignty of Good*, p. 52.
57. Murdoch, *Metaphysics*, pp. 140, 352, 354.
58. Murdoch, *The Unicorn*, p. 198; 'automatically' is repeated, pp. 203–4. See my discussion earlier, pp. 94–5.
59. Weil, *Notebooks*, p. 303; Weil, *Gravity and Grace*, p. 107, my emphasis.

However, we must take seriously Murdoch's early dissent from Weil over impersonality. This lends weight to the suggestion that, while in Weil nothing seems left of the self after the exercise of loving attention, in Murdoch it is only the self-centred *ego* (as in Freud) that needs to be put to death. As Julia Meszaros has maintained, rather than denying the reality of the self in general, in her mature thought Murdoch only denies the self with which we commonly identify, that which bestows on the human being – in Murdoch's words – 'a comforting sense of a unified self, with organised emotions and fearless world-dominating intelligence, a complete experience in a limited whole'.[60] Meszaros comments that 'it is this fantastical, self-contained and selfish "ego" which Murdoch would seem to have in mind when she writes that "the self, the place where we live, is a place of illusion".'[61] It is this illusory self that must be 'suppressed' or even die.[62] Murdoch envisages the self as 'a substantial and continuing developing mechanism of attachments'.[63] Thus, while the self is not unified in itself (this Murdoch learned from Freud), there is nevertheless something 'substantial' about it, as a project for self-becoming – this much Murdoch learned from Sartre while rejecting his isolationism. It appears that Murdoch views the human self as flourishing when it is 'attached' to the transcendent Good, when the ego which mechanically makes attachments for its own survival has been decreated or put to death, and this process is in accord with Plato's view of the 'highest part' of the soul which is 'rational and good and knows the truth which lies behind all images and hypotheses'.[64] Nevertheless, Murdoch's treatment of the self remains strangely elusive, and Sabina Lovibond is surely right to discern a continuing tension between the 'death of selfish desire' and 'the conversion of such desire' into a higher form.[65] Perhaps we can find a signpost for interpretation of the later work in Murdoch's early broadcast, where we find expressed a greater unease with Weil's 'decreation'.

In a second major critique, Murdoch in this broadcast is uneasy about Weil's rejection of social institutions. Weil declares that 'rootedness lies in something other than the social',[66] and Murdoch judges that for Weil 'the world of purposes and actions, of human planning' along with all political parties – in short, the area of ideology – is committed to the realm of the illusion-making imagination.[67] Murdoch wants to defend the making of 'theory' as a work of the intellect, as making

---

60. Julia Meszaros, *Selfless Love and Human Flourishing in Paul Tillich and Iris Murdoch* (Oxford: Oxford University Press. 2016), p. 139, citing Murdoch, *Metaphysics*, p. 88.

61. Meszaros, *Selfless Love*, p. 139, citing Murdoch, *Sovereignty of Good*, p. 91, cf. p. 63.

62. Murdoch, 'Sublime and the Good', p. 218.

63. Murdoch, *Sovereignty of Good*, p. 69.

64. Murdoch, *Fire and the Sun*, pp. 4–5. My interpretation here is based on Meszaros, *Selfless Love*, pp. 140–2.

65. Sabina Lovibond, *Iris Murdoch, Gender and Philosophy* (London: Routledge, 2011), p. 127.

66. Weil, *Gravity and Grace*, p. 149.

67. Murdoch, 'Waiting on God', p. 14.

attention possible, and 'this is why institutions and ideologies are important'.[68] Weil regards thinking only as an individual matter (within the limits described above) and is deeply suspicious of any claims to collective thinking: 'Intelligence resides solely in the human being, individually considered. There is no such thing as a collective exercise of intelligence.' Weil continues dismissively that 'it follows that no group can legitimately claim freedom of expression, because no group has the slightest need of it'.[69] Trades unions can, in her view, associate to protect the interests of their members, under supervision of the authorities, but must not formulate ideas.[70] Good social order, in Weil's view, consists in obedience within a hierarchy, at every stage of which everyone recognizes their 'obligations' to relieve fellow human beings of distress and deprivation.[71] In her later work, Murdoch continues – in effect – to dissent from Weil, being much less anxious about the collective creation of political and social axioms, or theory which is constructed socially; she prefers to encourage a healthy conflict between different axioms, as a way of deterring slavish adherence to any ideology: 'Political liberalism is pluralism, the cost must always be counted, and there are different ways of counting.'[72]

This very pluralism will, however, mean a suspicion of any model of society 'as a whole', which can come curiously close to Weil's view without her particular reasons for it. In her late work Murdoch actually quotes Weil in allocating the state to the powers of darkness, in a passage paraphrasing Hobbes's theory of sovereignty but which seems written sympathetically.[73] Beginning 'The whole cannot be saved. Society must be thought of as a bad job to be made the best of,' she continues citing Weil: 'The social domain is unreservedly that of the Prince of this World. We have but one duty in regard to the social element, which is to try to mitigate the evil therein.'[74] Murdoch shows most affinity with Weil's suspicion of organized society, however, in reacting strongly against any philosophy which seems to her to make social structures ontologically *prior* to the individual subject. This results in her lumping together a whole range of philosophies: structuralism, post-structuralism, deconstruction, modernism and postmodernism, with Derrida as the figurehead.[75]

---

68. Ibid., p. 15.

69. Weil, *Roots*, p. 26.

70. Ibid., pp. 28–9.

71. Ibid., p. 3: 'The notion of obligation comes before that of rights, which is subordinate and relative to the former'; cf. p. 19.

72. Murdoch, *Metaphysics*, p. 368; cf. pp. 355–7, 364–9.

73. Lovibond, *Iris Murdoch*, p. 35, simply takes this as Murdoch's point of view, as also in Lovibond, 'Iris Murdoch and the Quality of Consciousness', in Browning, *Murdoch on Love and Truth*, pp. 43–62 (57–8).

74. Murdoch, *Metaphysics*, p. 368; citing Weil, *Notebooks*, p. 296; also Weil, *Gravity and Grace*, p. 145.

75. Murdoch, *Metaphysics*, p. 185.

The common thread she finds in all these approaches, without sufficiently teasing out their differences, is their supposition that the individual is essentially formed by an environment of language and other social systems which exists ahead of them. I have already commented in a previous chapter on Murdoch's critique of Derrida, as manifested in the novel *The Black Prince*, but the suspicion of investment in language as a social tool already appears in Murdoch's first published novel, *Under the Net*. The title alludes to the 'net' of discourse in Wittgenstein's *Tractatus* (6.341),[76] which is necessary to identify and describe the particular details of the world, but which also conceals their reality. This means that all language and the 'theory' which weaves the net must be provisional. The saint-like character Hugo thus protests that 'there's something fishy about describing people's feelings', because 'things are falsified from the start'. Indeed, when we try describing any object in the world, 'the language just won't let you present it as it really was'.[77] Working up his conversations with Hugo into an artistic dialogue, the anti-hero, Jake, has one character, Annandine, declare that 'all theorizing is flight. We must be ruled by the situation itself and this is unutterably particular'.[78] Ironically, Jake himself is portrayed in contrast to Hugo as a notorious liar who seems, amusingly, unable to speak the truth. The novel ends with Hugo's retirement from business to become a watchmaker, to 'make little intricate things with my hands'. When Jake desperately enquires, 'What about the truth?,' Hugo replies, 'What more do you want? ... God is a task. God is a detail. It all lies close to your hand.'[79]

The influence of Wittgenstein on this novel has frequently been commented upon,[80] but we can also find traces of Murdoch's initial brush with Weil. In her broadcast talk Murdoch defended, against Weil, the creation of 'theory' by social intercourse and consent, and in the novel we can see at least a moderation of Weil's rejection of social thinking. In Jake's dialogue his character Annandine expresses an ambivalence about this: 'It is true that theories may often be a part of a situation that one has to contend with. But then all sorts of obvious lies and fantasies may be part of such a situation.'[81] Weil's image of the processes of life as a 'machine' finds its way into the text, as Hugo remarks that 'the whole language is a machine for making falsehoods'.[82] Other resonances with Weil are apparent too. There is Hugo's love of what is real in the contingent details of the world and the attention he gives to them: Jake recalls that 'for Hugo each thing was astonishing, delightful, complicated and mysterious. During these conversations I began to see the whole

---

76. Murdoch quotes from *Tractatus* 6.41 in her *Sartre* (1953, repr. 1967), p. 65, on the 'accidental' nature of being.

77. Murdoch, *Under the Net*, pp. 66–7.

78. Ibid., p. 92.

79. Ibid., 259–60.

80. E.g. Lovibond, *Iris Murdoch*, p. 50; Leeson, *Iris Murdoch: Philosophical Novelist*, pp. 23–4.

81. Murdoch, *Under the Net*, p. 92.

82. Ibid., p. 68.

world anew.'[83] We recall Weil's commendation of detachment – 'to detach ourselves from all good things and to wait'[84] – when Jake notes that Hugo 'was the most purely objective and detached person I had ever met'.[85] However, like Murdoch's response to Weil's embrace of impersonality, Murdoch's reaction against Weil's rejection of all social structures seems more raw, less nuanced, in her broadcast than in her subsequent work, including this novel.

Early reception of Weil: The Flight from the Enchanter

Murdoch's second published novel, *The Flight from the Enchanter*, shows, even more clearly than in the first, her increasingly nuanced reception of Weil. The context is overtly Weilian, with a number of the key characters suffering displacement from their roots and a consequent *malheur*. Murdoch says in her broadcast talk of 1951 that Weil 'moves us precisely because of the way that she has taken the impact upon herself of the particular extremities of the present time: the age of the factory worker, the D.P. [Displaced Person]'.[86] Weil herself voluntarily became a D.P. when she lost her own roots by moving from Nazi-occupied France to England in 1942; she chose to become a factory worker under harsh conditions in Ashford, Kent, in 1943 and finally died of tuberculosis in 1943 after virtually starving herself in sympathy with what she imagined the conditions of her fellow-countrypeople in France to be. The central figure in the novel, Rosa Keepe, has voluntarily become a factory worker despite having a small private income, because – says her brother, Hunter, gloomily – 'she wants to be in touch with the People'.[87] He attributes it to being named after Rosa Luxemburg by their (deceased) suffragette mother, but shades of Weil are hovering; Rosa does not, however, notably resemble Weil, apart – perhaps – for allowing the rhythm of the machine she works at to fill her body and for attempting to draw some 'harmonious or repetitive pattern' from the mechanical process (44).

Three of the characters are technically D.P.s. Mischa Fox, a sinister magnate possessing great power and riches who wants to repeat a previous 'enchantment' over Rosa, is a refugee from a mid-European country, as was Hugo in the previous novel. The two Lusiewicz brothers, Stefan and Jan, who graduate out of the enslaved group of machine-minders into the technical staff at Rosa's factory, and who share Rosa as their joint-lover (under increasing harassment from them), are refugees from Poland. Nina, a skilful dressmaker, who survives under the patronage of Mischa and eventually fails to survive through fear of deportation, is from another Eastern European country. Further, the youthful Annette Cockeyne, though living

---

83. Ibid., p. 66.
84. Weil, *Gravity and Grace*, p. 13.
85. Murdoch, *Under the Net*, p. 64.
86. Murdoch, 'Waiting on God', p. 16.
87. Iris Murdoch, *The Flight from the Enchanter* (London: Chatto & Windus, 1956), p. 16.

temporarily with Rosa while attending a finishing school, is effectively displaced, living a life of travelling from one country to another with her brilliant and wealthy parents as a 'cosmopolitan ragamuffin' and calling herself a 'refugee' (8, 271).

Contributing to this context of displacement, John Rainborough, a friend of Rosa and her family, is a former civil servant who now works in a government organization for administering the entry of refugees into the country – SELIB. The plot of the novel actually turns on the issue of refugees and displacement, since Mischa, at the request of Rosa, uses his influence to get the House of Commons to activate a policy decision of SELIB that refugees should only be settled in England if they come from a country west of a line arbitrarily drawn through the map of Europe. This achieves the desired end of causing the Lusiewicz brothers to disappear and so remove themselves (especially the oppressive and threatening Stefan) from her life. It also wreaks the collateral damage of prompting Nina to take her life, fearing deportation to a country where she has no roots any longer, and feeling now 'a soul without a nationality, a soul without a home' (289). Conradi points out that an earlier draft of the novel was even more far-reaching in its treatment of displacement, also making Rosa and the saint-like character Peter Saward refugees.[88]

While the setting of the novel picks up Weil's concern with the affliction created by displacement, it also draws on Murdoch's own experience of working for the United Nations Relief and Rehabilitation Administration from 1944 to 1946. In January 1946 she writes, 'God! So few people in this great relief organisation can make any imaginative effort to understand what the displaced person problem really is.'[89] Later that year she worked in Graz in the Hochsteingasse Displaced Persons camp for students,[90] from which she writes expressing her affection for those she has left behind in England: 'On these occasions I feel a sort of I-and-Thouish warmth and am no longer in the desert.'[91]

Describing the organization of SELIB, Rainborough reflects that 'the realm represented by the Board resembled Renaissance Italy in its profusion of lively independent centres … Each department showed a vigorous sense of its own autonomy, which it often carried to the point of ignoring completely the existence of the other departments' (93). Labour was rendered void 'by an entire lack of liaison between one department and another' (94). In the reference to 'Renaissance Italy' there is a remarkable resonance here with Weil's account in *The Need for*

---

88. Conradi, *Saint and the Artist*, p. 65.

89. Murdoch to David Hicks, 25 January 1946, in Peter J. Conradi, *Iris Murdoch: A Writer at War: Letters and Diaries 1939–45* (London: Short Books, 2010), p. 287.

90. This had been set up by the British Allied military government for students who had been accepted at the University of Graz.

91. Murdoch to Raymond Queneau, 2 June 1946, in Horner and Rowe, *Living on Paper*, p. 73; this oblique reference demonstrates that she had read Buber's book *I and Thou*. Also see her passing reference to Buber a few months earlier, Horner and Rowe, *Living on Paper*, p. 69.

Roots of the structure of the state in 'the second half of the Renaissance'; Weil diagnoses at that point the loss of a sense of overall purpose and 'method'[92] in public activities which makes for the spiritual health of the soul, and thinks that 'since then [these activities] have never been visualized in this light, but solely as a means of establishing a particular form of power regarded as desirable for one reason or another'.[93] For Weil, the overarching purpose is not an ideology but a recognition, within a fixed hierarchy of obedience, of mutual *obligations* between people, resting on a respect which derives from the eternal destiny of all human beings. Murdoch may well be agreeing with Weil's insistence on the need for an overall vision of reality, in which even the maintenance of industrial machinery requires 'a definite notion of mechanical relationships'.[94] But, as in the broadcast of 1951, she does not entirely follow Weil in her suspicion of modern institutions. Rainborough has a nostalgia for his old civil service job, in which 'an age-old hierarchy, ancient values and hallowed modes of procedure reduced to a minimum the naked conflict of personalities' (94). This description of hierarchy could have come directly from Weil's *The Need for Roots*, where Weil writes:

> Hierarchism is a vital need of the human soul. It is composed of a certain veneration, a certain devotion towards superiors, considered not as individuals, nor in relation to the powers they hold, but as symbols. What they symbolize is that realm situated high above all men and whose expression in this world is made up of the obligations owed by each man to his fellow-men ... The effect of true hierarchism is to bring each one to fit himself morally into the place he occupies.[95]

But Rainborough's desire for hierarchy is portrayed ironically and as one of the causes for his utterly ineffective activity. He is shortly to be swept aside by his own personal assistant, Miss Casement, one of a new, ambitious breed of women who are appointed as 'Organizing Officers' by the mysterious 'Establishment'. She aims, it transpires, both to get his job and to get him into marriage. While the rise to supremacy of these 'beautiful adventurers' over the old order is also depicted ironically, as the kind of desire for power deprecated by Weil, Murdoch seems to register her approval of the exercise of liberal values over established social hierarchy by the place she allots in the novel to a journal called *Artemis*. Part-owned by Rosa, managed by her brother, Hunter, this failing enterprise is what survives of a feminist magazine founded by their mother. Mischa Fox is to be thwarted in his attempt to buy it by a hilarious meeting of aged women shareholders who once shared the ideals of Rosa's suffragette and militantly socialist mother, and who now band together, chaotically and absurdly, to protect it from a rapacious man. The

92. Weil, *Roots*, p. 186.
93. Ibid., pp. 187–8.
94. Ibid., p. 187.
95. Ibid., p. 19.

dead mother represents, suggests Byatt, the generation of liberal thinkers which Murdoch celebrates in her essay 'Against Dryness'.[96] It is unclear why Mischa wants to take it over this 'wretched' journal into his print empire, but it is probably because it remains an independent voice, and so it is implied that it stands for the liberal value of pluralism.

The situation of displacement and consequent *malheur* is underlined by the images of machinery, familiar in Weil, which constantly occur as a means of enslavement. Rosa is in servitude to the factory machine she has dubbed 'Kitty', whose face she cannot find and whose song she cannot decipher (44). Misch's brutal 'enforcer', Calvin Blick, attempts to blackmail Hunter into selling *Artemis* by showing him a photograph he has taken, at Mischa's order, of Rosa in the arms of the Lusiewicz brothers; significantly, the disclosure happens in his basement workshop at Mischa's house, a space filled with complex machinery for developing photographs. Miss Casement, as Byatt perceptively points out,[97] uses the enticement of a machine to temporarily trap Rainborough into engagement – Rainborough wonders why he asked her to marry him, 'and the thought came to him that what had really happened in that moment was that he had become engaged to Miss Casement's red M.G.' (269). Most vividly, Nina has a dream in which her sewing machine becomes malevolent, turning into a beast with savage jaws, chasing her through a dark wood, issuing streams of cloth which bind her like a winding sheet.

For Weil, while the physical machines of the age are brutalizing, emphasizing the 'gravity' of *malheur*, there is a spiritual machinery of grace to whose momentum we simply need to submit, and so 'the mechanism of necessity' can be 'transposed' into obedience.[98] Murdoch however, as we have seen, has criticized this process as being *too* 'automatic', using Weil's own word. This critique seems to be continued in the inability of either Rosa or Nina to transpose the rhythms of the machinery into a meaningful pattern; when Nina finally sees the pattern of her enveloping cloth clearly, it 'was a map of all the countries of the world' (149), in none of which she has a home.

With the exception of Nina, all the characters who suffer affliction typify Weil's observation that those afflicted aim to pass on affliction to others,[99] an idea which Murdoch selects as one of Weil's key thoughts.[100] This syndrome takes the form of first attempting to evade *malheur* by constructing an imaginary universe around the self, situating oneself (in Weil's words) 'in the centre of the world'[101] and then imprisoning others in one's own orbit. It is to become the 'enchanter' of the title, of whom the key instance is Mischa, who uses Nina for his own ends, and who wants

---

96. Byatt, *Degrees of Freedom*, p. 52; see Murdoch, 'Against Dryness', pp. 293–5.
97. Byatt, *Degrees of Freedom*, p. 48.
98. Weil, *Waiting on God*, p. 72.
99. See Weil, *Notebooks*, p. 122.
100. Murdoch, 'Knowing the Void', p. 158; the breaking of this pattern is attributed to Hannah, *The Unicorn*, p. 116: see above, p. 92.
101. Weil, *Waiting on God*, p. 98.

to recapture Rosa who has broken free. Paying the rent of Nina's room in Chelsea, as well as an allowance, he has not allowed her to expand her business and requires her to be alone and available to speak privately with him at any hour. She had become convinced 'that she was playing, in the strange economy of Mischa Fox's existence, some quite precise part – though what part that was she would perhaps never know'. She had at first succumbed to what seemed 'great authority' and 'a kind of oriental magic', but was becoming increasingly uncomfortable about his manipulation of her; she had come to imagine that 'perhaps he was keeping her in reserve to play a part in some plot or conspiracy which had not yet matured' (154). It seems to the reader that, lonely himself in his *malheur*, the plot is simply that he wishes to keep someone else in that condition, to 'pass the affliction on' to another. Annette's self-constructed world is much less sinister, but also extends to Nina, who is her dressmaker. Annette 'liked to believe that Nina was always working for her … She must be like a princess for whom all over her realm people toiled night and day to make her trousseau'. The essence of freedom for Annette, comments the narrator, 'was the feeling that someone else was making or doing something for her the fruit of which she would soon enjoy' (82). When Annette and Mischa meet in Nina's room there is a kind of conflict of worlds. He admits that he is 'not famous for anything in particular', but 'just famous', and she responds that she hopes to 'manage that too' (87). When he touches her she springs back 'with a moan', and it seems that they have collided with each other, and that at some point one will need to gain mastery over the other.

In fact, she tries to make him part of her world by trying to 'save him'. After a disastrous party at his grand house, 'he looked so melancholy that Annette … felt, and with it a deep joy, the desire and the power to enfold him, to comfort him, to save him' (215). Later, Murdoch's novels are going to portray a number of such characters, who try to bind others into their universe either by making them a saviour or by trying to be a saviour for another (what Mischa calls 'unicorn' women) (412). Annette's attempt is a miserable failure. Just as he had required Nina to sit with him in isolation, he takes Annette to experience his own *malheur* by facing a stormy sea in the night: 'He was staring at the waves like a man cornered by a strange animal. Terror and fascination were upon his brow' (217). But when she perceives he is giving her no 'attention', she tries to gain control of the situation by running into the sea; as he pulls her out, 'they swayed to and fro upon the stones and the great wave drenched them' (218). Others, in future novels, will also slip on the stones as they fail to cope with the sea. Here, Mischa concludes that Annette is of no use to him and wants nothing more to do with her: 'She had the feeling that he was not looking at her, that he was looking past and through her' (220). Like all enchanters, he does not notice her as she is. The party had already been a disaster because it had failed in its purpose to draw Rosa back into his world, when she had broken his 'magic' spell (208) by the unexpected, arbitrary action of shattering a huge fish bowl, full of costly specimens, by throwing a paperweight. To the stones and the fish we shall return. Blick has the last word to Annette about the crisis at the sea: 'The notion that one can liberate another soul from captivity is an illusion of the very young' (240).

The two Polish brothers also exert an enchantment of a different kind, with their lively talk, their charm and animal spirits; their habitual dance to the student drinking-song *gaudeamus igitur* has the force of a ritual. Rosa, in helping them settle and teaching them English, had regarded them as her own private world, but now finds that she is bound by them in *their* world: 'It was profitless to ask now whether the bond that tied her to them was love. The darkness in which those two held her was profound beyond the reach of names. She could not of her own will break the spell' (110). Finally they occupy the centre of her world by actually taking up residence, in succession, in her own house. They fail to notice her in her own right, any more than they had recognized the existence of the woman teacher in their home village on whom they had taken a sexual revenge for her humiliation of them in school. As Byatt comments, they have 'a dangerous, rootless freedom', and 'only the same kind of rootless power in Mischa can dispose of them'.[102] Grateful to Mischa, Rosa is very nearly dragged back into his self-made world from which she earlier escaped, but is prevented by Blick's revelation to her of two facts: that Mischa had instructed him to take the compromising photograph of her, and that Nina has taken her own life. Commentators usually think that Blick is referring to Rosa when he comments that 'someone ought to have explained matters to her, someone who knew her situation through and through' – since she did not realize that the authorities would almost certainly have made an exception for her. No doubt Rosa is the 'someone', but the 'someone' is even more clearly Mischa, who was the one who put her in what Blick calls a 'peculiarly isolated' position. Rosa recognizes again Mischa's controlling strategy and leaves him to his servant – and self-appointed guardian – Blick, watching him on the beach, staring out to the horizon in his tragic loneliness.

Although Rosa occupies the main line of the story, which ends by her taking up ownership and editorship of *Artemis*, the counterpoise between the nineteen-year-old Annette and the middle-aged Mischa occupies the main thematic interest – one should surely say Weilian interest – of *malheur*, of constructing the world of the self and of the flourishing of the self that is possible through giving attention. Annette survives and grows because she has learned to give attention to other things outside herself, objects of beauty in the world; as Murdoch summarizes Weil in 1956, 'we are helped by meditating on "absurdities which project light"'.[103] Chief among those things are the 'stones' she has collected over the years, which in her privileged case are actually unset jewels; she arranges the selection on view every day, 'sometimes putting them in symmetrical patterns, sometimes laying them out in constellations, and sometimes just scattering them about at random'. She 'looks into the heart' of them (65), and she is the first of Murdoch's characters who find in collecting stones a witness to the hard reality of the world, its 'thinginess', challenging solipsisms. When she tries to make herself the centre of attention in Mischa's sea moment, she slips on the stones of the shingle.

102. Byatt, *Degrees of Freedom*, p. 48.
103. Murdoch, 'Knowing the Void', p. 158, citing Weil, *Notebooks*, p. 454.

When we first meet Annette she is depicted as someone who is always 'looking around' at interesting things (14), and when she travels on a train with her parents towards the end of the book, she 'looked at the world' and was 'absorbed in watching the landscape', observing its contingent detail with wonder – 'a house, a dog, a man on a bicycle, a woman in a field, a distant mountain' (310). These glimpses from a train, their 'green detail', had seemed to her earlier to be indicators of her own lack of roots, as she was unable to 'cross the barrier' into their reality, but now they are transformed into signs of delight. She makes the decisive move when she allows the precious stones their own life, abandoning possessiveness by throwing them away into the Thames (though most are appropriated by Jan, who promptly deserts Stefan). As Murdoch comments in her 1951 broadcast on Weil, for her 'to *know* the world is to recognize the independence of its order', and 'imagination veils us from the sharp independence of things'.[104] We are glad when Annette survives her attempt at suicide, her last throw at drawing others into the machinery of her own world, where 'within her all things lived and moved and had their being' (267).[105] Not yet having learnt the proper 'death' of the self, she determines to make a theatrical death for herself in the middle of a party, placing her at the centre of attention. She is thwarted by mistakenly taking an overdose of milk of magnesia instead of sleeping tablets. One of those at her suicide party is Rainborough, who also seems to be saved from entering the prison of his intended marriage by his capacity to look at the world beyond himself. Earlier he had watched a snail: 'Can it see me? He wondered. Then he felt, how little I know, and how little it is possible to know; and with this thought he experienced a moment of joy' (132).

Mischa Fox also observes the details of the natural world, but without joy, as his policy is to absorb them into himself. Talking with Rainborough, he tells him of noticing a bird with only one foot and directs Rainborough's attention to a moth: 'What a beautiful moth there is over there on the wall … Have you seen it, John?' Later, he confesses to Peter Saward that when he was young he was so full of pity for small, vulnerable animals that he would kill them: 'They were so defenceless. Anything could hurt them … Someone gave a me a little kitten once … and I killed it.' He remembers, 'That was the only way to help it, to save it' (225–6). When Rosa breaks the giant fish bowl, he apparently feels compassion for the fish, but makes no effort to keep them alive. He finishes his session with Saward by enquiring, 'Did Rainborough tell you – about the fish?' (227). Mischa is presented as someone who notices contingent objects and persons of beauty, but does not actually 'attend' to them; he cannot allow them to be 'independent', but in accord with his view of salvation, he must capture them as dead specimens within his world (like the insect he takes in a matchbox to his conversation with Saward) or literally kill them, as he does effectively with Nina. In Blick's last conversation with Rosa, she exclaims, 'I cannot think … why Mischa has not killed you years ago,'

---

104. Murdoch, 'Waiting on God', p. 12, original emphasis.
105. This is a quotation from Acts 17:28, where it applies to God.

and Blick replies softly, 'Mischa did kill me years ago' (306). Rosa concludes that 'in the past I always felt that whether I went towards him or away from him I was only doing his will. But it was all an illusion' (308). This is the lesson Murdoch learnt from Weil, that exerting the will is an illusion, while reality lies in waiting and attention; as she quotes Weil in her review of 1956, 'we should pay attention to such a point that we no longer have the choice'.[106]

Peter Saward, a gentle, saint-like scholar, is in love with Rosa and approaching the end of his life. He gives scrupulous attention to the details of the ancient manuscripts which he is attempting to decipher, but he never thinks he owns them. When, at the end of the story, another scholar discovers the key to unlocking them, he is not sad. Rosa cries out that 'all your work was for nothing', but he only replies 'one reads the signs as best one can' (315). He does not think, with Calvin Blick, that the many ciphers for the solution of Reality are 'all of them right ones' (305). He gives the same attention to 'reading the signs' in other people and never seeks to possess; so when Rosa finally asks 'what would you think of the idea of marrying me?', he deters her with the calm reply, 'you don't really want it. Ah! if only you did, but you don't' (315). He exemplifies not only Weil's theory of attention but also her view of the way that truth in scholarship comes through patient waiting, an attitude commended by Murdoch: something, Murdoch records, 'comes to us out of the dark of non-being, as a reward for loving attention'.[107] Saward would 'remain quiet and receptive, almost in a dream, writing down ideas as they came to him', and what he wrote down would be 'plans for future work, intuitions about present problems, or ... visions of the past' (24). Later he would 'work more systematically' and subject his 'intuitions' to criticism. We recall Weil's reflections on 'the right use of school studies with a view to the love of God' when she writes that 'there is a special way of waiting upon truth, setting our hearts upon it, yet not allowing ourselves to go out in search of it ... a way of waiting, when we are writing, for the right word to come of itself at the end of our pen'.[108] Her *Notebooks* have many references to waiting for moments of intuition in scholarly study, which is a kind of intellectual contemplation superior to discursiveness: 'Moments of pause, of contemplation, of pure intuition, of mental void, of acceptance of the moral void. It is through such moments that [man] is able to approach the supernatural'.[109] The influence of Platonic *anamnesis* ('recollection') is apparent,[110] and Weil also references Bergson. Already, in her early *Lectures in Philosophy* (prepared for a

---

106. Murdoch, 'Knowing the Void', p. 159; citing Weil, *Notebooks*, p. 205.
107. Murdoch, *Metaphysics*, p. 505. See above, p. 160, cf. p. 20.
108. Weil, *Waiting on God*, p. 57.
109. Weil, *Notebooks*, pp. 156; cf. 118, 125, 509, 520, 550.
110. Cf. Murdoch, *Metaphysics*, p. 399. Murdoch seems to have elided Weil's approach to intuition with the 'ethical intuitionism' that she discovered in G. E. Moore's *Principia Ethica* (IML 656, edition of 1903) and which she attempted to revive in the Oxford philosophy of the 1950s: on Murdoch and Moore, see Kerr, 'Back to Plato with Iris Murdoch', pp. 69–71; also Patricia Waugh, 'Iris Murdoch and the Two Cultures', pp. 35–8.

girl's *lycée* in 1933–4), she commends Bergson's conversion of Kant's 'intuition' which is limited to the senses: for Bergson, 'intuition would be knowledge of the hidden workings of the universe'.[111]

The waiting and the passion

In all the ways I have explored, *The Flight from the Enchanter* is full of resonances of Simone Weil, and in particular of those aspects with which Murdoch showed herself intrigued in her broadcast of 1951. It seems that the dissension from Weil that is quite rawly expressed in the talk has become more nuanced. In this novel which – quite exceptionally for Murdoch – deals with a world of public affairs as well as the convoluted relationships within a privileged social class, there no longer appears the defence of institutions and ideology that Murdoch mounts in the talk.[112] Further, with the character of Peter Saward we can detect a little more sympathy with the kind of epistemology that Murdoch dismisses in the broadcast as a 'too simple' idea of the operation of the truth. There is, however, one element of the process of coping with *malheur* that I have not yet considered. Murdoch, I suggest, does not seem to know what to do with it in her earlier work, and so it will give a clue about the nature of Murdoch's rediscovery of Weil in the later 1950s.

In her 1951 talk, introducing *le Malheur* as 'the main fact of human life' for Weil, Murdoch continues immediately: 'For her the centre of Christianity is the passion and the central moment of the passion is the cry of dereliction'[113] – that is, Jesus's cry 'My God, why have you forsaken me'. Murdoch perceives, correctly, how closely associated in Weil's mind are the general human experience of affliction (Weil's 'the void') and the particular affliction of Christ. Later in the talk she remarks that 'it is not a sovereign but a suffering God that she desires'. Murdoch understands Weil's view to be that Christ provides an *example* of enduring affliction:

> [Weil] says carefully of Christ that his death was not like the death of the martyrs – it was nearer to that of a common criminal.[114] It had its moment of complete blackness ... the best that religion can do for a man in these days, she says, is to prepare him for affliction. The church which should embrace such a view would be a church careless of temporal sovereignty and prepared to be dismembered.[115]

---

111. Weil, *Lectures on Philosophy* (trans. Hugh Price) (Cambridge; Cambridge University Press, 1978), pp. 200–2.
112. However, Gary Browning, 'Murdoch and the End of Ideology', in Browning, *Murdoch on Truth and Love*, pp. 133–57 (146–54), maintains that Murdoch remains interested in social ideology until the end of her writing career.
113. Murdoch, 'Waiting on God', p. 11.
114. Citing Weil, *Waiting on God*, p. 69.
115. Murdoch, 'Waiting on God', p. 15.

It is this unity between the affliction of Christ and that of all afflicted humanity that Nina perceives on the very brink of her suicide, as she contemplates the crucifix hanging on the wall of her room. Annette had disliked the crucifix, since it did not fit into her own world.[116] Nina, however, now finds it central to her crisis of fear. She pays attention to it and 'she saw it for the first time in her life as a man hanging most painfully from his hands'. At first, she assumes with conventional piety that Christ, being divine, could not have suffered in the same way as a mortal man: 'It was not the senseless blackness of death, the senseless blackness as it was for her.' There are resonances here of Weil's contemplation of the cross as relayed by Murdoch, except that Weil stresses that there *was* in fact 'complete blackness' for Christ. Nina goes on to contemplate the alternate possibilities if Christ were indeed really identified with her, as a suffering human being: if he did *not* suffer blackness, then neither should she, but if she *does*, then surely he must have done so as well:

> If not so for him, then not so for her. If for her, then for him too. A dark confusion rose to cover her. For an instant she felt the terrible weight of a God depending on her will. It was too heavy. Her song came to an end. She gathered her feet under her and pitched head first from the window.[117]

The only question here is whether Christ suffered *malheur* in the same way that any person does. If he did, it has consequences for the passibility of God. But Weil, despite Murdoch's account, does not simply see Christ as the prime example of human affliction. She develops a more complex relation between the passion of Christ and the affliction of human beings generally, which is deeply integrated into the whole process of escaping from the void. The passion of Christ is at the centre of the mechanisms of gravity and grace, because human beings can participate in the abandonment of Christ by God his Father and enter the distance that opened between them in that moment:

> Our misery gives us the infinitely precious privilege of sharing in this distance placed between the Son and his Father. This distance is only separation, however, for those who love. For those who love, separation, although painful is a good, because it is love. Even the distress of the abandoned Christ is a good. There cannot be a greater good for us on earth than to share in it.[118]

Those 'who are struck down by affliction are at the foot of the cross'. The necessity of the 'blind mechanism'[119] of *malheur* makes us 'nailed down to the spot', but this offers the opportunity to share in the relation of love in God which continues

---

116. Murdoch, *Flight from the Enchanter*, p. 83.
117. Ibid., p. 291.
118. Weil, *Waiting on God*, p. 71.
119. Ibid., p. 72.

despite the 'infinite distance between God and God' caused by the immensity of space and time introduced into God by 'Creation, Incarnation and Passion'. Thus, necessity can become obedience. This participation in the love of God is not a willed effort by us, but is the result of a prevenient act of God: supernatural love has been planted in the human person by the creator, and the 'tree of love' which grows up within us becomes the tree of the cross in the experience of affliction and the void.[120]

While Murdoch evidently read this passage in Weil's essay 'The Love of God and Affliction', since she quotes from it in the 1951 broadcast, it seems that she could do nothing with it. In the broadcast and in *The Flight from the Enchanter*, the passion of Christ is presented simply as an example of human affliction, which is of course a part of Weil's account. But as Murdoch's thought develops, she becomes discontented with the image of a 'suffering Christ'. There is a stark contrast between Nina's seeing Christ as 'a man hanging from his hands' and Christ's own brisk dismissal of the picture in his conversation with Anne Cavidge: 'They did not pierce my hands. They drove the nails through my wrists. The flesh of the hands would have torn away.' Of course, nailing the wrists would hardly have been less painful; Murdoch is trying to undermine the conventional pietistic image of 'pierced hands' in order to relativize suffering in favour of another reality – enduring death. When Anne looks at the wrist of Christ, 'the wrist was unscarred too'. Christ explains, 'if there was suffering it has gone and is nothing'. The pain is not 'the point … though it has proved so interesting to you all'.[121]

As we have already seen in other chapters, for Murdoch in her mature thinking an indulgence in suffering is a way of evading the need to face the death of the ego-self. This, we can now see, is what Murdoch finally 'does' with Weil's placing of the passion at the heart of the dynamic of affliction. As in Weil's account, it is not enough to see Christ as an example of human suffering. But Murdoch does not follow Weil into her theology of participating in the 'infinite distance' within God, an idea which stands at the centre of the theology of the cross developed extensively by the Catholic theologian Hans Urs von Balthasar.[122] Rather, Murdoch is to make the cultivating of suffering through identification with Christ into one more exercise of what Weil identifies as the consolations of the imagination with which we try to fill the void: 'My wounds are imaginary,' says Christ to Anne. Murdoch thus sets up a dialectic between suffering and death with regard to Christ which is not in Weil. As Father Brendan affirms in *Henry and Cato* (1976), Christ did not 'cheat death by suffering instead'.[123] Further, urges Murdoch, we can be

---

120. Ibid., pp. 76–7.
121. Murdoch, *Nuns and Soldiers*, pp. 290–1.
122. See above, p. 130, and Hans Urs von Balthasar, *Mysterium Paschale* (trans. Aidan Nichols) (Edinburgh: T&T Clark, 1990), pp. viii–ix; he notes (*Mysterium Paschale*, p. 65) that Weil interprets the cross 'anthropologically or ontologically' in her *Intuitions Préchrétiennes* (1951).
123. Murdoch, *Henry and Cato*, p. 338. See above, pp. 38–9.

helped towards the death of the ego and an obedient turning towards love of the Good when we realize that the death of Christ was without reward, that is, without resurrection: 'If Christ be risen our faith is vain.'[124] We too must be 'good for nothing'. She thus makes Weil's critique of the consolation-making imagination a way of interpreting the compelling image of the passion of Christ. Like Weil, the passion is thus at the centre of the human experience of the void, but in a quite un-Weilian way.

Murdoch's review of the English translation of Weil's *Notebooks*[125] for the *Spectator* in November 1956, 'Knowing the Void', contains surprisingly little more analysis of Weil than her broadcast talk of October 1951. Although Justin Broackes rightly judges that it is 'a real achievement' in some 1,500 words, to 'weave together for the review a presentation of ideas so clear, expressive, and fundamental out of the six hundred pages of Weil's wandering and brilliant text',[126] Murdoch largely follows the lines of her earlier broadcast in which she had commented on *Gravity and Grace* as well as *Waiting on God*. The earlier volume was after all, as Murdoch points out herself, a kind of condensed version of the *Notebooks*. Broackes is also doubtless right that the *Notebooks* made 'a huge impact upon her', but the review in itself does not allow us to see very much of what the new impact – taking her beyond her first encounter with Weil – might have been. Murdoch follows her previous critique by labelling Weil as 'in a sense non-liberal' about institutions and society, though she nuances this judgement by suggesting that 'considering her, our political categories break down; and this is perhaps instructive'.[127] Her previous unease about the 'automatic operation' of gravity and grace is repeated with the comment that 'she seems at times almost too ready to embrace evil and to love God as its author', so that 'many readers may find a repellent and self-destructive quality in her austerity'.[128] Again, however, a nuance is introduced; 'the union of a passionate search for truth with a simplicity and austerity of personal living' gives her writings an air of 'authority'. The review does, however, give just a hint of the way that Murdoch might have begun making a key distinction between suffering and death:

> [Weil] observes that we can only think that suffering purifies because we see it as pure affliction, whereas the sufferer sees not the affliction but the imaginary

---

124. Father Bernard in Murdoch, *Philosopher's Pupil*, p. 188.
125. The *Notebooks* were published in 1956 in two volumes by Routledge and Kegan Paul, translated by Arthur Wills; the 2004 Routledge one-volume edition I have referenced throughout this book is identical to the 1956 printing, including pagination. Murdoch's Oxford library contains heavily annotated copies of the two original volumes in English (IML 931–2), as well as the three volumes of the French *Cahiers* (Paris: Plon, 1951, 1953, 1956; IML 481–3) from which they were translated.
126. Broackes, 'Introduction', p. 19.
127. Murdoch, 'Knowing the Void', p. 159.
128. Ibid., p. 160.

consolation. Her concept of 'the void', which must be experienced in the achieving of detachment, differs from the *Angst* of popular existentialism, in that *Angst* is usually thought of as something that circumstances may force upon a man, whereas experience of the void is a spiritual achievement, involving the control of the imagination.[129]

Here she echoes Weil's view that affliction and suffering may not produce spiritual profit because we are inclined to make imaginary 'consolations' to avoid their impact; see, for example, 'imagination can fill the void. That is why average human beings can ... pass through no matter what suffering without being purified'.[130] But in Murdoch's convoluted expression we may perhaps trace another reason in her own mind for the mistaken view that 'suffering purifies' – that this sentiment itself is an 'imaginary consolation'. Behind the determination to make 'experience of the void ... a spiritual achievement', we may sense a contrast developing between suffering and 'the void' which Weil herself does not intend; for Murdoch we must turn *from* suffering *to* the void, or the death of the ego.

If there is an incipient contrast between suffering and death appearing here, it does not yet appear in her novel *The Unicorn* (1963), where Hannah's devotion to mental suffering is indistinguishable from a death wish. The mythical unicorn, a beautiful, solitary animal destined to be betrayed and killed, was a symbol for Christ in medieval thinking,[131] and here is associated with Hannah. Effingham reflects that 'I know one mustn't think of her as a legendary creature, a beautiful unicorn,' but he clearly does. Max Lejour replies, 'The unicorn is also the image of Christ.' However, despite the title of the book, any analogy between the suffering of Christ and her suffering seems somehow unsatisfactory. Max goes on, 'but we have to do too with an ordinary guilty person', and if she is 'expiating a crime', she's just guilty 'like us'.[132] The solution to which Murdoch is working, not yet expressed in this novel, is that Christ is not essentially a representative of human suffering, but of the need to face death in the fullest sense.

Broackes's own answer to the question as to what Murdoch does with Weil's writings in the late 1950s, in so new an adoption that she sees it as a new discovery, is that she substitutes 'God' in Weil with 'the Good'. He judges that:

> In Weil, the renunciation of the self leaves, quite literally, God operating in us; in Murdoch, it will become Good that operates in us ... She has transposed much of Weil's thought into a new key, and made it her own. Where Weil had talked of God and the methods and training for coming to a love of God, Murdoch will talk of Good and the methods and training for coming to a love of the Good.[133]

129. Ibid., p. 159, original emphasis.
130. Weil, *Notebooks*, p. 145; see also pp. 211, 218, 227, 526, 610.
131. See Adolfo Salvatore Cavallo, *The Unicorn Tapestries at the Metropolitan Museum of Art* (New York: Harry N. Abrahams, 1998), pp. 45–51.
132. Murdoch, *The Unicorn*, p. 115.
133. Broackes, 'Iris Murdoch's First Encounters', p. 19.

Broackes has identified an important shift of thought here, but we must observe that it is not altogether clear-cut. Weil herself, of course, writes of attending to the 'good' as well as to 'God'; in the review of 1956, Murdoch refers to Weil as a Platonist who 'believes that Good is a transcendent reality'.[134] Summarizing Weil's thought she remarks that 'during our apprenticeship good appears negative and empty', and that 'when we truly realise the impossibility of good we love it, *as we love* the mysteries of religion'.[135] She almost appears to be crediting Weil, in advance, with a later book title, 'The Good Apprentice'.[136] This is thoroughly in accord with such statements of Weil as 'if we turn our mind towards the good, it is impossible that little by little the whole soul will not be attracted thereto'.[137] Rather than speaking of a 'transposing' of Weil's thought, we might then speak of a 'selecting' or 'cropping' of her thought from 'God *as* the good' to simply 'the good'. Moreover, as I have suggested in a previous chapter, there remains something ambivalent about Murdoch's rejection of 'God' along with her denial of a 'personal' God, given what she herself writes about the power of symbols.[138] She ends her 1956 review with the declaration that 'as Simone Weil points out, mysteries will yield truths only to religious attention', and she anticipates her later *Metaphysics* with the conclusion that 'the Notebooks may also be recommended to those who imagine that current philosophical techniques can readily show theological statements to be empty'.[139]

Broackes's proposal is insightful, then, but I suggest that we might add to it another 'transposition' of Weil's thought by Murdoch: that too much embrace of affliction (*malheur*) may not lead us into the 'void' but distract us from it, and that the image of the passion of Christ can warn us of this imaginary consolation. Later, in Murdoch's *Metaphysics as a Guide to Morality*, we can detect transposition going on when she cites a passage in Weil's *Notebooks* in which Weil is making her own use of Kant's aesthetic of purposeless beauty:

> God is the sole and unique end. But he is not really an end at all, since he is not dependent on any means. Everything which God has for an end is finality without end [purposiveness without purpose] … The suffering which goes hand in hand with necessity leads us to finality without end. This is why the spectacle of human misery is beautiful.[140]

134. For Weil's strong influence on Murdoch's reading of Plato, see Peter J. Conradi, 'Platonism in Iris Murdoch', in Anne Baldwin and Sarah Hutton (eds), *Platonism and the English Imagination* (Cambridge: Cambridge University Press, 1994), pp. 330–42.

135. Murdoch, 'Knowing the Void', p. 158, my emphasis. See my Chapter 2.

136. On 'apprenticeship', see Weil, *Waiting on God*, pp. 74–5.

137. Weil, *Gravity and Grace*, p. 106; Weil, *Notebooks*, p. 414.

138. See earlier, pp. 74–5.

139. Murdoch, 'Knowing the Void', p. 160; cf. Murdoch, *Metaphysics*, pp. 229–30, 327, 425–6, 432–3, 468, 510–12.

140. Weil, *Notebooks*, p. 613, as cited in Murdoch, *Metaphysics*, p. 106 with Murdoch's parenthetical gloss.

6. The Void and the Passion

Confirming Broackes's suggestion, Murdoch interprets Weil's statement he 'God is not really an end at all' to mean that 'the "true saint" believes in "God, but not as a super-person who satisfies all our ordinary desires "in the end", since 'there is no end, there is no reward'. God, rather, is the Good, as Murdoch goes on to explain, with reference to Plato's *Timaeus*.[141] Further, however, Murdoch comments that human misery can be 'beautiful' when we enjoy great tragedy, which she has just affirmed (going beyond Weil) to be about 'the difference between suffering and death'. Tragedy 'must contain some dreadful vision of the reality and significance of death', since 'tragedy, like religion, must break the ego, destroying the illusionary whole of the unified self'.[142] The exhibition of literal death causes us to accept the death of the ego-self. She thus understands Weil's sentence that 'suffering leads to finality' to mean that suffering, or the 'horrors' of contingency, should always be seen as 'an aspect of death'. She cites twice in three pages a phrase that she claims is by Weil, that exposure to God condemns what is evil in us 'not to suffering but to death' (she supplies the French, *pas à la souffrance mais à la mort*). The same phrase appears, attributed to Weil, on the last page of *The Sovereignty of Good*.[143] If the words 'not to suffering but to death' were indeed written by Weil,[144] and Murdoch is not misremembering a quotation, Murdoch is using them as a key to Weil's thought in a way that Weil herself does not. Weil's urging us to face the reality of *both* 'suffering and death' has become in Murdoch's transposition 'death *not* suffering'. Murdoch adds that 'I expressed this once in an aphorism: the false God punishes, the true god slays'. Weil has a similar aphorism, but without a *dialectic* between suffering and death: 'The false God changes suffering into violence, the true God changes violence into suffering.'[145]

Either Murdoch has independently come to typify the dialectic 'not suffering but death' in the passion of Christ, or her reflection upon what to do with Weil's focus on the crucified Christ has prompted this more general contrast. It is significant that, as distinct from Murdoch's emphasis that 'Christ did not cheat death by suffering', Weil commends Aquinas: 'St. Thomas on the suffering of Christ. Not to seek not to suffer, or to suffer less (in affliction), but to seek not to be affected by sufferings.'[146] Further, from the 1970s onwards, Murdoch finds she can do something else with Weil's picture of finding ourselves nailed, with Christ, to the 'very centre of the universe'.[147] It is to affirm the presence of the 'mystical Christ'. While these ideas may be found in several of the later novels, I am choosing her penultimate novel to explore them.

---

141. Murdoch, *Metaphysics*, p. 107.
142. Ibid., p. 104.
143. Murdoch, *Sovereignty of Good*, p. 104.
144. Murdoch offers no reference, and the phrase cannot be found in Simone Weil, *Oeuvres*, édition établie sous la direction de Florence de Lussy (Paris: Gallimard, 1999).
145. Weil, *Notebooks*, p. 507.
146. Ibid., p. 106.
147. Weil, *Waiting on God*, p. 78.

Reworking Weil: The Green Knight

Where the nineteen-year-old Annette has a collection of stones in *The Flight from the Enchanter*, here they belong to the sixteen-year-old Moy, one of the three daughters of the widowed Louise Anderson who have created a kind of court for themselves in the family home in Kensington Gardens. In the ironic view of Louise's lifelong friend, the divorced Joan Blackett, they have set up an 'all-singing, all-laughing, all-crying show' (9), or they are 'fairy-tale damsels, grail bearers, sleeping princesses inside an enchanted castle' (11). Joan's son Harvey is generally expected to fall in love with the eldest and most beautiful sister, Aleph, but we learn later that Moy has been passionately in love with him since she was a child. Right at the beginning we learn that Moy is an artist in the making, and that she 'cries over things ... like stones. She thinks things have rights'.

Moy is the figure in the book who gives most attention to objects and small animals in the world and is the least inclined to build her own universe around her own centre. She has such deep sympathy for the existence of her 'grotesque, ugly flint stones', that she has the telekinetic gift of moving them and attracting them to slide into her hands, which she understands as a force that 'joined her life with the life of things' (20). She is aware, however, of the ambiguity of her attachment: it could become an attempt to exercise control, and she is so sensitive about things having their own reality that she is worried about having imprisoned the stones, having taken them from their natural environment into her world. She fears that one stone in particular, her favourite flint, conical and stained with lichen, has resentful feelings about being severed from its natural location on its granite hillside. Each day she 'rescued the tiniest almost invisible creatures who were in some wrong place where they might starve or be crushed', but, as with the stones, she doubts whether she knows 'what little living creatures, and even *things, wanted* her to do' (109, original emphasis). This acute sense of the independence of beautiful things reflects Weil's vision of a world where objects are beautiful because materials are being obedient in their own way, not to human beings, but to God.[148] The self-identity of non-human things takes symbolic form when – in the course of gathering stones from the Thames – Moy is violently attacked by a swan. Also carrying sexual undertones of the myth of Leda and the Swan, and happening at a moment when she is becoming increasingly aware of her own sexuality, the incident leaves her badly shaken.[149]

When Moy falls into a deep *malheur* towards the end of the book, as a result of discovering that Harvey loves the second sister, Sefton, and intends to marry

---

148. Ibid., pp. 72–4.
149. Sharon R. Wilson, 'Enchantment, Transformation, and Rebirth in the Green Knight', in Simone Roberts and Alison Baumann (eds), *Iris Murdoch and the Moral Imagination: Essays* (Jefferson: McFarland Press, 2010), pp. 92–106, shows the interaction of this myth with other mythological patterns in the book, but does not relate it to Moy's sense of interaction with the natural world.

her, the contingency of the world generally becomes hostile and alien to her; she loses her power of telekinesis and her sense of 'contact with innumerable entities whose relationship with her she had taken for granted' (461). Like Annette, she has a crisis on the edge of the sea, and like Anne Cavidge, it relates to stones. Visiting the coast, in the area from which her favourite flint had come, she leaves the stone on a rock by the sea's edge and decides not to retrieve it: 'What did it matter? It was just a stone. It was nothing. She was nothing' (463). She throws herself into the sea, and Anax, the dog for whom she has been caring in the absence of its owner, Bellamy James, tries in vain to pull her back. But just as Mischa drags Annette out of the wild sea in *The Flight from the Enchanter*, Bellamy drags Moy out of the violent beating waves, plunging into the water by running over the stones, 'the big wet stones shifting under his boots … then onto the sand which was strewn with smaller stones' (468). At that moment, Anax finds the exact place from which the stone had been taken. Restoring it to where it belonged on the hillside ('kneeling, she kissed it') she finds herself lifted out of her void of deadly despair. In all, Moy exemplifies Weil's (and Murdoch's) theory that paying proper attention to things and people and 'waiting' patiently under the gravity of affliction without ceasing to love good things will (almost 'automatically') be answered by a movement of grace. Here, the seals which had apparently abandoned the coastline suddenly return: 'It's wonderful that the seals are back,' comments Bellamy, 'I expect they came to say hello to you.' She replies 'Well – yes – I think – they did,' and he reflects, wonderingly, 'something's happened' (471).

Others in the novel are suffering affliction. A prime example is Bellamy himself, the owner of the dog Anax, and a former university friend of Louise's deceased husband. He separates from his most-loved companion for a while in an attempt to deprive himself of all pleasures and to 'give up the world' in preparation for entering a monastery. Though English, he is a kind of displaced person, unable to settle into any kind of job and ill at ease in society: 'He wanted to get closer to something – perhaps life. But life continued to reject him' (23). Using one of Weil's favourite words, he reflects that as soon as he got into the 'mobile machine' of life, the 'machine would soon eject him' (22). Later he reflects that 'the dark is just the old dark of meaninglessness and falsehood, which separates me from my friends and from the real world where people love' (154). He has entered Weil's void, the 'black sickness which almost no one else, certainly not his nearest dearest friends, could understand at all. He thought … I am crammed with darkness' (116). Echoing the 'decreation' which Weil desires, he writes to his spiritual director, Fr Damien, a monk at the monastery he wants to enter, 'I want to be destroyed' (40), and 'I desire to be struck down like St Paul' (114); giving almost everything he owns away (including his dog) 'he had enjoyed this stripping' (74), and he associates his affliction with 'my own notion of dark night' (114).

Fr Damien makes exactly the diagnosis of his condition that Murdoch makes of those who identify with the sufferings of Christ. The desire to suffer is an evasion of facing the death of the ego-self: 'You think of the dedicated life as a form of death, but you will be alive and crying. The false God punishes. The true God slays' (95). The desire to be punished and to be hurled to the ground are a form of 'masochism' and 'worldly obsessions in disguise' (154); in these fantasies, Damien advises him, 'you are in danger of exalting a sentimental Christ. You are secretly attached to magic, which is the enemy of religion.'[150] Bellamy correctly understands Damien to be saying that he is making a 'consolation' out of suffering and protests 'I want not consolation but to be destroyed' (155).

In Bellamy's response, Murdoch seems to be imagining what Weil might have replied to her own criticism that suffering should be distinguished from death: 'I crave for suffering, perhaps physical suffering, something so extreme that my false fantasising mind may be shattered and into that great dark void God may enter' (155). Murdoch's point is that the desire for suffering *is* precisely a mood of the 'fantasising mind'. Bellamy links his masochism with what he believes to be the presence of 'the mystical Christ'. He knows that 'the resurrection is a spiritual mystery, and that what matters is the living Christ whose reality we *experience*', and so he asks Fr Damien, 'If we have a mystical Christ can that be the real Christ? Is a mystical Christ "good enough"? Could there be a Christ if *that* man never existed at all?' (41). Bellamy is asking exactly the questions that Murdoch was considering in the 1960s, in the wake of Bishop Robinson's *Honest to God*: Does a demythologizing of Christ also involve a dehistoricizing? As I have suggested earlier, Murdoch stands with Bultmann and against Robinson in affirming both.[151] For Bellamy, the detachment of the 'mystical Christ' entirely from history is a kind of 'stripping' of Christ, a stripping that he wants to emulate in his own suffering. As for God, he writes, 'God can look after himself.' Fr Damien does not answer his question directly, but rebukes him for presuming that he can know a 'mystical Christ' so quickly and easily in his spiritual quest: 'The mystical vision is the reward of long ascetic pilgrimage and not to be compared with the emotional experiences to which you refer.' He adds: 'Do not sit all day reading Eckhart! Later you may meditate upon what he means when he says seek God only in your own soul' (95).

Like all Murdoch's characters, Fr Damien voices only partially Murdoch's own opinions. He articulates her mature response to Weil, that ego-death and suffering must be separated out, but Bellamy expresses Murdoch's conviction that knowing the presence of the 'mystical Christ' can accompany the death of the self and rejection of a literal resurrection. With Bellamy, she is an avid reader of Eckhart. Fr Damien comes over somewhat to Bellamy's side in his last letter, which announces that he has lost his Christian faith, left the monastery, abandoned the priesthood and thus effectively joined the group of Murdoch's atheist-spiritual clerics or former clerics. In this letter he is much more encouraging about finding one's own mystical Christ than he was formerly, and he no longer advises that Eckhart's theology should be left for 'later':

---

150. Cf. Fr Damien, in Murdoch, *Green Knight*, p. 39: 'Religion is but too easily degraded into magic.' See my Chapter 1, pp. 24–8.

151. See earlier, pp. 65–6.

You should stay with Christ, that presence need not fade, it can be an icon. But do not be miserable seeking for moral perfection. Remember Eckhart's advice (for which he was condemned as a heretic):[152] 'do not seek for God outside your own soul' ... Do not seek solitude ... And do, as a sign of sanity, go back to your dog! (266)

Bellamy, like Eckhart (and as quoted by Murdoch),[153] senses 'the vast extension of his soul wherein God seethed and bubbled' (98). Later he finds himself suspended 'in some warm fluid, which was indeed God, the perfect love of God', and he concludes that it is not so much a case of God in the soul as the soul in the womb of God (292). The language is still from Eckhart, who writes of the divine being, as Murdoch reports, 'in process of giving birth to itself'.[154]

Another character to experience *malheur*, and one who is more central to the main line of the plot, is Lucas Graffe. This eminent historian, who is another former acquaintance of Louise's late husband from university days, confesses that he lives 'in hell' and has done since he was a child (252). Although an academic rather than a tycoon, he resembles Mischa Fox in being a sinister 'ringmaster' of his world (59), attempting to control all people, events and objects that come into his orbit with a Nietzschean will.[155] As Mischa had been rejected by Rosa, so Lucas has been rejected by Louise, to whom he offered marriage after her husband's death. But his *malheur* has deeper roots. As a very young child he was adopted, as his parents thought themselves unable to have children. Then they did have a natural child, Clement, now a relatively successful actor and theatre manager and yet another university friend of Louise's husband. Clement realizes that Lucas's ideal early 'world of pure undivided love', of which he was the sole centre, had been shattered by the irruption of the strange 'other', 'an outsider, an intruder, a spoiler, a wrecker' (93), whose reality he was totally unwilling to recognize. Lucas, already a child displaced from his natural family and possibly his home country, was now displaced again. All those afflicted, finding their self-made world threatened, are likely – as Weil discerns it, and Mischa earlier displayed it – to hurt and afflict the other. Clement recalls many acts of cruelty towards him by his brother when they were growing up, but Lucas can see the world only from his viewpoint, telling Clement condescendingly that 'I forgive you ... for all the suffering which

---

152. See earlier, p. 113, when Fr Damien had denied that Eckhart was declared to be a heretic.

153. See earlier, pp. 75–6.

154. See Murdoch, *Good Apprentice*, pp. 145, 246; *Metaphysics*, pp. 464–5, 501.

155. Bellamy, *Green Knight*, p. 172, describes his morality as 'beyond good and evil'. Leeson, *Iris Murdoch: Philosophical Novelist*, p. 122, suggests that the conflict between Peter Mir and Lucas Graffe is an argument between Neoplatonism and Nietzsche, though he finds (pp. 126–8) Schopenhauer's development of Nietzsche's 'will' to be even more influential, citing Murdoch's statement that 'Other debased descendants of Eros are the "wills" of Schopenhauer and Nietzsche and the libido of Freud'; *Metaphysics*, p. 490.

you caused me when we were children' (322). This shocking absolution is in the wake of his own recent attempt literally to kill Clement with a savage blow from a weighted baseball bat (a relic from childhood), after luring him, half-drunk, one night into a dark and deserted place. Clement survives because a stranger rushes between them and takes the stroke instead. The man is thought to have died in hospital from the terrible wound, and Lucas has maintained successfully in court that he acted in self-defence as the victim of a street robbery.

It is this man, Peter Mir – whose family name, as he explains, means both 'world' and 'peace' in Russian – who now appears, apparently risen from the dead (he speaks of 'after my resurrection') or at least as a miraculous survivor of deadly injury. He visits Lucas and Clement, with a vague demand for justice, vengeance, retribution and restitution, but it is unclear what he means by any of this. Above all, he explains that he needs love, or at least 'lovingkindness' and friendship (130). He is troubled by a deep *malheur*, complaining that his life is 'ruined'; he is no longer able to concentrate, has lost his vocation – which he claims to be that of a psychoanalyst – and feels that the blow to the head has made him forget something of huge importance (162). Clement simply admits 'he died for me' (91), but Lucas tries to dismiss him as a nuisance, though admitting for the first time that he had tried to kill Clement. With deep insight, Peter Mir claims that he and Lucas are 'eternally connected'. He suggests that Lucas is a Jew, as he is himself, and points out that by preventing him from killing his brother, 'I saved you from the sin of Cain' (123). Mir, like Mischa, is an immigrant from Eastern Europe and – like Mischa Fox – is immensely wealthy; in the end he is to be revealed not as a psychoanalyst but as the retired owner and director of an international meat business, founded in Russia. In this novel, the attributes of Mischa appear in fact to be distributed between Lucas and Mir, with Lucas assuming the negative features, and Mir exhibiting the mystique and aura of power. Lucas himself is evidently displaced in some way, and now Mir is hinting that he is nothing other than the ultimate displaced person, the mythical Wandering Jew, Cain condemned to wander without ever finding a home.[156] 'I am not a Russian Jew,' protests Lucas, but Mir replies, 'How do you know you are not?' (131).

Mir, if not technically displaced, is like Lucas in having lost his place in life, in his case through Lucas's terrible blow. When he gets to know Louise's family with the (somewhat unwilling) help of Clement, in his quest for love and friendship, Moy sees him as the Minotaur of Greek legend (195). She pities him, like the Minotaur – part human, part bull – having no home in the palace of King Minos and trapped in a maze. At a family fancy dress part to which he is invited, he

---

156. The motif of the Wandering Jew appears in the next and final novel, in the rootless and enigmatic figure of Jackson: Murdoch, *Jackson's Dilemma* (London: Chatto & Windus, 1995), p. 64: ' "Jackson is suffering," said Mildred, "for something, perhaps for something terrible".' Significantly, Owen responds that in Jackson he recognizes 'my brother' (p. 65)—cf. pp. 188, 232, 248–9. Rowe, in *Iris Murdoch*, p. 76, regards him as 'another of Murdoch's Christ figures', but the identities are not incompatible.

chooses to wear the head of a bull (209)[157] and later he appears 'bullish' to Clement (277). Here we have another curious throw-back to the early *Flight*. There, on the very first page, we read that Annette disliked the passage about the Minotaur in Dante's *Inferno*: 'Why should the poor Minotaur be suffering in hell? It was not the Minotaur's fault that it had been born a monster. It was God's fault.'[158] As Byatt suggests, this anticipates the situation of the refugees in the novel who have been born in the wrong place, on the wrong side of the line drawn by SELIB.[159] Moy's sister Aleph, however, sees another mythical character in the mysterious Peter Mir: 'I think he's the Green Knight' (195). He dresses in green, carries a green umbrella, and Lucas thinks his eyes are green, but this is not the fundamental reason for the reader to identify him with the figure in the Middle English poem of that name. Already we have been given, seventy pages before, the clue that his story and that of Lucas will run in some way parallel to that of the Green Knight and Sir Gawain. When Peter Mir bursts in on Lucas, he declares that a just punishment for Lucas would be 'the reception of a blow upon the head delivered with equal force' (126), just as the Green Knight proposes that after one year Gawain should suffer a blow with an axe to cut off his head, having first inflicted such a blow on the Green Knight, 'whatever the outcome'.[160] The title of the novel is also no doubt working away in our minds, and Bellamy has already had a dream of a man standing and holding a tall axe (153). At the fancy dress party, Mir carries his bull-head as the Green Knight carried his head away from Arthur's court at Camelot after Gawain's stroke, and not long after that, Lucas declares, 'He wants my head' (199).

It is not until 230 pages later that Clement recalls, in detail, the romance of *Sir Gawain and the Green Knight* and reflects that it fits approximately the story they have been living through, but that 'it's all mixed up' (432). Some readers will learn of the poem for the first time, but others, who know it, will have been anticipating with curiosity the working out of the plot. Those 'in the know' will be startled by what actually happens, and in particular at the version of the meeting of Gawain/Lucas with the Green Knight/Peter Mir when in the poem the Knight is expected to take his just recompense of an 'equal blow' (126). In the novel, Lucas and Mir, with Clement and Bellamy, have set up a ritual re-enactment of the scene when Lucas struck the original blow. Mir describes it as 'a sort of rite of purification – a sort of mystery play – a gamble, a gesture – the intervention of a god', and Lucas calls it in advance 'a symbolic revenge without bloodshed' (268). Mir hopes that the re-enactment will restore his memory and describes his loss as a form of *malheur*,

---

157. Rebecca Moden, '"Liberation through Art": Form and Transformation in Murdoch's Fiction', in Browning, *Murdoch on Truth and Love*, pp. 159–81 (173–8), suggests that the masks in the story symbolize the 'trickery and magic' of aesthetic form, which nevertheless has power to reveal truth.

158. Murdoch, *Flight from the Enchanter*, p. 7.

159. Byatt, *Degrees of Freedom*, p. 45.

160. Anon., *Sir Gawain and the Green Knight* (ed. J. R. Tolkien and E. V. Gordon) (Oxford: Oxford University Press, 2nd edn, 1967), lines 380–90 (p. 11).

a 'dark' from which he needs to be drawn: 'I feel increasingly sure that there is something, some great thing, which that blow has annihilated, as if a huge part of my personality has been blotted out' (250). Bellamy, in a heightened mystical state, prays, 'I can see the blackness, oh let it be withdrawn … let there be light' (281). The reader with the Middle English poem in mind is surprised when there is no blow inflicted on Lucas at all, but as they face each other, Mir suddenly appears to Bellamy as a 'pillar of light' or 'shooting star' and – 'still rigid, still glowing' – collapses (282). When he recovers consciousness, he finds he has recovered his memory. What he says later is that 'I have remembered God' (298).

Mir explains that he has now remembered how he was following the Buddhist path of enlightenment towards the death of the self at the time when Lucas struck him down, and this is what he had forgotten: 'I felt … that I must change, I must change myself or die, change by dying to my awful self.' Bellamy objects that 'Buddhists don't believe in God,' and he replies: 'In a personal God, no. I used the word as a brief way of indicating a spiritual path.' Bellamy contributes his own favourite quotation from Eckhart, 'Do not seek for God outside your own soul,' and Mir readily responds that 'as Buddhists speak of the Buddha in the soul. As Christians might speak of the Christ in the soul' (298). We are now on familiar Murdoch territory of the 'mystical Buddha', 'the mystical Christ' and the death of the ego-self, but we have been brought here unexpectedly by a conversion of the myth of Gawain and the Green Knight. Bellamy declares that 'Buddhists say that enlightenment is found by a blow' and concludes that the first blow from Lucas took it away, while a second blow brought it back: 'Last night you were struck down, an angel struck you, and you became that angel' (299). Moreover, Murdoch has used the myth to portray Weil's theory that when we 'fix our will on the void' without seeking consolations, but continuing to love the good as best as we can (as Mir has sought to do good and exchange love with Louise's family), 'we shall come through all right, for God fills the void'.[161] Clement had exclaimed, 'He's been struck by lightning,' and Weil also writes, 'Man only escapes from the laws of this world in *lightning flashes*. Instants when everything stands still … of the void, of acceptance of the moral void. Whoever endures a moment of the void either receives the supernatural bread or falls.'[162] As Bellamy maintains later, looking back, 'Peter remembered his goodness' (373), a phrase that combines Weil with Plato's *anamnesis* of the soul.

Now he has been lifted from his void, Mir can abandon all thoughts of revenge and resolves to bring about a reconciliation with Lucas. But, as Harvey asserts to Aleph, thinking about the remarkable change in Mir, 'Punishment isn't the same as revenge. There are crimes and there must be punishments' (304). When Mir next meets Lucas, he says similarly that 'reconciliation involves two persons. I used to want retribution, now I want reconciliation – I want something clear – like equivalence' (317). Here he, and Harvey earlier, is echoing Weil's views on

---

161. Weil, *Gravity and Grace*, p. 13.
162. Ibid., p. 11, my emphasis.

punishment as 'a vital need of the human soul': she avers that the punishment 'must be *in keeping with the kind of obligation* which has been violated, and not with the interests of public security'.[163] The 'equivalence' of the blows in the Middle English poem again comes into play, and now Mir in the role of the Green Knight inflicts the stroke we have been expecting all along. Mir suddenly slides a sharp knife out of his umbrella and, with the consent of Lucas, quickly makes a slight slit between his ribs. In the poem, the Green Knight gives Gawain a superficial nick on the neck with an axe because he has lied by omission;[164] given hospitality in a rich castle before the appointed time of meeting with the green giant, he fails to tell his host that the host's beautiful wife has given him a magic girdle which (she claims) can save him from death when he meets his judgement at the hands of the Green Knight. In the poem, the host and the Green Knight are of course one. It seems that the nick in Lucas's side is both what Lucas calls 'choos[ing] to despatch me with a symbolic retribution' (322) and punishment for Lucas's failure to tell the truth to Louise's family, which is the fact that he had injured Mir in trying to kill Clement. Immediately after the ritual wounding, Lucas recognizes that justice has been done, exclaiming that 'the sword and the scales have had their day', and the two antagonists smile and laugh together; Lucas tells Mir that he feels 'much better' (320). Later Clement remembers 'the two sorcerers, delighted with each other, dancing together like goats in a love-scene' (456).

While Harvey, in his insistence on punishment, and Mir in his search for 'equivalence' appear to be echoing Weil, we must not assume that Murdoch herself is simply underwriting her, and their, perspective. Once more we have a nuanced reception of Weil. Frances White, in her study of justice in Murdoch, points to the conversation between Rupert Foster and Julius King in *A Fairly Honourable Defeat*. Rupert believes that 'a sense of being justly judged consoles', but Julius replies that the very concept of a 'perfectly just judge' is 'empty and senseless'. We hear a note of authorial warning in Rupert's desire for 'consolation', and White is surely right to underline Rupert's response to Julius that 'I don't believe in a judge ... but I believe in justice'.[165] White suggests that in *The Green Knight* Murdoch is challenging readers to fill for themselves the space between justice and judgement.[166] The ambiguities here are thrown into relief by Aleph's response to Harvey's cry, 'there must be punishment': she explains, 'Of course I'm not suggesting we abolish Law Courts ... I mean something quite simply really, we

---

163. Weil, *Roots*, p. 21, my emphasis.
164. Anon., *Sir Gawain*, lines 2358-61 (p. 65).
165. Murdoch, *Fairly Honourable Defeat*, p. 201.
166. Frances White, '"It's like brown, it's not in the spectrum": The Problem of Justice in Iris Murdoch's Thought', in Browning, *Murdoch on Love and Truth*, pp. 183-210 (198-9, 204). Anne Rowe, *The Visual Arts and the Novels of Iris Murdoch* (Lampeter: Edwin Mellen Press, 2002), p. 111, proposes that Murdoch demands that readers 'study and admire' concepts of justice, mercy and love rather than the characters in whom these qualities 'may be temporarily manifest'.

should try to overcome our egoism and see the unreality and futility of so much of our instinctive thinking' (304).

We might indeed hope that Lucas has himself now been finally lifted out of his 'hell' of his 'egoism' and will give up wanting to control the world around him. Clement wistfully wonders, 'will Lucas cherish that scar?', as Gawain valued the green girdle as a sign of his moral failure, but there is little sign of this. His 'forgiveness' of Clement is ambiguous, to say the least, admitting no fault on his part. Lucas is not a simple character: he inspires not just admiration for his intellect but love for him as a person in Clement, Bellamy, Sefton, Aleph, (once at least) Louise, and something like love from Mir himself. His unflinching quest for the truth in his historical discipline seems to make him loveable, since (as Sefton reflects) he inspires an 'invigorating sense of truth which was love' (272). He is *almost* elevated in the eyes of the reader by his final eloquent disquisition to Sefton on the values of scholarship, especially since he includes within these the attention to intuitions that we know Weil urges, and which Murdoch's character Peter Saward had lived by:

> Meticulous tracings of facts need not exclude the warmth of passions, provided these are controlled by truthful vision. The Lord whose shrine is at Delphi does not say yea or nay but gives a sign. Meditation upon such signs may prove a richer guide than an acceptance of simpler safe conclusions in terms perhaps of general tendencies. (273)

But we are less ready to admire Lucas when we recall his lack of truthfulness about his attack on Clement, and when we consider his final advice to Sefton: 'Do not marry. Marriage ends truthfulness in a life ... Solitude is essential if real thinking is to take place' (274). This admonition causes her to draw back at first from Harvey's love, fearing the eros which is prompting her to lose herself, protesting 'I want my solitude' and holding on to a freedom of the self which makes her love for Harvey 'seem like death' (393). But 'the awful presence of the god' (384), Eros, can – as we know extensively from Murdoch's writings – precisely be the power that breaks open the self-enclosed ego towards the Good. Not only does Lucas's prescription seem wrong, the kind of generality he has just condemned, but he breaks it himself by eloping with Aleph to an academic job in America. Playing about with the details of the poem *Gawain and the Green Knight*, trying to make their own story fit it, Clement wonders whether Aleph's role was that of the lady of the castle: 'Wasn't she the temptress, wasn't she what they both wanted?' (431).

Others – indeed, virtually all the characters – suffer some kind of affliction. Louise has lived for most of the book in the *malheur* into which her husband's early death sank her, and by the end of the story, though she is content to be newly married to Clement, the sight of the sea causes her 'more violently to enact, in her soul and body, the deep horror of all that happened'; her 'sickness' includes the loss of Aleph and the death of Peter Mir, who has returned to hospital after his brief remission from brain injury and has only survived a few weeks (455).

Harvey suffers an acute sense of displacement from society when he badly injures his ankle in an accident, and it seems that he might be lame for the rest of his life; he feels estranged from healthy society by being 'disabled', feeling that 'the Harvey who had been once so handsome, so long-legged and athletic did not exist any more' (60). He is rescued from his void of despair by Sefton's love and by the experience one evening of a *passeggiata*, or evening parade, in a little Italian town which gives him the sense of being immersed into the sheer reality of others as if in a religious procession, 'carried along by the flow of people, by their physical presence, pushed, brushed, gently jostled'.[167]

While the afflicted in the earlier *Flight from the Enchanter* include the working class, this novel is typical of the bulk of Murdoch's novels in exploring the particular 'displacements', usually more metaphorical than literal, of a privileged middle-class set.[168] We are, however, returned to the world of Nina and the machine-minders in the factory at one point. Visiting a women's refuge, Harvey comes across a woman desperately crying, 'the voice jerking forth like the regular movements of a machine, the high piercing scream, the desolate agonizing wail, the raucous drawing of breath, growling then dying to a moan, then the scream again' (241). She is caught in the 'machine' of affliction, and we recall Weil's appeal to give attention to the 'cry' of the poor. What is needed, she writes, is a regime which provides an 'attentive silence' in which the cry of the oppressed against evil can be heard; but political parties concerned with keeping themselves in power 'can discern nothing in these cries except a noise'.[169] Harvey hears the cry and is appalled by the 'noise', but he can do nothing to help her; she simply interrupts his life as an erratic incident and never appears again. Unlike Nina in *The Flight from the Enchanter*, she plays no part in the plot of the story, but she is at least present at this penultimate moment of Murdoch's novel writing. It may be indicative of the range of Murdoch's portrayal that the general affliction of humankind is most clearly symbolized in the cries of Bellamy's dog, miserable at being deprived of its

---

167. Murdoch had experienced such a *passegiata* in Ascoli Piceno in September 1988: Conradi, *Iris Murdoch*, p. 567. Moden, 'Liberation through Art', p. 172, interprets the parade as a 'troubling image' of 'human beings enclosed in masks of fantasy', in my view against the spirit of the passage.

168. Dipple, 'The Green Knight and Other Vagaries of the Spirit', pp. 146–7, accepts the criticism that the moral action of *The Green Knight* is presented against a background with no socio-economic depth, but thinks the criticism irrelevant. Gary Browning, 'Murdoch and the End of Ideology', p. 153, maintains that Murdoch's later novels provide a 'critical frame for assessing society and the politics of liberalism'. Anne Rowe and Sara Upstone, 'Iris Murdoch, Ian McEwan and the Place of the Political in Contemporary Fiction', in Rowe and Horner, *Iris Murdoch: Texts and Contexts*, pp. 59–73 (70–1), argue that Murdoch allows political implications to be subsumed within her commitment to art as 'a truth-telling enterprise, not a polemicizing one'.

169. Simone Weil, 'Human Personality', in Miles, *Simone Weil: An Anthology*, pp. 69–98 (73).

master. Hearing his whining at night, 'Moy thought it must be like God hearing the endless wail of suffering humanity and realising He can't do anything about it' (201).

Angels and avatars

In this complex novel – evidence of an artist at the height of her powers – the mythology of the Green Knight offers Murdoch a vehicle for fleshing out familiar Weilian themes – the need to give attention to the other, the void and its association with displacement, the temptation of building a world around oneself, the power of love to release from the void and the danger of looking for compensation. But it also offers the opportunity for Murdoch to explore her modification, or reuse, of Weil. The death of the self, administered at the point of the Green Knight's axe, the butcher's knife of Peter Mir and even the baseball bat of Lucas, is contrasted with the self-indulgent suffering of Bellamy and Harvey and, to some extent, of Louise. At the same time, this theme is interwoven with knowing the presence of the 'mystical Christ', which is Murdoch's alternative to Weil's identification in the void with the Christ who is forsaken by God.

This subtle intertwining of images is given yet further depth by another mythology, which Murdoch had been developing since the 1960s, and which, until this point, had most clearly appeared in the novel *The Time of the Angels*, in the wake of the 'Death of God' movement. There, however, the scattering of the Good into multiple powers, or 'angels', was not yet associated with the idea of the 'mystical Christ' which does not seem to have appeared until the 1970s. In this penultimate novel, the presence of the mystical Christ, the danger of evading of death by suffering instead and the 'angels' are finally woven together in a way that shows – I suggest – Murdoch's final modification of Weil. The image of angels is mostly used by Bellamy and is plurivalent in this novel, with meanings constantly overlapping; but in order to see *how* they overlap, it is worth separating out four distinct kinds of angel that appear in its pages.

The first is the notion of angels as a dispersal of powers of the Good. Lucas, sitting in his study in the dark, explains to Bellamy that 'we are surrounded by strange invisible entities, possibly your angels'. In answer to his response, 'I hope so', he exclaims, 'Ah, you think that that they are good, they cannot be good, there is no good, the tendency to evil is overwhelming' (72). Here Lucas speaks with the voice of Carel from *The Time of the Angels*; since now 'God is dead' (254), the Good also is not a unified reality ('there is no good') and so its 'angels' or messengers have become malicious. Lucas is not quite as nihilistic as Carel: he does think that a limited truth remains, 'but it is on a short lead' (254). Murdoch, we know, believes that there *is* a unity of the Good, but that it can only be known *through* its scattered fragments. Some of these are the many beautiful objects in the world that can become signposts to the one Good. This appears to be the view of Fr Damien, when he writes to Bellamy of 'pure and holy things that are lights and guides', and Bellamy interprets these as angels (96).

Second, Bellamy has a more traditional understanding of angels as spiritual beings, messengers of God, who can be the objects of religious visions.[170] Bellamy constantly sees and dreams of angels in this sense and has a feeling of 'special affinity' with the archangel Michael (96); this is an aspect of his religious experience which causes Fr Damien a good deal of suspicion, even vexation. When leading a derived existence in western art or in orthodox icons, these spiritual beings exert an influence on Bellamy and excite in him feelings of love and veneration. In this form they overlap with the objects of beauty as messengers of the Good, and among them Bellamy mentions in passing the icon that plays a central role in *Time of the Angels*, the three visitors to Abraham by Rublev ('Does not the Orthodox Church represent the Trinity as three angels?'). This traditional kind of angel also blurs in Bellamy's spirituality with a third sense – a human being who is an 'avatar', or a special incarnation of God or the good; Bellamy knows that such avatars are venerated in other religions than Christianity. Finally, Bellamy is inclined to apply the designation 'angel' to ordinary human beings who have some aspect of an avatar about them, or who reflect avatars; these may be 'gurus' or authoritative teachers or may simply act unwittingly as agents of the Good. Certainly, when Mir refers to Lucas as an angel he is speaking in this sense: 'If an angel was present,' he says of the moment when he recovered his memory, 'it was Lucas ... An angel is a messenger of the divine, a messenger is an instrument of the divine, sometimes an unconscious one' (299).

The mysterious nature of Peter Mir, with his strange eruption into the lives of Louise, her family and friends, inheres in the impression he himself gives of shifting between the different senses of an angel. Rationally he can be understood in the fourth sense, but for the characters in the novel, and for the reader, he constantly evokes the other senses as well, so that he seems, as Louise puts it, 'like some bizarre instrument of justice, coming from some other court upon some other planet' (455). We readily suspend our disbelief, because we can always resort to the fourth, minimal sense of 'angel', but the other senses are hovering around him. When Bellamy dreams of the man with an axe, he fuses him in his imagination with the archangel Michael leaning on his sword and with Lazarus, behind whom stands the greater figure of Christ: 'So the victim had risen wonderfully from the dead like Lazarus' (153). To Mir, after the ritual 'game' he exclaims, 'Last night you were struck down, an angel struck you, and you became that angel ... I saw your spiritual being.' His appearance to Bellamy, like a pillar of light or a shooting star, may associate him with Lucifer ('light-bringer' and fallen angel),[171] and this phenomenon is not limited to Bellamy's highly suggestive consciousness; even Clement cries, 'He's been struck by lightning' (282). Bellamy and the publican, Kenneth Rathbone, who befriended Mir after he left hospital without medical

---

170. About angels of this kind, Weil writes in *Notebooks*, p. 428: 'Angels; gods in Plato. At precisely the same moment of eternity they are transported into being, and, out of love, cease to be.'
171. Cf. Isaiah 14:12, 'Lucifer, Son of the Dawn', applied to the king of Babylon.

permission, slide from one meaning to another as they recall Mir after his death. Rathbone says, 'I think he's some kind of holy being. Or was, I should say, I can't think of him as not existing,' and Bellamy replies:

> Nor can I. I think of him as an avatar, I mean an incarnation, a pure sinless creature, a very special visitor to this earthly scene, like an angel – I can't express it. (450)

In Christian theology, Christ is more than an angel, but in the spectrum of angelology expressed in this novel, he fits into the classification of an 'avatar', like the Buddha. The association between Mir and Christ is pervasive. Mir says of himself, 'You thought I was dead, perhaps I was dead, perhaps I am dead' (123), and Bellamy tells him, 'You died and rose again. You became an angel' (297). The revelation that Mir is not after all a surgeon and a psychoanalyst but a butcher's son and a butcher himself (though 'a very rich butcher … a tycoon' [352]) comes with the same impact as labelling Christ as a 'carpenter's son'.[172] Mir holds a last supper, a dinner party, at his house before returning to hospital and his death, and assures Bellamy, as Christ did the dying thief, 'You will be with me later' (359).[173] It may not be incidental that Murdoch, in her radio talk of 1951, had recalled that 'the person in the New Testament that Weil envies most is not St. Paul but the good thief'.[174] In recounting this promise, Bellamy affirms that earlier on 'I saw him transfigured' (452), as the disciples saw Jesus.[175] Reflecting that 'something huge and strange has shot up in our midst and we simply cannot conceptualise it', Clement recalls that Mir's last words to him were, 'Look after your brother' (456). The words recall one of the last words of Christ on the cross, an injunction to John and Mary to look after each other.[176] Even Lucas had told Clement, 'one man can die for another' (91), echoing the words of the High Priest about Jesus that 'it is expedient that one man should die for the people'.[177]

All this does not mean that Mir is an allegorical figure standing for Christ, or even that we are being asked as readers to think that he is literally an avatar, as Bellamy supposes. After all, when Mir inflicts his reconciling blow on Lucas he makes him also reminiscent of Christ: he wounds him in the side, and Lucas picks up the Christic image when he tells Clement, 'Yes there was blood. I'll show you. Dear me, this is like doubting Thomas. Do you want to touch me too?' (321). Mir, of course, has already told Lucas that they are 'eternally connected', and here they share some signs of Christ. The point is that, in the sliding of meaning from one

---

172. Matthew 13:55 = Mark 6:3.
173. Luke 23:43: 'Today you will be with me in paradise.'
174. Murdoch, 'Waiting on God', p. 15, citing Weil, *Waiting on God*, p. 14.
175. Matthew 17:2 = Mark 9:2. At the same time, Mir's words recall the question of God to Cain, 'Where is your brother?' and his reply, 'am I my brother's keeper?' (Genesis 4:9–10).
176. John 19:26–7.
177. John 11:30, 18:14.

sense of 'angel' to another, all human beings can become 'messengers' of the Good, witnessing to those who are actually incarnations of the Good. In Murdoch's Christology, people can mediate the 'mystic Christ' to others.[178] Mir is a mediator; despite Bellamy's adulation, he is not presented as a 'pure sinless creature', in fact beginning his relationship with Lucas in the mood of seeking revenge.

In this very slipping from the role of teacher to that of avatar, Lovibond finds, however, a problematic influence of Weil on Murdoch. With her proper concern for the oppression inflicted on women, Lovibond is troubled by Weil's acceptance of authoritarianism, urging obedience to the person next above one in a social or spiritual hierarchy, as if in obedience to God. Weil commends, we have seen, 'a certain veneration, a certain devotion towards superiors, considered not as individuals, nor in relation to the powers they hold, but as symbols' of a higher realm. Lovibond suggests that some of this sense of hierarchy lingers on in Murdoch, who makes 'an emotional investment in (say) Buddha or Jesus Christ',[179] whom Murdoch regards, while being imperfect men, as serving for 'images and tokens of perfect spiritual ideas'.[180] This might not be too dangerous for a sense of the self, except that for Murdoch – Lovibond points out – the teacher or guru belongs to 'the same imaginative cluster'. It is easy then to slip from the exceptional avatar to some 'holy' person encountered in everyday life, or (we might say) from one kind of angel to another. Here she quotes Murdoch as asking, 'Can there still, now, be avatars, great teachers, pure of heart in whom we can believe?'[181] Citing Murdoch's reflection that 'we may think of a person as an image of God or of the soul',[182] Lovibond finds her novels persistently suggesting that an investment in such persons 'is both possible and potentially valuable'. She does not name any candidates, but Peter Mir is an obvious one, along with – to a lesser extent – Fr Damien. As Bellamy exclaims of Mir, 'he is an angel … He is an avatar … I wanted him to teach me, to enlighten me' (363).

This tendency to exalt everyday persons to the status of avatar or even angel, with a consequent danger of authoritarianism, is however moderated by Murdoch's continual critique of making another person one's 'saviour'. We become suspicious of Bellamy's identification of Mir as an avatar, when he continues, 'I wanted to be with him forever, for all of my life' (363). Earlier he had appealed to Mir, 'Let me be your patient, let me be your servant, heal me,' and Mir had replied, 'Stop, please stop! I need to heal myself' (299). Earlier he had expressed himself in similar terms to Fr Damien, 'When I write to you I feel you are already enlightening me' (42) and 'I bow before you' (97). Harvey is another, in his displacement, who wants to find a saviour. First he tells Aleph that his love for her is 'like prayer, it's like salvation' (264), and when she leaves to go travelling he thinks that 'if only he

---

178. Dipple, 'The Green Knight', p. 166, regards Mir as an 'apocalyptic figure' like Christ.
179. Lovibond, *Iris Murdoch*, p. 46.
180. Murdoch, *Metaphysics*, p. 478.
181. Ibid., p. 249.
182. Murdoch, *Metaphysics*, p. 306; Murdoch is more positive in *Metaphysics*, p. 455.

could have lived in Aleph's house, slept in Aleph's bed, the magic power which he so desperately longed for would have been granted to him' (328). When he consequently falls in love with Sefton, he tells her, 'You have made me into an angel, you have made me into a god ... I worship you' (389). As we have seen in other novels, making someone else into a saviour is a way of evading the harsh reality of the death of the self and simply positions them in the orbit of one's own world. Correlatively, a similar fantasy attaches to the opposite mood of wanting to be another's saviour. Bellamy had thought at one point about Mir that 'only I can help him', and Fr Damien had written in response, 'Such attempted "rescues" often drag down both the "saver" and the "saved". This can be the region of the demonic' (222). In his last letter, Damien writes that he himself no longer believes in what he once took to be his lifelong mission, 'the saving of souls' (265). Louise, in the depth of her *malheur*, thinks that if she had shown Lucas affection and love 'I might have saved him ... then I would have saved Peter – and saved Aleph' (429). All this saviour-thinking is, in Murdoch's view, illusory. Towards the end of the story, Bellamy's friend and benefactor, Emil, says of Peter Mir, 'They seemed to think he was a magician – well, they thought that of Jesus too. And do you think that he has saved you?' The 'he' is ambiguous, perhaps deliberately, but in any case Bellamy replies 'I'm not saved!'

Mir's physician, Dr Fonsett, is quick to dismiss the thought of finding any image of an avatar in another with a rational explanation: 'Religion is connected with the fantasising aspect of the mind, it is connected with sex ... I suggest simply that you have all, with various deep motives, elected Peter, about whom you know very little, to be your guru!' (357). Joan is quick to reply, 'Well, what's wrong with sex? ... a great spirit has been released.' Murdoch is more subtle than her creation, Fonsett, and is more on the side of Joan. It is possible to find another person becoming an 'image' or living 'icon' of the Good, or being a signpost to it, but making another into a saviour, or making *oneself* into a saviour, is indeed a fantasy. Murdoch is adding it to the illusory 'compensations' for affliction that Weil identifies.

In this penultimate novel, before the tragic decline in artistic skill evident in the last book, when Alzheimer's disease began to take its cruel grip on Murdoch, we have what is the final stage of Murdoch's long conversation with Simone Weil. *The Green Knight* takes up many echoes from *The Flight from the Enchanter*, not least exploring the nature of displacement and the need to give attention to another. Weil had been steadfast in avoiding all compensations that might detract from facing the 'void', and yet Murdoch evidently thinks that her central idea of 'redemptive suffering' in identity with Christ[183] is just one such illusion, inhibiting us from accepting the death of the ego-self. Weil believes that Christ is a saviour, because we can share – in our own void – in the forsakenness of Christ by God his Father and so know the bridging of that terrible gulf by love.[184] Further, she writes that 'an innocent being who suffers sheds the light of salvation upon evil. He is the

---

183. Weil, *Gravity and Grace*, pp. 82, cf. 79–80.
184. Weil, *Waiting on God*, pp. 67–70.

visible image of the innocent God. That is why a God who loves man and a man who loves God have to suffer.'[185] Thinking of the cross of Christ, she writes that 'the tree that nourishes kills, and the tree of suffering saves.'[186] Making Christ a saviour is for Murdoch a fantasy. So what can she do with this element in Weil? There is still what Bellamy recalls on the last page of the novel as 'something about the presence of Christ not fading' and the possibility of finding an image – however faint – of the mystical Christ in others.

185. Weil, *Notebooks*, p. 234.
186. Ibid., p. 269.

CODA: WITH AND BEYOND SIMONE WEIL: THE DIALOGUE BETWEEN MURDOCH AND THEOLOGY

In Murdoch's dialogue with Simone Weil we can find recapitulated many of the aspects of the two-way dialogue between theology and Murdoch that I have been identifying in this book. In their process of making doctrine, Murdoch's suspicion of Christ as a symbol of suffering should lead Christian theologians to prefer theories of atonement that stress the creative power of love revealed in the cross of Jesus over forensic theories that associate the death of Christ with some kind of divine punishment for human sins.[1]

Weil does not in fact suggest that the cross of Christ is a vicarious punishment, but she does envisage a *deliberate* abandonment of Christ by God, in order that, in our own experience of an absent God, we can know that the divine love shown us by Christ can remain unbroken. For her, unity and abandonment are two forms of the 'love which is God himself'.[2] I suggest that atonement theory that centres on the persuasive love of God revealed in the cross will certainly affirm – with Weil – that human forsakenness enters into the relational space or 'infinite distance'[3] in the Trinity; but it will understand – beyond Weil – the universal condition of estrangement in which Christ participates to be entirely due to *human* lack of love rather than a divine strategy.[4] In this area of thought, nevertheless, Murdoch's adoption of Weil's 'void' should show theologians the possibilities of placing the negative sublime within both theology and spiritual experience, introducing a necessary shock of the apophatic where language fails.[5]

Murdoch's suspicion that talk of a suffering God undermines the very notion of a God may be answered theologically by locating the vulnerability of God within God's own will and desire to be a creator of a free and vulnerable universe, rather than having any conditions imposed upon God externally.[6] But Murdoch's

---

1. See earlier, pp. 39–40.
2. Weil, *Waiting on God*, pp. 70–1.
3. Weil, *Notebooks*, pp. 126, 208.
4. See earlier, pp. 40, cf. 176–7.
5. See earlier, pp. 100, 108.
6. See Moltmann, *Trinity and the Kingdom of God*, pp. 105–8, 56–9; Fiddes, *Creative Suffering of God*, pp. 71–6; Barth, *Church Dogmatics*, II/1, pp. 280–1.

pressing of the logic of Bonhoeffer's phrase 'as if there were no God' should prompt theologians to develop a theology of the suffering God that exceeds mere sentimentality. Weil uses the phrases 'crucified God' and 'suffering God' with regard to Christ,[7] but she is not explicit about carrying this mutability from his incarnate state into an eternal divine nature, although her location of a sense of abandonment within the Trinity might well imply this. Beyond Weil, a theology that takes divine passibility seriously and not just sentimentally ('how comforting to think God suffers too') is willing to work out the implications of passibility and empathy in terms of a radical self-limiting of divine knowledge and power and a mutability of God in the sense of divine openness to new experience arising from creation.[8]

The theologian who takes seriously the uniqueness, unclassifiability and mystery of God will agree with Murdoch that God cannot be a 'super-person'. By contrast, Weil conceives God as some kind of 'person' by understanding the Trinity in terms of a single divine subjectivity which diversifies itself into 'subject, object, and desire which unites them'. Mysteriously, God is one 'I' and yet also three 'I's:

> This union is a Person, that is to say it differs from the union between subject and object with which we are familiar, and which is an abstract relationship. Here, the subject is subject, and the object is again subject, and the union is also subject. God regarded as subject says 'I', God regarded as object says 'I', and God regarded as wisdom or love says 'I'. In whichever quality we may consider him, he always says 'I'.[9]

I have already suggested that God as Trinity may be understood as 'personal', in so far as God is infinitely relational, but that conceiving God as three movements of relationship need not mean that God is either one personal being or three.[10] I would now add that, contrary to Weil's trinitarian proposal, it does not entail God as either one *subjectivity* ('I') or three. Trinity is a symbol for participating in inexhaustible yet distinguishable currents of love that are always excessive to our own love and that we can only call relational. Moreover, these relations can be known only in and through relations with other people and things, while Weil's model makes the Trinity, in an Augustinian way, a self-enclosed circle: 'Trinity – God's relationship to himself ... man is related to something other ... God alone knows and loves himself.'[11] Murdoch's dismissal of God as 'a' person, however subtly conceived 'a divine person' might be, is helpful in taking us beyond Weil here.

---

7. Weil, *Notebooks*, pp. 343, 490, 541.

8. Fiddes, *Creative Suffering of God*, pp. 68–71; Catherine Keller, *Face of the Deep: A Theology of Becoming* (London: Routledge, 2003), pp. 180–2, 226–8.

9. Weil, *Notebooks*, p. 336.

10. See earlier, pp. 74–5, 131.

11. Weil, *Notebooks*, pp. 263–4.

While Murdoch can help the theologian to make theology in these ways the other direction of the dialogue the theologian can also open up a critique of Murdoch. A theological perspective alerts us to an inconsistency in maintaining the validity of 'the Good' as a symbol of ultimate reality, while rejecting 'the personal' on the grounds that it is only symbolic;[12] the theological approach suggests that, without the challenge of an existence of God over against the world, signs of the Good are always liable to become 'compensations';[13] and it prompts us to see that characters in her novels who are warned against seeking salvation from others – 'you must do it all yourself' – tend to become isolated from community.[14]

But Murdoch's penultimate novel, *The Green Knight*, offers us perhaps the clearest example of the two-way dialogue, in being a novel about resurrection. Peter Mir has, mysteriously, risen from death: the improbability of his survival is constantly stressed: Mir himself refers to 'my resurrection'; Clement confesses that 'he died for me';[15] Bellamy affirms 'you died and rose again'; and Moy remarks on meeting him, 'He seems to me to be dead.'[16] But the story tells us that, like the story of Lazarus, but unlike the Gospel story of Christ, Mir must die in the end without further resurrection, and that he is reconciled to this fate. For Murdoch, belief in resurrection is the archetypal illusion, since it promises a reward for doing the good and deflects from the reality of death. Unless we can accept the finality of physical death, we will always be trying to evade the death of the ego-self. This does not seem to trouble Weil, who apparently affirms resurrection, despite insisting that we must live life under the horizon of death:[17] of Christ she writes: 'The entire being becomes deprivation of God: how proceed beyond this? There is nothing after this, except the resurrection.'[18]

If (in the first direction of the dialogue) we allow Murdoch's art to help us to make theology, it will challenge us to construct a theology of resurrection which does not undermine the tragedy of the cross. One who has attempted this is D. M. MacKinnon, Murdoch's former teacher of philosophy, with whom she remained in conversation on theology and whose works she read and annotated assiduously. He insists that the cross of Jesus must be understood as belonging within the class of events that are human tragedies, which means that neither Christ nor the Christian believer can interpret the darkness of the cross by resort to any metaphysical solace. There is an 'intractable' element of 'sheer waste' in the 'failure and defeat' of Christ.[19] The resurrection, whatever its nature, cannot alleviate or

---

12. See earlier, pp. 73–4.
13. See earlier, p. 35.
14. See earlier, pp. 44–5.
15. Murdoch, *Green Knight*, p. 91.
16. Ibid., pp. 101, 91, 297, 168.
17. Weil, *Notebooks*, p. 56: 'We should orientate ourselves, not towards another mode of life, but towards death'; cf. pp. 48, 52.
18. Weil, *Notebooks*, p. 26; cf. pp. 479, 535, 539, 545.
19. MacKinnon, *Borderlands* (IML 25), pp. 102–3; cf. MacKinnon, *Explorations in Theology* (IML 379), pp. 185, 187.

cancel the tragedy of the death of Christ. 'It is only in the light of the resurrection,' writes MacKinnon, that Christians can say with Pascal that 'Christ will indeed be in agony unto the end of the world'.[20] The resurrection narratives are 'literary projections' of a 'victory' in which Jesus enters upon a life that 'does not move towards an inescapable horizon of death, a life over which death is affirmed no longer to have any sovereignty', but this very victory 'remains mysteriously and inescapably tragic'.[21] MacKinnon emphasizes that the resurrection is a 'unique' event, of its own kind,[22] not to be easily classified among events of history, but both cross and resurrection are acts of God in Christ which are 'objective, as something built into the structure of the world'.[23] MacKinnon admits that 'my own bias is always in the realists' direction, and that therefore I am (perhaps quite unfairly) hostile to views which seem to me to move in the direction of saying that faith creates its own objectives'.[24] Something unique and creative has happened, objectively in the resurrection, in an 'event which is more than event',[25] which requires 'discovery' by faith and reason. He asserts:

> We are left asking questions in a process of interrogation that is partly, though not entirely, self-interrogation, to which we see no easy end; but this may be as it is because the mysteries that set our inquiring in motion have their authority over us, thus continually to disturb our minds, only because they do touch what is ultimate, which is at once within and yet wholly beyond our comprehension.[26]

The passion and resurrection of Christ call us to exploration and questioning as events that have 'authority over us', and we must take care not to cancel out one uniqueness by another. Such an epistemology does not, of course, simply disprove Murdoch's own rejection of anything objective about the resurrection. But it can be developed in a way that learns from her insistence on tragedy.

The dialogue between Murdoch and theology also works in the other direction, to open up an exposition of Murdoch. A theologian with the kind of perspective adopted by MacKinnon will point out that she shows some perplexity about her own affirmation of the presence of a 'mystical Christ'. She writes, referring to Weil:

> For a true religious ideal should we not turn to the de-individualized individual of Buddhism or mystical Christianity, the 'empty' soul of Eckhart, the 'decreated'

---

20. MacKinnon, *Borderlands*, p. 96.
21. MacKinnon, *Explorations in Theology*, pp. 194–5.
22. Donald MacKinnon, 'Good Friday and Easter: An Interpretation', in Lampe and MacKinnon, *The Resurrection*, pp. 71–86 (84).
23. Mackinnon, 'Further Reflections', in Lampe and MacKinnon, *The Resurrection*, pp. 105–12 (110).
24. Ibid., p. 111.
25. MacKinnon, 'The Resurrection', p. 64.
26. MacKinnon, 'Good Friday and Easter', p. 85.

person of Simone Weil? ... Christ is seen as the guarantor of the irreducible individual, seen in all his particularity by God, and incarnate in a particular man. Yet is Christ himself 'really there', is he not hallowed, in the remarkable accounts of him out of individuality? Is he not described at last and seen (as perhaps other instances are not) as the perfect mystical *non-individual*?[27]

The questions betray a puzzlement and are not satisfactorily answered in the succeeding text. From the very first encounter with Weil, Murdoch has wanted to affirm a greater particularity of the human person than she has found in Weil, and while she has adopted her language of 'decreation', she has limited its impact to the egocentric self, not the whole self: so she wrote earlier in her *Metaphysics*: 'The tragic image of death in art is a counterpart or reflection of *selfless* decreated being,'[28] and she goes on to write, 'The mystical man, "decreated" to use Weil's term, who has broken the barriers of the ego is an ever-present religious ideal, a magnetic moral picture.'[29] Christ ought then to be what he seems to be in the Gospel narratives, a particular person with the moral attractiveness of someone who has conquered the selfish ego. But as a mystical presence he appears to have lost particularity, 'hallowed ... out of individuality'. Murdoch does not resolve this dilemma; in the succeeding text she simply blurs the issue by proposing that there are a number of different types of human beings who balance each other out in actualizing human nature – 'the demonic man [i.e. a highly individualized man], the mystical man, the Platonic-Kantian good man, and the Hobbesian-Humian political fiction man'.[30] This hardly deals with her question which seems to be about how the non-individualized mystical Christ might be the same as, or at least be related to, the particularized figure of the Gospels.

A theologian could propose an answer to this question from the viewpoint of the resurrection of Christ. Human individuals are always related to others; while having a core of individual particularity, this is always formed in relationship not in a private isolation, so that our own individuality is less our possession than a gift to us from the love of others. The particularity of Christ in the Gospels derives from his being 'the man for others', as Bonhoeffer stresses in his final *Letters and Papers*, read by Murdoch.[31] In the resurrection, which can only be a metaphor for the life of a new creation,[32] or what MacKinnon calls a life which no longer moves 'towards an inescapable horizon of death', this being for others takes the form of a more corporate and universal life. The metaphor for this state of being in the New

---

27. Murdoch, *Metaphysics*, p. 352, original emphasis.
28. Ibid., p. 140, my emphasis.
29. Ibid., p. 354.
30. Ibid.
31. Bonhoeffer, *Letters and Papers* (Murdoch's copy, 1966), p. 165; passage with marginal lines, possibly by Murdoch. But on annotations, see above, p. 30 n.131.
32. See Wolfhart Pannenberg, *Jesus: God and Man* (trans. Lewis Wilkins and Duane Priebe) (London: SCM, 1973), p. 74.

Testament is 'the body of Christ', an image for the way that the risen Christ now lives embodied in countless lives.[33] The risen Christ is thus both particular and a non-individual, universal presence. In his book *The Origin of Christology*, the New Testament scholar C. F. D. Moule expresses the phenomenon in this way: 'A person who had recently been crucified, but found to be alive, with "absolute life", the life of the age to come [...] is found, moreover, to be an inclusive, all-embracing presence.'[34] Murdoch possessed Moule's book in her Oxford collection, though we cannot know – unlike the books by MacKinnon – whether she read it.

Murdoch's Christ is 'the perfect mystical non-individual' and yet is also to be identified in some way with the particular Christ of the Gospels, as well as with the Christ 'whom we make our own'[35] and who is perhaps over-privatized by one character as 'the Christ that belonged only to her'.[36] Despite these tensions in her picture, I am not suggesting that a theological understanding of the resurrected Christ *must* be viewed as more coherent than Murdoch's 'mystical Christ'. Rather, the theology makes us sensitive to the question that Murdoch is asking – is Christ really there? – and the way that she tries to answer it. At the same time, theology can alert us to the way that Murdoch's attention to the Good is always diffused through the many signs of the Good that the particularities of the world represent, among which is the Christ.[37]

It is in this kind of conversation with a theologian, Paul Tillich – and with his understanding of God as our 'ultimate concern' – that Murdoch concludes her most substantial piece of moral philosophy, published as she was writing *The Green Knight*, her most theological novel:

> Paul Tillich describes theology as a response to 'the totality of man's creative self-interpretation in a particular period'. We need a theology which can continue without God. Why not call such a reflection a form of moral philosophy? All right, so long as it treats of those matters of 'ultimate concern', our experience of the unconditioned and our continued sense of what is holy.[38]

---

33. In the New Testament this concept is restricted to the bodies of Christ's disciples, the church, but Bonhoeffer rightly extends this to 'the form of Christ in the world': see Bonhoeffer, *Ethics*, 100–1.

34. C. F. D. Moule, *The Origin of Christology* (Cambridge: Cambridge University Press, 1977), p. 53 (IML 367).

35. Murdoch, *Metaphysics*, p. 429.

36. Murdoch, *Nuns and Soldiers*, p. 304.

37. On Derrida, Murdoch and a doctrine of the triune God, see above, pp. 151–2.

38. Murdoch, *Metaphysics*, pp. 511–12.

BIBLIOGRAPHY

Note: IML in the footnotes refers to a volume in the Iris Murdoch Oxford Library, preserved in the Iris Murdoch Archive at the Kingston School of Art, Kingston University.

Altorf, Marije, *Iris Murdoch and the Art of Imagining*. London: Continuum, 2008.
Anon., *Sir Gawain and the Green Knight*, ed. J. R. Tolkien and E. V. Gordon. Oxford: Oxford University Press, 2nd edn, 1967.
Antonaccio, Maria, and William Schweiker (eds), *Iris Murdoch and the Search for Human Goodness*. Chicago: University of Chicago Press, 1996.
Armstrong, Charles I., 'Echo: Reading the Unnamable through Kant and Kristeva', *Nordic Journal of English Studies* 1.1 (June 2002), pp. 173–87.
Bagnoli, Carla, 'Constrained by Reason, Transformed by Love: Murdoch on the Standard of Proof', in Gary Browning (ed.), *Murdoch on Truth and Love*. Cham: Palgrave Macmillan, 2018, pp. 63–88.
Balthasar, Hans Urs von, *The Glory of the Lord: A Theological Aesthetics. Vol. I: Seeing the Form*, trans. E. Leiva-Marikakis, ed. J. Fessio and J. Riches. Edinburgh: T&T Clark, 1982.
Balthasar, Hans Urs von, *The Glory of the Lord: A Theological Aesthetics. Vol. III: Studies in Theological Style: Lay Styles*, trans. Andrew Louth, John Saward, Martin Simon, and Rowan Williams. Edinburgh: T&T Clark, 1986.
Balthasar, Hans Urs von, *The Glory of the Lord: A Theological Aesthetics. Vol. VII: Theology: The New Covenant*, trans. Brian McNeil. Edinburgh: T&T Clark, 1989.
Balthasar, Hans Urs von, *Mysterium Paschale*, trans. Aidan Nichols. Edinburgh: T&T Clark, 1990.
Balthasar, Hans Urs von, *Theo-Logic. Theological Logical Theory, Vol. I: The Truth of the World*, trans. Adrian J. Walker. San Francisco: Ignatius Press, 2000.
Barth, Karl, *Church Dogmatics*, trans. and ed. G. W. Bromiley and T. F. Torrance, 14 vols. Edinburgh: T&T Clark, 1936–77.
Battersby, Christine, *The Phenomenal Woman*. Cambridge, MA: Polity Press, 1998.
Battersby, Christine, *The Sublime, Terror and Human Difference*. London: Routledge, 2007.
Bauerschmidt, Frederick Christian, 'The Theological Sublime', in John Milbank, Catherine Pickstock and Graham Ward (eds), *Radical Orthodoxy: A New Theology*. London: Routledge, 1999, pp. 201–19.
Bayley, John, *Iris and Her Friends: A Memoir of Memory and Desire*. New York: W.W. Norton, 1999.
Bayley, John, *Iris and the Friends: A Year of Memories*. London: Gerald Duckworth, 1999.
Bellamy, Michael, 'An Interview with Iris Murdoch', *Contemporary Literature* 18 (1977), pp. 129–40.
Bethge, Eberhard, 'The Challenge of Dietrich Bonhoeffer's Life and Theology', in Gregor Smith (ed.), *World Come of Age: A Symposium on Dietrich Bonhoeffer*. London: Collins, 1967, pp. 22–88.

Betz, John R., 'Beyond the Sublime: The Aesthetics of the Analogy of Being', part 1 in *Modern Theology* 21.3 (2005), pp. 367–411, part 2 in *Modern Theology* 22.1 (2006), pp. 1–50.
Boehme, Jacob, 'Clavis Specialis', in G. Ward and T. Langcake (eds), *The Works of Jacob Behmen*, 4 vols. London: Richardson, 1764–81.
Boff, Leonardo, *Passion of Christ, Passion of the World*. New York: Orbis, 1987.
Bonhoeffer, Dietrich, *Ethics*, trans. Reinhard Krauss, Charles C. West, and Douoglas W. Stott, Dietrich Bonhoeffer Works 6. Minneapolis: Fortress Press, 2009.
Bonhoeffer, Dietrich, *Letters and Papers from Prison*. London: Collins/Fontana, 1966 (repr.).
Bonhoeffer, Dietrich, *Letters and Papers from Prison*, trans. Isabel Best, Lisa E. Dahill, Reinhard Krauss, and Nancy Lukens, Dietrich Bonhoeffer Works 8. Minneapolis: Fortress Press, 2010.
Bradley, F. H., *Appearance and Reality: A Metaphysical Essay*. London: Oxford University Press, 2nd edn, 1897.
Broackes, Justin (ed.), *Iris Murdoch, Philosopher*. Oxford: Oxford University Press, 2011.
Broackes, Justin, 'Introduction', in Justin Broackes (ed.), *Iris Murdoch, Philosopher*. Oxford: Oxford University Press, 2011, pp. 19–20.
Broackes, Justin, 'Iris Murdoch's First Encounters with Simone Weil', *Iris Murdoch Review* (2017), pp. 17–20.
Browning, Gary, 'Murdoch and the End of Ideology', in Gary Browning (ed.), *Murdoch on Truth and Love*. Cham: Palgrave Macmillan, 2018, pp. 133–57.
Browning, Gary (ed.), *Murdoch on Truth and Love*. Cham: Palgrave Macmillan, 2018.
Brümmer, Vincent, *The Model of Love*. Cambridge: Cambridge University Press, 1993.
Buber, Martin, *Eclipse of God*. Sussex: Harvester, 1969.
Bultmann, Rudolph, 'The Idea of God and Modern Man', in Gregor Smith (ed.), *World Come of Age: A Symposium on Dietrich Bonhoeffer*. London: Collins, 1967, pp. 256–73.
Bultmann, Rudolph, *Jesus Christ and Mythology*. London: SCM Press, 1963.
Bump, Jerome, '"The Wreck of the Deutschland" and the Dynamic Sublime', *English Literary History* 41.1 (1974), pp. 106–29.
Burke, Edmund, *A Philosophical Enquiry into the Origin of Our Ideas of the Sublime and Beautiful*, ed. Adam Phillips. Oxford: Oxford University Press, 1990.
Butler, Judith, *Gender Trouble: Feminism and the Subversion of Identity*. London: Routledge, 1990.
Byatt, Antonia, *Degrees of Freedom: The Early Novels of Iris Murdoch*. London: Vintage, 2nd edn, 1994.
Byatt, Antonia, *Possession: A Romance*. London: Chatto & Windus, 1990.
Calvin, John, *Institutes of the Christian Religion*, trans. Ford Lewis Battles, ed. John McNeill, 2 vols. London: SCM Press, 1961.
Caputo, John D., *The Prayers and Tears of Jacques Derrida: Religion without Religion*. Bloomington: Indiana University Press, 1997.
Cavallo, Adolfo Salvatore, *The Unicorn Tapestries at the Metropolitan Museum of Art*. New York: Harry N. Abrahams, 1998.
Chappell, Sophie-Grace, 'Love and Knowledge in Murdoch', in Gary Browning (ed.), *Murdoch on Truth and Love*. Cham: Palgrave Macmillan, 2018, pp. 89–108.
Chevalier, Jean-Louis (ed.), *Recontres avec Iris Murdoch*. Caen: Centre de Recherches de Littérature et Linguistique des Pays de Langue Anglaise, Université de Caen, 1978.
Clements, Keith, *Dietrich Bonhoeffer's Ecumenical Quest*. Geneva: WCC, 2015.

Clines, David J. A., *Job 38–42*, Word Biblical Commentary 18B. Nashville: Thomas Nelson, 2011.
Conradi, Peter J., *Iris Murdoch: A Life*. London: HarperCollins, 2001.
Conradi, Peter J., 'Platonism in Iris Murdoch', in Anne Baldwin and Sarah Hutton (eds), *Platonism and the English Imagination*. Cambridge: Cambridge University Press, 1994, pp. 330–42.
Conradi, Peter J., *The Saint and the Artist: A Study of the Fiction of Iris Murdoch*. London: HarperCollins, 2nd edn, 2001 (repr.).
Coward, Harold, and Toby Foshay (eds), *Derrida and Negative Theology*. Albany: State University of New York Press, 1992.
Cupitt, Don, 'Iris Murdoch: A Case of Star-Friendship', in Anne Rowe and Avril Horner (eds), *Iris Murdoch: Texts and Contexts*. New York: Palgrave Macmillan, 2012, pp. 11–16.
Cupitt, Don, *Radicals and the Future of the Church*. London: SCM, 1989.
Cupitt, Don, *Taking Leave of God*. London: SCM, 1980.
Derrida, Jacques, 'Afterward: Toward an Ethic of Discussion', in *Limited Inc*, trans. Samuel Weber. Evanston: Northwestern University Press, 1988, pp. 111–54.
Derrida, Jacques, 'Différance', in *Margins of Philosophy*, trans. Alan Bass. Chicago: University of Chicago Press, 1982, pp. 1–28.
Derrida, Jacques, 'How to Avoid Speaking: Denials', trans. Ken Frieden, in Harold Coward and Toby Foshay (eds), *Derrida and Negative Theology*. Albany: State University of New York Press, 1992, pp. 73–142.
Derrida, Jacques, 'Of an Apocalyptic Tone Newly Adopted in Philosophy', trans. J. Leavey, in Harold Coward and Toby Foshay (eds), *Derrida and Negative Theology*. Albany: State University of New York Press, 1992, pp. 25–72.
Derrida, Jacques, *Of Grammatology*, trans. G. C. Spivak. Baltimore: Johns Hopkins University Press, 1976 (repr.).
Derrida, Jacques, *On the Name*, trans. T. Dutoit. Stanford: Stanford University Press, 1995.
Derrida, Jacques, *Parages*. Paris: Galilée, 1987.
Derrida, Jacques, 'Plato's Pharmacy', in *Dissemination*, trans. Barbara Johnson. Chicago: University of Chicago Press, 1981, pp. 61–171.
Derrida, Jacques, *Positions*, trans. Alan Bass. Chicago: University of Chicago Press, 1971.
Derrida, Jacques, *Psyché: L'Inventions de L'Autre*. Paris: Galilée, 1987.
Derrida, Jacques, *Rogues: Two Essays on Reason*, trans. Pascale-Anne Brault and Michael Naas. Stanford: Stanford University Press, 2005.
Derrida, Jacques, *Speech and Phenomena*, trans. David Allison. Evanston: Northwestern University Press, 1973.
Derrida, Jacques, *The Truth in Painting*, trans. Geoff Bennington and Ian Macleod. Chicago: University of Chicago Press, 1987.
Derrida, Jacques, 'White Mythology', in *Margins of Philosophy*, trans. Alan Bass. Chicago: University of Chicago Press, 1982, pp. 207–72.
Derrida, Jacques, *Writing and Difference*, trans. A. Bass. London: Routledge, 1978.
Dipple, Elizabeth, 'The Green Knight and Other Vagaries of the Spirit; or Tricks and Images of the Soul; or the Uses of Imaginative Literature', in Maria Antonaccio and William Schweiker (eds), *Iris Murdoch and the Search for Human Goodness*. Chicago: University of Chicago Press, 1996, pp. 138–70.
Dipple, Elizabeth, *Iris Murdoch: Work for the Spirit*. London: Methuen, 1982.
Faber, Roland, *God as Poet of the World*. Louisville: Westminster/John Knox, 2008.

Fiddes, Paul S., 'Concept, Image and Story in Systematic Theology', *International Journal of Systematic Theology* 11.1 (2009), pp. 3–23.

Fiddes, Paul S., *The Creative Suffering of God*. Oxford: Oxford University Press, 1988.

Fiddes, Paul S., *Freedom and Limit: A Dialogue between Literature and Christian Doctrine*. Basingstoke: Macmillan, 1991.

Fiddes, Paul S., *Participating in God: A Pastoral Doctrine of the Trinity*. London: Darton, Longman and Todd, 2000.

Fiddes, Paul S., *The Promised End: Eschatology in Theology and Literature*. Oxford: Blackwell, 2000.

Fiddes, Paul S., 'Relational Trinity: Radical Perspective', in Jason Sexton (ed.), *Two Views on the Doctrine of the Trinity*. Grand Rapids: Zondervan, 2014, pp. 159–85.

Fiddes, Paul S., *Seeing the World and Knowing God: Hebrew Wisdom and Christian Doctrine in a Late-Modern Context*. Oxford: Oxford University Press, 2013.

Forsberg, Niklas, '"Taking the Linguistic Method Seriously". On Iris Murdoch on Language and Linguistic Philosophy', in Gary Browning (ed.), *Murdoch on Truth and Love*. Cham: Palgrave Macmillan, 2018, pp. 109–32.

Fraser, G. S., 'Iris Murdoch and the Solidity of the Normal', in John Wain (ed.), *International Literary Annual, Vol. 11*. London: John Calder, 1959, pp. 37–54.

Freud, Sigmund, *Standard Edition of the Complete Psychological Works of Sigmund Freud*, trans. James Strachey and Anna Freud, 18 vols. London: Hogarth Press, 1953–74.

Freud, Sigmund, *Totem and Taboo: Some Points of Agreement between the Mental Lives of Savages and Neurotics*, trans. James Strachey. Oxford: Routledge Classics, 2001 (repr.).

Gardner, W. H., *Gerard Manley Hopkins: A Study of Poetic Idiosyncrasy in Relation to Poetic Tradition*, 2 vols. London: Oxford University Press, 1961.

Haffenden, John, *Novelists in Interview*. London: Methuen, 1985.

Harris, Daniel A., *Inspirations Unbidden: The 'Terrible Sonnets' of Gerard Manley Hopkins*. Berkeley: University of California Press, 1982.

Hart, David Bentley, *The Beauty of the Infinite: The Aesthetics of Christian Truth*. Grand Rapids: Eerdmans, 2003.

Heidegger, Martin, 'The Onto-theo-logical Constitution of Metaphysics', in *Identity and Difference*, trans. J. Stambaugh. Chicago: Chicago University Press, 2002, pp. 42–76.

Hertz, Neil, *The End of the Line: Essays on Psychoanalysis and the Sublime*. New York: Columbia University Press, 1985.

Hick, John (ed.), *The Myth of God Incarnate*. London: SCM, 1977.

Hopkins, Gerard Manley, *Oxford Essays and Notes, Vol. 4*, ed. Lesley Higgins. The Collected Works of Gerard Manley Hopkins, 9 vols. Oxford: Oxford University Press, 2006.

Hopkins, Gerard Manley, *The Poems*, ed. W. H. Gardner and N. H. Mackenzie. London: Oxford University Press, 4th edn, 1967.

Hopkins, Gerard Manley, *The Sermons and Devotional Writings*, ed. Christopher Devlin, S.J. London: Oxford University Press, 1959.

Horner, Avril, 'The "Wondrous Necessary Man": Canetti, *The Unicorn* and *The Changeling*', in Anne Rowe and Avril Horner (eds), *Iris Murdoch: Texts and Contexts*. New York: Palgrave Macmillan, 2012, pp. 163–76.

Horner, Avril and Ann Rowe (eds), *Living on Paper: Letters from Iris Murdoch 1934–1995*. London: Chatto & Windus, 2015.

Johnson, Deborah, *Iris Murdoch* (Key Women Writers). Brighton: Harvester, 1987.

Johnson, Elizabeth A., *She Who Is: The Mystery of God in Feminist Theological Discourse*. New York: Crossroad, 1992.

Jones, Ernest, *Hamlet and Oedipus*. London: Gollancz, 1949.
Julian of Norwich, *Revelations of Divine Love*, trans. Elizabeth Spearing. Harmondsworth: Penguin, 1998.
Jüngel, Eberhard, *God as the Mystery of the World*, trans. D. Guder. Edinburgh: T&T Clark, 1983.
Jüngel, Eberhard, 'Von Tod des lebendigen Gottes', *Zeitschrift für Theologie und Kirche* 65 (1968), pp. 93–116.
Jüngel, Eberhard, 'The World as Possibility and Actuality', in J. B. Webster (ed. and trans.), *Theological Essays*. Edinburgh: T&T Clark, 1989, pp. 95–123.
Kant, Immanuel, *The Critique of Judgement*, trans. James Creed Meredith. Oxford: Oxford University Press, 1973 (repr.).
Kee, Alistair, *Constantine Versus Christ*. London: SCM Press, 1982.
Keller, Catherine, *Face of the Deep: A Theology of Becoming*. London: Routledge, 2003.
Kerr, Fergus, 'Back to Plato with Iris Murdoch', in *Immortal Longings. Versions of Transcending Humanity*. London: SPCK, 1997, pp. 68–88.
Kierkegaard, Søren, *Works of Love*, trans. H. V. Hong and E. H. Hong. Princeton: Princeton University Press, 1955.
Kristeva, Julia, *Black Sun: Depression and Melancholia*. New York: Columbia, 1989.
Kristeva, Julia, *Desire in Language: A Semiotic Approach to Literature and Art*, trans. T. Gora, A. Jardine and L. Roudiez. Oxford: Blackwell, 1980.
Kristeva, Julia, *In the Beginning was Love: Psychoanalysis and Faith*, trans. Arthur Goldhammer. New York: Columbia University Press, 1987.
Kristeva, Julia, *Murder in Byzantium*, trans. C. Jon Delagu. New York: Columbia University Press, 2006.
Kristeva, Julia, *Powers of Horror: An Essay on Abjection*, trans. Leon S. Roudiez. New York: Columbia University Press, 1982.
Kristeva, Julia, *Revolution in Poetic Language*, trans. M. Waller. New York: Columbia University Press, 1984 (repr.).
Kristeva, Julia, *Tales of Love*, trans. Leon S. Roudiez. New York: Columbia University Press, 1987.
Lacan, Jacques, *Écrits: A Selection*, trans. A. Sheridan. London: Tavistock/Routledge, 1977 (repr.).
Lacan, Jacques, *The Ethics of Psychoanalysis: The Seminar of Jacque Lacan: Book VII*, trans. Dennis Porter. London: Routledge, 2008.
Lacan, Jacques, *The Four Fundamental Concepts of Psychoanalysis*, trans. A. Sheridan. Harmondsworth: Penguin, 1979.
Lampe, G. W. H., and D. M. MacKinnon, *The Resurrection: A Dialogue between Two Cambridge Professors in a Secular Age*, ed. William Purcell. London: A. R. Mowbray, 1966.
Leeson, Mike, *Iris Murdoch: Philosophical Novelist*. London: Continuum, 2010.
Leibniz, G. W., *Die Philosophischen Schriften, Vol. 7*, ed. G. J. Gerhardt. 7 vols. Hildesheim: G. Olms, 1875–1890, pp. 389–420.
Lello, Ronald (ed.), *Revelations*. London: Border Television, 1985.
Lenehan, Kevin A., '*Etsi deus non daretur*: Bonhoeffer's Useful Misuse of Grotius' Maxim and Its Implications for Evangelisation in the World Come of Age', *Australasian Journal of Bonhoeffer Studies* 1/1 (2013), pp. 34–60.
Leeson, Mike, *Iris Murdoch: Philosophical Novelist*. London: Continuum, 201.
Levinas, Emmanuel, 'Meaning and Sense', in Adrian T. Peperzak, Simon Critchley and Robert Bernasconi (eds.), *Basic Philosophical Writings*. Bloomington: Indiana University Press, 1996, pp. 33–64.

Levinas, Emmanuel, *Otherwise than Being, Or Beyond Essence*, trans. Alphonso Lingis. Pittsburgh: Duquesne University Press, 1998.
Lochhead, Judy, 'The Sublime, the Ineffable, and Other Dangerous Aesthetics', *Women and Music: A Journal of Gender and Culture* 12 (2008), pp. 63–74.
Lovibond, Sabina, *Iris Murdoch, Gender and Philosophy*. London: Routledge, 2011.
Lovibond, Sabina, 'Iris Murdoch and the Quality of Consciousness', in Gary Browning (ed.), *Murdoch on Truth and Love*. Cham: Palgrave Macmillan, 2018, pp. 43–62.
Luther, Martin, *Confession Concerning Christ's Supper* (1528), ed. H. T. Lehmann, American Edition of Luther's Works 37. St Louis: Concordia, 1961.
Luther, Martin, *D. Martin Luthers Werke: Kritische Gesamtausgabe*. Weimar: H. Bohlaus Nachfolger, 1883–1929.
Lyotard, Jean-François, *Lessons on the Analytic of the Sublime: Kant's 'Critique of Judgment'*, trans. Elizabeth Rottenberg. Stanford: Stanford University Press, 1994.
MacKinnon, Donald, *Borderlands of Theology and Other Essays*. London: Lutterworth, 1968.
MacKinnon, Donald, *Explorations in Theology 5*. London: SCM Press, 1979.
MacKinnon, Donald, 'Further Reflections', in G. W. H. Lampe and D. M. MacKinnon (eds), *The Resurrection: A Dialogue between Two Cambridge Professors in a Secular Age*. London: A. R. Mowbray, 1966, pp. 105–12.
MacKinnon, Donald, 'Good Friday and Easter: An Interpretation', in G. W. H. Lampe and D. M. MacKinnon (eds), *The Resurrection: A Dialogue between Two Cambridge Professors in a Secular Age*. London: A. R. Mowbray, 1966, pp. 71–86.
MacKinnon, Donald, *The Problem of Metaphysics*. Cambridge: Cambridge University Press, 1974.
MacKinnon, Donald, 'The Resurrection: A Meditation', in G. W. H. Lampe and D. M. MacKinnon (eds), *The Resurrection: A Dialogue between Two Cambridge Professors in a Secular Age*. London: A. R. Mowbray, 1966, pp. 61–70.
Macquarrie, John, *Principles of Christian Theology*. London: SCM, rev. edn, 1977.
Magee, Bryan, *Men of Ideas. Some Creators of Contemporary Philosophy*. Oxford: Oxford University Press, 1982.
Magliola, Robert, *Derrida on the Mend*. West Lafayette: Purdue University Press, 1984.
Mariani, Paul, *Gerard Manley Hopkins: A Life*. New York: Viking, 2008.
McGinn, Bernard (ed.), *Meister Eckhart: Teacher and Preacher*. New York: Paulist Press, 1986.
McGrath, Alister E., *Luther's Theology of the Cross*. Oxford: Blackwell, 1985.
Meszaros, Julia, *Selfless Love and Human Flourishing in Paul Tillich and Iris Murdoch*. Oxford: Oxford University Press. 2016.
Milbank, John, 'Sublimity: The Modern Transcendent', in Regina Schwarz (ed.), *Transcendence*. London: Routledge, 2004, pp. 211–34.
Milbank, John, *Theology and Social Theory: Beyond Secular Reason*. Oxford: Blackwell, 1993.
Miles, Siân (ed.), *Simone Weil: An Anthology*. London: Penguin, 2005.
Milligan, Tony, 'Murdoch and Derrida: Holding Hands under the Table', in Anne Rowe and Avril Horner (eds), *Iris Murdoch: Texts and Contexts*. New York: Palgrave Macmillan, 2012, pp. 77–90.
Moden, Rebecca, '"Liberation through Art": Form and Transformation in Murdoch's Fiction', in Gary Browning (ed.), *Murdoch on Truth and Love*. Cham: Palgrave Macmillan, 2018, pp. 159–81.
Moi, Toril (ed.), *The Kristeva Reader*. Oxford: Blackwell, 1986.

Moltmann, Jürgen, *The Crucified God: The Cross of Christ as the Foundation and Criticism of Christian Theology*, trans. R. A. Wilson and John Bowden. London: SCM Press, 1974.
Moltmann, Jürgen, *The Trinity and the Kingdom of God: The Doctrine of God*, trans. Margaret Kohl. London: SCM Press, 1981.
Moule, C. F. D., *The Origin of Christology*. Cambridge: Cambridge University Press, 1977.
Murdoch, Iris, *An Accidental Man*. London: Chatto & Windus, 1971.
Murdoch, Iris, 'Against Dryness', in Peter Conradi (ed.), *Existentialists and Mystics: Writings on Philosophy and Literature*. London: Chatto & Windus, 1997, pp. 287–96.
Murdoch, Iris, 'Art Is the Imitation of Nature', in Peter Conradi (ed.), *Existentialists and Mystics: Writings on Philosophy and Literature*. London: Chatto & Windus, 1997, pp. 243–58.
Murdoch, Iris, *The Bell*. London: Chatto & Windus, 1958.
Murdoch, Iris, *The Black Prince*. London: Chatto & Windus, 1973.
Murdoch, Iris, *The Book and the Brotherhood*. London: Chatto & Windus, 1987.
Murdoch, Iris, *Bruno's Dream*. London: Chatto & Windus, 1969.
Murdoch, Iris, 'Christ and Myth', interview with F. W. Dillistone, *Frontier*, Autumn 1965, pp. 219–21.
Murdoch, Iris, *Existentialists and Mystics: Writings on Philosophy and Literature*, ed. Peter Conradi. London: Chatto & Windus, 1997.
Murdoch, Iris, 'Existentialists and Mystics', in Peter Conradi (ed.), *Existentialists and Mystics: Writings on Philosophy and Literature*. London: Chatto & Windus, 1997, pp. 221–34.
Murdoch, Iris, *A Fairly Honourable Defeat*. London: Chatto & Windus, 1970.
Murdoch, Iris, *The Fire and the Sun: Why Plato Banished the Artists*. Oxford: Oxford University Press, 1988 (repr.).
Murdoch, Iris, *The Flight from the Enchanter*. London: Chatto & Windus, 1956.
Murdoch, Iris, *The Good Apprentice*. London: Chatto & Windus, 1985.
Murdoch, Iris, *The Green Knight*. London: Chatto & Windus, 1993.
Murdoch, Iris, *Henry and Cato*. London: Chatto & Windus, 1976.
Murdoch, Iris, 'The Idea of Perfection', in Peter Conradi (ed.), *Existentialists and Mystics: Writings on Philosophy and Literature*. London: Chatto & Windus, 1997, pp. 299–336.
Murdoch, Iris, *The Italian Girl*. London: Chatto & Windus, 1964.
Murdoch, Iris, *Jackson's Dilemma*. London: Chatto & Windus, 1995.
Murdoch, Iris, 'Knowing the Void', in Peter Conradi (ed.), *Existentialists and Mystics: Writings on Philosophy and Literature*. London: Chatto & Windus, 1997, pp. 157–60.
Murdoch, Iris, *The Message to the Planet*. London: Chatto & Windus, 1989.
Murdoch, Iris, 'Metaphysics and Ethics', in Peter Conradi (ed.), *Existentialists and Mystics: Writings on Philosophy and Literature*. London: Chatto & Windus, 1997, pp. 59–75.
Murdoch, Iris, *Metaphysics as a Guide to Morals*. London: Chatto & Windus, 1992.
Murdoch, Iris, *The Nice and the Good*. London: Chatto & Windus, 1968.
Murdoch, Iris, 'The Novelist as Metaphysician', in Peter Conradi (ed.), *Existentialists and Mystics: Writings on Philosophy and Literature*. London: Chatto & Windus, 1997, pp. 101–7.
Murdoch, Iris, *Nuns and Soldiers*. London: Chatto & Windus, 1980.
Murdoch, Iris, *The Philosopher's Pupil*. London: Chatto & Windus, 1983.
Murdoch, Iris, *The Red and the Green*. London: Chatto & Windus, 1965.
Murdoch, Iris, *The Sacred and Profane Love Machine*. London: Chatto & Windus, 1970.
Murdoch, Iris, 'Salvation by Words', in Peter Conradi (ed.), *Existentialists and Mystics: Writings on Philosophy and Literature*. London: Chatto & Windus, 1997, pp. 235–42.

Murdoch, Iris, *The Sandcastle*. London: Chatto & Windus, 1957.
Murdoch, Iris, *Sartre, Romantic Rationalist*. London: Collins/Fontana, 1967 (repr.).
Murdoch, Iris, *Sartre, Romantic Rationalist*. London: Chatto & Windus, 2nd edn, 1987.
Murdoch, Iris, *The Sea, The Sea*. London: Chatto & Windus, 1978.
Murdoch, Iris, *A Severed Head*. London: Chatto & Windus, 1961.
Murdoch, Iris, *The Sovereignty of Good*. London: Routledge and Kegan Paul, 1970.
Murdoch, Iris, 'The Sublime and the Beautiful Revisited', in Peter Conradi (ed.), *Existentialists and Mystics: Writings on Philosophy and Literature*. London: Chatto & Windus, 1997, pp. 261–86.
Murdoch, Iris, 'The Sublime and the Good', in Peter Conradi (ed.), *Existentialists and Mystics: Writings on Philosophy and Literature*. London: Chatto & Windus, 1997, pp. 205–20.
Murdoch, Iris, *The Time of the Angels*. London: Chatto & Windus, 1966.
Murdoch, Iris, *The Unicorn*. London: Chatto & Windus, 1963.
Murdoch, Iris, *Under the Net*. London: Chatto & Windus, 1950.
Murdoch, Iris, *An Unofficial Rose*. London: Chatto & Windus, 1962.
Murdoch, Iris, *A Word Child*. London: Chatto & Windus, 1975.
Murdoch, Iris, '"Waiting on God": A Radio Talk on Simone Weil (1951), with a Prefatory Note by Justin Broackes', *Iris Murdoch Review* (2017), pp. 9–16.
Nancy, Jean-Luc, 'The Sublime Offering', in Jean-François Courtine et al. (eds), *Of the Sublime: Presence in Question*, trans. Jeffrey S. Librett. Albany: State University New York Press, 1993, pp. 31–45.
Nicol, Bran, 'Philosophy's Dangerous Pupil: Murdoch and Derrida', *Modern Fiction Studies* 47.3 (2001), pp. 580–601.
Niebuhr, Reinhold, *The Nature and Destiny of Man: A Christian Interpretation. Vol. I: Human Nature*. London: Nisbet, 1941.
Nussbaum, Martha, '"Faint with Secret Knowledge": Love and Vision in Murdoch's *The Black Prince*', in Justin Broackes (ed.), *Iris Murdoch, Philosopher*. Oxford: Oxford University Press, 2011, pp. 135–54.
Nygren, Anders, *Agape and Eros*, trans. Philip Watson. London: SPCK, 1982.
Ong, Walter J., 'Sprung Rhythm and English Tradition', in Geoffrey Hartman (ed.), *Hopkins: A Collection of Critical Essays*. Englewood Cliffs: Prentice Hall, 1966, pp. 151–9.
Osborn, Pamela, 'Minding the Gap: Mourning in the Work of Murdoch and Derrida', in Anne Rowe and Avril Horner (eds), *Iris Murdoch: Texts and Contexts*. New York: Palgrave Macmillan, 2012, pp. 110–28.
Pannenberg, Wolfhart, *Jesus: God and Man*, trans. Lewis Wilkins and Duane Priebe. London: SCM, 1973.
Peters, W. A. M., *Gerard Manley Hopkins: A Critical Essay towards the Understanding of His Poetry*. London: Oxford University Press, 1948.
Pettigrove, Glen, 'Forgiveness without God?', *Journal of Religious Ethics* 40.3 (2012), pp. 518–44.
Prenter, Regin, 'Dietrich Bonhoeffer and Karl Barth's Positivism of Revelation', in Gregor Smith (ed.), *World Come of Age: A Symposium on Dietrich Bonhoeffer*. London: Collins, 1967, pp. 93–130.
Rahner, Karl, *Foundations of Christian Faith: An Introduction to the Idea of Christianity*, trans. W. V. Dych. London: Darton, Longman and Todd, 1978.
Ramsey, Ian, *Religious Language: An Empirical Placing of Theological Phrases*. London: SCM Press, 1957

Robinson, John, *In Extremity: A Study of Gerard Manley Hopkins*. Cambridge: Cambridge University Press, 1978.
Robinson, John A. T., *Honest to God*. London: SCM Press, 1963.
Robinson, John A. T., *The New Reformation*. London: SCM Press, 1965 (repr.).
Robinson, John A. T., 'Our Image of God Must Go', *Observer*, 17 March 1963, p. 21.
Rowe, Anne, *Iris Murdoch* (Writers and Their Work). Liverpool: Liverpool University Press/British Council, 2019.
Rowe, Anne, *The Visual Arts and the Novels of Iris Murdoch*. Lampeter: Edwin Mellen Press, 2002.
Rowe, Anne, and Avril Horner (eds), *Iris Murdoch: Texts and Contexts*. New York: Palgrave Macmillan, 2012.
Rowe, Anne, and Sara Upstone, 'Iris Murdoch, Ian McEwan and the Place of the Political in Contemporary Fiction', in Anne Rowe and Avril Horner (eds), *Iris Murdoch: Texts and Contexts*. New York: Palgrave Macmillan, 2012, pp. 59–73.
Sartre, Jean-Paul, *Being and Nothingness. An Essay on Phenomenological Ontology*, trans. Hazel E. Barnes. London: Routledge, 2003.
Saussure, Ferdinand de, *Course in General Linguistics*, trans. Roy Harris. London: Duckworth, 1995 (repr.).
Schweiker, William, 'The Sovereignty of God's Goodness', in Maria Antonaccio and William Schweiker (eds), *Iris Murdoch and the Search for Human Goodness*. Chicago: University of Chicago Press, 1996, pp. 209–35.
Smith, R. Gregor (ed.), *World Come of Age: A Symposium on Dietrich Bonhoeffer*. London: Collins, 1967.
Soelle, Dorothee, *Suffering*, trans. E. Kalin. London: Darton, Longman and Todd, 1975.
Tillich, Paul, *Systematic Theology, Combined Volume*. Welwyn: James Nisbet, 1968.
Tillich, Paul, *Systematic Theology, Vol. 1, Reason and Revelation; Being and God*. London: SCM Press, 1978 (repr.).
Tillich, Paul, *Systematic Theology, Vol. 2, Existence and the Christ*. London: SCM, 1978 (repr.).
Todd, Richard, *Iris Murdoch: The Shakespearian Interest*. London: Vision, 1979.
Todd, Richard, 'The Plausibility of the Black Prince', *Dutch Quarterly* (1978), pp. 82–93.
Tracy, David, 'Iris Murdoch and the Many Faces of Platonism', in Maria Antonaccio and William Schweiker (eds), *Iris Murdoch and the Search for Human Goodness*. Chicago: University of Chicago Press, 1996, pp. 54–75.
Vaizey, Wendy, 'Language, Memory and Loss: Kristevan Psychoanalytical Perspectives on Intertextual Connections in the Work of Murdoch and Banville', in Gary Browning (ed.), *Murdoch on Truth and Love*. Cham: Palgrave Macmillan, 2018, pp. 192–206.
Waugh, Patricia, 'Iris Murdoch and the Two Cultures: Science, Philosophy and the Novel', in Anne Rowe and Avril Horner (eds), *Iris Murdoch: Texts and Contexts*. New York: Palgrave Macmillan, 2012, pp. 33–58.
Weil, Simone, 'Draft for a Statement of Human Obligations', in Siân Miles (ed.), *Simone Weil: An Anthology*. London: Penguin, 2005, pp. 221–30.
Weil, Simone, *Gravity and Grace*, trans. Emma Craufurd. London: Routledge and Kegan Paul, 1952.
Weil, Simone, 'Human Personality', in Siân Miles (ed.), *Simone Weil: An Anthology*. London: Penguin, 2005, pp. 69–98.

Weil, Simone, *Lectures on Philosophy*, trans. Hugh Price. Cambridge: Cambridge University Press, 1978.
Weil, Simone, *The Need for Roots: Prelude to a Declaration of Duties towards Mankind*, trans. Arthur Wills. London: Routledge, 2002 (repr.).
Weil, Simone, *The Notebooks of Simone Weil*, trans. Arthur Wills. London: Routledge, 2004 (repr.).
Weil, Simone, *Oeuvres: édition établie sous la direction de Florence de Lussy*. Paris: Gallimard, 1999.
Weil, Simone, *Waiting on God*, trans. Emma Craufurd. London: Routledge and Kegan Paul, 1951.
White, Frances, ' "It's Like Brown, It's Not in the Spectrum": The Problem of Justice in Iris Murdoch's Thought', in Gary Browning (ed.), *Murdoch on Truth and Love*. Cham: Palgrave Macmillan, 2018, pp. 183–210.
Wilder, Amos, *Theopoetics: Theology and the Religious Imagination*. Philadelphia: Fortress Press, 1976.
Williams, Daniel D., *The Spirit and the Forms of Love*. London: Nisbet, 1968.
Wilson, A. N., *Iris Murdoch as I Knew Her*. London: Hutchinson, 2003.
Wilson, A. N., *Jesus*. London: Sinclair-Stevenson, 1992.
Wilson, Sharon R., 'Enchantment, Transformation, and Rebirth in the Green Knight', in Simone Roberts and Alison Baumann (eds), *Iris Murdoch and the Moral Imagination: Essays*. Jefferson: McFarland Press, 2010, pp. 92–106.
Žižek, Slavoj, *The Fragile Absolute: Or Why Is the Christian Legacy Worth Fighting For?* London: Verso, 2008.
Žižek, Slavoj, *The Sublime Object of Ideology*. London: Verso, 2008.

INDEX

abjection 116–18, 119, 120, 122–3, 127, 130
abyss 75–7, 97, 120
affliction (*le malheur*) 58 n.65, 76, 158–9, 161, 162, 163, 168, 170–1, 175–7, 178–9, 180, 181, 183, 185, 190–1, 196
Altorf, Marije 63 n.82, 85 n.29, 142 n.52
analogy 2, 71, 72, 74, 96–7, 100–1, 108, 131–2, 179
angels 21–2, 27, 27 n.121, 60, 61, 64, 95, 192–3, 196
art 4, 7, 9, 16–17, 17 n.65, 18, 19, 20, 23, 24–5, 27, 34, 35, 37, 71, 72, 84, 85–6, 87, 91, 98–9, 103, 112, 113, 115, 117, 118, 126, 129, 139–40, 142–5, 149, 161–2, 193, 203
ascesis 124, 129, 148
attention 7, 8 n.9, 9, 17–18, 19, 24, 33, 37, 46, 51, 53, 59, 66, 82, 87, 93, 94–5, 96, 100, 103, 110, 113, 121–5, 129, 132, 134, 136, 142, 149, 153, 156 n.7, 157, 161, 162, 163–6, 172–3, 174, 176, 180, 182, 183, 191, 192, 196
  to the Good 25, 27, 30, 32, 49, 52, 56–8, 60, 63, 70, 85, 125, 129, 132, 136, 152, 160, 166, 204
  See also: Good – as respect for the other; waiting
atonement 39–40, 44, 199
avatars 192–6

Bagnoli, Carla 112 n.17
Balthasar, Hans Urs von 100–4, 101 n.102, 122 n.48, 130, 152, 177, 177 n.122
Barth, Karl 1, 34–5, 34 n.157, 47, 58, 62, 78, 97, 101, 108
Battersby, Christine 109 n.3, 119 n.41
Bauerschmidt, Frederick Christian 81 n.2
Bayley, John 1
beauty (the beautiful) 41, 56–7, 81–108, 109, 112–15, 121, 122–3, 130, 131–2, 149, 152, 161, 162, 163, 172, 173, 180, 181, 182, 192, 193
Being 59, 63, 64, 65, 71, 72, 73–4, 75, 76, 96–7, 117, 149, 151 n.75
Bellamy, Michael 148 n.59

Bethge, Eberhard 29 n.130, 44
Betz, John R. 96–7, 101, 108
Boehme, Jacob 76
Boff, Leonardo 40
Bonhoeffer, Dietrich 1, 28–35, 29 nn.128–9, 41–4, 44 n.202, 47, 54–5, 55 n.34, 65, 66, 200, 203, 204 n.33
Bradley, F. H. 54, 54 n.29, 139–40, 143
Broackes, Justin 149 n.62, 156 n.6, 157, 178, 179, 180–1
Browning, Gary 111 n.7, 112 n.17, 140 n.35, 165 n.73, 175 n.112, 187 n.157, 189 n.166, 191 n.168
Brümmer, Vincent 130 n.80
Buber, Martin 47, 55, 56, 73 n.157, 74 n.161, 77, 168 n.91
Bultmann, Rudolph 1, 31–2, 48, 48 n.2, 53, 57, 65–6, 71 n.139, 184
Bump, Jerome 105, 107 n.135
Burke, Edmund 82
Butler, Judith 119 n.42
Byatt, Antonia 14 n.52, 92, 93, 93 n.70, 98 n.88, 156, 157, 170, 172, 187

Calvin, John 39, 40 n.183, 46
Caputo, John D. 47, 151
Cavallo, Adolfo Salvatore 179 n.131
Chappell, Sophie-Grace 19 n.74
the *chora* 117, 131
Clements, Keith 44 n.202
Clines, David J. A. 41 n.189
coherence 139–40, 142–3, 144
Conradi, Peter J. 9 n.12, 45 n.207, 71 n.136, 89 n.52, 90 n.54, 124, 125, 127, 145 n.55, 149 n.62, 155, 155 n.2, 156 n.7, 158 n.17, 168, 180 n.134, 191 n.167
consolation 17, 25, 35, 41, 44, 55, 60, 67, 68, 92, 98, 113, 115, 121, 159, 177–9, 180, 184, 188, 189
contingency 4, 7, 9, 11, 12–13, 1, 16, 17, 19, 20–2, 23, 26, 33, 36, 50, 56–7, 61, 68, 78, 84, 85–6, 88, 90, 95, 98–100, 103, 105, 112, 113–14, 115, 124, 126–7, 129, 134, 135–6, 138, 139, 142–3, 145–6, 147, 148, 149, 151, 152, 160–1, 166, 173, 181, 183

Cupitt, Don 47, 56, 57–8, 58 n.61, 59, 63, 68, 72

death 37, 42–3, 44, 46, 61–2, 67, 93, 109, 115, 118, 121, 122, 181, 190, 201, 201 n.17, 203
  of the self 9, 13, 35, 38, 62–3, 66, 68, 69, 71, 77, 93–5, 121, 163, 164, 173, 177–9, 183–4, 188, 192, 196, 201, 203
  See also: Jesus Christ – death of; decreation; love – and loss of self; unselfing
deconstruction 134, 135, 137, 147, 151, 165
decreation 62, 164, 183, 203
  See also: death – of the self; love – and loss of self; unselfing
de-historicization 65–6, 184
the 'demonic' 64–5, 196
demythologization 30, 35, 43, 53–5, 57, 59, 65–6, 67–8, 70, 71, 79, 184
Derrida, Jacques 1, 3, 95, 108 n.137, 109, 118, 118 n.35, 133–42, 133 n.2, 137 n.19, 137 n.23, 140 n.41, 143, 147, 149–53, 151 n.75, 165–6
dialogue 1–5, 9, 23, 34, 53, 56, 79, 82, 110–11, 129–30, 152, 158, 199–204
Dipple, Elizabeth 4 n.9, 21, 22 n.93, 191 n.168, 195 n.178
displacement 155 n.2, 158, 167–8, 170, 183, 185, 186, 191, 192, 195–6
Dunbar, Scott 66 n.99

ego 2, 10, 13, 15, 16, 19, 20, 23, 45, 50, 57, 62–3, 66, 68, 69, 71, 77, 93, 122, 127, 139, 159–60, 163–4, 177–8, 179, 181, 183–4, 188, 190, 196, 201, 203
  See also: death – of the self; decreation; individuality; unselfing
empathy 28, 123–4, 129, 130, 132, 200
existentialism 40, 58, 62, 65, 90, 116 n.26, 136, 162, 179
experience 3, 7, 18, 31, 43, 51, 56, 65, 73, 74, 77, 78, 83–4, 86, 88, 90, 94, 96, 97, 100, 105, 108, 110, 111, 114, 117, 121, 122, 123, 125, 131, 135–7, 138–9, 152, 164, 175, 178, 179, 184, 199, 200, 204

Faber, Roland 131 n.82
fallenness 9, 10–11, 11 n.25, 13, 23, 36, 51, 188
fantasy 10, 13, 14, 17, 22, 23, 25, 28, 37, 85, 91, 92–3, 115, 124, 145, 147, 166, 184, 196, 197
  See also: illusion
Fiddes, Paul S. 2 n.3, 3 n.5, 8 n.7, 41 n.189, 74 n.167, 100 n.99, 100 n.100, 130 n.80, 131 n.85, 151 n.78, 199 n.6, 200 n.8

forgiveness 25, 26, 36–7, 50, 121, 122–3, 124–5, 129, 130, 132, 190
form 17, 33, 37, 44, 81, 83, 84, 86, 88, 89, 97–100, 101, 102–4, 107, 112–13, 115, 149, 152, 162, 204 n.33
formlessness 17, 83, 84, 86, 96, 98–100, 149
Forsberg, Niklas 140 n.35
Fraser, G. S. 127 n.69
freedom 8–9, 11, 23, 31, 34, 35, 41, 60, 63, 83–5, 86, 89, 112, 115, 136, 141, 143, 171, 172, 190
Freud, Sigmund 10, 10 n.22, 14, 14 n.50, 61–2, 75, 92, 109, 116, 118, 118 n.38, 122, 127, 148, 148 n.60, 164, 185 n.155

Gardner, W. H. 24 n.99, 107 n.133
God
  death of 21, 28–9, 31, 42, 52, 60, 73
  hidden 31–3, 34, 35, 42, 43, 46
  non-objectifiable 34–5, 131–2
  personal 7, 15, 25–6, 34–5, 38, 42, 52, 53–9, 63, 65–6, 71, 72–5, 77, 79, 97, 100, 112, 113, 127, 129, 131–2, 163, 180, 188, 200–1
  and participation 31, 40, 64, 74–5, 76, 96–7, 98, 104, 106, 108, 131, 132, 151, 152, 176–7, 200
  self-limitation of 41, 130, 200
  suffering of 29, 31, 41–2, 72, 130, 175–6, 199–200
  as triune 22, 27, 57, 60, 74, 100–1, 106, 108, 131, 151–2
the Good
  as force 30, 35, 61, 62, 64, 77, 78, 124
  impersonal 20, 34, 45, 124, 162, 163–4, 167
  necessary 52, 56, 57, 60, 61, 63
  objective 21, 25, 52, 53, 56, 57, 58, 60, 62, 64, 68, 85, 121, 144
  scattered 21, 22, 30, 32, 34, 35, 60, 61, 64, 87, 100, 152, 192
  signs of 35, 51, 57, 61, 78, 123, 173, 174, 190, 201, 204
  sovereignty of 20, 35, 52, 56–7, 59–60, 67, 77, 112
  transcendent 52, 53, 55, 56, 57, 58, 60, 62, 64, 73, 77, 78, 104, 112, 115, 125, 131, 136, 140, 141, 153, 164, 180
  unity of 21, 21 n.87, 34, 52 n.16, 59–61, 63, 100, 152, 192
'good for nothing' 21, 21 n.84, 22, 39, 41, 57, 60, 85, 112, 178
grace 9, 15, 17, 19, 21, 23, 41, 44, 103–6, 159–60, 162, 163, 170, 176, 178, 183

gravity 100, 159–60, 162, 162 n.48, 170, 176, 178, 183

Haffenden, John 4 n.8, 142 n.48
Harris, Daniel A. 104
Hart, David Bentley 68 n.117, 82, 91, 95–6, 97–8, 100, 102, 108, 108 n.137, 131 n.86, 152 n.83, 152 n.85
Heidegger, Martin 47 n.1, 64, 95, 97, 137 n.19, 137 n.23, 151 n.75
Herz, Neil 109 n.3
Hick, John 47, 66 n.99
Hicks, David 168 n.89
Hopkins, Gerard Manley 1, 8, 8 n.7, 24, 81 n.3, 82, 82 n.6, 101–8, 102 n.109, 107 n.134
Horner, Avril 47 n.1, 93 n.67, 155 n.1

Idealism 54, 118 n.38, 136, 139
illusion 10, 20, 24, 25, 37, 39, 62, 89, 91, 96, 120, 124, 125, 127, 159–60, 162, 163–4, 174, 181, 196, 201
See also: fantasy
imagination 2, 17, 28, 39, 53, 63 n.82, 67, 69, 82–3, 85, 85 n.29, 89, 92, 111–13, 117, 120, 121, 122–3, 131, 143, 147, 159–60, 163, 164, 170, 173, 177–8, 179, 180
immanence 100, 152
imprisonment 10, 49, 90, 92, 161, 170, 182
individuality 8, 12, 21, 32 n.142, 45–6, 71, 81, 84, 86–7, 98, 102–3, 107, 116, 122, 134, 135–6, 137, 139, 140, 141, 146, 148, 149, 160, 165–6, 169, 195, 202–4

Jesus Christ
 death of 26, 39, 66–7, 68–9, 175–8, 181, 183, 194, 199, 201–2
 as mystical Christ 3, 26, 31, 35, 39, 66, 69–70, 71, 72–3, 181, 184, 188, 192, 197, 202–3, 204
 resurrection of 26, 39, 42–4, 57, 67, 68–9, 71, 72, 130, 178, 184, 201–2, 203–4
 See also: de-historicization; demythologization
Johnson, Deborah 14 n.52, 126 n.66
Johnson, Elizabeth 74 n.166
Jones, Ernest 148 n.60
Julian of Norwich 8, 114
Jüngel, Eberhard 31, 32, 42, 42 n.193, 78 n.192, 130
justice 60, 131, 150, 186, 189–90, 193

Kant, Immanuel 17 n.64, 18, 30, 81–6, 85 n.29, 87, 88, 89, 90, 91, 94, 97, 98, 100, 105, 106, 107, 108, 109, 111–13, 114, 115, 116–17, 118, 118 n.38, 121–2, 128, 139–40, 175, 180, 203
Kee, Alistair 28 n.127
Keller, Catherine 200 n.8
Kerr, Fergus 58 n.61, 174 n.110
Kierkegaard, Søren 162 n.46
Kristeva, Julia 1, 3, 109–11, 109 n.3, 110 n.6, 111 n.7, 115–21, 116 n.26, 122–4, 122 n.48, 127, 129, 130, 130 n.78, 131–2

Lacan, Jacques 109, 114, 116, 116 n.26, 118, 119, 122, 129, 130
Lampe, G. W. H. 47, 202 nn.22–3
language 24, 43, 45, 58–9, 67, 74–5, 76, 98, 111 n.7, 116–17, 120, 122–4, 134–6, 139–40, 140 n.35, 142–3, 147–50, 151, 152, 166, 199
Lebowitz, Naomi 110 n.4
Leibniz, G. W. 131
Lenehan, Kevin A. 29 n.129
Levinas, Emmanuel 95, 97–8, 108 n.137, 109
Lochhead, Judy 109 n.3, 113 n.21
love
 as *agape* 130–1
 as controlling 13–14, 16, 22, 36–7, 45, 69, 89, 196
 as *eros* (desire) 19–20, 53, 122, 124, 125, 127, 128, 129, 130, 136, 145, 148, 149 n.62, 185 n.155, 190
 and God 75–6, 92, 103, 108, 122, 123, 131, 151, 160–2, 174, 176–7, 179, 185, 196–7, 199, 200
 and the Good 7, 9, 13, 20, 25, 26, 27, 34, 53, 56, 57, 77, 85, 92, 98, 113, 125, 129, 136, 145, 178, 179, 180, 188
 and loss of self 9, 18, 19–20, 21, 36, 94–5, 129, 136, 144–5, 160
 reciprocal 97–8, 122, 129
 as respect for the other 19, 19 n.74, 57, 84, 93, 94–5, 96, 98–9, 112, 115, 121, 122, 124, 129, 144, 146, 160, 163, 166; *see also*: attention; waiting
 of truth 7, 8, 9, 39, 174, 190
Lovibond, Sabina 164, 165 n.73, 166 n.80, 195
Luther, Martin 29, 42, 42 nn.192–3, 78, 78 n.192
Lyotard, Jean-François 95, 97 n.81, 109, 109 n.3, 113

MacKinnon, Donald 1, 47, 47 n.1, 48, 48 n.2, 68–9, 68 n.114, 68 n.117, 73, 77, 78, 201–2, 203–4
Macquarrie, John 15 n.56, 47, 47 n.1, 71 n.138, 75

Magee, Bryan 5 n.14, 17 n.63, 17 n.65, 24 n.101, 98 n.85, 133 n.2
magic 11, 16, 17, 18 n.68, 23–8, 34, 35, 36–7, 38, 39, 41, 61, 69, 135, 143, 171, 184, 187 n.157, 196
Magliola, Robert 152
Mariani, Paul 107 n.134
Marsyas, myth of 19, 39, 62, 148
masochism 20 n.78, 38, 40, 45, 147, 184
materiality 17, 17 n.65, 27, 58, 97, 182
McGrath, Alister E. 42 n.192
Meszaros, Julia 164, 164 n.64
metaphor 2, 52, 74, 75, 104, 132, 163, 191, 203
Milbank, John 81 n.2, 96 n.78, 108
Milligan, Tony 137 n.23
Moden, Rebecca 187 n.157, 191 n.167
Moltmann, Jürgen 28 n.127, 40, 42 n.193, 74 n.166, 199 n.6
morals 7, 9, 11, 15, 18, 20, 21, 30, 32, 33, 35, 36, 38, 41 n.190, 48, 51, 52–4, 60, 64, 67, 73, 79, 83–5, 86, 91, 99, 107, 112, 112 n.17, 115, 134, 136, 141, 149, 174, 185 n.155, 188, 203, 204
Moule, C. F. D. 47, 47 n.1, 204
Murdoch, Iris
  An Accidental Man 9 n.12, 10 n.21, 28 n.126, 37
  'Against Dryness' 170
  'Art is the Imitation of Nature' 133 n.2
  The Bell 9, 17, 18–19, 20, 23–4, 27, 125–9, 156–7
  The Black Prince 19–20, 125, 133–4, 139–40, 141–9, 166
  The Book and the Brotherhood 7, 8, 10 n.18, 11, 12 n.31, 15 n.58, 16 n.60, 18, 19, 21, 25–6, 37, 39, 45–6, 71 n.134, 72, 87
  Bruno's Dream 87–8, 89
  'Christ and Myth' 17 n.66
  'Existentialists and Mystics' 21, 45 n.207, 85, 112
  A Fairly Honourable Defeat 8 n.8, 9 n.12, 10 n.17, 11–12, 20 n.78, 38, 45, 88–9
  The Fire and the Sun 7, 8, 10, 18, 19, 20, 23, 25, 27, 127, 135 n.2, 136 n.16, 141 n.47, 162, 164
  The Flight from the Enchanter 162, 167–75, 176, 177, 182, 183, 187, 191, 196
  The Good Apprentice 7, 11, 13, 21, 23, 26 n.111, 27, 28 n.126, 36–7, 38, 45, 47, 48, 49–53, 54–7, 59, 61–65, 67–70, 73, 75–6, 78–9
  The Green Knight 158, 182–97, 201–2
  Henry and Cato 9 n.15, 20, 26, 26 n.111, 27, 37, 38–9, 70, 76 n.172, 87, 93 n.69, 94 n.71, 104, 177

  'The Idea of Perfection' 32 n.142
  The Italian Girl 19
  Jackson's Dilemma 186 n.156
  'Knowing the Void' 76 n.177, 110, 156, 162, 170, 172, 178–80
  The Message to the Planet 12–13, 135, 138–9
  'Metaphysics and Ethics' 58 n.60
  Metaphysics as a Guide to Morals 15, 30, 32, 34, 35, 39 n.177, 48, 52 n.18, 54–6, 57–8, 58 n.65, 59, 61, 62, 63–4, 66–7, 68, 70–4, 75–9, 113, 116 n.26, 124 n.67, 129, 133–8, 139–42, 143 n.53, 148, 149, 151, 160, 161 n.38, 162 n.49, 163 n.54, 164 n.60, 165, 174, 180, 181, 185 n.154, 195, 203, 204
  The Nice and the Good 8, 12, 21 n.84, 112 n.15
  'The Novelist as Metaphysician' 136 n.18
  Nuns and Soldiers 26 n.111, 39, 45, 67, 69–70, 111–15, 121, 124, 126, 177, 204
  The Philosopher's Pupil 9 n.12, 21 n.87, 25, 26, 27 n.121, 34, 39, 71, 178
  The Red and the Green 45 n.206, 61
  The Sacred and Profane Love Machine 10, 10 n.18, 16–17, 36, 37
  'Salvation by Words' 17 n.64, 24, 85 n.33, 144 n.54
  The Sandcastle 17–18
  Sartre, Romantic Rationalist 11 n.30, 14, 15, 134, 160–1, 164, 166 n.76
  The Sea, The Sea 9 n.12, 10, 10 n.18, 49 n.4, 87, 90, 93 n.69, 146
  A Severed Head 13–14, 15 n.55, 116 n.26, 125 n.61, 149 n.61
  The Sovereignty of Good 8, 9, 10, 10 n.17, 13, 15, 17, 18 n.71, 21 n.85, 30, 34, 48, 52, 54, 55–7, 60, 62–3, 66, 70, 74, 84 n.22, 94 n.71, 104 n.119, 112, 124, 136 n.14, 136 n.17, 152, 157, 160, 162 n.43, 163, 164, 164 n.61, 181
  'The Sublime and the Beautiful Revisited' 17 n.64, 82–3, 85–6, 88, 90, 98, 99, 140, 149 n.63
  'The Sublime and the Good' 18 n.70, 82–6, 98, 112, 115, 121, 136 n.15, 144 n.54
  The Time of the Angels 10 n.18, 10 n.21, 11 n.28, 21–2, 23 n.95, 25, 27–8, 33–4, 37, 41, 41 n.190, 49, 50–1, 52, 53–5, 56 n.49, 57, 59–61, 64 n.88, 65–6, 67, 69, 79, 95, 100, 192, 193.
  The Unicorn 9 n.12, 10 n.20, 39, 49 n.4, 81, 87, 91–5, 125, 157, 163, 170 n.100, 179
  Under the Net 89, 142, 166–7
  An Unofficial Rose 99–100
  A Word Child 9 n.12, 124–5

'Waiting on God' 156, 158–65, 167, 173, 175, 194
mystery 2, 3, 4, 34, 40, 44, 71, 75, 77, 100, 105, 138, 166, 180, 184, 200, 202
mysticism 8, 11, 70, 85 n.31, 87, 90, 188, 202–3
  See also: Christ – as the mystical Christ
mystification 4, 17, 24–5

Nancy, Jean-Luc 97, 109
Neoplatonism 19, 148, 185 n.155
Nicol, Bran 4, 4 n.9, 142 n.51
Niebuhr, Reinhold 11 n.24, 13 n.38
Nussbaum, Martha 149 n.62
Nygren, Anders 162 n.46

Ong, Walter J. 102 n.109
ontological argument 52, 57, 63, 66
Osborn, Pamela 147 n.57
the other, *see*: attention; love – respect for the other; waiting

Pannenberg, Wolfhart 203 n.32
particularity 20, 27, 40, 46, 84–6, 94, 95, 96, 98, 102–3, 108, 112, 128, 149–50, 151, 152, 162, 203
Peters, W. A. M. 103 n.112
Pettigrove, Glen 124
Platonism 30–1, 37, 56, 58, 62 n.74, 63, 74, 76, 78, 87, 92, 112, 115, 117, 125, 127, 128 n.71, 136, 140, 141, 145, 152, 161, 164, 174, 180, 180 n.134, 181, 188, 193 n.170, 203
politics 18, 28, 85, 156, 164–5, 178, 191, 191 n.168, 203
post-structuralism 134–5, 165–6
prayer 18, 26, 32, 57, 62, 66, 107, 162, 195
Prenter, Regin 34 n.157

Queneau, Raymond 5 n.13, 168 n.91

Rahner, Karl 3 n.4
Ramsey, Ian 48, 48 n.2, 53, 57
reason 63, 82–5, 89, 91, 106, 107, 109, 111–13, 115, 118, 121, 202
revelation 2–3, 9, 20, 21, 34, 34 n.157, 55, 101, 118, 145
Robinson, John A. T. 34 n.152, 47, 47 n.1, 53–4, 55, 55 n.34, 57–8, 65–6, 107 n.134, 184
Romanticism 62, 85, 88, 90, 91–2, 94, 105, 107, 108, 156, 160
Rowe, Anne 34 n.153, 47 n.1, 155 n.1, 186 n.156, 189 n.166, 191 n.168

sacrament 18, 34–5, 40, 78
Sartre, Jean-Paul 4, 11, 14, 41, 58, 62, 63, 134, 136, 137, 143, 145, 156, 160–1, 161 n.38, 162, 164, 166 n.76
Saussure, Ferdinand de 134, 135, 137 n.23
saviours 26, 36–40, 44–5, 50, 69, 72, 121, 171, 195, 196, 197
Schweiker, William 56 n.45
the sea 8, 9 n.12, 12, 70, 83, 89, 90, 91, 105, 113, 115, 171, 172, 183, 190
self, *see*: decreation; ego; individuality; love – and loss of self; unselfing
shock 15, 16, 23, 43, 50–1, 94, 100, 113, 199
society 45, 116, 119, 120, 123, 125, 131, 165, 178, 183, 191, 191 n.168
Soelle, Dorothee 40
spirit 12, 21, 27 n.121, 32, 52, 54, 56, 61, 75, 87, 103, 122, 135, 150, 161
stones 8, 12–13, 21, 70, 87–88, 90, 91, 94, 98, 103, 113–114, 126, 146, 171, 172–3, 182–3
structuralism 133, 133 n.133, 134–5, 137, 137 n.23, 142, 165
the sublime, 7, ch. 3 *passim*, ch. 4 *passim*, 149
  according to Kant 82–4, 111–12
  according to Kristeva 117–19
  according to Murdoch 84–6, 112–13
  negative 61, 88–9, 90–2, 92–4, 96, 100–1, 105–7, 108, 113–14, 126, 128, 131, 152, 199
  positive 86–8, 89, 93–5, 104–5, 106, 128
  and sublimation 118–19, 120, 121, 122–3, 127, 129, 130, 132
subjectivity 20, 58, 116, 122, 127, 200
suffering 12, 13, 20, 37–40, 66–9, 72, 92–4, 122, 123, 138–9, 159, 170, 187, 190–2
  contrasted with death 9, 38, 44, 94, 94, 121, 177–9, 180–1, 183–4, 186–7
  See also: affliction; God – suffering of
symbol 3, 18, 21, 25, 26, 27–8, 34, 35, 54, 70, 74–5, 77, 79, 84, 87, 116–17, 119, 120, 122–3, 129, 130–1, 132, 151, 169, 180, 195, 201

Tillich, Paul 1, 11, 11 nn.25–6, 40 n.185, 47, 47 n.1, 58, 59, 59 n.66, 63–5, 64 nn.86–8, 64 n.92, 71–8, 74 n.161, 78 n.196, 130 n.79, 164 n.60, 204
Todd, Richard 10 n.19, 148 n.60
Tracy, David 10 n.22
Trinity, *see*: God – as triune

the unexpected 15, 31–2, 50–1
unselfing 9, 19, 25, 104 n.119, 124, 148

See also: death – of the self; decreation; love – and loss of self

Vaizey, Wendy 111 n.7
voice 19, 23–4, 101, 126, 133 n.2, 141, 147–9, 150, 191
the void 12, 55 n.34, 77–8, 79, 90, 92, 93, 95, 109, 114, 116, 119, 159–62, 174, 175–9, 180, 183–4, 188, 192, 196, 199

waiting 32–3, 34, 160, 161, 161, 163, 174, 183
See also: attention; love – as respect for the other
Waugh, Patricia 142 n.52, 174 n.110
Weil, Simone 1, 32, 48, 48 n.2, 62, 69, 76, 77, 90, 92, 93, 110, ch. 6 *passim,* 156 n.7, 167, 177 n.122, 180 n.134, 181 n.144
  'Draft for a Statement of Human Obligations' 60 n.28
  Gravity and Grace 32 n.142, 92, 155–6, 155 n.2, 157, 159–60, 159 n.22, 161–2, 163, 164, 167, 178, 180, 188, 196
  'Human Personality' 191 n.169
  Lectures on Philosophy 175–6
  The Need for Roots 155, 155 n.2, 156, 159, 159 n.22, 162 nn.48–9, 165, 165 n.71, 168–9, 189
  The Notebooks 40–1, 92, 99–100, 156, 157, 163, 163 n.55, 165 n.74, 170 n.99, 172 n.103, 174, 178–9, 180–1, 180 n.140, 193 n.170, 197, 199 n.3, 200, 200 n.7, 201
  Waiting on God 32, 55 n.34, 155–6, 157, 158, 159–60, 161, 162–3, 164 n.67, 170, 174, 175 n.114, 176–7, 180 n.136, 181 n.147, 182, 194 n.174, 196 n.184, 199 n.2
White, Frances 189
Wilder, Amos 131 n.82
the will 28, 84, 86, 143, 160, 174
Williams, Daniel D. 130 n.79
Wilson, A. N. 3, 4, 58 n.61, 79
Wilson, Sharon R. 182 n.149
'world come of age' 29 n.128, 34, 34 n.157, 35, 43, 44
writing 34 n.153, 48, 85–6, 120, 133 n.2, 137–8, 141, 143, 145, 147–9

Žižek, Slavoj 109 n.3, 129–30

CPSIA information can be obtained
at www.ICGtesting.com
Printed in the USA
LVHW080156070622
720675LV00004B/22